If This Be Magic

Also by Daniel Hahn

Catching Fire: A Translation Diary

If This Be Magic

The Unlikely Art of
SHAKESPEARE in TRANSLATION

Written in English by
DANIEL HAHN

CANONGATE

First published in Great Britain in 2026
by Canongate Books Ltd, 14 High Street, Edinburgh EH1 1TE

canongate.co.uk

1

Copyright © Daniel Hahn, 2026

The right of Daniel Hahn to be identified as the
author of this work has been asserted by him in accordance
with the Copyright, Designs and Patents Act 1988

Canongate supports copyright, which exists to encourage creativity by making sure that authors, artists and other creative people can be fairly rewarded for their work. Copyright allows authors control over the use and reproduction of their work. No part of this book may be used or reproduced in any manner for the purpose of training artificial intelligence technologies or systems. Canongate expressly reserves this work from text and data mining (Article 4(3) Directive (EU) 2019/790). By buying books (as well as borrowing them from the library) you are supporting authors and publishers and making new and original work possible.

British Library Cataloguing-in-Publication Data
A catalogue record for this book is available on
request from the British Library

ISBN 978 1 80530 162 2

Typeset in Dante by Palimpsest Book Production Ltd,
Falkirk, Stirlingshire

Printed and bound by CPI Group (UK) Ltd, Croydon CR0 4YY

The manufacturer's authorised representative in the EU
for product safety is BGC Sustainability & Compliance,
7 avenue du Général Leclerc, Paris 75014
(gpsr@baldwinglobalconsulting.com)

For my parents

Contents

Prologue: Hvis du ku glæde mig ved at tale til mig . . . 1

1. **this storie/The World may reade in me** 5
   (*on translation*)

2. **Comment mettre cela en vers?** 19
   (*on verse*)

3. **O teu beijo é um soneto** 34
   (*on Juliet and Romeo's sonnet*)

4. **ये दोनों एण्टीफोलस शक्ल से एक-से ही हैं** 38
   (*on rhyming*)

5. **. . . Om nieuwe raadzelen mijn zelven in te scherpen** 50
   (*on irregularity*)

6. **그가 얘기를 다시 하게 만들겠습니다** 60
   (*on archaism*)

7. **Milý pane, mluvte i vy téż jenom jako dřiv** 70
   (*on translating into English*)

8. **Podrę wiersz. Proza lepiej usposobi**   77
   (*on prose*)

9. **Սպասիʼր, շունչ աʼռ**   86
   (*on commas, and other things*)

10. **Thou ferlies at my words, but haud thee still**   93
    (*on ambiguity and wordplay*)

11. **Ni chaiff peryglon fy nychrynu ddim**   111
    (*on extreme wordplay*)

12. **Uthando ayilothando**   121
    (*on meaning/s*)

13. **จะเลยยกเอาเป็นญาติวงศาของเจ้าเองเสียกระมัง**   134
    (*on uncles, and boldness*)

14. **jIH jIH 'e' yInISQo'. 'ej chochoH 'e' yInIDQo'**   139
    (*on pronouns*)

15. **እዚሁ ላይ ነው ችግሩ**   148
    (*on 'To be . . .'*)

16.   I am a-mazed ——— at your pas-sion-ate words   154
    (*on words and their effects*)

17. **нуждата превръща всичко . . .**   162
    (*on gender and other opportunities*)

18. **不用多说了**   168
    (*on economy*)

19. **Und sein so schlichter Schein herbergt Verrat**   184
    (*on deceptive simplicity*)

20. **Todas sus palabras son meritorias**   190
    (*on Latinate vocabulary*)

21. **kad jūsų iždas kupinas žodžių**   200
    (*on influences, kinships and etymologies*)

22. **קוקנדיק אף מיר, ווערן שארפזיניק אויך אנדערע**   205
    (*on humour*)

23. **Red' gelahrt on weise**   226
    (*on research*)

24. **che l'ordine va spezzato . . .**   232
    (*on word order*)

25. **Таква музика е слатка сал**   239
    (*on languages of other kinds*)

26. **正当な順序の継続**   246
    (*on bridges*)

27. **ти људи бесконачног језика**   252
    (*on Shakespeare's languages*)

28. **ანუ რაოდენ ჩვენთვის ჯერერთ უცნობ ენაზედ**   261
    (*on accents, dialects and representation*)

29. **أرجوك ألا تفرضي القيود على لسان**   268
    (*on reasons to translate*)

30. **Jó hírnév nevű áru**   276
    (*on names*)

31. **ते हे सुंदर नवं जग!**   282
    (*on cultural adjustment*)

32. **αν δεν την καταλαβαίνετε ούτε σεις, δεν πειράζει**   297
    (*on understanding, and multilingualism*)

33. **bir kaç diyarda / Aynı dili kullanmakla**   308
    (*on multipolar languages*)

34. **Why, now you speak as I would have you speak**   312
    (*on actors*)

35. **O, daardie verruklike speeltuig van haar gedagtes** (*on thoughts, and more actors*)	324
36. **. . . galdramann, ramman að kynngi** (*on all of it at once*)	339
37. **No coneixem ses obres?** (*on the literary canon*)	354
38. **Сколь естеству твои дела противны** (*on translations without translators*)	364
39. **doni al li sian vočon per sia propra lango** (*on the translators*)	369
Epilogue: If this be magic . . .	379
Appendix (*on chapter titles*)	382
Further Reading and References	389
Acknowledgements	401

Prologue

Hvis du ku glæde mig ved at tale til mig . . .*

I don't speak Danish. But in September 2023, as I was beginning my research for this book, I spent two days in Copenhagen, where the Royal Danish Playhouse were staging a production of *Richard II* that I was keen to see. And I had another reason for making the trip: I'd arranged to spend the day after the performance with Niels Brunse, the translator whose work I would have just heard spoken on that stage.

Copenhagen was sunny, in a lovely, crisply autumnal way, and very beautiful. The production was not altogether to my taste, though interesting enough. But day two proved to be what really mattered.

I knew that my book on Shakespeare translation would draw on the insights and experiences of actual Shakespeare translators, and sitting down with Niels for a 'general chat' (as I pitched it, mildly) seemed a good first step. I'd met him before, thanks to some events with mutual friends at the Globe, and was looking forward to this conversation. And because, occasionally, some things are just delightful in the state of Denmark, I got to meet him not in Copenhagen but

---

* 'If thou couldst please me with speaking to me . . .' (from *Timon of Athens*), as translated into Danish by Niels Brunse. You'll find the sources for all other chapter titles in the Appendix (p.382).

an hour's train ride away, in the town of his youth: Helsingør, Shakespeare's Elsinore, home also to one Prince Hamlet.

Niels walked me around 'Elsinore' Castle (really Kronborg Castle), a grand, atmospheric complex in a dramatic coastal setting, where it's easy to imagine standing watch on the ramparts at night, peering through the cold mist, waiting for the old king's ghost to stalk the darkness once again . . . Then we crossed the road to the offices of the HamletScenen theatre festival to talk.

Shakespeare is big business in Denmark, and especially here in Helsingør. The festival offices where Niels and I talked are decorated with photos of generations of famous Hamlets, the meeting-room dotted with little ornamental glass skulls. But the intended 'general chat' I had with Niels that afternoon was not about Shakespeare's global popularity and global cultural influence and the global Shakespeare industry in general. It wasn't about historic Danish productions, or historically how Shakespeare has been received. It was about about the numbers of syllables in certain Danish verbs, about irregular verse patterns in two *Hamlet* lines, about one specific word in one specific line in one specific edition of *The Merchant of Venice*. I'm aware that not everyone would consider this a good time. I loved it.

Nobody reads more closely than a translator. If you're translating a literary text that you think worthwhile, you will consider all of it, you'll be aware of every comma, every little unstressed syllable. As a translator myself, working mostly on fiction, the detail-focus is a phenomenon familiar to me; where any other reader might give a novel, say, ten hours of their attention, I will spend many months living deep in the book's guts.

You will meet many translators in this volume, and, pleasingly, most are even more obsessive than I am.

Niels is one of the few contemporary translators who has worked through the entire canon of Shakespeare plays, a labour of several decades, which meant our Helsingør afternoon focusing on a handful of micro-examples was – of course – only the tiniest tip of a very large iceberg. So after a few hours talking, as he ran me back to the station,

I warned him that he'd be getting a few follow-up email questions. Ever generous, ever gracious, he told me he would welcome them. If he came to regret this at any point in the eighteen-month barrage that followed, he was too kind to mention it.

Since that time, I have had conversations – often more than one, often at great length – with people who have rewritten Shakespeare in many languages. We've met in cafés and in their homes and in Zoom boxes, while waiting outside theatres and over long lunches. Each of those conversations made me see fresh things in pieces of 400-year-old writing I thought I knew well, things I hadn't bothered to stop and notice before, though they'd been there all along.

Here are a dozen of the translators you'll meet in these pages:

- Abhijit Gupta (*Bangla*)
- Ádám Nádasdy (*Hungarian*)
- José Francisco ('Chico') Botelho (*Brazilian Portuguese*)
- Emine Ayhan (*Turkish*)
- Frank Günther (*German*)
- JC Niala (*Swahili*)
- Jean-Michel Déprats (*French*)
- Lawrence Flores Pereira (*Brazilian Portuguese*)
- Niels Brunse (*Danish*)
- Shoichiro ('Sho') Kawai (*Japanese*)
- So Kwok Wan (*Chinese*)
- Te Haumihiata Mason (*te reo Māori*)

They are my cast of recurring characters. And you'll see the work of many others besides. More than anything, I hope you will reach the end of this book with the same awed admiration for them that I have.

And my Danish trip in September 2023 proved a fine place to begin those conversations: in real-world Elsinore, a couple of hundred yards from Hamlet's castle, studiously ignoring all the conspicuous manifestations of the Shakespeare tourism industry and instead worrying nerdily at a line that Shakespeare decided to launch with a stressed syllable, and trying to understand how 'The rest is silence' can be such pesky trouble to a long-suffering Danish translator.

It's the spirit of that conversation that I've tried to capture in the pages that follow.

Chapter 1

this storie/The World may reade in me

(on translation)

Shakespeare is a very good writer. This is not news. We know how clever he is, how versatile, how compassionate, how insightful, how constantly contemporary. But while this book might make a familiar case for Shakespeare's brilliance, it will simultaneously argue that he can be appreciated for all his qualities even if we don't hear a single one of his words. That Shakespeare with every word changed can still be great, and can remain Shakespeare. And that this possibility – that a play might be capable of surviving a full text transplant, from those 25,000 old words into these 25,000 different, entirely new ones, and surviving it somehow *intact* – isn't simply a factor of his pretty good storylines, or his perceptiveness about general human experience, or the universality of his 'themes'.

I work as a literary translator, which means that I am daily faced with that task: to replace the words in a book – all of them – in such a way that when I'm done, it is nonetheless still itself.

There's that old idea that within a seven-year cycle, all the cells in our bodies are replaced. People who understand these things better than I do tell me that this is not exactly true – but nearly. A substantial number of the thirty-six trillion cells in my body (give or take) will have been formed in the last few years, yet I still remain essentially the same person. Over a period of thirty-plus years, Niels Brunse replaced almost all the component cells in the works of William Shakespeare, but his *As You Like It* is still essentially *As You Like It*; his Rosalind is still essentially Rosalind.

So one of this book's questions will be about what that 'essentially' means, and what preserving that essence of expression entails. I am not naturally given to talking about the resilience of some transcendent *soul* while the gross cladding around it changes; I'm more interested in the mechanisms that go into *physically* regenerating this thing in such a way that, despite its being made up of new constituent parts, the differences are not what matters.

I often encounter doubts as to whether a great writer like Shakespeare can 'survive' translation – indeed, a very clever friend who knows Shakespeare far better than I do said, on hearing that I was writing this book, 'But Shakespeare *can't* be translated, isn't that the whole point?' The assumption being, I suppose, that translation is merely a destructive process – or a process, at best, of damage limitation. And it *is* destructive, of course, but it's creative, too. And in good translation, Shakespeare does not merely survive, he thrives.

Shakespeare's ability to connect with actors and audiences beyond his own language and place – and indeed outside his own time – is predicated on a general agreement that there is something universal about his writing. The plays resonate because everybody falls in love, and power invariably corrupts, and death comes to us all. But it is not, of course, as simple as 'everyone gets sad sometimes, so a play about someone getting sad will resonate with everyone everywhere across all time'. In Shakespeare, people get sad with *precision*. King Lear dies and Desdemona dies and Falstaff dies and their experiences of death are entirely specific, and different from each other. Nobody dies generically. Cordelia and her intransigent father don't have the same relationship as Celia and *her* intransigent father or Hermia and hers.

And this precision of character and experience is located in its expression. When I argue that Shakespeare is actually very good (I know!), my argument is rooted in his management of the very smallest units of writing – words, syllables, pauses – and not simply that he's managed correctly to sequence four basic narrative building-block events into a story that makes people cry at the end. *Precision* is a word you'll see a lot in this book – translation is about change, but that change obviously cannot be indiscriminate. Start swapping out our cells carelessly, or entirely at random, and we quickly become some other person altogther, or, I don't know, a lobster or an avocado.

(Translation is too often described through metaphors, incidentally, and this replacing-cells one is as imperfect as any other; so for the most part, this book will work by example, rather than abstraction.)

Underlying this focus on precision in our translators' work is a simple enough idea: language is not merely a delivery mechanism for basic dictionary-limited meaning. If you speak a word, what that word 'means' is not the only thing that's happening. It's rare that you can paraphrase a bit of Shakespeare – dress the basic meaning in alternative words – without diminishing it. He puts the language under pressure, makes every part of it work hard. A line in a Shakespeare play is custom-designed to have an effect – activating the actor who speaks it (because expression here is indissoluble from stagecraft), the audience listening. Replace the line with an approximation (maybe a couple of syllables shorter, an alternative collection of consonants, a differently placed breath), and the effect will change.

Drastically? Well, no. I don't believe that getting a couple of words wrong in *Hamlet* would bring the whole edifice clattering down. But these things are cumulative. The whole play is nothing but one syllable after another, and even small alterations will threaten the integrity of the structure if you make enough of them.

The version of *Kiss Me, Kate* I saw last year in London opened with director Fred Graham giving his actors notes on their rehearsal of Shakespeare's *The Taming of the Shrew*. One of the actors wasn't quite on top of his lines, but protested that he had managed at least to convey their gist. Fred's response is at the heart of this book: *People don't come to a Shakespeare play for the gist.*

And, crucially, a translation needs the same precision as the source text. Making a show in which, well, at least the boy's still called Romeo and she Juliet, or near enough . . . and rival families, and there's a nurse . . . That's it. Oh, and some people definitely die at the end? I feel that is probably not enough.

In a good piece of writing, every word might have a dozen different functions – the better the writing, the more precise, and perhaps the more subtle, will be the roles each word fulfils. It will operate syntactically, it will convey information, it will have a distinctive shape, texture and sound, resonating with other words, precisely influencing the rhythm of a sentence. No word operates without context. So the translator is trying to find words in his own language that deliver all of those dozen things, not to mention preserving several simultaneous formal features of the writing (a fixed verse pattern, sounds that rhyme when spoken aloud on a stage, etc.). Impossible? No matter.

Shakespeare has done quite well over these past 400 years, and his success is by no means limited to the Anglosphere. But discounting the language, one might ask: what's left, apart from some variably robust plots? Well, of course, I don't think we *should* discount the language; in translation, at least in good translation, the language is there, all the things that the language is *doing* will survive. A translator – a good translator – will work very hard to ensure that. Great literature survives as still great, not despite translation but because of it.

There's a much-paraphrased line from the American poet Robert Frost about poetry being 'what gets lost in translation'. We translators are inclined to roll our eyes whenever it's deployed. As much as anything, this book is about why we do.

Dog, the noun, is *chien*, *perro*, كلب (*kalb*), *Hund*. Easy. That's the basic information. But the word has other qualities. It also rhymes with log, can be used as a verb (as Shakespeare does), it's a monosyllable, and can be a nice pun if there's a nearby God. Suddenly *chien*, *perro*, كلب and *Hund* don't quite cut it. (My *Oxford English Dictionary* devotes half a dozen densely packed pages to the word 'dog' and its derivatives.

The majority of what's covered there will not overlap with what you might imagine as the 'direct' translation of the word into another language.) The more sophisticated, complex, layered and playful a text's language, the more a translator must struggle to find a replacement. Inevitably, that equivalent – a word in the new language with all the same dozen properties as the original word – cannot exist. So what's a translator to do? And Shakespeare, of course, is about as sophisticated, complex, layered, playful, and – again – as insistently *precise* as they come.

Look at these lines not from *Hamlet*:

> Being or not being? One can't help wonder!
> To be, or to be not – thus goes the matter.
> Existence or its absence? You tell me.
> Here's the question: should we be, or not?

A well-tuned translator would produce something different for each of these lines, despite the fact that the basic *meaning* they all convey is the same. What if Shakespeare had written <u>This</u> is the question rather than <u>That</u>? Or *That is <u>my</u> question*? What's the difference between *to be* and *being*? Well, the rhythm of the line for starters – that's no accident, either. Because translators don't traffic in meaning alone. Recreating meaning is often the easy bit.

Some years ago, a friend was working with a group of actors on a practical criticism exercise – rigorous close analysis of the functioning of a text, without much context – using a scene from *Macbeth*, and she commented, pleased, 'It really *does work* on Shakespeare, doesn't it?' In that good, careful writing, you can find a useful explanation for the abrupt shift from long words into a sequence of staccato monosyllables, for a speech curtailed prematurely, for a word here echoing a word there. A translation – like any writing, like any poetry, like Shakespeare – is specific. If a translation is doing its job, you should be able to make practical criticism work just as well on the new text, too.

Which is not to stay that we aren't engaged in a process of absolute change. Romeo says:

> But soft, what light through yonder window breaks?
> It is the East, and Juliet is the sun.

while same-but-different Rómeó says:

> *De csönd – ott fény gyullad egy ablakon!*
> *Az ott kelet, és Júlia a nap!*

(via Hungarian translator Ádám Nádasdy). But as we'll discover, in important ways, *nap* is not the same as *sun*; and *fény* is not the same as *light*; nor indeed are any of the Hungarian words the same as their English counterparts. (Even Júlia is not the same as Juliet.) There's a rough overlap of meaning, but meaning is not a simple one-dimensional thing, nor – as I've said already – is it the only thing that matters.

Often, in writing that's interesting, there are plenty of other things that matter more. Sometimes when translating I do need to jettison other aspects in order to preserve that basic semantic (meaning-related) data: it says 'lagosta', so I say 'lobster'. But sometimes I have other priorities, and that 'lagosta' might end up as a 'wolf'. A source text might say 'Cleopatra' or 'Coriolanus', and a translation – a very good, faithful translation, mind – might render those names in French as 'Julés César' or 'Roi Lear'.

Languages are different, so sometimes they need to be manipulated differently in order to achieve the same thing. Which is less complicated than it sounds.

'As a writer,' – said Arundhati Roy – 'one spends a lifetime journeying into the heart of language, trying to minimise, if not eliminate, the distance between language and thought.' But what if you're a translator, and it's someone *else's* thought you're trying to reach with your language? This might be a particular challenge in drama, where a playwright is not working with a default single consistent narrator, but always inhabiting every character; every character has a distinct voice that needs shaping (or, for a translator, reshaping).

The translator's job is to preserve their source text intact – alert to nuance and references and effect and rhythm – and to keep the voice lively and the prose propulsive and make sure that when you're done with it, the jokes are still funny. To avoid loss, if at all possible. In short, to change absolutely nothing about this piece of writing – except, of course, for all the words.

When translating is actually mentioned in Shakespeare, it is seldom about language, and usually to do with transformation – focusing, in other words, on how the thing is *changed*: 'I kill thee, make thee away, translate thy life into death, thy liberty into bondage . . .' Likewise even in those rare cases where the sense specifically concerns movement between words:

> Wherefore do you so ill translate yourself
> Out of the speech of peace, that bears such grace
> Into the harsh and boist'rous tongue of war . . .*

But my interest is principally in how translation keeps things *unchanged*. As one translator put it, we engage in a peculiar alchemy of turning gold into gold. My focus in this book, then, is on those translators who seek to preserve / recreate as closely as possible. (Whatever that means.) As an audience member, I tend to like Shakespeare direction that feels *revelatory*, rather than more adaptive or exploitative – I think translation, too, should usually work to express or to reveal what is already there. (Not that I think other kinds of production or translation are without value or desecrating, they just tend not to be what I'm looking for today.)

I'll be writing about what *has* been done in this language or that; but also about what *can* be done – or what can't. Every language has strengths and possibilities and opportunities for a translator to muster. Shakespeare provides the blueprints – in *a lot of* detail – and each translator works with their language as the medium in which to realise the reconstruction.

---

* These lines are from *As You Like It* and *Henry IV, Part 2*, respectively.

You can make your model of Brighton Pavilion* out of Lego, or out of woodblocks or out of matchsticks or clay. Each model will be good at conveying different aspects, each will be clearly Brighton Pavilion. Some changes might be revealing – you make your Lego model and think, oh, doesn't that original look rather dull all of a sudden? But whatever materials you're using, it must retain what you consider to be the main properties of Brighton Pavilion, and it must not fall over.

This is especially true if it's a model of something really tricky like the Leaning Tower of Pisa; then you *really* need to understand structure if your Lego model isn't going to topple.

That's Shakespeare.

(And there you go: another metaphor.)

Translation is not just a mechanical thing you do in the shadows to allow you access to the *real* work. It's a piece of creative work of its own. Dependent, but not without its own substance, its own materiality.

So *If This Be Magic* is about two things: about the precision of Shakespeare, a writer we might think we know; and translation, which is a practice that seeks to avoid approximation and paraphrase and settling too easily for a 'gist', but which is also limited by what different languages allow or require. In one sense, all translation is surely an approximation – if one could express oneself identically in language A and language B, then A and B would have to be the same language. And only English is English. No single word in one language maps exactly onto a single word in another (remember *dog*), and it's obvious that languages are infinitely more complicated than any individual word could be. So what does happen when Shakespeare gets translated? When the countless demands of a precise dramatic moment are combined to put pressure not onto English, but French? Or Japanese? Or Arabic? What makes the task so difficult – and when you've done it, well, what's

---

* The seaside palace built for the Prince Regent (later George IV). I thought of using something more internationally known for my metaphor – a model of the Eiffel Tower? – but I'm the sort of translator who likes to keep his cultural references local and trust the reader to do a little work if necessary. Those of you who are translating *If This Be Magic* can do with this example what you please.

actually left? Shakespeare is performed all over the world to considerable enthusiasm, so there must be something . . .

A translator of Shakespeare must be a rigorous, almost obsessively analytical reader of the text (and context, of course), seeking to identify what Shakespeare is doing with each line besides conveying semantic data: giving us clues about the speaker, telling an actor where to breathe, making an almost unnoticeable (but revealing) tweak to the default regular metre, subtly prefiguring an image that will be reignited a couple of scenes hence, making an audience laugh. But then she must also be a sufficiently brilliant and supple writer to construct a line in her language with all the same moving parts. That is the hard bit. (She also mustn't be deterred when she's done that and realises she has another 2,999 lines still to go.)

One of the weirder characteristics of translation is its combination of great reverence for an author, and total irreverence. The translator must assume that every tiny detail of the work is significant and worth preserving (as I said, the translations I'm interested in here are at least attempting some kind of fidelity; I'm less concerned with versions that might be deliberately distorting, whether for political, artistic, ideological or practical reasons); yet at the same time they must be willing to change it all. A careful translator is constantly teetering between these. After all, over-reverence can manifest itself in unfortunate ways, which can include attempting to reflect Shakespeare's status as 'high culture' by using much higher-flown poetry than is needed. (Shakespeare in English leaps between registers and tones, and for good reasons. If all the characters talked like Othello, Shakespeare would sound ever so grand, but would be much diminished as a result.)

A translator will recognise the precision in a piece of writing (and with such a multivalent writer as Shakespeare, there's a lot going on), and seek to do – to keep – many different things.

I work as a literary translator myself, as I've mentioned, from Portuguese, Spanish and French, the first two being my heritage languages. And like many translators, I started by accident. My friend Daniela asked me to translate an Angolan novel and I carelessly agreed (*how hard can it be?*), and here we are. That I've been translating regularly for nearly twenty years feels unlikely, though it shouldn't. I was a bookish kid (I remain a bookish kid), though without any fiction-writerly aspirations, and I was raised with the great privilege of not being monolingual. Both of my parents, when recent immigrants to the UK, had earned money doing bits of translation work. When my grandfather died, in 2006, my grandmother decided she needed A Big Project, and set about translating my debut book into Portuguese. My great-grandfather (as I learned much later) had translated with some distinction, too. Oh, and I did write an essay on translation – in relation to Shakespeare – in my university finals. The fact that this is my life should not, perhaps, be a surprise.

Back in Copenhagen, after my day with Niels, I bought several volumes of Danish-language Shakespeare, counting on Danish-speaking friends to help me to decipher them. Then I went online and ordered every cheap edition of a Shakespeare translation I could get my hands on. If I'm being honest, I paid little attention to what I was buying. So for a month or so after I arrived back home, books would show up at my door as a random surprise. One day it was *The Merchant of Venice* in Polish; the next it was 'The Comedies' in Italian (volume II); a couple of days later, two different *Tempests* in Welsh; then a Hindi *Taming of the Shrew*. Then one day, through the letterbox, came a Hebrew translation of . . . what? I don't know any Hebrew.

Not only could I not read many of the books I'd ordered, but in many cases – especially when dealing with languages that don't use the Roman alphabet – I couldn't even tell which play I was looking at. This was going to be trickier than I'd expected. Because while I'm writing this book in English, it's in conversation with other languages, some of which I can read, most of which I cannot. (Depending on who you are, I might take examples from languages you know, too; I will certainly take examples from languages you do not.*) Beyond the source

---

* I am confident in this claim. The languages quoted in this book include Arabic, Azeri, Bulgarian, Cape Verdean Creole, Danish, French, Hebrew, Hungarian, isiXhosa, Italian, Japanese, Kurdish, Latin, te reo Māori, Portuguese, Russian, Swahili, Thai, Turkish and Yiddish (and several dozen others). If you are a comfortable reader of *all* of these, drop me a note, and I'll gladly refund your purchase.

languages I translate from, and the target language I translate to, I have scraps of reading competence in a only few others (all of them European languages). But I didn't want to be limited by the languages I can read myself. Thanks to the Shakespeare translators I met, who helped me to understand what it is – *precisely* – that they did, and to many other helpful friends (who are named in the manifold Acknowledgements at the end), I have been able to range much more widely. After all, there is a lot to choose from.

'Shakespeare in translation' is a phenomenon that began very slowly. About eighty or a hundred years after Shakespeare's death, translations did exist but a mere handful – he was performed many times in Europe in translation (as well as by touring English companies), but any translations were seldom published. The idea that he would attain today's global cultural near-ubiquity was absolutely not a sure thing.*

The eighteenth century did see some international admirers proselytising for Shakespeare within their own cultures, and translating bits and pieces. Significant milestones include Christoph Martin Wieland's twenty-two prose translations into German, and the first complete works (actually very curtailed) by Pierre-Antoine de la Place, in French. Even Voltaire enthusiastically turned out a quick 'To be or not to be'. (This is what we translators do – if I find a non-Anglophone book I really want my friends to be able to read, I will rewrite it myself, all over again, just for you.) Still, the available volume remained small – mostly just the odd desultory *Hamlet* here and there – and the quality variable.

It was only in the nineteenth century that the great flourishing really began. Non-Anglophone Shakespeare came to be more widely published and performed in a few (principally European) countries. France and Germany in particular would produce translations that were widely read even outside their borders – by educated Russians, say, who were far more Francophone than Anglophone. Germany was an early adopter,

---

* Indeed, eighty years after his death, few people would have put money on his work thriving long-term even *in England*, but that's another story . . .

and an especially enthusiastic one – indeed, in the 1820s and 1830s, it was a veritable hive of Shakespeare translation activity; most notable, and enduring, was the Schlegel-Tieck edition (begun by the poet, translator, scholar and Sanskritist August Wilhelm von Schlegel, and completed by his fellow Romantic writer Ludwig Tieck and others), an early complete works that was systematic and serious about preserving what was remarkable about the plays in poetic and dramatic terms – including retaining the verse, which many early translations did not. The Schlegel-Tieck edition comprised texts of great literary sophistication, though German speakers tell me they have dated now (translations tend to date even as originals don't, curiously), and the local early-nineteenth-century sensibility meant a toning down of things like sexual jokes.*

By the end of the nineteenth century, there were over a dozen *Hamlets* to choose from in Russian alone, and they were in fine company. In this book, we'll see work by several nineteenth-century translators, including Edvard Lembcke, János Arany and François-Victor Hugo, working respectively into Danish, Hungarian and French. (Lembcke and FVH followed Schlegel and Tieck in scaling the entire canon.) However, as I said, this nineteenth-century flourishing, rich and diverse though it was in many respects, remained mostly confined to European languages. There were exceptions to this trend in India – for imperial reasons one might guess at – with Indian-language versions of the plays recorded as early as 1852, with a Gujarati adaptation of *The Taming of the Shrew*.

As the nineteenth moved into the twentieth, we saw first-time translations into languages including Japanese (1883, *Julius Caesar*) and Arabic (the oldest surviving being a 1901 *Hamlet* – with a happy ending), launching not only a great increase in productivity, but a global spread eastward and south. Shakespeare came to China at the start of the twentieth century – in this case, introduced first through his plots (Charles and Mary Lamb's *Tales from Shakespeare* were translated by Lin

---

* This was the age of bowdlerisation – quite literally, with the publication in London in 1807 of the English-language *Family Shakespeare*, courtesy of one Thomas Bowdler.

Shu in 1904) and the plays themselves only subsequently, and so the phenomenon grew and spread. From the late nineteenth century to today, things have only been accelerating.

Volume III of the Birmingham Shakespeare Library catalogue is a little over 300 pages long, and it's mostly just a *list* of those foreign-language editions of Shakespeare that happen to be in that one collection, enumerating translated texts from Albanian to Wendish – and only going up as far as 1932. Even if I'd limited this book's scope to pre-1932, that would have been plenty to be getting on with, I feel. And this massive pre-1932 tally is still *relatively* small, and with conspicuous linguistic/regional gaps, compared to the much greater global Shakespeare saturation we find today. I mention this so you understand why this book makes no attempt to be comprehensive, or indeed even properly representative.

This book will look at Shakespeare with a translator's eye, and listen with a translator's ear. As we dip into his plays in multiple languages, we'll encounter the work of some amazing contemporary translators, as well as glimpsing the translation habits of famous writers like Pasternak, a couple of Kings, and – making a surprise appearance – my great-grandfather. We will look at some big policy decisions (verse or prose, rhymed or unrhymed, what *sort* of language?) and small word choices. We'll look at some general features of Shakespeare's writing (if you know Shakespeare well, you'll find parts of this book generalising in ways that might annoy you), and things that the particularities of English allow him. We'll see how every other language brings its own challenges, and its own possibilities. We'll consider what audiences need; and what actors need (translating for the stage has its own special features); and who all these amazing translators actually are.

But we'll start by looking at the writing from *outside*, as it were – looking at bits of text but only at their shape, verse structure, line stops, rhyme schemes, punctuation and other architectural features. Let's not worry about the actual words for now – there'll be time enough for them.

Each moment in Shakespeare's English text will be a – sometimes fiendish – problem for the translator to solve, a multi-dimensional choice for them to make. Translation is theoretically impossible. Practically, well, it's just very, very difficult. But . . . might this be magic . . . ?

Spoiler alert: it isn't.

While doing my research, I happened to be in Stratford-upon-Avon for the town's Shakespeare birthday celebrations. Attached to the lamp posts on the high street were wooden boards painted with a selection of national flags. Italy, Brazil, Hungary, Iceland, Ireland and Austria ran down the west side (outside the branches of Debenhams, Robert Dyas, Lush . . .); the Slovak Republic, Belgium, Kazakhstan, Armenia, Denmark and Finland on the east (WH Smith,* Whittard, Superdrug . . .).

Shakespeare was being celebrated as a global writer – 'rather the world's than ours', as John Ruskin said. For centuries, people in all these places have been reading Shakespeare, just like us.

But . . . have they really? Or have they not?

Well, вот в чем вопрос,† as Hamlet says, sometimes.

---

* The stationer-newsagent lately translated into 'TGJones'.
† 'there it is in what question', or something.

Chapter 2

Comment mettre cela en vers?

(on verse)

A translator's work is a sum of choices, mostly tiny ones that combine to great effects. Individual words, individual commas, a monosyllable rather than a disyllable – that sort of thing. There will be thousands upon thousands of these. But there are also occasional big choices to be made, strategic ones, policy decisions to be taken up front which will affect all the rest. So that's where we'll begin.

Any translator tackling Shakespeare needs to grapple with the iambic pentameter, the shape of verse line that he uses most regularly. It's a simple pattern, each line containing ten syllables with alternating stresses:

de-DUM de-DUM de-DUM de-DUM de-DUM

It's his default, and the engine that drives a lot of the writing.
Here's some Shakespearean verse in action:

> But soft, what light through yonder window breaks?
> It is the East, and Juliet is the sun.
> Arise, fair sun, and kill the envious moon,
> Who is already sick and pale with grief
> That thou, her maid, art far more fair than she.

Or this:

> You common cry of curs whose breath I hate
> As reek o'th' rotten fens, whose loves I prize
> As the dead carcasses of unburied men

Or this:

> There is a lady in Verona here
> Whom I affect, but she is nice and coy,
> And naught esteems my agèd eloquence.

Or this:

> Discomfortable* cousin, knowst thou not
> That when the searching eye of heaven is hid
> Behind the globe that lights the lower world,
> Then thieves and robbers range abroad unseen . . .

(Those were: Romeo in *Romeo and Juliet*, Coriolanus in *Coriolanus*, the Duke in *Two Gentlemen of Verona*, and King Richard in *Richard II*, respectively.)

In this case what we've got is specifically 'blank verse' – that is, *unrhymed* iambic pentameter. Most of Shakespeare's verse either takes that regular form or is a subtle variation on it. (If you were reading those examples aloud – which I'd recommend – you will have felt that, say, *As the dead carcasses of unburied men* does not fit into the same pattern as the rest.)

Where the beat is regular, a line tells an actor how to speak it. If you see the words:

> spending your wit

---

* Read this word with all five syllables: Dis-<u>com</u>-for-ta-ble.

without any context, you have no way of knowing which of those words to stress; but here's that phrase set in a neatly formal frame, from the Princess in *Love's Labour's Lost*:

> I am less proud to hear you tell my worth
> Than you much willing to be counted wise
> In spending your wit in the praise of mine.

Read it aloud. The regular alternating beat of the second and third lines will make you want to put some stress on the word 'your' – which might not be what you expect, but it's actually how best to make sense of the line. She is setting up *your* wit against *mine*.

This is what the *Two Gentlemen of Verona* bit quoted above looks like in Danish:*

> *Der er en dame fra Verona her,*
> *som har behaget mig; men hun er knibsk,*
> *og min erfarne talekunst forgæves.*

If I tell you that Niels Brunse (about whom you will tire of my enthusing) has produced three lines that are also in pretty regular iambic pentameter, then you can make a decent stab at how those words are to be spoken, more or less. With a bit of guesswork, try reading it aloud – roughly alternating soft and hard stresses, ten syllables per line with an extra one at the end (*for-gæ-ves* has a light third syllable):

> *Der er en da-me fra Ve-ro-na her,*
> *som har be-ha-get mig; men hun er knibsk,*
> *og min er-farn-e ta-le-kunst for-gæ-ves.*†

---

* Don't worry if you don't know Danish – I don't either. We'll both have to get use to a lot of this sort of thing as the book develops.

† Not, incidentally, how Danish is commonly spoken today – it's much more elided; this is the old-fashioned, performative version.

We can't assume that every translator would be capable of constructing something that resembles this – but nor, indeed, would they all want to. This is one of those up-front policy decisions: *do* I translate Shakespeare's verse into verse, and if so, what form do I use?

The iambic pentameter happens to be perfect for English, a language that falls quite naturally into iambs. As I wrote a moment ago:

> then you can make a decent stab at how
> those words are to be spoken, more or less.

Any translator will be constantly pulled between preserving formal aspects of the source and relocating the play within the traditions of the world in which they are fashioning this new text. I don't mean transposing the culture – making Macbeth the Thane of Jakarta or Lear the ageing one-time strongman losing his grip on a Rio favela, or having Falstaff drinking with the Dauphin in the taverns of the Marais (though such things happen a lot in production and I would watch all of these); rather I'm talking about literary conventions. If your local poetry has historically been built around alliteration (*soft sweet sounds*) and assonance (*the sound of cows meowing*) rather than rhyme, why force your text to rhyme just because English does it? Maybe you need much more singing in your translation, if that's a major part of the language of theatre for you? Or, as Welcome Msomi did in his Zulu Macbeth, *uMabatha*, could you replicate some effects of the language not simply with another language but with drumming? And how about using the oratorical devices common to your own tradition rather than having to shoehorn in the same old Latin- and Greek-influenced rhetorical ones Shakespeare was using? Why wouldn't you, if you can?

So it is with metre. The iambic pentameter suits English. It's the form favoured by a long tradition stretching from well before Shakespeare – Chaucer's *Canterbury Tales*, say – to well after, where it's the foundation for Milton's *Paradise Lost*, Wordsworth's *Prelude*, and much work by Pope, Keats and countless others. But cross the Channel, and you'll find Molière, Corneille and Racine building their oeuvres instead around the French alexandrine, lines of twelve syllables usually with a caesura (break) in the middle.

So, a choice: you keep to ten syllables, something resembling iambic pentameter (as we've seen Niels do), or use something established as more common in the target theatre. You might turn Shakespeare's natural ten-syllable lines into your own literary tradition's default fourteener, say.

Though keep in mind that every choice has consequences. If you're allocating your material differently (Shakespeare's seventy syllables now spread over five longer lines rather than seven shorter ones), then you will instantly lose the line integrity – matching which lines run on, which thoughts end where in which lines, what rhymes with what. Alternatively you keep it line for line, replacing half a dozen ten-syllable lines with half a dozen fourteen-syllable lines, but this has its problems, too. Because while I do love *Hamlet*, truly, I have never wished it forty per cent *longer* than it is.

While – for example – Polish translators often expand Szekspir's iambic pentameter into alexandrines, Józef Paszkowski in the nineteenth century went for something closer to the source – a quite regular eleven-syllable line (like an iambic pentameter with an extra syllable at the end), which leans in to the fact that the stress on Polish words always falls on their penultimate syllable. So for Shakespeare's line *And by opposing end them; to die: to sleep* . . . (in Hamlet's *To be or not to be* . . . speech), Paszkowski has

Przez opór wybrnąć z niego? – Umrzeć – zasnąć . . .

Eleven syllables, alternating stressed and unstressed, with every word stressed on its penultimate, very tidily.

There are currently two great Brazilian translators working on new versions of Shakespeare's plays, whom you'll meet many times over the course of this book. José Francisco ('Chico') Botelho and Lawrence Flores Pereira are translating Shakespeare's plays concurrently, divvying out the canon between them. While both are incredibly sensitive to the rhythms of their lines, they're taking quite different approaches to the verse. And neither is simply recreating something like iambic pentameter, as their recent predecessor Barbara Heliodora* did:

Ha uma dama que habita em Verona
A quem estimo; é boa e recatada
Mas não vê bem minha eloquência idosa . . .

An insistence on decasyllables at all costs means Heliodora has to cut anything that doesn't fit. (I do find Heliodora's verse rather inelastic. I like my Shakespeare elastic.)

Lawrence bases his verse on a twelve-syllable line. In part, this is to maintain some of the structure of Shakespeare's lines, their semantic unity – and, very simply, he needs more space to do this because Portuguese has longer words. (Of such practical constraints is poetry made!) But he acknowledges this sort of dodecasyllabic line is an unusual choice for Brazil – 'I didn't know if the experiment would work . . .' He's very familiar with the French theatre tradition that does use twelve-syllable lines as standard – though interestingly, he says that if he were translating Shakespeare into French then he would actively *not* use twelves, for fear of sounding too much like a Racine play.

Lawrence avoids the fixed shape of the French-style classical alexandrine, which is also rhymed; instead, within his basic dodecasyllabic frame, his lines are in constant fluctuation. The twelve-syllable span allows for translations that are, he says, more *acidentada* than he could do in ten. (I'd translate that as 'bumpier', perhaps, though without the English word's negative connotation.)

---

* Barbara's real name was Heliodora Carneiro de Mendonça; she took her pen name from an eighteenth-century woman described by Wikipedia as 'poet, activist and gold-miner'. Sounds about right for a translator.

'I'm not making a transcription of Shakespeare's rhythm,' he says, 'I just want to understand how it works, to give me a platform to reshape that in a different way, to produce effects.' So yes, Lawrence observes carefully that the twelve-syllable line allows for detailed mirroring, each half-line balancing the other . . . but actually, once he gets going, he forgets the counting entirely, and responds to the intelligence of the thing, and 'the rhythmic effect it's having on me'. The lines have movement, to which the translator is obsessively attuned.

José Francisco ('Chico') Botelho is every bit as obsessive about rhythm in his translations, though his form is more variable. Some of his speeches are in twelve-syllable lines, others in tens. Each speech employs whatever the translator feels it demands, guided by many factors but sound pre-eminent above them.

When he was translating *Julius Caesar*, Chico ran into some trouble while working on a twelve-syllable version of a famous passage. It's the angry speech that comes shortly after Caesar's assassination, beginning:

> O pardon me, thou bleeding piece of earth,
> That I am meek and gentle with these butchers.

and building to a climax at:

> Cry havoc and let slip the dogs of war . . .

But *havoc* is a problem. It is, Chico realised, a sort of battle-cry. The word is shouted, urgently, as if to rouse others to action. His first option in Portuguese, however, was *devastação*, which is a really feeble battle-cry – it's four syllables long, without a stress until the last syllable (de-va-sta-ção). Even your most loyal soldiers aren't going to wait around for you to get to the end. What Chico came up with instead was *matança* – which means *killing*. One syllable shorter, and it's the second syllable that's stressed – matança – so it's shoutable. (And the meaning might be slightly altered but it's within range. *Cry 'Slaughter!' and let slip the dogs of war . . .*)

His line, then, becomes:

Grita 'Matança!' e solta os cães da Guerra

And, as a result of this single-word decision, he went back and reconstructed the entire speech in decasyllabic (ten-based) lines.

Chico's choice of formal variation allows him to conjure other nice effects, not all of them with exact equivalents in Shakespeare's seeming regularity. In the Brazilian rendering of Caesar's funeral, Brutus and Antony address the crowd in twelve- and ten-syllable lines, respectively; when the citizens respond to these speeches, they too change – twelve syllables when responding to Brutus, ten when responding to Antony – their own speaking swayed by the last orator they heard.

The first full Shakespeare play translated in Brazil (*Hamleto*, 1933) dodged this what-sort-of-verse issue entirely, using nothing but prose throughout. It's by a translator who published under the name Tristão da Cunha, and he wrote in his translator's note that rhythmic, accentual English verse simply does not fit Brazilian Portuguese syllabic norms; rather it more closely resembles the free verse introduced by Symbolism – which he calls a kind of 'melodic prose'.

And many other translators over the centuries have made the same choice, deciding that the gains that come from translating into fixed verse aren't worth it for the losses and inevitable infelicities it can entail (especially if you're not great at it). The wonderful Argentine novelist César Aira has produced some prose-only Shakespeares, arguing in his preface to *Cymbeline* that 'this meant that there was no need to skip anything or to come up with idiomatic equivalences, which have always seemed questionable to me. This method may mean that, although the (abundance of) jokes and obscenities may be less effective, they can all at least retain their place in the text'. And it's true: adopting artificial line constraints can entail the enforced loss of things for which you simply haven't the space.

Committing to a metre will force your hand on other choices, after all – any rigidity will mean certain things just won't fit. I say this, bitterly, as the person who once foolishly decided to translate a funny children's picture book into anapaestic tetrameter – *da-da-DUM/ da-da-DUM/da-da-DUM/da-da-DUM*, a metre used often as the basis for Anglophone rhyming picture books (*And we looked! And we saw him! The Cat in the Hat!*); but there's no place in that particular line pattern for you to slot in a word like, say, *watermelon – DUM-da-DUM-da*, which is fine except when you're translating a funny children's picture-book *about watermelons*.

When Gabriele Baldini produced his Italian translations of Shakespeare in the mid-twentieth century, he – like Aira, like Tristão – decided wholesale against verse, in order that he should not be compelled to omit anything. And I do mean *anything*.

Here's a couple of lines from Baldini's *Cymbeline*, with Shakespeare's to compare:

. . . and Sinon's weeping	*E il pianto di Sinone calunniò*
Did scandal many a holy tear,	*molte pie lacrime e tolse il*
took pity	*conforto della compassione*
From most true wretchedness . . .	*molte veraci miserie.*

Not *too* bad, arguably; Baldini's prose has eighteen words to the fifteen of Shakespeare's verse; though it has certainly spread, and the syllable count is much more alarming – Shakespeare's twenty-two has now become Baldini's forty.

And here's another pair:

You have abused me.   Mi avete offeso, con quella frase.

The Italian means 'You have abus'd me <u>with those words</u>.'

You'll notice how comprehensive the Italian is. (By which I mean, how very *long*.) Not being limited by the constraints of fixed verse, Baldini allows himself to keep everything, and to add supplementary clarifications besides.

There is perhaps some usefulness to translating in this expansive way, but these are not especially pleasing, speakable lines. And even if they were, Baldini's ungainly version of *Cymbeline* would take, what, six hours to perform? This is a lesson that translators learn fast: *constraints can be useful*.

Now, take a quick flick through Baldini's translations and you'll notice that there are exceptions to his doggedly maximalist prose policy. He recognises that at least Shakespeare's songs need to sound song-like, and at those moments, sprawling prose very clearly won't cut it. (Many other prose translators, like the above-mentioned Tristão, make the same exceptions.)

So this, from that same Baldini *Cymbeline*, is actually lovely:

GUIDERIUS	GUIDERIUS
Fear no more the heat o'th' sun,	*Dell'arsura d'agosto non aver più timore*
Nor the furious winter's rages,	*Il gelo dell'inverno più non ti farà male.*
Thou thy worldly task hast done,	*Sei arrivato a casa, hai riscosso la paga;*
Home art gone and ta'en thy wages.	*E ti puoi riposare, ch'è finita la strada.*
Golden lads and girls all must,	*Giovani dalle chiome bionde e fanciulle in fiore*
As chimney-sweepers, come to dust.	*Muoiono, come il nero spazzacamino muore.*

And a few lines from later in the same song:

GUIDERIUS	GUIDERIUS
Fear no more the lightning flash,	*Non aver più timore del baleno che abbaglia.*
ARVIRAGUS	ARVIRAGUS
Nor th'all-dreaded thunder-stone.	*Né del tuono che romba come suon di battaglia.*
GUIDERIUS	GUIDERIUS
Fear not slander, censure rash,	*Non aver più timore di calunnia o impostura.*
ARVIRAGUS	ARVIRAGUS
Thou has finished joy and moan.	*Per te non c'è più lagrime, né gioia, né sventura.*

Baldini is having a good day. The Italian has relatively regular line lengths (round about fourteen syllables), and there's a pattern of rhyming, albeit a different one to Shakespeare's. (The last four lines are ABAB in English, AABB in Italian.) The Italian is still on the long side – which is an unavoidable factor of the language itself, a subject to which we'll return – but nothing like the wild expansiveness we've seen in the prose. It's actually quite controlled here.

A couple of other details to notice:

- *arsura d'agosto* in line one: it's about a fear of *the August heat* rather than *the heat o'th' sun*. That's quite a free translation for the typically un-flighty Baldini. So it's not clingingly loyal in terms of meaning, word for word or line for line; but it is – as you'd hope any song would be – *singable*.
- That word *lagrime*, meaning tears. The same word appeared in our earlier quotation as *lacrime*. Uniquely in this song, Baldini seems to be using a slightly archaic spelling. At some point, we'll need to work out why.

* * *

We should keep in mind, of course, that broad statements about Shakespeare tend to be only generalisations, and the reality is always more complex.

Self-contained ten-syllable lines, with alternating beats? Well, yes and no. It's trueish for *The quality of mercy is not strained*, but otherwise there are structural irregularities everywhere you look. We'll examine many of these in due course. For now, though, just three *commonly recurring* irregularities:

First: none of the examples of iambic pentameter I've mentioned thus far are made up exclusively of ten-syllable lines that are self-contained. Some lines are end-stopped (*It is the East, and Juliet is the sun.*), but others are 'enjambed' – the sense runs on. It's one thing that can give a speech its momentum.

> Now is the winter of our discontent
> Made glorious summer by this sun of York,
> And all the clouds that loured upon our house
> In the deep bosom of the ocean buried.

There, in the opening to *Richard III*, line one runs straight into line two (then a pause), then line three straight into four.

From the punctuation alone you can see the general shape maintained here, albeit stretched to five lines:

> *Kaygılarımızın kışı şimdi*
> *Muhteşem bir yaza döndü*
> *Bu York güneşi sayesinde.*
> *Hanemizin tepesinde dolaşan kara bulutlar*
> *Okyanusun dibine gömüldü.**

We aren't always using a single line to round off a single thought, then. And the shape usually has a logic to it.

---

*   A Turkish translation by Bülent Bozkurt.

Though perhaps not so much in this bit of Prospero's 'Our revels now are ended' speech from *Y Dymestl* – that's *The Tempest*, in Gwyn Thomas's Welsh translation:

Ac, megis defnydd disylfaen y dychymyg
Hwn – y tyrau mewn cymylau, y
Palasau gwychion, y temlau cysegredig,
Y byd mawr ei hun . . .

You don't need to know what the speech means, only that 'y' means 'the' (the play's title is your clue), including the lone 'y' that comes after the comma in the second line. (*Y palasau* – the palaces.) Even without knowing Welsh, I'd wager that fixed line length is being over-favoured as a criterion here. It's hard to believe this is the most natural place to break a line.

Second common irregularity: that last line from the *Richard III* snippet – 'In the deep bosom of the ocean buried' – is eleven syllables long, not ten. We'll be seeing plenty of those lines, with an extra syllable at the end, unstressed. (A so-called 'feminine ending'.)

To be, or not to be – that is the ques-
(tion)

The extra syllable is weaker, more doubtful.
Compare with this, without an unstressed extra syllable:

To be, to be, to be! Ay, that's a <u>fact</u>.

Third irregularity: lots of lines of iambic pentameter in Shakespeare don't *really* have five equally stressed syllables. When Lady Anne spurns Gloucester (soon to be King Richard III):

Av<u>aunt</u>, thou <u>dreadful</u> <u>minister</u> of <u>hell</u>!

you don't really need to stress the 'er' of 'minist-er' too heavily. It's a regular-looking ten-syllable line, but speak it naturally and you'll find there are four heavy downbeats, not five.

Likewise Titania's:

> What angel wakes me from my flowery bed?

If an actor knows what their words mean, they don't really need to over-stress the 'from' just because it's technically one of the iambic on-beats.

And likewise Enobarbus in *Antony and Cleopatra* beginning his description of Cleopatra's arrival with these famous lines:

> The barge she sat in, like a burnished throne,
> Burned on the water . . .

The first line is to all intents and purposes an iambic pentameter, though in reality you will stress 'barge' and 'sat' and 'burn-' and 'throne' more than you would ever naturally stress 'like'.

All of which is important for translators like Niels, Chico, Lawrence and co. to notice, if they want to shape their lines closely to Shakespeare's.

Though you might encounter a more fundamental challenge still, depending on your language. English (like Danish, Arabic, Russian, etc.) is a 'stress-timed' language, meaning the gap between stressed syllables when we speak is roughly even, regardless of how many weak syllables might fall between them; so we use accentual verse most effectively. Languages like Mandarin, French, Cantonese, Turkish, Korean, Italian, etc. are predominantly 'syllable-timed', using syllabic verse that prioritises a fixed syllable count over a fixed stress count.*

---

* Here, Portuguese causes some trouble (as a Portuguese translator, I feel this often and deeply) – it tends towards the syllable-timed in Brazil and the stress-timed in Portugal.

So if you're translating into a syllable-timed language, no attempt at this sort of metric match is going to work anyway . . .

(A French speaker visiting London for the first time, despite having studied English extensively, can struggle to acclimatise to such a heavily accentual language where discerning meaning is made much harder because – unlike in French – you can barely hear some of the hastier unstressed syllables.)

And so the patterns go, and oftentimes,
a scene will end with formal verse that rhymes.

Which is my way of telling you we're talking about rhyme next. Including clunky rhymes, like that one. 'Oftentimes' not being a word I use (you won't find it anywhere else in this book) so it's clearly being shoehorned in to force a rhyme. We'll see many egregious examples of this sort of thing, too.

But first, a brief interlude, for Juliet to meet her Romeo . . .

Chapter 3

O teu beijo é um soneto

(on Juliet and Romeo's sonnet)

In 2017, the Colombian novelist and translator Juan Gabriel Vásquez was invited to produce a new translation not of a Shakespeare play, exactly, but of Lee Hall's script for *Shakespeare in Love* (based on the Oscar-winning screenplay), to be performed on the stage of Bogotá's Teatro Colón.

Shakespeare in Love is set in the days when young Will Shakespeare is trying to write what would become *Romeo and Juliet*, so bits of that play appear in the script. Sometimes they are in imperfect, unfinished form (when we begin, he's still tussling with a draft of *Romeo and Ethel the Pirate's Daughter*), but in moments of magic, his brilliance comes into focus and suddenly we're hearing what is essentially a fully finished bit of writing, freshly composed Shakespeare that should give the audience goosebumps. No pressure for the translator, then.

Among those moments is the first exchange between Romeo and ~~Ethel~~ Juliet (played respectively by Viola and Sam), here written by Shakespeare and reconstructed by Vásquez:

VIOLA/ROMEO
Si con mi mano indigna yo profano
Este santuario, dulce es el pecado:

> *Mis labios, sonrojados peregrinos,*
> *Con un beso lo habrán desagraviado.*
>
> SAM/JULIETA
> *Buen peregrino, mal juzgas tu mano*
> *Que cortesía devota muestra en eso:*
> *La mano santa el peregrino toca,*
> *Y palma a palma es de palmeros beso.*
>
> VIOLA/ROMEO
> *¿No tienen labios santos y palmeros?*
>
> SAM/JULIETA
> *Sí: labios para usar en oraciones.*
>
> VIOLA/ROMEO
> *Que sean entonces labios como manos.*
> *Que recen por la fe sin condiciones.*
>
> SAM/JULIETA
> *No mueve al santo el rezo concedido.*
>
> VIOLA/ROMEO
> *No se mueva, que tomo lo pedido.*

A few things to notice in the Spanish:

There are four perfectly rhyming pairs (lines 2 and 4; lines 6 and 8; lines 10 and 12; and the closing couplet). It sustains Shakespeare's extended metaphor about pilgrims (*peregrinos*), saints (*santos*), palmers (*palmeros*), prayers (*oraciones*), lips (*labios*) etc. – many of which words you might guess at even without being a Spanish speaker, as they relate to Latinate-origin words we have in English. And we're looking mostly at hendecasyllabic lines (eleven syllables, like an iambic pentameter with an extra unstressed syllable – that *-tion* at the end of 'To be, or not to be'). So by Spanish standards – and compared, say, to the Italian we've seen – these are pretty compact lines, barely less taut than the source text. Take a look – this is that source, in Shakespeare's words:

ROMEO
> If I profane with my unworthiest hand
> This holy shrine, the gentle sin is this:
> My lips, two blushing pilgrims, ready stand
> To smooth that rough touch with a tender kiss.

JULIET
> Good pilgrim, you do wrong your hand too much,
> Which mannerly devotion shows in this,
> For saints have hands that pilgrims' hands do touch,
> And palm to palm is holy palmers' kiss.

ROMEO
> Have not saints lips and holy palmers too?

JULIET
> Ay, pilgrim, lips that they must use in prayer.

ROMEO
> O then, dear saint, let lips do what hands do –
> They pray; grant thou, lest faith turn to despair.

JULIET
> Saints do not move, though grant for prayers' sake.

ROMEO
> Then move not while my prayer's effect I take.

This is the first time Juliet and Romeo have spoken, and their fourteen lines, their rather formal words, somehow construct a perfect sonnet. Their lines rhyme with each other's; each builds on the other's thoughts, around a single metaphor. The audience might not register consciously that they're hearing a sonnet, but should sense that this couple are supposed to be together. The play is about these two young people's attempt to build a world where they are united and safe, and here it all slots into place – just right. (Shakespeare had probably just finished the first burst of his sonnets at this point in his career so was amply proficient.) Very straightforwardly, the form is *doing something*. This is not one of those moments when you can just decide to use seventeen lines instead of fourteen, loosen up the rhymes or dispense with them altogether. A sonnet it is in English, so a sonnet it must be in Spanish.

This doesn't mean relentlessly strict adherence for the sake of it. The French translator Jean-Michel Déprats – general editor of the complete Pléiade Shakespeares, who's done about thirty of the plays himself – talked about two possible bad choices when working on Shakespeare's sonnets. One of these was translating a sonnet into prose (people really do this), so that without the structure, you lose the *density* of the thing, 'it becomes a sort of commentary, an explication', but the other is total adherence to form that *over*-privileges keeping the rhyme. It should feel natural, not forced.

After line fourteen, the line that rounds off the sonnet, the lovers kiss.

But just before Juliet's Nurse bustles in, bringing their poetic encounter to an end, Juliet says: 'You kiss by th' book'. Where 'by th' book' means something like 'suitably according to the rules of formal courtship', which is a pretty tricky meaning to convey in just *two syllables*. Oh, and they're still rhyming – this one rhymes with . . . 'the sin that they have took'.

In Brazil, Carlos Alberto Nunes used *Beijas como os sábios* – you kiss like the wise men, which seems an odd way of complimenting somebody's proficiency, and is presumably only there because *sábios* rhymes obligingly with *lábios* (lips).

Nunes's near-contemporary Onestaldo de Pennafort doesn't stoop to kissing like wise men – just *sois perito na conta de beijar* – you are an expert in the matter of kissing.

But our friend Chico sets up the ending by having Juliet say:

Tenho um pecado, então, nos lábios — e o cometo . . .
[I have a sin, then, on my lips – and I commit it]

Then comes the second kiss, and she concludes, rhyming delightfully:

. . . O teu beijo é um soneto.

Your kiss is like a sonnet.

Chapter 4

ये दोनों एण्टीफोलस शक्ल से एक-से ही हैं

(on rhyming)

JULIA
> *Das Bild erhört, doch darf sichs nicht bewegen.*

ROMEO
> *Beweg dich nicht, ich hol mir selbst den Segen.**

When translating a writer I believe to be a really *good* writer, one of my starting assumptions is that their choices have reasons behind them. That's not to say that those choices – or indeed those reasons – are something the writer has grappled with consciously, but if two characters speak in quite different registers, I should be able to deduce something about them from this; if there's a section narrated by a lizard, I shouldn't assume this is an authorial oversight my translation should correct; if the final chapter suddenly cuts off mid-sentence, then the author wants the reader to feel something very particular in that moment, and whatever that is, I want my readers to feel it too.†

---

* Tr. Frank Günther, *Romeo and Juliet* (German).

† Some things *are* just mistakes, obviously, and I do check. 'Dear brilliant author, in your magnificent novel (did I mention I <u>love</u> it?), I couldn't help noticing you've used this word four times in one paragraph . . . oh, and a recently murdered character wanders past the café two chapters later . . . and it's not actually clear which of the characters is speaking here – I presume the ambiguity is . . . deliberate?'

In Juliet and Romeo's first meeting, we have seen them instantly rhyme, and that – needless to say – is no accident.

Of course, the challenge isn't necessarily just producing translations that rhyme – in many languages, it isn't especially hard. But when Shakespeare uses rhymes, they're often doing something more precise than merely ending pairs of lines with randomly chosen sounds that handily echo one another. It might matter, for example, exactly *which* word rhymes with *which* other word. *Bread* may rhyme with *head* in English, but it rhymes with *hand* in Portuguese or French, with *voice* in Greek, and so on. If we take Puck's closing speech of *A Midsummer Night's Dream*, I'm sure it wouldn't be hard to make a pair of rhyming lines in many languages whose meaning is, very roughly speaking:

If we shadows have offended,
Think but this, and all is mended . . .

but it's not irrelevant that it's the *offending* and the *mending* that are placed in balance. Two words set up in contrast, and in this case there's a good reason why *these* should be the words that rhyme.

This is not happening, for example, in this Welsh translation by Gwyn Thomas:

Os bu I mi gysgodion bechu
Ystyriwch hyn, a maddau wnewch-chwi . . .

where the lines do rhyme, but the rhyming words are *bechu* and *wnewch-chwi* (meaning *sin* and *what you'll do*, respectively), which are not a match with the English pair.

Abhijit Gupta's translation took advantage of the fact that Bengali is rich in rhymes and rich in synonyms (and also uses Sanskrit-derived suffixes that you can play around with), to do this:

আমাদের পালা যদি লেগে থাকে মন্দ,
এটুকু রাখলে মনে কেটে যাবে ধন্দ ।

The rhymed words are underlined: *mondo* (dislike) in the first line, *dhondo* (puzzle) in the second. The direct meaning is something like, 'If you have not liked our play / then think of this and your puzzlement will clear'.

Puck concludes the speech, and the play:

> So, good night unto you all.
> Give me your hands, if we be friends;
> And Robin shall restore amends.

The last line is a nice regular iambic tetrameter, ending on a solid stressed syllable, and yes, a perfectly satisfying, reconciliatory – and heartwarming – rhyme.

I'm always concerned, even when translating prose, about which word a phrase will end on, which sound will be left echoing in the ear in the quiet moments before the next phrase steps in. In rhymed verse, if you're going for closure and/or satisfaction (rather than surprise), you hit the end of each line and the effect should usually be that the rhymes feel inevitable. Inevitable, but not too predictable.

Shakespeare sets it up:

> When in that moment, so it came to pass,

and delivers the comic rhyme:

> Titania waked, and straightway loved an ass.

So Ádám Nádasdy must do the same. *Szamár* is a Hungarian donkey, so his set-up

> Titánia – mintha csak erre várna –

embeds that parenthetical phrase meaning 'as if this was what she was waiting for' (for the English filler 'so it came to pass') . . .

fölébredt, s most szerelmes egy <u>szamárba</u>.

Now, Shakespeare might be a natural-seeming deployer of rhyme, but not all of his characters are equally expert. Orlando in *As You Like It* pins love verses to the trees, but he insists on rhyming everything with 'Rosalind', and it is not good:

> From the east to western Inde
> No jewel is like Rosalind.
> Her worth being mounted on the wind
> Through all the world bears Rosalind.
> All the pictures fairest lined
> Are but black to Rosalind . . .

Touchstone the Fool mocks him:

> Winter garments must be lined,
> So must slender Rosalind [. . .]
> Sweetest nut hath sourest rind,
> Such a nut is Rosalind.
> He that sweetest rose will find
> Must find love's prick – and Rosalind.

('I pray you mar no more trees with writing love songs in their barks,' says Jaques. Fair, I think.)

Jean-Michel's French version of the Fool – *le bouffon* – produces a parody like the original, using variants of Rosalind's name:

> *Habits d'hiver fourrés d'hermine,*
> *Fourrée sera ma Rosaline.*

> *Le moissonneur engrangera,*
> *À la charrette Rosalinda.* [. . .]
> *Qui cherche rose très câline*
> *Trouve l'épine, et Rosaline.*

The English 'prick' in the last line reads today with a vulgarity that isn't there in the French *épine*, alas. But translators *compensate*. Look at that first couplet again:

> Winter garments must be lined,
> So must slender Rosalind.

> *Habits d'hiver fourrés d'hermine,*
> *Fourrée sera ma Rosaline.*

The French loses the 'slender', and gains specificity of what winter garments must be lined *with* – in this case 'ermine' (there for the rhyme – hermine/Rosaline). But you'll see that the French also repeats *fourré* – lined (or filled, stuffed). So the second half of the couplet means 'lined will be my Rosaline'. Why? Absent the possibility of a *prick* joke to give a modern touchstone some fun, Jean-Michel is playing on the fact that *fourrée* when referring to a woman (hence that extra 'e' on the end) has a NSFW usage – less common or explicitly vulgar than the English word 'fucked', but that's the idea . . .

Falstaff in *The Merry Wives of Windsor* is as grimly heavy handed as Orlando, and he (typically) doesn't know when to quit; his love letter to Mistress Page signs off:

> By me, thine own true knight, by day or night,
> Or any kind of light, with all his might
> For thee to fight,
>
> *John Falstaff*

You keep thinking, *surely* he's got to stop now . . .

While researching this book, I visited Jean-Michel a couple of times to sit in his Paris apartment and discuss his translations. He speaks confidently about his choices – except when I asked him about this one moment, and we looked at his version. Ah, he said, somewhat ruefully, I'm not sure I made those bits bad enough.

'Inevitable but not too predictable', I said earlier with regard to rhymes – so a couplet will 'feel right' when you complete it, but it won't feel like you've had to contort yourself too much. Coleridge's 'Kubla Khan' ends with these four lines:

> Weave a circle round him thrice,
> And close your eyes with holy dread,
> For he on honey-dew hath fed,
> And drunk the milk of Paradise.

Paradise being a lovely word to end a poem on (and the satisfaction is withheld a little by separating the rhyming pair – the pattern is not ABAB but ABB . . . A), but you don't see that word 'thrice' and immediately think, hmm, that's a weird choice but, oh, I suppose he's got to put this word in because there's probably a *paradise* coming. Far too many old songs have lines that end with 'skies *above*' and you just know there's an imminent 'love'. (Far more *doves* than one would otherwise expect to feature in popular song, too.)

Also, remember that 'You kiss like the wise men' foolishness?

Jean-Michel advocates using rhymes if they come, not forcing them – otherwise 'you make a genius into a talented versifier'. Though admittedly French has some odd precedents. I've mentioned the nineteenth-century translator, François-Victor Hugo who published an eighteen-volume Shakespeare complete works; he was the son of the more famous novelist Victor Hugo who once, when writing a poem based on the Book of Ruth, invented an entire Biblical city – Jérimadeth – just to land a funny rhyme.

When the constraints are tough, translation can be a matter of trade-offs. Here's a couple of lines from *The Merchant of Venice*, with the Greek translation by Errikos Belies (who did the complete plays in Greek):

Like one of two contending in a prize
That thinks he hath done well in people's eyes

Σαν ένας απ' τους δυο σε αγώνα όπου ήρθανε στήθος
   με στήθος
και είναι σίγουρος πως ευχαρίστησε το πλήθος

(San énas ap'tous dío se agóna ópou írthane stíthos me
   stíthos
Ke íne sígouros pos efharístise to plíthos)

In line one, the word αγώνα (agóna) is a *fight/struggle* – related to our *antagonist*; and the concluding word στήθος (stíthos) is a *chest*; the second line ends on πλήθος – *crowd* (he's sure to please the crowd). Only . . . what's the word *chest* even doing there? The English doesn't mention it. In this instance, the translator has the two contenders facing off, *contending chest-to-chest* – because στήθος rhymes with πλήθος. Here, the price to be paid for the rhyme is a line that's soooo long . . .

It's not uncommon to adjust natural sequencing to land a rhyme, too. Conventional English word order has adjectives preceding nouns (*green and yellow melancholy, multitudinous seas, true love, blue sky, green sea, yellow submarine*). But we sometimes break that rule for poetic or dramatic effect (*murder most foul!*), or to complete a rhyme artificially. So we might then sing about a sky of blue and a sea of green (as seen from one's yellow . . . submarine).

And talking about The Beatles . . . there's at least one couplet in a Beatles song that resists cover versions because it only rhymes if you're from Liverpool – the moment you leave the city limits, the rhyming stops. Which is worth remembering when we read, because my assessment of what is a perfect rhyme or an imperfect one is determined by where my English is from, and when. Your vowels might not be mine, and nor might Shakespeare's. When I speak the words *prove* and *love*, they do not sound alike; in Shakespeare's voice, they did.

Rhyme plays different roles in different poetic traditions. So just as a translator might decide on a metrical line based on what's common to their language (e.g. taking a French alexandrine as basically an 'equivalent' to Shakespeare's iambic pentameter), similarly a translation can accommodate its own language's traditional devices in matters of rhyme.

Thai poetry is particularly rich in rhyme, for example, and its default is structured with more sophistication than just our end-line rhymes; so Thai Shakespeare might rhyme more extensively and with greater complexity than its English predecessor. The *klon pad* form of Thai poetry (the 'eight poem') rhymes its line endings but also reuses the same rhymes in the middle of lines. You'll find something similar in this Thai translation, from the start of the Prologue to *Romeo and Juliet* (โรเมโอและจูเลียต). The rhymes are highlighted:

กล่าวถึงสกุลสอง, กิติศักดิ์เสมอ<u>กัน</u>,
อยู่ร่วมณถิ่น<u>บรร</u>พะบุเรศเวโรนา,
จากโทษะเก่าแก่ทุษะใหม่ก็เกิด<u>มา</u>,
จนญาติวงศาคณะมิตระผิด<u>ใจ</u>.
จากเบื้องอุทรโทธิแรงกำแหง<u>ไซร้</u>
เกิดบุตรชะ<u>ไม</u>ใจมนะรักสมัคสุมาน;
กล่าวเรื่องชะไมบุตร์ฤก็สุดจะสง<u>สาร</u>
สองบุตระวายปราณและระงับกลีบร.*

Some traditional forms in Turkey's varied poetic traditions use in-line rhymes as well as the end-line rhymes we find in Shakespeare, so translator

---

* Thai does not put spaces between its words, which doesn't make pattern-spotting any easier.

Emine Ayhan had both of these quite different potential resources at her disposal. Or think of a language like British Sign Language. BSL poetry uses rhyme, but the echoes happen to be visual/physical rather than sonic. (Deafinitely Theatre's great *Love's Labour's Lost*, performed at Shakespeare's Globe in 2012 in a BSL translation, was full of such intricacies for even us non-BSL users to spot.)

But what do you do in a language where the use of rhyme is not common at all?

Japanese translator Shoichiro (Sho) Kawai is currently working his way through all Shakespeare's plays. At the point at which we meet on Zoom, he has translated seventeen of them; these don't include *The Winter's Tale* or *Cymbeline*, but both will have been crossed off the list by the time you're reading this. Sho hopes to be the first Japanese translator to do what he considers the full set of forty-one. (Other translators have done most of these, but not the maximal forty-one including the most recent – sometimes contentious – additions to the canon.)

Sho's first Shakespeare translation was *Hamlet* back in 2003. He was diligent about many things, but decided against maintaining the rhymes. His rationale was simple enough: rhyme is much less used in Japanese, so including it feels much more emphatic, less natural than it can be in English. Rhyme isn't one of those things Japanese just *does*, so why force it?

Over the years, Sho worked his way through more of the plays, till he got to *A Midsummer Night's Dream*. And, more specifically, to Act III, Scene 2, in which Demetrius and Lysander are both professing their adoration for Helena and she believes she is being mocked – and even Hermia seems to be in on the sport. The scene is all in verse, and the previous 190-ish lines have also been consistently rhymed, in what's called 'heroic couplets' (rhymed pairs of iambic pentameter lines), when suddenly this happens:

LYSANDER
> . . . Fair Helena, who more engilds the <u>night</u>
> Than all yon fiery oes and eyes of <u>light</u>.
> Why seek'st thou me? Could not this make thee <u>know</u>,
> The hate I bare thee made me leave thee <u>so</u>?

HERMIA
> You speak not as you think. It cannot <u>be</u>.

HELENA
> Lo, she is one of this confedera<u>cy</u>.
> Now I perceive, they have conjoined all <u>three</u>
> To fashion this false sport in spite of <u>me</u>.
> Injurious Hermia, most ungrateful maid,
> Have you conspired, have you with these contrived
> To bait me with this foul derision?

Three lines into Helena's speech – when she has realised that (as she thinks) her beloved friend is mocking her – she drops the rhyming entirely. It's all the more conspicuous because the last rhyme covered not two lines but four, ending with *be*, *confedera-cy*, *three*, *me* – and then . . . nothing. The next time Helena rhymes is 160 lines later, when she makes a dramatic exit on a rhyming couplet – until that time, she plays this scene in a minor key. There's a chill in the midsummer night air, and this is no longer a game.

(A similarly significant pattern break happens earlier in the play, where we first met Titania and Oberon. Some consistently rhyming spirits hurriedly vacate the stage to allow the fairy queen and king to enter, and these two are arguing, their dissent distinctly *un*rhymed. Like Helena in the passage above, they are talking about a break in the natural order.)

One reason to have rhyme, Sho concluded, is to create contrast with those moments when you do not. And so, from then on, he began to deploy it in his Japanese. He even went back to reinstate some carefully placed rhyming into a new edition of his old *Hamlet*.

Here's that same moment in Sho's *Dream*:

ライサンダー
　. . . あの空に輝く満天の星々よりも、
　夜を煌 きら めかせる美しいヘレナを、誰よりも。
　なぜ俺のあとを追う？　まだわからないか？
　君が嫌いになったから、君のもとを去ったんじゃないか。
ハーミア
　本気じゃないでしょう。ありえない！
ヘレナ
　まあ、この人もぐるなんだ！　信じられない。
　やっとわかった。三人で示し合わせてたのね。
　そして私をいじめようと悪ふざけを仕掛けたのね。
　ひどいわ、ハーミア！　なんてつれない人なの。
　あなたまでが、この人たちとこそこそ企んで、
　こんないやらしいやりかたで私を嘲るの？
　. . .

Look at the pairs of characters down the right-hand edge,* and you can see where it rhymes, and then you can see where all that nice fun rhyming suddenly stops.

The solution might be a matter of degree – Sho wants the positives of rhyme without the negatives (that heightened over-emphatic effect it has in Japanese), so might deploy it a little more sparingly than it's used in English. It's important for closure, or when there's a tonal shift, but maybe you don't need ten rolling pages of this.

Back in France, Jean-Michel once had a disagreement with an actor who wanted Puck's lines to rhyme *always* as they do in English. But Jean-Michel felt that in French, too much rhyme ends up with *des vers de mirliton* – a kind of artless doggerel – and being forced to reproduce

---

* Traditionally, the text wouldn't have looked like this – this horizontal presentation is an option nowadays, but Japanese has traditionally been printed in *tategaki*, meaning vertical columns (rather than horizontal rows), which is how all of the published Shakespeare translations I've got have been set. So if, as a Japanese reader, you wanted to run your fingers along the rhymes, you track right to left along the bottom of the page.

the rhyme constantly 'brings formality to what has to be quick'. He chooses to prioritise it in moments like this where there's a dramatic impact.

He did, however, keep plenty of rhyming in 'Pyramus and Thisbe' (the play-within-a-play peformed in the *Dream*), which is *supposed* to be inexpert writing. We will definitely be looking at 'Pyramus and Thisbe' later . . .

But first, we need to go back to those iambic pentameters, and complicate them.

Chapter 5

. . . Om nieuwe raadzelen mijn zelven in te scherpen

(on irregularity)

As we saw in Chapter 2, iambic pentameter is a sort of default, but you won't just find Shakespeare churning out hours of identically regular verse – his verse is incredibly limber, in fact. Rhyme isn't the only thing that's set up so as later to draw attention to its inevitable absence – with verse, too, he also makes a pattern in order to break it. So Shakespeare's lines of verse are made up of ten syllables of alternating soft-hard stresses (like *this*, and *this*, and *this*, and *this*, and *this*!) – except when they are not. His adherence to that regularity is not relentlessly strict, and every variation has an effect, so the translator needs to be right there with him.

In Shakespeare's Sonnet 18, which begins 'Shall I compare thee to a summer's day?', which of the first two words do you really stress? Speaking this as a perfect iambic opening would mean beginning 'Shall <u>I</u> compare thee to a summer's day?' (Or would you rather be compared to a summer's day by somebody else?) The more likely reading, to my mind, is '<u>Shall</u> I compare thee . . .' – or shall I not?

It's common to find similar ten-syllable lines where natural speech patterns suggest the first foot is flipped – instead of an iamb (soft-<u>hard</u>) we get a trochee (<u>hard</u>-soft). 'Trochaic substitution', it's called.

When Juliet is desperate to see Romeo, she begins her speech

*Ga*llop apace, you fiery-footed steeds . . .

(For the avoidance of doubt: the first word is not pronounced gall-*op*.) When Iago is trying to strike panic into Desdemona's father, he says:

Look to your house, your daughter and your bags!*

Look to them! Do it now! There's a sense of urgency that comes automatically to the actor speaking a line like that.

Reto Rossetti's Esperanto translation of *Othello* includes this line:

Zorgu la domon, sakojn kaj filinon!

The translator has spotted the shape of that opening, and its effect. *Zo*rgu is stressed on the first syllable, breaking a pattern that would otherwise be neatly iambic.

In *The Taming of the Shrew*, when Baptista Minola is talking with the wooers of his younger daughter Bianca, he finally says:

Gen-tlemen, importune me no farther . . .

It's a very stressed start, as he cuts them off from speaking and sort of throws his hands in the air. Please just stop talking to me! And here it is in Danish, where Niels is recreating the effect not by flipping two syllables but by adding an initial emphatic *Nej – no!*:

Nej, mine herrer, plag mig ikke mere . . .

Or, for an even more Danish example, consider the moment when Hamlet sees his father's ghost. At this peak of emotional drama, he exclaims:

---

* One of those that doesn't really have five heavy stresses, unless for some strange reason you're desperate to stress the word 'and'.

> Angels and ministers of grace defend us!

Angels! If he'd said 'Angelic ministers of grace', that would have been neatly *de-dum de-dum de-dum de-dum*. But we need a start to the line that's much more explosive – the actor hits that first word, with its first stressed syllable, just that bit harder.

It is not Hamlet offering a considered appraisal of the situation. As he launches into this line, he is seeking protection from celestial beings, but he is also *exclaiming*. As one does.

> <u>Oh</u> those <u>stu</u>pid <u>mo</u>****-<u>fu</u>**ing <u>ass</u>**les!

These, too, are all trochees. Which are much more satisfying to say with passion. The pleasing explosiveness of punchy expletives, in the reverse of the iambic foot.

Compare the beat to a similar line we've seen before. If you say these lines one after another, you'll hear the different rhythm:

> A-<u>vaunt</u>, thou dreadful ministers of hell
> <u>An</u>-gels and ministers of grace defend us!

Angels and ministers of grace! Here's Niels's line for his Danish Hamlet:*

> *<u>Him</u>lens engle, stå os nådigt bi!*

He's dropped the first weak syllable here, thus giving us a nine-syllable line beginning with a hard stress. <u>Him</u>lens <u>en</u>gle!

That dropped syllable at the start, said Niels, manifests as a beat, an almost audible gasp in Hamlet's terror at seeing his dead father returned.

To see how a line like this might look without that syllable dropped, just compare it to the moment in the next scene where Niels gives

---

* I mean the *really* Danish Hamlet. They're all Danish, obviously.

Hamlet a similar expression but without such a metrically punchy start; here there's an initial *Åh* to fill in the gap, keeping it regular:

Åh, Himlens englehær! Åh jord! Hvad mer?

(*O all you host of heaven*, it starts in English-Shakespeare.)

You'll remember I've already quoted the first line from Enobarbus's speech about Cleopatra's arrival, which is iambic enough, but look what happens next:

[The barge she sat in, like a burnished throne,]
Burned on the water; the poop was beaten gold;
Purple the sails, and so perfumed that
The winds were love-sick with them . . .

No actor with an ear for natural speech is going to get to that second line and stress the word 'on'. The regular metrical alternation of line one doesn't last long

The <u>barge</u> she <u>sat</u> in like a <u>burn</u>-ished <u>throne</u>
<u>Burned</u> on the . . .
<u>Pur</u>-ple the . . .

Or, as Enobarbus might say if he were German (rather than, um, English),

*Die **Bark**-e, **drin** sie **saß** – ein **glühn**-der **Thron**,*
***Flam**-mend im Fluss* . . .
***Pur**-purn die Segel* . . .

The sonnet that begins 'My mistress' eyes are nothing like the sun' doesn't require that we hop past that first little word and launch into the more important 'mistress', because he's actually comparing this mistress in particular to other mistresses conjured by other poems – I'm not talking about *your* mistress, you understand, or about any generic mistress, but rather:

My mistress' eyes (are nothing like the sun)

Or consider:

—When to the sessions (of sweet silent thought)
—When in disgrace (with fortune and men's eyes)
—Let me not to (the marriage of true minds)

Four famous sonnet openings – all different, none of them starting iambically.

Verse, then, is not all about pleasant-sounding regularity; it's about conveying more granular information (you must notice *this* word! speak faster, pause here!), about establishing a frame within which you can change things up. Not just making your play entirely regular from end to end without any variety, but setting the rhythm up de-dum de-dum and then OMG AN-GELS AND MINISTERS OF GRACE DEFEND US!

Regularity is itself revealing – characters in control tend to control their language; only then, when their grip on the situation comes apart (jealous Leontes or jealous Othello, say), does their line structure go all to hell, too. As I said in the last chapter, the assumption is simple: if the writer is a good one, even tiny features of the writing will have their rationale.

Of course, that assumption naturally underpins much of a translator's work. My writer moves suddenly from long sentences to sharp staccato ones, so I need to figure out what the intended effect is so I can recreate it. I don't want readers to encounter a line in another language and think, well yes, I can understand what it *means* now, but I don't see what all the fuss is about . . . A good translator will pick up every tiny literary gesture. Like any good reader, but with deliberateness, and some self-consciousness about this hyper-detailed experience.

So, because these lines with choriambic openings (trochee then iamb) have a bit of extra propulsion to them, often a bit of urgency, the effect should be retained. *Antony and Cleopatra* actually begins with such a line:

> Nay, but this dotage of our general's
> O'erflows the measure . . .

and it feels not as though somebody's embarking upon a formal speech but that we're in the middle of a conversation, already with some momentum to it.

> Nein, *aber dies Geschmachte unsres Feldherrn* . . .

Richard III begins with another, because:

> Now is the winter of our discontent
> Made glorious summer by this sun of York

doesn't begin with an iamb ('So nów the wínter of our díscontént' would be more like it) but a more forceful trochee. An actor strides confidently onto the stage, looks the audience in the eye, in total control, and says Now. Not now *is*, but **Now**.

> Now is the winter . . .

Incidentally, if you're a French speaker, you'll know that the everyday French word for 'now' is 'maintenant', which does helpfully start on a stressed syllable, but there its usefulness ends. It's three syllables long, for one thing, really lacking the pith of now. We might find a better alternative in due course.

Now (if I may), when translating into a language like French, where the length of each syllable is mostly equal, you can't exactly follow rhythmic/metrical irregularities. But you can mark *a* difference.

Take the Witches in Act IV, Scene 1, of *Macbeth*. Their verse is distinct, starting with a stressed syllable, and that trochaic impetus:

> **Fill**et of a fenny snake,
> **In** the cauldron boil and bake;
> **Eye** of newt and toe of frog,
> **Wool** of bat and tongue of dog, . . .

While he couldn't do this exact thing (French not having the same tools of iambs, trochees, dactyls, etc., as constitutive units of accentual verse), Jean-Michel was adamant that the witches' lines remain distinct. The dramatic stakes are high, after all – their magic is in their words. So he translated them into unexpected seven-syllable lines:

> *Duvet de chauve-souris,*
> *Dans le chaudron bous et cuis,*
> *Tranche de serpent des mares*
> *Et une patte de lézard . . .*

which are not the basis for the rest of his play. He's also using as many monosyllables as he can, working against French's natural fluidity. And the unusualness (vis-à-vis the rest of the play, and vis-à-vis common French) is a particular strength. One critic praised Jean-Michel's translation for allowing one to hear the English *en filigrane* – beneath the surface, as a kind of watermark. This is definitely a compliment here.

Over his career, Shakespeare increasingly freed himself from rigid strictures of verse (using more variable lengths, strangely placed breaks, dropping rhymes, run-on lines etc.); and when Shakespeare changes gear, so does Lawrence: 'Every translation is a statue of David – you make a hand that isn't in proportion, but it looks to a spectator like it is.' So when Shakespeare drops from ten syllables to eight, Lawrence curtails his lines too, for the contrast.

A translator can use the shape of a structured verse line to ensure that an actor stresses the right word, as Shakespeare did. But they can also resort to other modern tools he did not have at his disposal. Here's a couplet from Romeo, who's about to go to a party where Benvolio wants him to find a new girl:

> I'll go along no such sight to be shown,
> But to rejoice in splendour of mine own.

The sense of the couplet is about a contrast (not *that*, but *this*); so Shakespeare builds the line to end on 'mine *own*', adding the emphasis that comes with rhyme. (And with that, they exit, and there ends the scene.)

And here it is now, in Chico's Portuguese:

> *Irei, não para achar um outro amor,*
> *Mas ver a* minha *bela em esplendor.* [emphasis the translator's]

In this version, the terminal rhyme words are 'love' and 'splendour'; so the 'mine own' – 'minha' – is slightly lost in the middle of a line. It's the 'my' in a couplet that means roughly 'I will go, not to find another love, / But to see my beauty in splendour'.

However, as mentioned, the emphasis in the Portuguese 'mine own' is not mine own; the translator's published text uses an italic to mark out that *minha*. And one of the functions of the modern italic is to indicate the stress on a syllable. No, no – not that syllable there, *this* one. The metre might not force any obvious extra emphasis onto the 'minha', but the printed text makes it clear, through those italics, that while there are inevitable light natural Portuguese stresses on *MIN*-ha, *BE*-la, and es-plen-*DOR*, the first must be emphasised for Romeo's meaning to come across. Not just to see my beauty in splendour, but – please note, this is the point – to see my beauty in splendour.

Italic fonts were used in Shakespeare's day, but not for emphasis as now. The First Folio by convention italicises personal names, stage directions, foreign words, and other quoted texts (letters, songs, etc.).

The modern italic has other functions; the modern translator will use the tools at their disposal.

Back to English-Romeo's line:

> But to rejoice in splendor of mine own.

Say it aloud naturally and you don't really put much stress on the 'to', do you? But note how you speak the word 'splendour' in that line – there's a significant emphasis on it.

And now also note 'there's a significant emphasis on it' – eleven syllables, but in normal English speech there are really only two that you'd give a full stress.

> there's a sigNIFicant EMphasis on it

One final verse-line irregularity we should look out for: Shakespeare sometimes sneaks in an extra syllable mid-line – he puts in a strong caesura (a mid-line break), and an extra syllable is slotted in, and it acts like a pause marked in musical notation. (You can do this more flexibly in English with all its unstressed syllables.)

An extra unstressed syllable creates a forced stop in the second line here:

> Or to take arms against a sea of troubles
> And by opposing end them; // to die: to sleep . . .

We've seen this pair of lines in Józef Paszkowski's very regular Polish translation – only in this line, 'very regular' isn't what we want! More recently, Stanisław Barańczak did this:

> *Czy ten, kto stawia opór morzu nieszczęść*
> *I w walce kładzie im kres? Umrzeć – usnąć –*

Apparently Barańczak *did* notice Hamlet's little anomaly, because his second line reverses the stresses in the middle, so without adding an extra syllable, you still get a jolt like in the English, with two irregular consecutive stresses and an enforced pause:

*I w **walce kładzie** im **kres**? **Um**rzeć – **us**nąć –*

(Though Polish is more syllable-timed than stress-timed, so the line's not quite as accentually marked as that might suggest.)

Each of Shakespeare's plays is a very detailed dramatic score. In translation it must remain so. The translator needs to notice what the source is doing, and do the same – assuming it's been done for a reason. This means following patterns and breaking them, like those trochaic starts – or indeed whole stretches that are trochaic rather than iambic. Think of the bit from Puck we looked at when we were first considering rhyme: *If we shadows have offended, / Think but this, and all is mended . . .*

When King Lear says: 'Never, never, never, never, never . . .', a fivefold repetition of 'jamais' would get as close as French ever comes to an iambic pentameter; but that's just what Shakespeare's ten-syllable line *isn't* – in this moment he's actively going against it. (It's not nev-ER, nev-ER.) He could have said, oh, 'But never, never, never, never more' and kept to regular iambs if he'd wanted. His solution is starker.

Vicente Molina Foix's Spanish translation opts for *Nunca* (×5) rather than *Jamás* (×5). The latter would have been more emphatic in its meaning, more absolute, it's true; but the former has the superior virtue of being stressed on the first syllable.

Núnca, núnca, núnca, núnca, núnca.

Yeah – bleak.
  (It's perfect.)

Chapter 6

그가 얘기를 다시 하게 만들겠습니다

(on archaism)

I'm starting to write this chapter in Istanbul. It's late September, and still summer. I'm just a couple of hundred metres from the Sultan Ahmet Camii, and from this café table it's possible to glimpse little patches of the dome and walls through the leaves. Shakespeare never came to Turkey, but if he had, he would have found this place a building site; in the years when he was in London writing *Cymbeline*, *The Winter's Tale* and *The Tempest*, and his collaborative *Pericles*, the people of Constantinople were working on this astonishing building, known today as the Blue Mosque.

Shakespeare did visit Turkey in his imagination, more than once. *The Comedy of Errors* is set in Ephesus, *Troilus and Cressida* in Troy, *Pericles* in Tarsus and Antioch (among other places). Besides these settings, there are dozens of disparaging references to 'Turks', in a sort of vague, threatening, barbarian way, often as a comparator to our more apparently 'civilised' manners. ('This is the English, not the Turkish, court,' says the newly crowned Henry V, reassuringly. 'Not Amurath an Amurath succeeds, / But Harry, Harry.') The Turks are the enemy fleet in Cyprus-set *Othello*, whose malignant and turbanned Turk we'll meet in Chapter 24.

I look at the menu and order a *Duble Türk Kahvesi* – a double Turkish coffee. I don't know any Turkish, but I can guess that much. But only because in 1928, under Ataturk's reforms, the country shifted from the

Ottoman Turkish alphabet – Arabic-based – to the modern Turkish alphabet, a twenty-nine-letter set largely coinciding with the Latin.

The abrupt top-down deliberateness of the changes to Turkish is unusual, but all languages evolve – at different rates, in different ways, subject to different influences. Since Shakespeare we've had four centuries of uninterrupted linguistic evolution, so some linguistic gap between him and today's audiences is inevitable.

Here are some lines from *The Taming of the Shrew* – where old Baptista is trying to get his elder daughter Katherine to stop terrorising her younger sister, Bianca – in a Dutch translation (*De Dolle Bruyloft*) by A. Sybant.* A Dutch speaker could tell at once this is not a recent text. My friend Mattho identified these markers.

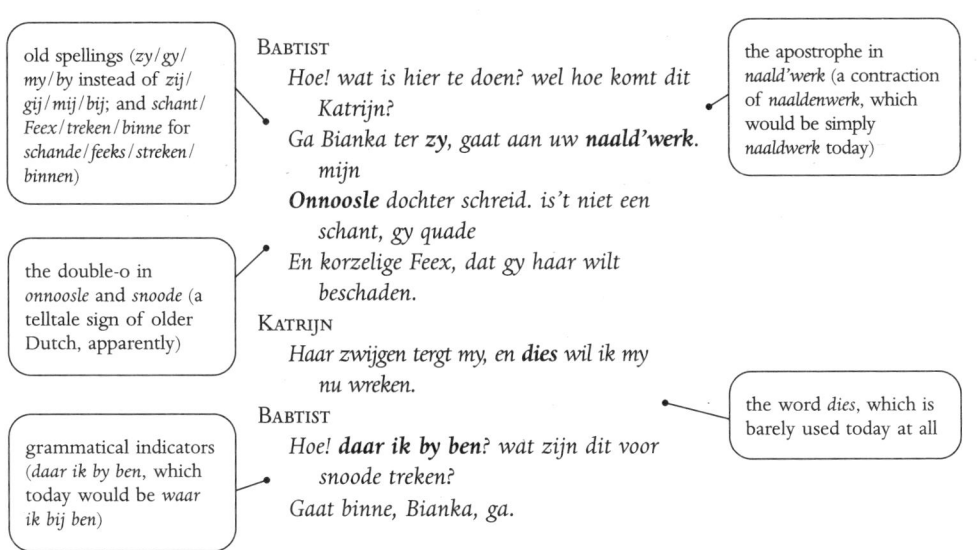

This conversation is written in seventeenth-century Dutch, because it's from a translation published in 1654.†

But now we turn back to that early twentieth-century Brazilian

---

* This was the translation quoted in the title of the last chapter.
† Seemingly the oldest surviving (sort-of) translation of a Shakespeare play, though the line's slightly arbitrary – I'm deciding that e.g. Jan Vos's *Aran and Titus* (1641) is more adaptation than translation, that the 1654 Sybant is more translation.

all-prose *Hamlet* by the jurist and writer Tristão da Cunha. His decision to drop the verse altogether and render the whole play anew in poetic prose was, he said, prompted by a desire for 'fidelity' – verse would involve too much collateral loss. Changing things in order to preserve things is a standard translator manoeuvre.

Overall my feelings about the effectiveness of Tristão's translation are mixed. Not so much because of the all-prose choice, though, but mostly because, in the height of modernism, this translator decided the greatest fidelity he could offer the play was to reproduce it in seventeenth-century language. (Or at least language heavy with pseudo-seventeenth-century markers.) Unlike the Dutch *Shrew* that used seventeenth-century language because it was by a seventeenth-century translator, this was a twentieth-century archaicising *choice*. And a strange one, not only being out of step with the literary movements of his own time (and the literary translation movements), but also because it would have entailed a distancing effect for a new audience in 1930s Brazil. The language a seventeenth-century English or Dutch audience heard wouldn't have been alienating, archaically distant, it would have been totally fresh and innovative to them. So the fact that translations typically bring a text closer to their new actors and their new audiences is not anachronistic, but entirely appropriate.

There's a logic to wanting to convey some sense of oldness (Shakespeare doesn't sound like Sally Rooney in English, so why should he in Italian?), but this cannot be done through any kind of temporal purity. For one thing, languages change at a different pace. Sure, translate Dante into early fourteenth-century English if you like, but Dante can be quite readily understood by Italians today, whereas *The Canterbury Tales*, nearly a century later, is taxing for the modern Anglophone. And if you're hoping to read Homer translated, by some kind of pure equivalence, into the same English that was spoken in the eighth century BCE, we might have a problem. (OK, two problems.) I do understand the temptation to archaicise – I've succumbed to it myself occasionally, and it's a treat to be able to play with language in that particular way – but, well, I don't love the Tristão. I only hope his ghost will forgive me.

The English language has travelled some distance since Shakespeare; but most translators will position themselves linguistically somewhere approximately *now*, not *then*, so the great distance isn't something their new audience will experience. Meanings that would have been clear to a Globe audience four centuries ago, and that have faded into obscurity (because our English is no longer Shakespeare's), are now clear again in Ukrainian or Korean.

By bridging the distance, translation can mitigate what to contemporary Anglophones could be anachronistic misunderstandings, or difficulties in understanding altogether. Words change their meanings (the 'nice' in the *Two Gentlemen* . . . quotation on p.20 doesn't mean 'pleasant', it might actually mean 'shy', per the Arden notes, or 'fastidious', per the Penguin) – but there's no such confusion in translation. When Juliet stands on her balcony and asks 'Wherefore?', there's no bafflement even to an audience member encountering the play for the first time – почему are you Romeo? *Por quê?* Simply, in translation: *why?*

Tristão wrote that 'the language should evoke the atmosphere of the period', rather than make the characters of Renaissance theatre speak as today. And my own reservations aside, many of his contemporaries didn't seem to mind – his translation was widely praised at the time, and in 1948, after his death, it was staged by a student company, with some success. The role of Gertrude was covered last-minute by an understudy – the young woman who, as 'Barbara Heliodora', would decades later come to translate all of Shakespeare herself.

Tristão da Cunha, incidentally, was a pen name, for a man called José Maria Leitão da Cunha Filho, born in Rio de Janeiro in 1878. By the time *Hamleto* was published in 1933, Tristão had married an English woman called Agnes, and they were back in Rio de Janeiro where they had raised three children. The youngest, twelve at the time, was my grandmother. When I wrote guiltily that I didn't love his translation, this biographical fact might help you understand my slight pangs.

This is not to argue that a new translation must be all insistently contemporary either. An audience's suspension of disbelief can be harder to earn if characters use conspicuously anachronistic slang, say. A certain timelessness is good – not that such a thing genuinely exists (language doesn't operate outside time), but the effect is fakeable. And in moderation, linguistic touches that feel slightly out-of-our-time can be valuable for situating the play in a not-quite-specific past. There are ways of opening a door to the late sixteenth century without having to commit wholesale to a funny olde voice.

Chico got fun bits of evocative nautical terminology for his *Tempestade* from the *História trágico-maritima*, an eighteenth-century collection of Portuguese shipwreck accounts (two volumes). Deciding when to use light archaic touches and when to use familiarly modern language – with or without what feels like jarring anachronisms – can be a matter of scholarship (which word would a speaker *actually* have used in year such-and-such?), but more often than not, the decision is the sort of sleight of hand (like much about translation) that's more impressionistic than rigorously researched. What would *feel* appropriate-vs-anachronistic for a reader or listener, rather than what *is*. When translating Machado de Assis, the late-nineteenth-century Brazilian novelist, I would have hesitated to have his characters talk about 'hanging out' in a tavern, even if Keats uses the phrase in a letter eighty years earlier. The question, for me, is when an anachronism is *perceived*. I probably wouldn't use 'tosspots' in a translation of a very old text either, even if it's technically fair game – which is why there's always a 'wait . . . what?' reaction in the audience when Feste sings of them at the end of *Twelfth Night* . . .

While there are interesting exceptions, translators do not on the whole fill their work with highly flagrant anachronism, but nor do they often (*pace* Tristão) ape 400-year-old vocabulary and diction – rather there's a sweet spot between the two. Frank Günther – another of that rare breed to have managed his own set of the complete works, his translations now used in countless productions – described his self-imposed rules when it came to using figurative language:

> a Shakespearean character cannot 'let off steam', because the steam engine that triggered this expression originally was not yet invented in Shakespearean times. So I draw a line where the vocabulary of

the Industrial Revolution starts; and I try to smuggle in as many colloquial words that do NOT sound like the twentieth century as possible.

I said earlier that translators work with whatever resource is at their disposal, but this is not quite true. Sometimes, unlike Shakespeare himself, they need to choose *not* to write with every resource at their disposal.

Still, contemporary translations are, more often than not, constructed from something at least *close* to contemporary French, or contemporary Farsi, or contemporary Thai. So today's English audiences might find Shakespeare more distant than an audience in another language, for whom he has been revived fresher, more immediate. Translating this sixteenth-century English into something like twenty-first-century Dutch changes the audience's relationship to what they're hearing. So instead of attempting to recreate a contrived sort of mock-Dutch of four centuries ago, should we go for modern Dutch jokes, idioms and slang?

The Bulgarian translator Alexander Shurbanov pointed out how much the natural language of communication on the Bulgarian street has changed even in the half-century since his predecessor Valeri Petrov's translations, but this doesn't mean that Alexander has aimed to imitate the contemporary exactly, but rather create a kind of 'linguistic neutrality'. Likewise, Niels isn't going for twenty-first-century Danish, not least because slang can date within six months – let alone fifty years – and he wants his translations to be used for some decades yet. (Translations of plays *can* be pitched to their exact time – this room, these people sitting here, in this theatre, tonight – in a way that the consumption of a novel on paper is less controllable. But to some translators, that specificity, for all its benefits, is also limiting.)

Niels describes himself engaged in a process of finding a Danish that isn't contemporary but also isn't pretending to be 400 years old. (His language has changed relatively fast in the last four centuries, in its words, spelling *and* grammar – twenty-first-century Danes would struggle with late-sixteenth-century Danish.) For him, this involves occasional deployment of words that might be fading from use but can still be understood within the context, but not words that are familiarly marked as old-fashioned that might create a sense of attempted archaicising.

When Hamlet's uncle says: 'My words fly up, my thoughts remain below. / Words without thoughts never to heaven go.', his Danish alter ego is given the lines *Mit ord kan flyve, tanken blir på jord. / Himlen er stængt for tankeløse ord.* That is to say, 'Heaven is closed to thoughtless words.' But for 'closed' Niels used the word *stængt*, which is an old-fashioned word meaning 'barred' (a *stang* being a long piece of wood) – the word, says Niels, is not in very common usage today, but it's 'not quite dead yet'. We'll later see both Jean-Michel and Emine drawing on older words – not because their translations were into faux-archaic French or Turkish, but because when they have problems to solve, they will use every stratum of language at their disposal. (In Turkish, because of its particular evolutionary journey, this is a choice that has distinct implications.)

The Māori translator Te Haumihiata Mason, with whom I had the pleasure of having lunch in Rotorua, did deliberately employ occasional older words and usages in her *Romeo and Juliet* – not because the play required it, but as a way of reviving some of the richnesses of her language among a population whose vocabulary has been gradually narrowing. For example, the word *mate* (pronounced *ma-te*, disyllabic). Today's *te reo* learners tend to focus on one cluster of meanings (*dead, injured, sick*), but it's a word with a lot more going on. It can mean *having no option* (but to), it can mean *being in dire need* (of), and more besides – a nice opportunity for a translator who wants to widen a sense of possibility in her language.

Te Haumihiata described her *Romeo and Juliet* as 'the door to a language that we're bordering on losing'. In this technologically changing age, she envisages an audience of young people, but the language she hears from them nowadays is quite unlike her parents' – so she is trying to preserve little bits of theirs. She teaches me some of the idioms and other colloquialisms that are no longer much heard, including lots of short (usually monosyllabic) exclamations that convey annoyance, disgust, relief, resignation. She still uses them herself, and now her granddaughter (and co-translator, sitting with us at lunch) uses them, too, with her kids.

In the opening to *Romeo and Juliet,* which begins with a conversation about fighting, the line:

I strike being quickly moved.

becomes:

E, kia riri nei au, he mate kei te haere

Where that little E is aggressive, threatening. Later in that scene, Romeo says:

Tut, I have lost myself.

Te Haumihiata gives him:

Ai! Kua hē hoki au;

That rather mild Elizabethan 'tut' is replaced by the very expressive 'ai!' which appears often in her translation – sometimes long drawn out – conveying varying degrees of irritation.

'Many of these native exclamations have mostly fallen into disuse,' Te Haumihiata says, 'and are now only used by the few native speakers we have left. New generations are developing their own expressions for such things.' But they mustn't be allowed to die, so they should be written somewhere. Unlike the Tristão approach, however, this isn't about creating a sense of archaism, a matter of literary curiosity or dramatic effect – and nor is it, she said, about the text as an archive. 'I want it kept *alive.*' She wants people to *use* these great resources.

Whenever her translation is staged, she hopes to be there in rehearsal with the young actors, specifically to tell them how these exclamations should be delivered.

On my last visit to Calcutta, I'd just missed a production of *Hamlet* that was still being raved about. The actors had been using a new, specially commissioned translation. The translator, Chaiti Mitra, described her acute awareness that she was translating for a more mixed audience than might have been traditional (the lead actor has an established film career). What this meant, she says, was that many in the audience don't speak very 'good' Bengali, but rather Bengali with a lot of Hindi mixed into it. Which required 'trying to translate a classical text into a Bengali that would be enjoyed by the young students sitting in the back row'. So definitely *not* using the formal heavy language (Sadhubhasha) which some translations have used, and specifically *avoiding* archaic vocabulary. Her Hamlet speaks in a language that's sometimes lyrical, but does not use dated words.

Our thoughts about even something as basic as which words rhyme with which other words – this changes over time, too. And once again, it's an opportunity for the translator to restore some closeness to the source. Shakespeare's Sonnet number 116 ends:

| If this be error and upon me proved, | А если я не прав и лжет мой стих, |
| I never writ, nor no man ever loved. | То нет любви – и нет стихов моих! |

Translator Samuil Marshak takes what looks like a not-quite-exact rhyme in English (*proved*/*loved*) and with some alteration concludes his sonnet on a perfect rhyme in Russian (*ст<u>их</u>*/*мо<u>их</u>*).* Except that, once

---

* See also: 'and if anyone disagrees with what i say, / i swear i never wrote this or loved in any way'; (from 'sonnets that slap: a collection of the littest shakespearean sonnets translated for a new generation').

again, a Russian's experience of the translation is in fact more 'accurate' than my reading of the source text today, because, as I've mentioned already, 'prove' and 'love' actually *would* have been perfect rhymes in Shakespeare's English, and now, in translation, they are again. Translation is solving the problem created by four centuries of distancing change. Plenty has been lost, within English, with the erosions of time; many of these things are regained, restored in translation.

Chapter 7

Milý pane, mluvte i vy též jenom jako dřiv

(on translating into English)

Almost every Shakespeare translation has some updating function, one way or another. The play might have been written *then*, but its translators use the resources made available by the new language *now*. Even while avoiding obvious anachronism, they're producing something that does not sound four centuries old to their audience. It is only those of us who live in English who are stuck with 400-year-old Shakespeare. That, said director Tim Supple, is 'both a treasure and a millstone'. Everybody else has the work nudged a few steps closer, so when Juliet and Romeo are speaking Spanish (in the translation by Josep María Jaumà), there's no distancing *wherefore*.

Oh, Romeo, Romeo, ¿por qué has de ser Romeo?

A little gap between actor and audience has been closed. But oh, I dare you to try 'Why are you Romeo?' on the London stage . . .

So – what about translating Shakespeare into English? This chapter will briefly look at some different extremes – major creative recreation vs straight contemporary simplifying 'translation'. (Those inverted commas are there for a reason, and to indicate general disapproval.) The former might include a children's retelling or a complete repositioning of the play in a new context with a new language to fit; among the latter, those countless versions in modern English, of the 'made easy' variety – 'Shakespeare for Idiots!' – some of which have their uses.

Most of these cases are essentially publishing propositions rather than theatrical ones – they aren't all-new English texts to be staged and spoken. But English-to-English translation is constantly happening in staged productions, even if on a small scale, and even if no one will draw your attention to it.

'Like a theatre director' is one among the many metaphors we translators use to explain our practice. We are taking a script as a starting point, and producing an interpretation of it; the new audience gains access to the source but only as mediated by our individual reading of it, re-expressed. But the British director Robert Icke allows himself the sort of liberties when working from pre-existing texts that we translators can only dream of. The changes he makes are structural, interventionist in the interest of a work's coherent dramatic function. (I say this as observation rather than criticism, incidentally – I love his work.)

But he also does things like this, in the first scene of *Player Kings* (his Falstaff multi-play mash-up):

> So shaken as we are, so wan with care,
> Find we a time for frighted peace to pant
> And breathe short-winded accents of new wars
> To be commenced in strands afar remote.

And this in the second scene:

> What a devil hast thou to do with the time of the day? Unless hours were cups of sack, and minutes chickens, and clocks the tongues of whores, and dials the signs of leaping-houses, and the blessed sun himself a fair hot wench in flame-coloured taffeta . . .

In the Shakespeare text, 'wars' used to be 'broils', and 'chickens' was 'capons', and 'whores' was 'bawds'.

I mentioned these changes to one of the translators in this book, and their immediate response was *Oh my God* . . . Yet evidently this Icke text is not more translated than any inter-language translation. The move certainly goes no further than (entirely acceptably) translating the whole thing into French, with *luttes, chapons, maquerelles*. The text is brought fractionally closer to its audience – again, as most translations do. The occasional speed bump to understanding is removed, making it comprehensible in the same way those original words would have been to Shakespeare's own audience, and it's not careless: yes, meaning for meaning, these are straightforward 'translations', but it's all done with due attention to the rhythms of the speeches (each word fits perfectly into the pre-existing slot), respecting the metre of the verse and the rhythm of the prose, syllable for syllable. And I know I've been saying thus far that a translator takes every word of Shakespeare's English seriously – precision, not paraphrasing gist, remember? – but I find myself entirely untroubled by this sort of change.

In 2016, Emma Rice, the then artistic director of Shakespeare's Globe, got in media trouble for suggesting in a *Today* programme interview that changing the odd word in a Shakespeare play might be justifiable. The example she gave came from these lines in the *Cymbeline* song we saw in that lovely Italian translation:

> Golden lads and girls all must,
> As chimney-sweepers, come to dust.

There was a theory, which gained currency in the 1970s, that 'golden lads' and 'chimney-sweepers' were Warwickshire dialect words for dandelions – and you can see the logic: they are golden-yellow first, then they open into what look like chimney-sweep brushes, before a puff of wind turns them to dust. Emma suggested that, seeing as few people would get this meaning, the word 'chimney-sweepers' might simply be replaced by 'dandelions'. This suggestion was, rather predictably, the end of the world.

A series of letters in the *Guardian* went under the headline 'The sin of smoothing out Shakespeare', and objected to today's stupid world with all its dumbing-down and miscellaneous idiocy. But Emma – in her interview and the *Cymbeline* production that followed – was not taking something that was *intended* to be obscure and 'smoothing it out' to make it inappropriately, nay, offensively comprehensible to those of us too stupid to appreciate it. She was taking something that was written for one audience to enjoy, and nudging it just a couple of little steps towards another. Again, as a translator, I find it hard to object.

It turns out the dandelion theory is unlikely to be correct (a shame – I thought it very pleasing), but had it been true, swapping in *DAN-de-LI-ons* for *CHIM-ney-SWEE-pers* would have been a neat enough solution. An outrage, a travesty, a monstrous betrayal! But also, again, that movement of sensitively managed convergence between text and audience that we translators are doing every day.

Across the road from the theatre where I saw *Player Kings*, there was a *Romeo and Juliet* in an English translation far more interventionist on a word-for-word level than Icke's. This was a hip-hop *Romeo and Juliet*, in partnership with Beats & Elements theatre company. Unlike 'made easy' versions, which I'll touch on in a moment, this version found what is essentially another rich, coherent language in which to express what Shakespeare is doing with his.

For the target language, which is the specific, detailed, consistent language of the south London characters in this translated production, the phrase '*Do you kiss your teeth at me, fam?*' proved to be a perfect translation of '*Do you bite your thumb at us, sir?*' The syllabic shape of the line, the rhythm, the tone and contemporary energy – everything.

A recurring theme in this book is the way translators can take advantage of the possibilities their particular language happens to allow. The word *cap* does things now that it did not do in the 1590s, so Shakespeare didn't have the option of making his Romeo say 'I'm gettin' capped by a Capulet', as he does in this version. But wouldn't he, if he could?

The least interesting propositions to my mind are those texts that exist only to provide a crib, texts produced with no interest at all in literary or dramatic effect. They might call themselves translations, but their aim is usually to convey only *meaning* in simplified form, and – as you'll have gathered by now – I make greater demands of translations than that. Even a sacred text can be rewritten very effectively in twenty-first-century English, into a language that's distinctive and coherent and energetic and expressly contextual (south London hip-hop *R&J*), just as it can be thrillingly crystallised in the language of *West Side Story*; and I have no queasiness at all about Shakespeare being entirely reconstructed in the medium of Norwegian or Tamil – these are all translations of sorts.

The 'made easy' versions I've seen – and maybe there are more interesting ones – privilege meaning over every other feature of Shakespeare's writing – actually, they don't just privilege it: meaning is the *only* thing they're interested in. And that, I feel, is paraphrase, not translation. 'Are you biting your thumb at us?' does *mean* the same as 'Do you bite your thumb at us?', but it's less compact and less energetic. I maintain that it's possible to clarify without simplifying. 'Are you biting your thumb at us?' is only simplification, and it is all loss.

Helpful publishers of versions in this vein have offered us, among other options:

> To live or not to live. That is the issue.

> The question is: is it better to be alive or dead?

I mean . . . yes, I guess?
    Also:

> Oh angels, protect us!

or:

> Angels and God's messengers defend us!

(There's a trochee to launch that one, at least, so I probably shouldn't complain.)

Also – Shakespearean text is not always *that* hard, so long as it's in the hands of an actor who knows how to tell a story with it. Sometimes it's simpler than you expect. In *The Merry Wives of Windsor*, when Mistress Page and Mistress Ford are deciding whether they might hide Falstaff in the laundry basket, Mistress Ford doesn't come out with some sort of parodic-Elizabethan *Yea, my liege, forsooth, methinks yon scoundrel be too corpulent to be capacity'd therein! Alas, what endeavours else remain that I might in all sagacity undertake?*

Shakespeare gives her:

He's too big to go in there.

That's it. And then:

What shall I do?*

In one of his lectures on Shakespeare, Jorge Luis Borges uses an example from the same *Hamlet* speech we've lately seen, in which the ghost is said to revisit 'the glimpses of the moon', a phrase Borges particularly likes:

I don't think it can be translated. Perhaps the words can be translated. Certainly Shakespeare cannot be translated. 'The glimpses of the moon' means exactly 'the glimpses of the moon.'

But note that Borges isn't describing the impossibility of interlingual translation here, but the inadequacy of a semantic paraphrase into some alternative English. He's talking about Shakespeare's *precision*.

Knowing the single central meaning of all the words in a line of Shakespeare is useful, but knowing their meaning without any other of the words' effects is a bloodless sort of experience. Of course there

---

* Admittedly, just ten lines later, we do get the somewhat less immediately comprehensible: '*Where's the cowl-staff? – Look how you drumble!*'

are plenty of inadequate translations into other languages, too, where a translator knew what all of the words meant and got all of them 'right', as it were – but got just about everything else wrong. The reason I'm so often excited about translation of Shakespeare is not that he 'survives' the ravages of translation because the meaning is just so great that it doesn't matter if we lose 'the poetry' (or whatever . . .); but because in the good translations, meaning and music and detailed dramatic effect are *all* still present and alive. Countless Shakespeare translations define their fidelity in a multivalent way, trying to construct something as sophisticated out of their particular language (and its possibilities) as Shakespeare was constructing from his.

In a 1960 performance, the line from the first (Quarto) edition of *A Midsummer Night's Dream*:

> I am amazed at your words.

was performed including a word added in the later (Folio) edition, as

> I am amazed at your passionate words.

Which, you will have noticed, is still definitely in English. But in this case, at least, other constraints meant there was a reason to choose that slightly expanded line. Good translation is inevitably all about change, but as we see so often, it's change that is justified by an attempt not to simplify but to preserve. Gold into gold.

Chapter 8

Podrę wiersz. Proza lepiej usposobi

(on prose)

Like rhyming vs not rhyming, like iambs vs trochees, prose has the useful property of being not-verse, and verse of being not-prose. Each offsets the other. The distinction drawn between noble patricians vs the common plebeians in *Coriolanus*, say, where the former tend to verse, the latter to prose. (It's not a hard and fast rule, but a good general one.)

That *Coriolanus* quotation on p.20, in verse, was spoken by patrician Coriolanus himself:

> You common cry of curs whose breath I hate
> As reek o'th' rotten fens, whose loves I prize
> As the dead carcasses of unburied men
> [etc.]

Meanwhile, here's a speech from a servingman:

> Let me have war, say I. It exceeds peace as far as day does night. It's sprightly waking, audible and full of vent. Peace is a very apoplexy, lethargy, mulled, deaf, sleepy, insensible, a getter of more bastard children than war's a destroyer of men.

(Like many of this play's socially inferior speakers of predominant prose, he is not even named.)

But of course prose isn't *only* not-verse, there to offset that other category of writing. It has its own characteristics and ample translation challenges. While all-prose translations of Shakespeare, those ones that erase the verse entirely, feel inadequate to me, actual prose well-used can of course be artful, its voices can be distinctive, with rhythmic and other 'poetic' devices employed for its effects.

And this artfulness will inevitably make demands on a translator. At an extreme, there can't be many parts in Shakespeare that are harder to get working than Lear's companion, the Fool – for an actor *or* for a translator. It's not the hugest part – with a couple of hundred lines, he's only the sixth most talkative character in this play. So why's he difficult?

One reason the Fool is hard to translate is that, simply, he isn't always easily *understood*. He often speaks sort of at a slant to the world, by allusion (often to things unfamiliar to us). He isn't easily transposed to other periods, or to a more naturalistic performance style, say. His untethered speech can feel like nonsense, but it's not arbitrary, so a translator must grapple with every reference, every quoted bit of song, every proverb, every allusion, till its working is comprehended.

Almost everything we know about the Fool we see for ourselves in his performance – it's rare that other characters talk about him.* And in English, he's linguistically and rhythmically different from every other character – so must he be in his new voice. And unlike, say, Feste in *Twelfth Night*, the Fool is, by design, not all that funny most of the time

---

* There's just one passing mention of a bond he shares with Cordelia, which will be echoed in the final scene. By that point, we haven't seen the Fool in a while, and when Lear sits on stage holding Cordelia's dead body, what he says is 'And my poor fool is hanged'. Niels was intrigued by the connection between the characters, each of them a kind of mirror to Lear. So he suggested the connection in Danish, too – taking advantage of the fact that 'lille nor' is an affectionate 'little darling', and 'lille nar' means 'little fool': *Mit lille nor, min lille nar er hængt* . . .

(there are glimpses). He seldom tells an Actual Joke. There are things a translator can preserve that might elicit a laugh, says Niels, 'but there's always a kind of bitter tone beneath it. There's a strange sadness about the Fool, and that's something you should keep, I'm not trying to make him just a comedian'. Here's a bit in English and also, in case you were wondering, what it looked like in Emine's Turkish:

Cry to it, nuncle, as the cockney did to the eels when she put 'em i'th' paste alive: she knapped 'em o'th' coxcombs with a stick, and cried 'Down, wantons, down!' 'Twas her brother that in pure kindness to his horse buttered his hay.	Amca, sen de, oldu olacak, şu Londralı kadın gibi seslen bari yüreğine: Hani kadın yemek yapayım derken yılan balıklarını canlı canlı hamura koymuş da, balıklar hamurun içinden kafa çıkardıkça sopayla vura vura 'serseriler, inin bakayım aşağı!' diyormuş ya, seninki de aynı o hesap. Bu kadının bir de erkek kardeşi.

If you don't know Turkish, you might still spot the *Londralı* – she's a London woman, the *cockney*. You can also see that there's barely any increase in word count (6.5%) but a large expansion in character count (34.5%, from 235 to 316), a phenomenon with which we'll become familiar.

'At a very early stage when I hadn't translated very much of Shakespeare,' Niels said, 'I thought, when I finished the verse passages and shifted into prose, "wow, now it's going to be easier, I can do this in a hurry!" But the more I did, the more I realised these prose passages also have their own aesthetic, they have their own way of influencing the audience, and much of it is about pace. There's a *drive* in it that's very important to keep up, and the tempo is very important.'

(Niels compares it with some energetic spoken-word poetry. We speak shortly after the opening night of his translation of *Cyrano de Bergerac*, translated not from Rostand but from the Martin Crimp version, and he noticed how much his experience with Shakespearean prose had taught him.)

The Fool doesn't follow most characters' conventions of social discourse, but there is an eccentric logic to him. The same play also gives prose to Edgar, a young nobleman who first disguises himself as Poor Tom, a mad beggar wandering the hostile landscape, then briefly takes on another voice to conceal his identity from his father (whose eyes have been torn out and who has just failed to jump off the cliffs of Dover).

Here's a bit of Poor Tom's prose – frantic, chaotic, jumpy:

> Bless thy five wits, Tom's a-cold! O do, de, do, de, do, de: bless thee from whirlwinds, star-blasting and taking. Do Poor Tom some charity, whom the foul fiend vexes. There could I have him now, and there, and there again, and there.

And here he is again (this time in Lawrence's translation) – equally dislocated rhythms and just the same nervy pacing, for this wretched man who's far too broken down to speak in verse:

> Salva tuas cinco faculdades, ai, Tom tá com frio. O do, dudi, didu, dadu: Bendito seja, e bem longe dos redemunhos, dos assopros astrais, dos contágios! Façam uma caridade pro Pobre Tom, que o bicho malino está atormentando. Eu podia pegá-lo agora – aqui, ali, agora, lá!

Lawrence didn't want Edgar's adopted voice to slot into any pre-existing Brazilian voice, such as a *caipira** (originally a rural person from São Paulo, the word is now used for a sort of 'hillbilly'); rather it should keep something of that spirit but is, in Lawrence's word, 'transfigured' so the audience feels a sense of familiarity with something they've never heard before. Because each translator uses whichever resources the new medium has at hand, Lawrence took as one of his touchstones the

---

* Yes, a *caipirinha* is a diminutive of this.

great Brazilian writer João Guimarães Rosa, author of the one of Brazil's twentieth-century masterpieces (now freshly Englished by Alison Entrekin as *Vastlands: The Crossing*), whose language is inventive, energetic, low-rural register, a language that feels real and spoken, but is an entirely original creation.

(We'll see more of Edgar's assumed voice later, in Bulgarian.)

Unconstrained by a formal structure, prose can more easily build momentum on a bigger scale, so it's no wonder this is what Kent uses when addressing Oswald (again in *King Lear*), calling him

> A knave, a rascal, an eater of broken meats; a base, proud, shallow, beggarly, three-suited-hundred-pound, filthy, worsted-stocking knave; a lily-livered, action-taking knave, a whoreson, glass-gazing, super-serviceable, finical rogue; one trunk-inheriting slave, one that wouldst be a bawd in way of good service, and art nothing but the composition of a knave, beggar, coward, pander and the son and heir of a mongrel bitch . . .

Even if you don't know what it all means, you can tell he is not a fan. And though it is prose, it's all about rhythm.

> *A bribón, a cafajéste, a slúbbert, and a tállerkenslíkker; a kof, a podléts, an infâme crapúle; a dikomanís, pornogenís, hundertpfündiger, schmútziger, grobstrümpfiger skurk; a truhán con hígado de azucéna, a villáno spiantáto, a Máitomáksainen káräjäpúkari, a grufolatóre, linge-blide, nemérnic, a szérvilis páraszt; a choramínga de tribunál, one that would be a sélvglad, smískende, skabágtig kholóp; and nothing but the composition of a tigger, kujón, svýnya, fils de pute and the syn and heir of a gryásnyi ploot.**

---

* Tr. Andrukhovych, Baudissin, Brunse, Déprats, Foix, Gheorghiu, Jylhä, Kapsalis, Kuzmin, Melchiori, Nádasdy, Nutku, Pasternak, Paszkowski and Pereira. (Non-Roman words have been transliterated, and some stress-accents added to help with pronunciation.)

You should test out how that sounds. Read it aloud. It's very satisfying.

Emine compared translating Lear's Fool to translating the Porter scene in *Macbeth*, for its sheer density. The Porter scene is a particular favourite of hers (though cut from the Turkish production I saw) because it allowed her to draw energy from the specific slang of the vibrant multicultural neighbourhood in Adana where she grew up. Vernacular prose is often quite high-tempo – think of the quick patter of a comic scene, especially – and certainly no less linguistically playful than verse. Jean-Michel cited *Much Ado about Nothing* as a play where the prose (the default mode here) is typically harder than the verse to translate, simply because it's more sophisticated, he said, 'more structured in terms of antitheses, grammatical structures, etc.', while the verse is easier to understand and hence to translate. Especially something like the clever, energetic bickering between Beatrice and Benedick, whose sparring uses all the possibilities of prose – we're witnessing two people showing off how clever they are, visibly flexing their wit, not just exchanging banal formalities.

Chico is a particular fan of prose swearing, referencing this moment from the start of *The Tempest*:

Hang, cur! Hang, you whoreson, insolent noise-maker!

Morre enforcado, vira-lata! Vai te enforcar, filho duma prostituta, insolente boca-suja.

The Portuguese takes longer to deliver (Shakespeare's 'Hang!' does a lot for one syllable), but it's energetic and percussive and full of relish – being longer than English, it fits in more hard consonants, plus an insistent rhythm sustained by those compound nouns, etc. This translator is definitely having fun, which I reckon is sometimes the main thing.

As he works through the plays, Chico is particularly keen to get to the *Henry IV*s, mostly I suspect because he can't wait to do Falstaff. It's easy to think of obvious formal aspects as the translator's big challenge to recreate, but Falstaff is another one of those characters who is overwhelmingly prosey yet has such distinctive rhythm and diction. In English, you can spot a line of his at 200 yards.

While a translator might not feel the need to count syllables as you would when constructing metrical verse, Ádám does try to stick to similar syllable lengths when making Hungarian prose speeches, because, he says, it does matter roughly how many seconds one person speaks compared to another. If Shakespeare's musical score gives three bars to you and five to me, that's the balance to maintain. Though that's an imperfect analogy, because what Ádám wants his audience to *feel* in the transition from verse to prose is, simply, 'OK, we're putting our instruments down, closing our music, and we're just going to *speak*.'

Syllable count notwithstanding, a translation might fall victim to other considerations entirely, of course. Lots of prose is humorous, so – says Ádám – '*everything* else is overridden by the necessity to have the audience laugh'.

It might seem odd today, but verse in Shakespeare isn't intended always to make his characters less natural, more contrived, rhetorical, artificially *heightened*. Characters are often just speaking as people, not as if constantly addressing a public meeting. Sometimes the transition to verse – even rhyming verse – happens as a character becomes more and more impassioned. But often, as I've mentioned, prose also serves as a useful contrast to that-which-is-not-prose. The extremes are *Richard II* (all verse) and *Merry Wives of Windsor* (nearly ninety per cent prose), but it's often the back and forth, the rhythm-switching, that provides the most interesting places for a translator to show off their virtuosity.

This even happens *within* conversations. In *A Midsummer Night's Dream*, Bottom speaks prose and Titania verse; when they are talking to each other, the rhythm alternates between speakers. (When he's with her and her fairies, he is the scene's lone prose speaker.)

And in *Coriolanus* we see prose/verse intermingled, too:

MENENIUS
>   Alack,
> You are transported by calamity
> Thither where more attends you, and you slander
> The helms o'th' state, who care for you like fathers,
> When you curse them as enemies.

SECOND CITIZEN
> Care for us? True, indeed, they ne'er cared for us yet. Suffer us to famish, and their store-houses crammed with grain; make edicts for usury, to support usurers; repeal daily any wholesome act established against the rich . . .

Like Sho's discovery that he needed to make his *Dream* rhyme specifically so that he could create the effect of not-rhyme alongside it, every *Coriolanus* translation I've found that could recreate this prose/verse back-and-forth did so. The only ones that did not were those that *could* not, because they had opted to make the play prose throughout, an initial policy choice that immediately limited their subsequent options.

The only adequate solution, then, is to commit to doing precisely, exactly what Shakespeare is doing, always absolutely all of the time. Simple!*

Kazuko Matsuoka has now completed the full Shakespeare canon in Japanese, but she began each play by first writing it out in English, in full, by hand. You get a sense of the weight of it, how the pacing works, how the shifts in macro-level form (very basically, verse and prose, rhymed or unrhymed, etc.) are patterned, which character has the most lines or the most broken sentences or the longest words. Apparently Hunter S. Thompson typed out *The Great Gatsby*, end to end, before he'd ever written a book of his own, just to see what it felt like.

When I translate, I like where possible to embark upon the work without even having read the source text, discovering it in the process

---

* Not simple.

of making my rough first draft. I am not, however, translating Shakespeare, and while there are countless decisions I need to make in the process of, say, constructing the voice of a novel's narrator, I seldom have *form* to worry about, and can usually make a start without big pre-emptive policy decisions.

But one thing that became clear when I was working my way through those books that appeared through my letterbox – those editions of Shakespeare plays in various languages – was that even without any access to the alphabet, I could usually tell what I was looking at *if I made certain assumptions*. I could get my rough bearings when the translator had chosen to maintain regular verse, to stick with the original title, to fragment the lines when Shakespeare did, not to make drastic cuts to alter the length, to shift into prose when Shakespeare shifted into prose, to repeat when Shakespeare repeated, to rhyme when he rhymed. There's a bit of repetition early in *Romeo and Juliet*'s opening scene in this Hebrew version, so I suspect it means *Do you kiss your teeth at me, fam?*, because the source material is patterned in just the same place and the translator must have recreated it.

Almost every solution we're looking at in a translator's work starts with their identifying something in the source, the thing that needs to be preserved. To recreate an effect, the translator needs to *notice* it initially, and see how it's achieved – and then figure out how to achieve it afresh. This applies to those big policy decisions (do I use verse? what *kind* of language am I using?), right down to the small-scale ones. And I do mean *really* small . . .

Chapter 9

Ստապի'ր, շուն չ ա'ո

(on commas, and other things)

Shakespeare begins *Twelfth Night* with Duke Orsino describing the effect of the music he's listening to.

Here are his first eight lines, in English and Hungarian (thanks to Ádám Nádasdy):

ORSINO	HERCEG
If music be the food of love, play on,	Ha a zene étel a szerelemnek,
Give me excess of it, that surfeiting	hát játsszatok! Sőt, tömjetek tele,
The appetite may sicken and so die.	hadd fojtsa meg a vágyat a csömör!
That strain again, it had a dying fall.	Ezt még egyszer! . . . Szép, elhaló a vége,
O, it came o'er my ear like the sweet south	suttog fülembe, mint édes lehellet,
That breathes upon a bank of violets,	mely ibolyák fölött az illatot
Stealing and giving odour.	teríti lopva. – Elég már, elég!
Enough, no more,	
'Tis not so sweet now as it was before.	Már nem édesek ezek a zenék.

IF THIS BE MAGIC

Apparently, that final word, *zenék*, means music – but in the plural. For some reason, the translator has chosen to say that *These musics (i.e. songs) are no longer so sweet.*

('K' used as a suffix is the marker of a plural in Hungarian.)

Eight lines that are not rhymed, except where in English they conclude – conclusively – on a pair that rhymes very neatly. *No more. Before.* I did initially think it a shame that the Hungarian can't do this, but I'm told by Hungarian friends that the terminal -g (*elég*) and the terminal -k (*zenék*) sound almost indistinguishable, so there *is* an end-line rhyme, just like Shakespeare's, but also a (new) perfect internal rhyme in that line. Shows how much I know . . .

So – aha – this also explains *why* the songs are in the plural, then, because unlike a singular music (*zene*), this plural *zenék* allows that perfect rhyme.

Punctuation was actually what I noticed first, though. Even without knowing the words, I expected to be able to make certain assumptions about the translator's intentions and map the text onto the familiar English, roughly shape for shape. But there are some small differences.

English punctuation usage is a fair guide for Hungarian punctuation, I've been told, so it reassures me that I can navigate the text using it. But while the passages look broadly the same, I did notice two unexpected commas. After the exclamation mark (which follows the 'play on', in this case shunted onto the second line), we have

> *Sőt, tömjetek telc,*
> *hadd fojtsa meg a vágyat a csömör!*

which has no possible correspondence in the English; and then in the next line, after the next exclamation mark (that strain again!)

> *. . . Szép, elhaló a vége*

Ádám's commas are clues that something has changed. The word *Sőt*, he tells me, means 'indeed' or 'Nay' – and it is, indeed, an addition, to bring some emphasis, and discreetly fill a syllabic gap.

Regarding the second, in the line 'it had a dying fall', Ádám is mitigating the fact that Hungarian doesn't have any equivalent to an 'it has' in a case like this, so he plugs the gap by here giving the *fall* a second adjective. It is not merely *dying*, but *szép* – *beautiful*. It's beautiful comma dying.

English does have 'it has', and so English fills out its phrase with a single adjective, and so English doesn't need an extra comma.

Here's the same speech again, this time in Vassilis Rotas's Greek translation:

Αν του έρωτα τροφή 'ναι η μουσική, ε, παίζετε,
παραχορτάστε με, ώσπου απ' την κατάχρησην
ο πόθος ν' αρρωστήσει, κι έτσι να πεθάνει.
Πάλι το ίδιο! Σιγοπέθαινε στο τέλος.
Ω, χάιδεψε τ' αυτί μου σαν αχός γλυκός
που, πνέοντας πάνω από βραγιά με μενεξέδες,
κλέβει ευωδιά και δίνει. Φτάνει! όχι άλλο πια:
τώρα δεν έχει πια τη γλύκα που είχε πριν.

In most respects, Greek also uses the comma (το κόμμα) like English, so some of Rotas's commas likewise reveal something that's been changed. That parenthetical ε in the first line is unexpected, but an insignificant bit of encouraging filler; and there's a comma where the English has none in line three – 'the appetite may sicken[,] and so die' – but again, that's not a big deal, since English could easily use it, too. The one that surprised me is the one near the start of line six (the line in bold) – the line whose English is 'That breathes upon a bank of violets' – the comma is after the first word.

What's happening? Well, it's just that πνέοντας is not *breathes*, but *breathing*. The Greek line is 'that, breathing upon a bank of violets, steals fragrance and gives it'. My guess is that this is only to do with space on the line – the next line is the crowded one, so this avoids needing to fit two participles in there, the way the English has it (stealing, giving). The stealing being the first word in line seven: κλέβει (klévei, hence our kleptomaniacs and kleptocracy).

Of course, some languages use punctuation entirely differently to English, thus allowing/requiring different things of a translated text. German has far more rigid rules – you put a comma where a comma goes and nowhere else. You don't mess around with them wantonly, for rhythm or breathing or whatever.

And note also that some languages have punctuation discrepancies that might look substantial, but are in fact only cosmetic – so, for example:

Armenian full stops look like :
Bangla full stops like ।
Greek question marks look like ;

but they still work like our full stops and question marks.

For the most part, translators are inclined to follow the adage 'punctuate the translation, don't translate the punctuation'.* Though here matters are complicated not only by grammatical structure and what a language allows or requires, but also the exigencies of performance – making lines that an actor can follow, in which an actor can breathe, and so on.

Niels has admitted (hmm, that's a loaded word . . .) that his use of punctuation can be unorthodox, not only compared to Shakespeare but also questionable from a Danish grammatical pedant's point of view. My friend Paul G., who teaches the language, explained the *old* Danish comma rules, including 'always use a comma before a conjunction'.† These rules have since changed (though, said Paul, the Danes do still

---

* I wish I knew which translator first put it like that. Translator friends reading this, please come out of the woodwork to claim it!

† In Paul's defence, when I wrote to ask him to explain Danish punctuation rules, he did start his answer with the word 'Ugh . . .'

love their commas), but that's how Niels's generation would have learned them – you use punctuation to reflect a sentence's grammatical structure. But Niels will cheerfully jettison those rules to make his words more speakable on the stage, to avoid an actor stressing the wrong word, and so on. The fixed precepts, he says, have:

> nothing to do with the way the sentence is spoken, and it has always annoyed me and I always refused to follow these rules. So instead I put commas to indicate breathing, or slow down the pace, or make something an aside . . . I have often been at odds with editors of printed editions who somehow expect me to follow the rules. And if I don't, then at least be consistent – which I'm not either, because it's all about the musicality of it.

When he punctuates, in other words, his frame of reference is more like musical notation than grammar.

> I have sometimes defended myself by saying that I use 'expressive punctuation,' and though the term is purely my own invention, it may at least give me a little breathing space until the zealots discover that it does not exist. If you are familiar with the erratic spelling and pronunciation of early modern English, you would hardly raise an eyebrow over such matters, but in an age of pedagogical punctiliousness you must fend for your faults. Or rather, your conscious transgressions . . .

As Niels reminds us, it's not as though Shakespeare was a rigorously consistent user of commas himself – nor working in a language that enforces entirely strict rules about them. Nor do we even know what all Shakespeare's own punctuation looked like; what we have comes from printed editions, rather than manuscripts, so the punctuation we can see today has been inherited from editors (and typesetters and others). The First Folio punctuation in some cases *might* be close to

Shakespeare's own – or not.* But the fact that it's even a question tells us something about English and where our flexibilities are.

We don't and can't know Shakespeare's exact intentions. So we're comparing these other languages not to them but to the requirements and possibilities that come with the English language. English doesn't have infinite flexibility as to where it puts its commas but it has quite a lot. (In that last sentence, I could have added a comma after the word *commas* if I'd wanted one; I could not have added one after *as to*.)

Shakespeare has King Richard II begin the last scene of his life with these words (punctuated here as per the First Folio):

> I haue bin studying, how to compare
> This Prison where I liue, vnto the World:

And this is the First Quarto (the first time the play was printed):

> I haue beene studying how I may compare
> This prison where I liue, vnto the world:

We'll leave aside the difference between 'how to compare' and 'how I may compare' (the first requires 'studying' to occupy three syllables).†

Most of the Shakespeare translators I've spoken to tend to take the Arden edition as their starting point. The latest Arden edition of *Richard II* loses that sole Q1 comma, giving the lines thus:

---

* The First Folio being his first large (posthumous) Collected Works, as opposed to the individual plays published as 'Quarto' editions.

† Nick de Somogyi, editor of the new 'Shakespeare Folios' edition of the play, suggested that this Folio wording likely comes from the poor-quality 'Second Quarto' edition. (The play's first publications in chronological order: Q1 1597, Q2 1598, Q3 1598, Q4 1608, Q5 1615, F1 1623.) And though the First Quarto's *how I may compare* is clearly better, Nick for his edition understandably retained the folio wording intact, albeit 'reluctantly'.

> I have been studying how I may compare
> This prison where I live unto the world;

If I were writing that sentence myself, today, I'd punctuate it as the Arden does: definitely no comma after 'studying' – that would be an odd choice in my English, I think.

Niels – punctuating his own translation, rather than translating Shakespeare's punctuation – has it thus:

> *Jeg grubler på, hvordan man sammenligner*
> *det fængsel, hvor jeg bor, med hele verden . . .*

He has commas around 'where I live' – which, he says, seems 'to make the character more passive, to suggest that this is something he's struggling with – instead of delivering it in one fell swoop as a conclusion he's reached earlier.' That pair of bracketing commas isn't essential in English, but they would be an option, so if such a sentence had them there it would be by choice, and for effect – so one might perhaps pause very slightly if they were there, the actor made hesitant, working it out as he goes. (Though Jonathan Bailey, the last Richard I saw, delivered those two lines in a single breath, as if comma-less.)

One of the writers I translate avoids commas where he can in Spanish, so his translators avoid them where possible in English, simply because with his very spare and delicate style, he doesn't like clutter on the page. Not all of his other-language translators would be able to avoid them even if they wanted to. Remind me to ask his German translator how he manages . . .

Chapter 10

Thou ferlies at my words, but haud thee still

(on ambiguity and wordplay)

Deck 12 of the *Queen Mary 2*, the Cunard liner that plies the Atlantic crossing between Southampton and New York, is where you will find the ship's kennels. British dogs and American dogs travel together and, I imagine, exchange amusing if predictable banter about the differences between their two cultures, just as the human passengers are doing on the decks below them. Cunard pride themselves on the thoughtfulness with which they design the customer experience for all their guests, and so the kennel area is supplied with both a lamp post *and* a fire hydrant. This is what we call 'equivalence'.

Sometimes a translator is not principally concerned with the thing, but its function.

I have, in the past, had to translate the word *azul* (conventionally referring to the colour blue) into the English word 'red'. Might there, then, be a situation in which you would translate 'Coriolanus' into French as 'Roi Lear'?

At the end of the last chapter, we looked at the hesitant commas Niels added to that *Richard II* line, but there was another reason why he wanted them there, which was nothing to do with pacing his actor's speech. In Danish, one compares things *with* other things; in English, we variously compare *with* and compare *to*. English Shakespeare has Richard compare his prison *unto* the world. In the same line, then, Danish Shakespeare compares his prison *with* the world. Which would be fine, only he isn't just comparing his prison (with . . .), he's comparing the prison *where he lives* (with).

> I have been studying how I may compare
> This prison where I live unto the world . . .

is fine. But replace the 'unto' with a 'with', and suddenly you find 'this prison where I live with the world' – an ambiguity that is not what's intended. Hence the disambiguating commas, making the middle part of the line parenthetical:

> *det fængsel, hvor jeg bor, med hele verden . . .*

So Danish Richard can now safely compare the prison (where he lives) with the world.

Ambiguity should be avoided when it is not intended. The bigger problem, however, is figuring out how to preserve the feature when it *is* deliberate. Ambiguity is the hardest thing of all to translate.

To find a word that means 'animal of the feline family', that's easy enough. To find a word that means 'to feel remorse', likewise. No problem – we have a lot of words. To find one word that means both of those things? Not so much.

Do we have a word in English that means both a doll and a pattern to be imitated? 'Model' might do. Or one that means both a doll and a number? Yes, 'figure' might work for both. But what about 'doll' and 'wrist'? I can't think of one. But Spanish does. A Spanish-language writer might deploy that word – *muñeca* – very deliberately. The Spanish word allows for two possible meanings, both of which might be intended, but which in English are mutually exclusive; how is a translator to produce an English translation of that word that doesn't close off one or other of those options?* Yes, context is relevant – usually with a word like *muñeca*, you'd know which one the author was intending, as dolls and wrists are typically not interchangeable in a narrative. Except for one novel I translated, where, unbelievably, that exact doll/wrist problem arose. Making a choice was easy enough, but the author's cleverly deployed ambiguity was the first thing to go.

Sometimes the very structure of a language can allow a kind of layeredness or a deliberate openness of meaning that English might struggle to preserve. Take Swahili, say. The writer JC Niala is currently working on a Swahili *Macbeth*, and she cited this cryptic moment from the witches' opening scene:

> Fair is foul, and foul is fair,
> Hover through the fog and filthy air.

Swahili grammar allows a speaker to draw distinctions between descriptive states and inherent qualities, JC explains, 'which can enrich the dualities and ambiguities in the witches' words'. She suggests this translation:

> *Mbaya mzuri, nzuri mbaya*

By using nouns rather than adjectives, the phrase both preserves the general paradox and also introduces a more personal dimension, hinting at types of people rather than abstract qualities, suggesting that someone who seems virtuous might, in fact, harbour malevolence. By leveraging the flexibility of Swahili grammar, the witches' lines could be crafted to layer general truths with specific insinuations.

---

* This particular example does not give the Spanish Shakespeare translator many new opportunities, since wrists are only mentioned in *Cymbeline*, *Hamlet* and *King John*. One of the less interesting things I have learned while writing this book.

Even in a large-vocabulary language like English, words can mean more than one thing. Just try to produce a compact and comprehensive definition, without context, for 'even'. Or 'like'. Or 'can'. Or 'mean'.

Jokes in particular are frequently language-rooted, built upon things sounding like other things or having multiple meanings. More often than not, Shakespeare's wordplay is constructed around these multiplicities. Multiplicities inherent within these *specific words*, and therefore ones that English allows him and that other languages – unless the translator is very lucky – will not.

If for some strange reason you were inclined to build complex wordplay around a *glass*, a *line of poetry*, the colour *green*, a *worm*, some movement *towards* – and, um, *squirrel fur* – you could find words for all these that sound identical – if, and only if, you are working in French.* But in English?

A writer will do things because they can. And so a translator must somehow contrive to do those same things, even if they can't.

When I asked Frank Günther why translating Shakespeare might be more difficult than translating anything else, he responded with a line from *Richard III*: 'I moralize two meanings in one word.' I've said before that translation – even of a text less complex than this most complex of texts – is all about making choices, but sometimes these are enforced, unwelcome ones.

(The French word for *choice* is *choix* – file that away for now . . .)

But maybe we can start with one of the lucky ones, with a moment in *The Merchant of Venice*, in Japanese.

BASSANIO
  We should hold day with the Antipodes,
  If you would walk in absence of the sun.
PORTIA
  Let me give light, but let me not be light;
  For a light wife doth make a heavy husband,
  And never be Bassanio so for me.

---

* The perfectly homophonous *verre/vers/vert/ver/vers/vair*.

Shakespeare is taking advantage of the fact that *light* has two quite distinct meanings. (Well, more than two, but we'll stick with these two for now.) Sho's Japanese conversation goes thus:

バサーニオ
　昼ですよ、地球の反対側と同様に。
　太陽がなくても、あなたがいれば**明るい**昼だ。
ポーシャ
　明るいならいいけど、「あ、**軽い**」と呼ばれるのは嫌よ。
　尻の**軽い**女は夫の心を重くする。
　私が**軽い**せいでバサーニオが重くなるのは嫌。

Look at those underlined words. 軽い in Japanese pertains to an object of negligible weight; and, as for the brightness such as one might obtain from a light bulb, that has now become 明るい. The cleverness of the choices lies in the fact that the first is pronounced *karui*, the second *akarui*. *Chapeau!** (Note that he's smuggled in an extra one of the latter in to Bassanio's lines, too.) How many translators does it take to change a light bulb? Well, that, as they say, depends on the context. And good news for the translator: having found this punning solution to the light/light problem, he'll have ample opportunity to reuse it. Shakespeare does.†

Now, imagine we're dealing with the brilliance not of a bulb but of the sun . . . or is that the *son*? Oh, because that's another pair Shakespeare reuses, too. Sometimes characters play on the homophony explicitly; at other times, there's one meaning clearly pre-eminent but Shakespeare is just taking advantage of a little flicker in the listener's mind – so when Prince Hal talks about his plan to:

---

* The French word for 'hat', sometimes used (even in English) as a congratulatory exclamation.
† Sho's translation was used for a Japanese-language production by an English director, who just assumed that, well, obviously all the wordplay and stuff was just going to work perfectly in Japanese too *somehow*, right? 'This one saved me,' says Sho.

> . . . imitate the sun,
> Who doth permit the base contagious clouds
> To smother up his beauty from the world . . .

we reach the end of the first line momentarily unsure which word we've just heard spoken – seeing as this is part of a speech about what sort of <u>son</u> he's going to be to his royal father.

There's no ambiguity when the word is sitting on the page – it's indisputable which word is written (even if we might get a faint sense of the other because we often read aloud in our heads); on stage, however, they are to all intents and purposes the same word. Speak them aloud, there's no difference. So back to that opening of *Richard III*:

> Now is the winter of our discontent
> Made glorious summer by this sun of York . . .

From the spelling that I have chosen to prioritise in the line above, you can see that he is, yes, talking about the sun turning winter to summer, with his family's victory in the lately ended wars, the rising of the warm sun of the house of York dispelling the Lancastrian chill. Meanwhile his brother, the new king Edward IV, is himself the eldest *son* of the house of York . . . (Richard is the youngest son; the next son up will appear shortly to interrupt this speech.)

Several translators I spoke to volunteered this as their first example of a place where loss is simply inevitable. I have not yet found any other language where *son* and *sun* are such a perfect match. The closest my friends have found thus far is Yiddish, where the same noun is indeed used, but there's a gender distinction, with *son* being דער זון (der zun) and *sun* being די זון (di zun), so the definite article will unambiguously mark which is meant.

But despite losing the double-thinking playfulness that Shakespeare exploits in the English word, Niels was keen that the two meanings be at least retained in Danish, even if not overlapping. So he squeezed everything in:

> *Nu er vort mismods vinter gjort til sommer:*
> *en søn af huset York er vores sol,*
> *han stråler, så hver sky der trued huset*
> *er sunket ned i oceanets skød.*

This keeps the reference to Edward and also the 'changing seasons' metaphor. A literal translation of this* might be:

> Now, the winter of our discontent is made into summer:
> a son of the house of York is our sun,
> he beams, so that every cloud that was threatening the house
> has sunk into the bosom of the ocean.

For lack of adequate real estate in his fixed-length line, he had to drop the 'deep', but impressively managed to fit everything else in.

Naturally, it's easier to explain each of the multiple meanings a listener is supposed to grasp if you're working in prose and therefore have all the space in the world to do it in. Here's our old friend Gabriele Baldini doing his thing with a pithy exchange from the opening of *Twelfth Night*. Orsino seems to suggest a play on the words *heart* (his own, suffering for love) and *hart* (the animal one might hunt).

CURIO
   Will you go hunt, my lord?
ORSINO
               What, Curio?
CURIO
                     The hart.

---

* The word 'literal' is annoyingly overused to suggest a sort of 'neutral' translation, which cannot exist. When I say 'literal' here, I just mean a translation that prioritises a word's commonly understood *meaning* over any other properties. (You can't have a neutral, purely literal translation of a text any more than you can have a neutral, purely literal production, or performance.)

ORSINO
   Why so I do, the noblest that I have.
   O, when mine eyes did see Olivia first,
   Methought she purged the air of pestilence;
   That instant was I turned into a hart,
   And my desires, like fell and cruel hounds,
   E'er since pursue me.

Now, here we go – deep breath . . .

CURIO
   Volete andare a caccia, signore?
ORSINO
   E di che cosa, Curio?
CURIO
   Del cervo.
ORSINO
   A caccia, infatti, io vado, ma non del <u>cervo</u>; della parte più nobile, bensì, di me stesso, del mio proprio <u>cuore</u>. Oh, quando i miei occhi videro Olivia per la prima volta, parvemi come se ella purificasse l'aria intorno di miasmi che vi stagnavano. In quell'istante io fui trasformato in un dàino, ed i miei desiderii, simili a veltri crudeli e feroci, hanno preso, da allora, a perseguitarmi senza tregua.

Meaning, roughly, *I do indeed go to hunt, but not for the <u>hart</u>; but rather for that noblest part of myself, for my own <u>heart</u>* . . . [etc.]

As usual, it's like Baldini has put Shakespeare's nice tightly bonded English into a centrifuge. (He does, though, get an extra point for the lovely word *miasmi* – that's the Italian plural of *miasma*, which is a word I do like.)

On a Folger Library podcast, Korean translator Hyon-u Lee discussed an example from *Hamlet*, in which the prince makes a joke linking the name Brutus to an actor playing 'a *brute* part', but he only makes the joke at all because English happens to allow it – because English happens to have a negative adjective derived from Latin 'brutus'. Most languages don't. Simply translate the word 'brute' into Korean and you might be faithful to the meaning, but that's about all – the joke has disappeared. The good news for Korean audiences, however, is that Lee achieved what we translators always aspire to in wordplay: he dismantled it and built an equally effective new joke with similar moving parts. There is a Korean word that sounds like Brutus, that means 'swollen'; and there is a Korean phrase, 'his liver is swollen', meaning that he is foolhardy – so:

의원 댁 송아지를 죽이다니 **브루터스가** 아주 간덩이가 **부르텄어, 부르터**.

[Eui-won dek song-aji-reul juk-i-dani <u>Bu-ru-teu-su-ga</u> ah-ju gan-dong-e-ga <u>bu-ru-tus-uh, bu-ru-tuh</u>]

The first word I've marked is 브루터스가, and that's Brutus: Bu-ru-teu-su-ga, the 'ga' particle indicating that he's the subject of the clause.

Then you have those last two words of the line – 부르텄어, 부르터 – which mean swollen, very swollen; they're pronounced bu-ru-tus-uh, bu-ru-tuh. (A slightly unusual verb to use for this idiom, but effective for its sonic similarity to Brutus's name.)

The English *Hamlet* has no mention of anyone's liver being swollen; the Korean *Hamlet* uses it as a way of deriving an insult from Brutus's name (just as the prince is supposed to do). It's not faithful to the exact meaning, but – more importantly – faithful to the joke, and to its effect.

The translator's job, then, is not simply to find semantic equivalents for each word. Meaning doesn't always matter much; words are also important for the effects they create. What matters is equivalence of function. Like a fire hydrant on the *Queen Mary 2*.

The Merry Wives of Windsor includes a scene in which Hugh Evans, the Welsh parson, is giving William a Latin lesson. The running joke is that several of the Latin words or phrases have potential mishearings, some sexually explicit, to the shock of Mistress Quickly who's listening in and commenting. Some are funnier than others:

EVANS
   . . . What is 'fair,' William?

WILLIAM
   Pulcher.

MISTRESS Q
   Polecats? There are fairer things than polecats, sure.
   . . .

EVANS
   What is the focative case, William?

WILLIAM
   O – *vocativo* – O –

EVANS
   Remember, William; focative is *caret*.

MISTRESS Q
   And that's a good root.
   . . .

EVANS
   What is your genitive case plural, William?

WILLIAM
   Genitive case?

EVANS
   Ay.

WILLIAM
   Genitivo horum, harum, horum.

MISTRESS Q
   Vengeance of Jenny's case, fie on her! Never name her, child, if she be a whore.

(You would have found the *Jenny's case* joke funnier if you'd lived at a time when *case* was slang for *vagina*.)

Now, while *pulcher* can be made to sound a bit like *polecat*, it does not sound like the French word for a polecat.* So co-translators Jean-Michel

---

* *putois*, I learn today.

Déprats and Jean-Pierre Richard did what any serious Shakespearean scholar would do in their place. They made a list of all the Latin words that made them giggle at school because they sounded rude, and they built a scene around them.

EVANS
William, conjuguez-moi le verbe « penser » au présent de l'indicatif.
WILLIAM
Puto, <u>putas</u>, putat.
MADAME PÉTULE
« <u>Putasse</u> » *? Ce n'est bien d'apprendre à cet enfant des mots pareils.*
[. . .]
EVANS
Cessez-nous votre babil ! William, maintenant, c'est quoi le verbe « aimer » au futur de l'indicatif ?
WILLIAM
Amabo, amabis, amabat.
EVANS
<u>Bit</u>, *William*, bit.
WILLIAM
<u>Amabit</u>. Amabim . . .
MADAME PÉTULE
Qu'est-ce que tu dis ? À qui tu parles là ?
WILLIAM
<u>Amabit</u>.

Then they move on to the singular relative pronoun:

WILLIAM
<u>Cujus</u>.
MADAME PÉTULE
<u>Couillon</u> *toi-même !*

The Latin word *putas* sounds like the French word *putasse* (meaning whore). The Latin word *cujus* sounds like the French word *couillon* (which is used to refer to an idiot, but from the Old French word for testicle).* And when William is conjugating the verb 'to love' in the future indicative, the boy incorrectly says not 'amabit' but 'amabat'. '*Bit*, William, *bit*,' says his exasperated teacher. And that *bit* sounds like a common French slang word for *penis*. The translators give us extra here, too – because 'à ma' is the French for 'to my'. So when Madame Pétule asks William who on earth he's talking to, he just says it again: *A-ma-bit . . .*

This is not a translation of the words *polecat* and *carrot* and *case*. It is, however, an excellent translation of the joke.

The scene is seldom played in English productions, incidentally, as it does little to advance the drama and requires work to land the jokes with a contemporary audience ('Who's Jenny?'). Like some of the wordplay in, say, *Love's Labour's Lost*, it works on the page if your edition is well annotated, but needs refocusing for the modern ear. Thank God for translation, then . . .

The critic J. Dover Wilson suggested that the nunnery in Hamlet's 'Get thee to a nunnery' might be an ironic (slang) reference to a brothel. While his view is not universally accepted, Chaiti Mitra found a way of keeping this echo in Bengali, just in case, by using a pair of similar-sounding words – *muth* (মঠ) and *kotha* (কোঠা) – a kind of Hindu monastery and a Hindi word used for a house of *tawaifs* (courtesans) – leaning particularly on the repeated 'th' (ঠ) sound.

And Sho (with his de-lightful *karui/akarui*) isn't the only one to catch an occasional break from his language. I asked Te Haumihiata about the challenges she faced, in particular when dealing whe the ruder jokes in Shakespeare, where – for example – plant or animal names do double duty, being used as slang for male or female genitalia. Oh, she said, *that's* not a problem. The English sexual double-meaning was almost

---

* (This also gave the Danes their word 'kujon' that our multilingual Kent used on p. 81.)

invariably contained in the Māori word too. ('That happened a *lot*,' she said.) In the rare instances when a language is as obliging as that, well, then translation can seem almost possible.

Or so you'd think, until you get to the moment in *Measure for Measure* where this happens:

> I have laboured for the poor gentleman to the extremest shore of my modesty, but my brother justice have I found so severe that he hath forced me to tell him, he is indeed Justice.

The judge Escalus has been trying to persuade Angelo to be lenient with the prisoner, but has found him cold and unyielding. The potential joke is in the final word – for Escalus has been forced to tell Angelo that he is, indeed, *justice*. Or is that . . . *just ice*? The second potential reading is not made explicit here, but earlier in the same scene, Lucio did remark that 'it is certain that when he makes water his urine is congealed ice . . .'

I've not yet found a translation that allows an actor this possibility, but I'm not done looking.

As so often, Shakespeare does things because English happens to allow them. Sometimes a translator writing in another language, however brilliant, simply cannot. Conversely, there are neat things that *don't* happen in his plays, not because Shakespeare lacks the capacity, but because English does, and a new language opens up a new possibility.

By way of illustration, indulge me in a non-Shakespearey parenthesis: Jean-François Ménard, the French translator of *Harry Potter*, couldn't keep the pun on that little street Diagon Alley – diagonally – because the French language wouldn't allow it, but when they needed a name for the Sorting Hat, French kindly offered them up the possibility of what I feel was a great improvement: *Le Choixpeau*. A blend of two words we've seen in this chapter already: *choix*, meaning *choice*, and *chapeau* meaning *hat*. Lovely! Meanwhile, in a Gaulish village, Asterix's dog is transformed from Idéfix to Dogmatix – keeping the basic properties of the name but adding – brilliantly – that doggy prefix, a joke the source text lacks. And the phrase used by *Asterix*'s Italian translators for the running joke 'These Romans are crazy!' is 'Sono pazzi questi romani!' – which they offer this as an explanation for . . . SPQR. Now, the source does no such thing with the acronym, simply because it can't. But translators will gratefully take a gift when a language generously insists upon it. A woman once told James Thurber how much she'd preferred his work in its French translation – 'Yes, madam,' Thurber replied, 'my work often loses something in the original.'

Or, dragging ourselves back to Shakespeare and *Love's Labour's Lost*, consider how pleasing it must be for a French translator to work on a text in which young people endlessly discuss abstemiousness (at the start of the play, the men agree to surrender three years of their life to study, chastity and fasting). The French word for 'young' or 'young person' is *jeune*. The French word for a fast is *jeûne*. (Hence the French call one of their meals *dé-jeuner*, just as we call one of ours *break-fast*.) Shakespeare is enabled by what English supplies, but also limited by it; the very apt emerging echoes of *young* and *fasting* – such as you find in *Peines d'amour perdues* – is nothing but gain.

Meanwhile, in this exchange in *Henry VI, Part 3*,

RICHARD
    Think'st thou I am an executioner?
KING HENRY
    A persecutor I am sure thou art . . .

Niels noticed that 'executioner' and 'persecutor' share an etymological root: *sequī*, to follow. As a bit of wordplay, it's not flashy – or indeed funny – but Niels made a point of constructing a subtle little hook of his own. I'm not sure many English audiences would notice the original etymological relationship, unless the actors pointed it up with their delivery. Yet there in the text it is. And if it's in Shakespeare, then it's in Brunse.

One of the reasons I emphasised the requirement that a translator be a great and careful reader, as well as a great and versatile writer, is that all this depends on the translator *noticing* these tiny little features of a text. The less flashy, the easier simply to miss.* But to recreate it, a translator must notice it first.

For my own silly amusement, I might decide, for instance, to make the first letter of each paragraph at the start of Chapter 9 spell out the word Shakespeare. (Well, strictly speaking, Shakespeáre.) A translator would need to notice that I've done it before they can start to figure out how to make it work in their language – if it's even worth the hassle, given that it might well be more difficult than it was for me. Honestly I wouldn't have bothered if it wasn't pretty easy. But Portuguese doesn't have many words beginning with a K; his name can be transliterated into some non-Roman scripts with a consonant sound that is more like an x than our k-s, which is a big ask, too, and some non-alphabetical languages will be trickier still . . .

So I should pause here to say sorry to *my* translators. Also for this book's hidden and entirely pointless echo of an early 1990s advertisement for a coffee liqueur. Moving on . . .

There's a whole category of wordplay that consists in characters misspeaking – often poorly educated characters trying to use big, impressive words and getting them wrong. The mechanism is similar – as a translator you need (1) a word that means something like X and (2) a word that sounds sufficiently like it but means something else, funnier. The mechanicals in *A Midsummer Night's Dream* are responsible for several of these.

Taking three brief examples, Ádám gave me an explanation of how he solved each one in turn:

* A Mexican translation of mine includes a bit of very subtle linguistic cleverness mirroring something equivalent in my source. It is *so* subtle that nobody has yet spotted it. I even made reference to it in my Translator's Note, citing the relevant page number, and still people have been unable to locate it. That doesn't bother me – I was glad to have noticed something in the source, and I was glad to preserve it, even if only for my own slightly smug benefit.

1. Bottom, reciting his part in 'Pyramus and Thisbe' says the line *'Thisbe, the flowers of odious savours sweet'*, but that's not right – the 'odious' is supposed to be 'odours'. The line Ádám gives him in his Hungarian script is 'you are like perfume to me', only Tompor (Bottom) reads *parföm* as *fartöm*: *Illatos fartöm vagy nekem*. You are like a lovely savoury *rump steak* to me.
2. Flute – also performing in 'Pyramus and Thisbe' – tells Pyramus he'll meet him at 'Ninny's Tomb' – rather than 'Ninus' tomb' (a mistake that's repeated, to Quince's desperation). Ádám has him change *A Nínusz sírjánál* to *A Nílus sírjánál* – at the tomb of the Nile. Then adds an extra line (ffs, it's a river, it can't have a tomb!) to make sure the joke lands.
3. When Bottom has been parted from his friends and they're lamenting his loss, Quince describes him as *'a very paramour for a sweet voice'*. Again, the humour is in his attempt to use a showy bit of vocabulary but without actual mastery. He means *paragon*, not *paramour*. The error is enhanced by the fact that we do know what Bottom's actually doing with Titania in her bower at this same moment . . . Ádám has the Hungarian Quince describe Bottom as heroic – *heroikus*. Only he says *herotikus* – neatly blending *heroic* and *erotic*.

In each case, Ádám constructed something in Hungarian that was different in meaning but almost identical in function and effect – not what the words *mean* but what they *do*. Later in our conversation, we were talking about some wordplay in *Twelfth Night* around the word 'accost', and Ádám explained his solution as 'just shameless fishing for fun'. Just as it should be.

It's worth remembering that while wordplay that rests on an ability to find matching ambiguities is one of a translator's biggest challenges, equally important is to avoid inadvertent *new* ambiguities, which can slip in if not checked. Context will sometimes focus things for you, at least. Yes, translation is often hard – but you knew without my specifying that I didn't mean translation is *physically unyieldingly solid* hard, but *difficult* hard.

It's not enough that words don't look alike on the page; so long as they are homophones, they can cause trouble in performance – just as *son* and *sun* are ambiguous to the ear even if not to the eye. The Japanese words 死者 (meaning a dead body) and 使者 (a messenger) have different initial characters, as you can see – but when *spoken*, both words are sounded as 'shisha'. There are plenty of dead bodies in Shakespeare, and messengers too, and we ought not mistake one for the other. So to avoid any misapprehension, Sho makes a point of avoiding these two words entirely.

The Greek word πουλί (poulí), which means simply *bird*, is also a kids' euphemism for *penis*; the English word 'bird' is not. I know this because I once taught *Romeo and Juliet* to a class of Greek thirteen-year-olds. It wasn't immediately clear to me why everybody's favourite bit was the lovers' whole 'I would I were thy bird . . .' conversation. Any translator who doesn't notice this innuendo slipping in will lose control of their audience fast.

That French translation of *The Merry Wives* . . . that I mentioned goes under the title *Les Joyeuses Commères de Windsor*. Likewise, the Spanish and Portuguese titles tend to use their equivalent, the word *comadres*. Which is just as well, seeing as the everyday Spanish word for *wife* is *esposa* (like our 'spouse'), but in the plural, *esposas* also means *handcuffs*. Now playing: The Happy Handcuffs of Windsor.*

And . . . many, many more examples besides.

The orderly Samuel Johnson was not keen on Shakespeare's insistent use of puns, which makes language so *untidy* . . .

> Whatever be the dignity or profundity of his disquisition, whether he be enlarging knowledge or exalting affection, whether he be amusing attention with incidents, or enchaining it in suspense, let but a quibble [= old word for pun] spring up before him, and he leaves his work unfinished. A quibble is the golden apple for which he will always turn aside from his career, or stoop from his elevation . . .

---

* Whereas *comadres* in both languages covers sort of *close female friends/godmother to your kids/female gossips/midwives*. And in Portuguese also *bedpans*. Language, eh?

So perhaps a translation could survive if forced to lose a few.

Wordplay that is built upon a single word's multiple meanings and associations won't usually survive the transit between languages without some translatorly intervention, then. But we know that those multiple meanings and associations aren't fixed, so it will not always translate across time, either. Just as two words might have rhymed perfectly four centuries ago and might not now, so the precise components of one word's reach and associations that allow it to be played upon might have altered, too. Which is really just to say that, yeah, I realise the 'case' joke above isn't funny *now*; the word had quite different potential *then*. At least non-English translators are allowed – indeed, expected – to do something about it.

Chapter 11

Ni chaiff peryglon fy nychrynu ddim

(on extreme wordplay)

There's a moment in *Richard II* where Henry Bolingbroke, the challenger to the throne, asks the king 'Are you contented to resign the crown?' There's been some equivocating up till now, so this is a clear, direct, yes-or-no question. Well, are you, or aren't you? We were never going to get a straight answer out of King Richard, though. His reply begins

    Ay, no . . .

Which is already a problem, because in English – and only in English – *ay* (yes) sounds like the pronoun *I* – so, wait . . . did he just say 'ay, no', or 'I know?'

And then it gets worse:

    Ay, no. No, ay; for I must nothing be.
    Therefore, no 'no', for I resign to thee.

It looks like a little literary flourish, Shakespeare showing off, not something of any substance. But this tricksy little ornament tells us about *character*, about Richard – a man who doesn't want to say yes, but isn't in any position to say no, who needs to answer – he's under pressure now – but doesn't want to commit, so he gives an answer but undermines it; a man, also, who might be losing his power but still knows he's clever (*surely* cleverer than Bolingbroke) and really likes to show it.

But two *ays*, and two *I*'s (all four homophones), all in a couplet with four noes – plus a rhyme? No translator would be so good, or so lucky, I thought.

Then I went to see that production in Copenhagen, with a text by Niels Brunse.

I had mixed feelings about the production. It was stylised, with almost everyone costumed alike and a non-realist set made up of fourteen beds, which meant that as a non-Danish speaker I had few clues to who was who and where we were. Lots of middle-aged white men talking to each other . . . but how do I know which is the king?

But there was a moment of tetchy confrontation between two of those men, where I recovered my bearings; so I waited – and there they are, one man holding out a crown to another. The question:

Indvilger I så i at opgi kronen?

(And I knew *krone* was Danish for *crown*, because it was the currency in which I'd bought my ticket.)

Then a two-line reply which said . . . well, I don't really know, but I could feel a ripple of laughter through the audience. Note to self: *What did Niels just do?* Had he found a solution to a seemingly insoluble problem?

The next day, I asked him what I'd just seen. What had Richard said? This was his answer:

Vil I, at jeg er villig? Vil jeg ville?
Min vilde vilje ville ville ilde.

It's even more homophonous than you'd realise, unless you're a Danish speaker – both *vilde* and *ilde* are pronounced with the 'd' silent.

The rough meaning is:

> Do you want me to be willing? Will I will it?
> My wild will would be willing to do ill.

It is not quite the *same* playing-around, but the effect is similar – and it's still Richard stalling for time, refusing to settle on a clear answer – because his will, as he says, is so ungovernable.

Wordplay that makes one word do two things (*light* and *light*, *sun* and *son*) is hard enough. But it gets more complicated where a character starts riffing on it, like Richard did; or when multiple characters build and build, elaborating on each other's jokes.

Here's a challenge. Produce a conversation with the following characteristics:

- two characters are discussing whether they're prepared to do hard, dirty work, but speculate that they might be driven to anger and violence, thus risking the hangman's noose;
- there are only four short lines;
- there need to be at least three words that are not etymologically related but nonetheless sound similar.

This is how Shakespeare does it:

SAMSON
    Gregory, on my word, we'll not carry coals.
GREGORY
    No, for then we should be colliers.
SAMSON
    I mean, an we be in choler, we'll draw.
GREGORY
    Ay, while you live, draw your neck out of collar. [etc.]

(It doesn't actually end there, but I'll spare you.)

It's the first exchange in *Romeo and Juliet*, though unless you know the play well, you might not recall it – it's often cut in English-language performance. (You may have views about whether that's frankly just as well.)

Shakespeare uses *coals* to set up *colliers* (coal merchants), and thence leads us to *choler* (anger) and *collar* (i.e. noose). He also gets extra points for 'draw' (. . . a sword) leading to 'draw' (. . . your neck back out of the noose).

Collier and *choler* and *collar* are neatly connected by sound. In English.

Any translator will face a challenge similar to the one I offered to you a moment ago: not to *translate* Shakespeare's four lines, meaning for meaning, but to construct a text that has its key properties.

Here's Raphael Eliaz's translation in Hebrew:

סמפסון: חי חיי, גרגורי, לא עוד נשא **ונסבל**
גרגורי: חלילה! לא עוד נהיה **כסבלים**
סמפסון: כוונתי לומר: כשפוקעת **הסבלנות** יש להוציא עז ממתוק.
גרגורי: כן, כל עוד אנו חיים יש להוציא את הצוואר מהקולר.

The meaning, roughly, is:

SAMSON
Upon my word, Gregory, we'll no longer carry and <u>suffer</u>.
GREGORY
Heaven forbid! We will no longer be <u>porters</u>.
SAMSON
I mean, when <u>patience</u> is lost, one should take the sweet out of the strong.
GREGORY
Indeed, as long as we're alive, we should free our necks from the collar.

The bold words in the Hebrew correspond to the underlined words in my translation: *suffer, porter, patience*. Most Hebrew words, like most

Arabic words, are built around three-consonant roots, and if you look at those three Hebrew words, you'll see that they all share a root in common:

סבל

(samekh-bet-lamed)

The translator is using words with this shared root three ways, to replicate the source's playfulness.

That first letter, you'll see, features twice in **Samson**'s name, too.

Incidentally, the unexpected line about 'take the sweet out of the strong', if you're wondering, is taken from the biblical Book of Judges, where it's part of a riddle posed by *Samson*. Translator Eliaz has our Samson quoting his Biblical namesake.

(And even more incidentally, there's a trace of the source still here too: the word קולר in line four is 'kolar' – an old Hebrew borrowing from the Latin, but stressed on the second syllable, unlike its English cousin.)

What the Hebrew and the English have in common, of course, is not exactitude of meaning, but equivalence of effect.

The Samson/Gregory dialogue continues thus, in Thai:

S: กูละทำเร็วนัก, ถ้าถูกคน**ผัด**.
G: แต่จะ**ผัด**ให้เพื่อนทำน่ะไม่สู้ได้เร็วนัก.
S: อ้ายหมาพวกมอนตะคิวตัวเดียวก็**ผัด**กูได้.
G: การ**ผัด**ก็คือล่อให้วิ่ง, และผู้ที่กล้าต้องยืนอยู่กับที่;
ฉนั้นถ้าเพื่อนถูก**ผัด**, เพื่อนก็คงวิ่งหนีละ.

Meaning, roughly:

SAMSON
I do things quickly if spurred to action
GREGORY
But to pass it on to a friend [to do] / to take turns doing it with a friend isn't quick.

SAMSON
>   Just one Montague dog can <u>move</u> me.

GREGORY
>   To <u>move</u> is to spur someone to run, and the brave must stand in place, therefore if you are <u>moved</u>, you would probably run.*

The translator uses this word – ผัด – five times in these four lines, in slightly differing functions, taking advantage of its convenient span of meanings.

I like this solution. And even if I didn't, I'd need to be circumspect about telling you, since the translation was done by King Rama VI of Siam, and Thailand has a still-active *lèse-majesté* law (criminalising the insulting of a monarch). Just as well we have nothing but praise for this perfect translation of high genius.†

Now we've seen this whole three-way coal/choler/collier/collar business, suddenly the old two-meanings-in-a-word or two-words-that-sound-the-same type of punning feels like child's play, doesn't it?

In the last chapter, I mentioned the two similar Japanese words that obligingly mean two different kinds of light. Easy! But then *Love's Labour's Lost* happens, and Shakespeare goes and does this:

>   Light seeking light doth light of light beguile;
>   So, ere you find where light in darkness lies,
>   Your light grows dark by losing of your eyes.

Where we have multiples of actual light (including that apparently produced by the eyes while seeing) and figurative light (the enlightenment of knowledge or truth) – plus *de-light* five lines earlier as a bonus.

---

* Source text: S: I strike being quickly moved. / G: But thou art not quickly moved to strike. / S: A dog of the house of Montague moves me. / G: To move is to stir, and to be valiant is to stand; therefore, if thou art moved, thou runn'st away.

† Despite being very keen on free speech, there are days when I'd quite like to have a law that could send people to prison for being mean about my translations.

IF THIS BE MAGIC

As well as Longaville's pun two scenes later:

LONGAVILLE
I beseech you a word. What is she in the white?
BOYET
A woman sometimes, an you saw her in the light.
LONGAVILLE
Perchance <u>light</u> in the light.

Where *light* seems to be contrasted with its common antonym *dark*, yes, but the underlined adjective has yet another meaning here – the woman in question is neither brightly lit nor lacking in weight; *light* here means unchaste, wanton.* So that last phrase, says the Arden, means 'Unchaste when seen properly'.

Here's Jean-Michel's:

BOYET
Une femme, si vous la regardez en plein jour.
LONGAVILLE
En pleine nuit aussi sans doute.

That's a clever substitution. In French, 'en plein jour' means 'in broad daylight' – you would know she is a woman, if you saw her clearly by daylight. *Yeah,* replies Longaville, *and if you saw her at night too.*

Longaville's name is itself a problem, by the way, with an immensely complicated play on *long* and *veal* in Act V, but that might have to be for another book . . .

Just changing scale slightly, how about a bit of complex wordplay that functions not on the level of ambiguous words but on the structure

---

* This was the one aspect our Japanese solution in the last chapter didn't cover, because while the Japanese/Venetian Portia uses the *brightness* and *not-heavy* meanings of two similar words, English/Venetian Portia is using *light* for *brightness* and *unfaithful* – but then by suggestion moves from light to heavy – a husband burdened by his wife's light-ness.

of sentences? As I've mentioned, the end of *A Midsummer Night's Dream* treats us to the play-within-a-play of 'Pyramus and Thisbe', artfully constructed as a hilariously bad piece of writing. The prologue is written in such a way that it tempts you to stop in the wrong places if you're a bad actor, but still makes some sense – albeit the *wrong* sense:

> If we offend, it is with our good will.
> That you should think, we come not to offend,
> But with good will. To show our simple skill,
> That is the true beginning of our end.
> Consider then, we come but in despite.
> We do not come, as minding to content you,
> Our true intent is. All for your delight,
> We are not here. [. . .]

A translator must arrange their sentences such that this double reading still works:

> *Ha nem tetszünk, a célunk éppen az.*
> *Hogy megmutassuk színészi tudásunk:*
> *hogy ügyetlenek vagyunk. Nem igaz*
> *történetünkkel mulattatni vágyunk.*
> *Kis játékunk komoly. Dolgokról szól,*
> *de unalmas. Percet ne várjanak:*
> *véletlenül se mulassanak jól.*
> *Nem. Szeretnénk, hogy bosszankodjanak.*

As with the source text, Ádám has arranged and punctuated sentences in such a way that you're encouraged to stop in the wrong places, creating meanings that are ridiculous. Translating it was 'like doing a crossword,' he said.

Here's a rough translation of the text as it stands, with deliberately incorrect punctuation:

If we please you not, that is our goal.
To show you off our actorly skill:
That we be clumsy. It's not true
our tale seeks to entertain.
Take our little play seriously. It has things to say,
though dull. Moments expect not:
not one jot you should enjoy.
No. We would like to see you gripe.

We started this chapter with a bit of extreme tricksiness on Shakespeare's part – and King Richard's part – playing with the homophony of 'I' and 'ay'. And we'll end with those same sounds – but, well, worse. Because 'I' (the one-letter word that is a first-person pronoun) and 'ay' meaning 'yes' also sound indistinguishable from 'i' (ninth letter of the Roman alphabet) and an 'eye' through which we see. So consider this speech, with similar homophonic trouble, in which Juliet is pressing her Nurse to tell her whether Romeo is alive or not:

Hath Romeo slain himself? Say thou but '<u>Ay</u>,'
And that bare vowel '<u>i</u>' shall poison more
Than the death-darting <u>eye</u> of cockatrice.
<u>I</u> am not <u>I</u> if there be such an '<u>Ay</u>',
Or those <u>eyes</u> shut that makes thee answer '<u>Ay</u>.' . . .

Shakespeare here is causing some severe *i* strain. Which is a bad pun that only works in English.

Look at the words I've marked: Juliet uses 'i' the vowel, and 'I' as the pronoun for herself, and a cockatrice's 'eye', and 'ay' meaning yes, all woven together – a total of *eight* of these – into just five lines. (We have the option of pronouncing cockatrIce with a long 'i', too, incidentally.) What are the odds that there's another language where the same trick would work? And what, then, is a translator to do instead when it inevitably doesn't? The German translator Frank Günther told me about his own struggles with this passage, resulting in a clever solution that among other things replaced the murderous cockatrice with a deadly jaguar. *Ja, ja,* a deadly *Jaguar.*

> *Hat Romeo sich getötet? Sag nur «ja»,*
> *Ja, diese Silbe «ja» trägt ja mehr Gift*
> *Als je ein Jaguarsblick den Tod ja trägt!*
> *Sagst du «jaja», bin ich ja nicht mehr ich,*
> *Ja, ich sag «nein», sagst du ein «ja» zum «ja» . . . .*

Sure, you can have a footnote with the 'meaning' if you really want it.* But even without knowing any German, you can just look at all those *ja*'s assembled in all those different ways. Amazing.

---

* The *ja*'s are yesses, but also emphatics and fillers and part of a ja-guar. *Did Romeo kill himself? If you say 'yes', then Yes, that syllable 'yes' carries more poison than a jaguar's gaze ever carries death! If you say 'yes, yes,' I am no longer me. Yes, I say 'no,' if you say a 'yes' to 'yes.'*

Chapter 12

Uthando ayilothando

(on meaning/s)

I don't buy the idea that languages have these special untranslatable words, unless you take the claim to mean words that can't be translated *using a single word*. The internet is full of charming lists of untranslatable words, assembled by a compiler who then helpfully *tells you what they all mean* – which, well, does seem to suggest . . .

The Portuguese word *saudade* doesn't map perfectly onto the Welsh *hiraeth*, but there's some overlap. Both are in the general homesickness/ missing/longing area of human emotion. One could explain how each is delimited slightly differently, and 'homesickness' might be inadequate as a one-word translation for either, but the variance is explainable. The word *saudade* lives at the core of some deeply tearful Portuguese music, while the word *hiraeth* is sewn into the ~~cholers~~ collars of the Welsh rugby team's away strip. I suspect the human feelings aren't all *that* different.

Of course you occasionally find certain words simply failing to exist in one language, because they're particular to the material trappings of another culture. A Spanish dictionary might include a *mesa camilla*, an old sort of table with a heater underneath it and a heavy tablecloth over the top, designed to keep one's legs warm. There is no English term that I'm aware of, because the English-speaking world has thus far survived without the item of furniture that the word describes. But these objects do exist in Spanish, and novelists seem to like including them in their novels in order to annoy me. But even the 'mesa camilla', which is not exactly one of the fundamental universals of human emotional experience, is still translatable, albeit perhaps into a phrase rather than a word. (My dictionary says 'table with a heater underneath' – that's good enough for most purposes.) The Japanese language has the word 'kotatsu', also referring to an under-heated blanketed table, though this one is much lower to the ground for sitting on the floor. A Japanese–Spanish dictionary might define 'kotatsu' as a 'low *mesa camilla*'. There isn't a single exact matching word, but there are always things a language can use for reference points.

The bigger problem for a translator comes where two languages might be able to express exactly the same things, but the dividing lines between words aren't comparable. For example, Spanish uses 'historia' for both history and story, and it's not always clear to a translator which is principally intended. It also has, like Portuguese, two different verbs for 'to be' – very roughly, one is provisional and one essential. (Not that 'to be' is going to be important in a Shakespeare play anytime soon . . .)*

English has *mornings* and *afternoons* and *evenings* and *night*; and again Spanish† has *madrugada*, *mañana*, *tarde* and *noche*, with *tarde* covering what we'd call afternoon and much of the evening. The Hispanophones' lack of a word for the band of time that we call *evening* (as distinct from either afternoon or night) doesn't of course mean they can't express it. The entire Latin American continent and Iberian peninsula don't just suddenly stop talking when the clock strikes 6 p.m. Of course, both languages have ways of referring to both 4 p.m. and 7 p.m., but in English they're on either side of a lexical dividing line. Similarly

---

* Russian is one of many languages with no *being* verb in the present tense at all. The technical term is a *zero copula* or *null copula* – in which the *copula* (a verb connecting a subject and a predicate) is omitted. Я переводчик. I translator.

† I was going to say 'I don't know why I'm picking on Spanish', but actually I do. I'm translating a book from Spanish today and it's annoying me.

madrugada covers a period between night and morning, only the earlier morning hours – the small hours, we might say, though we Anglophones cannot say it using one word alone.

And though *madrugada* doesn't correspond to a single English word – which causes trouble for me when I'm compelled to translate it – there are plenty of *madrugadas* to be found in translations of English-originating texts. For those moments where the English is referring to *the early morning*, this word is rather handy to have around.

There's a 'madrugada' in Lawrence's *Hamlet* St Valentine's Day song (it rhymes, too):

> *Amanhã é são Valentim,*
> *De casa saem, é <u>madrugada</u>;*
> *Jovem diante o varandim,*
> *Me torno sua amada.*

where the English was *All in the morning betime* – so this particular morning is definitely *first thing* in the morning (we know that from the 'betime').

In *Julius Caesar*, Brutus speaks to Portia of the morning, but we're to assume it is early here, too, rather than nearly lunchtime, because Brutus is asking Portia why she's already up, and saying it's not good for her health that she should be exposing herself to 'the raw cold morning'.

In Chico's Portuguese, Brutus remarks:

> *Não convém à tua frágil condição*
> *Expor-se à <u>madrugada</u> fria e inóspita.*

– she specifically shouldn't expose herself to the cold and inhospitable *madrugada*.

And Chico also has two of them in his *Romeo and Juliet*, when the lovers are in bed arguing whether the bird they can hear is the nightingale or the lark, and therefore if it's still early enough that Romeo might tarry a little longer . . . They have one *madrugada* apiece. Here's hers:

> *Pois esse canto vai puxar-te à <u>madrugada</u>,*
> *Como a trombeta matutina da caçada.*
> *Agora, vai! A luz à luz se soma, armando o dia.*

And here's his:

> *Direi que o olhar cinzento e azul da <u>madrugada</u> . . .*

For which Shakespeare has:

> I'll say yon grey is not the morning's eye . . .

– the coming dawn, in other words.

Madrugada isn't the only Portuguese word that doesn't cover the exact same territory as an English one. The above-mentioned *saudades* are famously tricky to find a match for, if you're translating outbound from Portuguese. But just because Shakespeare didn't have such a word in English doesn't mean that a lucky lusophone translator can't take advantage of it.

At the end of *Romeo and Juliet*, we learn that Lady Montague has died from grief at her son Romeo's departure, and her husband says:

> Grief of my son's exile hath stopped her breath . . .

The Portuguese could easily have ended up unwieldy. Portuguese doesn't have a possessive like English (my son's exile), so would need to say 'grief of the exile of my son', and the nouns are all longer – grief is *tristeza*, son is *filho*, exile is *exílio* – *tristeza pelo exílio do meu filho*. Apart from the unpleasantly echoey sounds (*filho* rhymes with *exílio*), it's also twelve syllables, twice as long as the English phrase – so you do what the language allows:

A saudade do filho a derrubou.

The thing that brought her down is simply *saudade for her son*.

Our old friend *saudade* – how we've missed it! – allows Chico a solution for the phrase that's almost as syllabically tight as the English.

In *The Tempest*, Prospero agrees to free Ariel but knows that he will feel that very human sense of loss and longing when it's time for him to leave:

Why, that's my dainty Ariel! <u>I shall miss thee,</u>	*Ariel, minha joia!* <u>*Eu sentirei saudades,*</u>
But yet thou shalt have freedom.	*Porém terás a liberdade que desejas.*

Useful word, for those lucky enough to have it.

By the way, don't you love that fact about the *hiraeth* in the Welsh away strip? I do.

I mean, I'm not in love with it, but I love it – though not in the way I love my family and friends. I also love ice cream. You wouldn't say 'I feel intense romantic/sexual desire towards your shoes'. (Or at least I wouldn't. Not judging.) And nor does saying 'I love your shoes' suggest a deep familial bond between them and me. Love is a many-nuanced word. In English, it has some serious range. We *can* specify feelings more precisely, but we also have this catch-all word of great general positivity that means we don't need to.

My English–Greek dictionary gives two initial options for the noun: αγάπη (agápi) and έρωτας (érotas) – the first general, the second specifically romantic/passionate/sexual, and Greek isn't alone in splitting the word into more distinct components than we do in English. So when Bassanio says to Antonio, in the opening scene of *The Merchant of Venice*:

> To you, Antonio,
> I owe the most in money and in love . . .

many a translator will have needed to make a determination about the exact nature of that 'love'. Because the English word is capacious (I love my friends and also pizza), an English-speaking Bassanio needn't testify to anything too specific; but not so in many languages. Various Spanish translations in the past have used *amistad* (friendship), *cariño* or *afecto* (both of these are sort of 'affection'). Vicente Molina Foix, more recently, chose *amor*, which is much more suggestive of an intimacy that is not simply a reasonably warm friendship. And the discrepancies aren't necessarily just a matter of earlier translators being nervous about the homosexuality suggested (and made explicit in many productions today); they had to make a choice one way or another, like it or not. The existence of the word love in English allowed Shakespeare to keep readings open (the shades of the word's meaning have changed in these 400 years, too, of course); for many people, Shakespeare translators among them, their language will force a choice upon them. You say 'love', Bassanio, but what *exactly* do you mean?

Another Antonio – this time in *Twelfth Night* – says: 'I do adore thee so', which specifies this as being of a different level from whatever vague affection you might have construed from *love*. But the word *love* certainly can carry that weight in English, too, of course. In the first half of *Much Ado about Nothing*, Beatrice uses the word *love* once, while the other characters in that same period speak it fifty-eight times, and when she finally says: 'I do love nothing in the world so well as you. Is not that strange?', it's a great discovery for her of a feeling that is profound. *No hay nada en el mundo que ame como a ti.**

Single words can split to multiple options when translation happens, not only in form (love/loves/loving) but also in precise meaning. So it is with love in Arabic.

The play in which 'love' has the most mentions is . . . *The Two Gentlemen of Verona*. Even if you've seen it – and not all that many people have – you perhaps didn't notice that the word *love* and its

---

* Tr. Edmundo Paz Soldán (Spanish).

associated words are spoken more frequently than in any other play. According to Bartlett's Concordance, *love/s* alone – and so disregarding *loved, lover, loving*, etc. – appears in 135 of the play's lines.

So, naturally, we consult a copy of *The Two Gentlemen of Verona* in Arabic.

Except we don't. I wasn't able to get my hands on an Arabic translation (though I have belatedly now learned that several exist!), so I'll look at it in Spanish instead.

Here is a sampling of the lines from the opening two pages of *The Two Gentlemen of Verona*:

> —the sweet glances of thy honoured love . . .
> —But since thou lov'st, love still . . .
> —Even as I would when I to love begin . . .
> —And on a love-book pray for my success . . .
> —Upon some book I love I'll pray for thee . . .
> —To be in love, where scorn is bought with groans . . .
> —Love is your master, for he masters you . . .

In the Spanish translation by José Mendez Herrera (who also, heroically, did a complete Spanish Dickens), each of those underlined words are, respectively: *amada, (sigue) amando, amar, de amor, amo, enamorado* and *el*. (The last of these being just 'he' – a pronoun standing in for 'amor', which is a masculine noun in Spanish.)

In English, *love* is a noun, but it's also the verb in the infinitive form, in the present tense in most instances. I/you/we/they *love* (it's only the third-person singular that love*s*), and all of us *will love* in the future and *did love* in the past. In Spanish, the shape of the word shifts much more than in English depending on use, so you'll see that the Spanish words are all different. The conjugating of Spanish verbs is part of it; but it's also because English has other idiosyncrasies (the basic word 'love' stands within 'in love'; the English ability to make a noun into a kind of adjective 'what kind of book? A *love-book*', etc.).

At least all of the Spanish uses in those lines are variations on the same word (*amor*), because the meaning across them all is deemed to be coherent. But not so here:

> . . . And that I love him not as I was wont.
> O, but I love his lady too too much . . .

Where the second love is *amo*, but the first is *aprecio*, which is slightly more affectionate than the English 'appreciate' that it resembles, but it's not really what we'd commonly call love. And here:

> I give thee this
> For thy sweet mistress' sake, because thou lov'st her.

> *por amor de tu dueña te la doy,*
> *pues que en verdad la quieres mucho.*

where again the verb isn't *amar*, but this time it's *querer* – a quite general, common-use word, not necessarily intense or romantic.

(Though confusingly the Spanish does include the word *amor* here, but it's to stand in for the English *sake*.)

The multifarious uses of the word 'love' that English allows means that Shakespeare can use its repetition deliberately for neat effect. When Richard III tells Lady Anne that he 'for thy love did kill thy love', the first of those is the abstract noun, the second is the person she loved. Other languages won't always have one dictionary word that can drop identically into both parts of that line.

As ever, swapping between linguistic systems mean we lose possibilities, but also that we gain them. And this particular Spanish translator did happily take advantage of the gifts that his language offered him. The Spanish word for *master* is *amo*, and for *mistress*, *ama*, which allowed him to do a few nifty things with lines like:

Confío en que reciba fríamente
las solicitaciones de <u>mi amo</u>,
pues que <u>el amor</u> respeta de <u>mi ama</u> . . .
¡Ay! ¿Cómo puede <u>amor</u>, de tal manera,
engañarse a sí mismo?

(I hope my <u>master's</u> suit will be but cold,
Since she respects my <u>mistres' love</u> so much.
Alas, how <u>love</u> can trifle with itself!)

There are many occasions in this play where *master/mistress* and *love* appear in close proximity. English has no scope to do anything with this. (Though the English *Two Gents* does manage a play on *lover* and *lubber* . . .)

Now, one of the plays I *have* found in Arabic is *As You Like It*, which obligingly does also feature the word *love* in many functions.

Look up 'love' in an English–Arabic dictionary, and the first thing you get is حب (*houb*) – the most simple and general, which works as both noun and verb; thus far not unlike English, then. But this basic word alters form depending on the lover, the lovee, etc. So, for example, when we are told in the opening scene that the Duke's daughter Celia 'so loves' her cousin Rosalind, the word in Mohammed Ayad Ibrahim Bek's translation is تحبها – (*tahibuha*), with a female prefix (ta-, for a female subject) and a female suffix (-ha, for a female object).

The one who is loved – the beloved – is مَحْبوب (*mahboub*) if male, مَحْبوبة (*mahbuba*) if female. The former is the word used when Orlando is described a couple of minutes later as 'enchantingly beloved'.

And when we're told that three or four loving lords have put themselves into voluntary exile with the banished Duke, those loving lords are المحُبّين (*almuhibbeen*) – they are the-ones-who-love-him, though not in a romantic sense.

Other variants of these words appear a lot. So for instance, Oliver's line:

> Charles, I thank thee for thy love to me

أشكرك على <u>محبتك لي</u> ولعلي أوفق لمكافأتك عليها

The relevant words here are محبتك لي – *mahabatok li*. I thank you for your <u>mahaba</u> to me.

But how about this?

> Your brother is but young and tender, and <u>for your love</u> I would be loath to foil him . . .

That 'for your love' is translated as:

و<u>لصداقتنا</u> لا أريد أن أهزمه

which is nothing to do with 'houb' at all. Here the word used by the translator is صداقتنا (*sadaqatuna*), which is commonly used for friendship (not romantic love) and it's specifically reciprocal – not one's affection for another but a feeling of positive attachment that is mutual. For *our friendship* I would be loath to foil him.

Incidentally, all these instances we've seen thus far occur in the space of sixty-five lines in Act I, Scene 1.

A few lines into the second scene, Celia says:

> Herein I see thou lov'st me not with the full weight that I love thee.

أوه أن هذا القول يدلني على أنك لا <u>تحبينني</u> بقدر ما أحبك

And it's another related one – the word is تحبينني (*tahoubinani*) with the female subject and a 'me' object.

But then a moment later, Rosalind asks her cousin, 'what think you of falling <u>in love</u>?'

ألم تجربي <u>العشق</u> أو<u>الغرام</u>؟

Here is no general *houb* or any derivatives; nor is this the reciprocal friendly version we've seen; this is something else again. Rosalind is asking here: have you experienced عشق (*ishq*) or غرام (*gharam*)? Where *ishq* is passionate love (one-sided, not necessarily reciprocal), and *gharam* is a kind of deep infatuation.

If I put حب (houb) into Google Translate, it gives me *love*. If I put عشق (*ishq*) into Google Translate, it gives me *Love*.* If I put غرام (*gharam*) into Google Translate, it gives me *love*. All of which are reasonable English translations.

The word مودة (*mawada*) doesn't happen to appear on this page in *As You Love It*, but apparently (thanks, Google T.), it's *love*, too.

Interestingly, if I enter all four in series – مودة حب عشق غرام – then Google Translate bothers to specify, and offers me not *love, Love, love, love*, but *affection, love, passion, infatuation*.

Though all Shakespeare needs is *love, love, love, love*.

While on matters of the heart . . . In *te reo* Māori, the word *manawa* means heart, the physical organ; but *ngākau* means one's heart as in one's soul, one's inner self. When Hurieta tells Rōmeo to 'swear not by the moon' but rather 'by thy gracious self' – it's an injunction to swear by your *ngākau*. Then when Friar Lawrence calls Romeo a young *waverer*, his *te reo* words are *ngākau rua*, where *rua* means two or double – a person of double mind, of double self. A connection is made that isn't there in the English.

Act I, scene 2 of *The Tempest* uses the word 'brave' to describe (among other things) both a ship and a person. The word here means something like *fine* or *splendid looking*, rather than *courageous*. At the urging of the director he was working with, So Kwok Wan wanted to find one Chinese word/expression to fit both instances. He ended up going with 无与伦比 – which means sort of *peerless*, an unusual choice but an apt epithet for both in context.

Internal consistency sometimes matters, but is often hard to sustain. In Chapter 1, I suggested some ways the simple word *dog* is not so

---

* Capitalised, for some reason.

simple, so would be hard always to replace with the same word, one for one. Scattered around this book, you'll find references to real dogs on the *Queen Mary 2*, fictional dogs in a comic, figurative dogs as an insult; there's a dog-matic pun, a useful rhyme with *frog*, 'dog' used as an example of a monosyllable, the phrase 'raining cats and dogs', also doggy, doggerel, dogged, etc.

If you've ever wanted to read a whole chapter that worries at the word *dog* and its complex multiple uses in *Timon of Athens*, I'd recommend William Empson's *The Structure of Complex Words*. Though if you're a translator about to start translating *Timon of Athens*, you might find it upsetting, so perhaps give it a miss . . .

We don't typically notice the lacks in whichever language we swim in on a daily basis. (Unless you're a translator, in which case social media algorithms will drown you in '18 cool things other languages have a word for!' listicles.) At a translation workshop the other day, we realised that there is no compact way in English of referring to two people who are a couple and who are your friends – 'a couple of friends' means something different. I'm having dinner tonight with a friend-couple? With a couple I'm friends with? With two friends of mine who incidentally are also a couple? That seems to place too much emphasis on information that's purportedly incidental. The workshop where this came up was for Portuguese-language translators, so I was able to say, 'You know, *um casal de amigos*,' which is simple and unambiguous. A 'casal' is one kind of couple (relational) and not only the other kind (numerical).

Again, we delineate things differently. In *Timon of Athens*, Timon refers to blue adders. In *Titus Andronicus*, Tamora speaks about green leaves. If you look at the work of Chinese translator Shenghao Zhu, who managed to get through 31 plays before his premature death from tuberculosis in 1944 (aged just 32), you'll find that he uses the word 青 to describe both. In Chinese, 青 (qīng) means green and also blue (among other things).

Yiddish, meanwhile, differentiates between *esn* and *fresn* – the first being the eating that humans do, the second being what animals do.

The latter is used for humans but only with that negative, animal connotation of gluttonous voracity. So when Lancelot in *The Merchant of Venice* refers to Christians as 'pork eaters', Y. Bovshover translates it as חזיר־פרעסער – *khazer-freser*. Not just pork-eaters but pork-*guzzlers*.

When I asked Niels about disagreements he might have had with an actor or director, his example was about another simple-seeming English word that splits in his language: silence. The director Eyðun Johannessen (father of the Danish Richard II actor I saw), wanted to use silence for dramatic effect at *Hamlet*'s final close. There's a moment of silence, then you hear the drums of the approaching army, their rhythm suggesting the heartbeat of the dying Hamlet – then Fortinbras arrives and the drums stop – and thus so does the heartbeat.

So when Hamlet says his final line, 'The rest is silence', the director insisted that the *silence* in question be *stilhed*, rather than *tavshed*, the classic translation of the word. The latter means no one is speaking, the former means there is just no sound at all.

Niels, however, prefers *tavshed*. Hamlet knows he can't speak any more, and Horatio has been given the task of telling his story – Hamlet's imminent *speechlessness* in particular is important, because he's asking his friend to speak for him. The published version of Niels's translation has no need to bow to any director, nor anybody else's interpretation but the translator's own. In print, Hamlet's last word is *tavshed*.

I particularly like this example – it sums up so much of why translation interests me. It is not a matter of looking a word up in a dictionary; it's about considering multiple dimensions, and about critical interpretation, and ultimately making a choice.

Needless to say, a director in Denmark – like a translator in Denmark – has options that Anglophones mostly do not. An English director might wish Hamlet had said something different, something more convenient, but rewrite the famous bits at your peril. An English director did once say to Niels: 'Ugh, I wish we could translate Shakespeare, too . . .'

Chapter 13

จะเลยยกเอาเปนญาติวงศของเจ้าเองเสียกระมัง

(on uncles, and boldness)

In many South Asian languages – and indeed in many other of the world's languages, too – it's common to distinguish between different types of uncle or aunt, where English is vague. If I tell you – in English – that my uncle is visiting London in August, you can't thereby deduce whether he's my maternal uncle or paternal; nor can you tell if he's their younger or older brother. Whereas to the children of a close Bengali-speaking friend, I am referred to as Danny-*mama*, because that friend is female and so I'm deemed to be, through friendship, an uncle on the maternal side.*

In Hindi, Claudius is Hamlet's *chacha* – which is to say, (younger) brother to his father. (This is important to the plot. If he were Hamlet's *mama*, then he would be Gertrude's brother, and things would be even worse than frankly they already are.)

I should point out, by the way, that it's hard to think of *mamas* – maternal uncles – in Shakespeare. With an interest in dynastic power and succession, the history plays are full of the other kind – Richard III is *chacha* to the Princes in the Tower, Worcester to Hotspur, York

---

* Also, I only needed to tell you explicitly that the friend in question is female because – unusually – the English word 'friend' doesn't contain that data already.

to Bolingbroke, and so on. This lack of maternal uncles and oversupply of paternal ones had never struck me, incidentally, until I started having to look through the lens of these other languages, and to consider how – unlike in English – these languages encode the distinction.

In the unusual case of *Richard III*, the young princes *do* also have *mamas*, *Richard III* being in general one of the uncliest plays.* When the king dies and the young prince inherits the throne, a couple of citizens recall the last time they had a child on the throne, at Henry VI's accession:

THIRD CITIZEN
   . . . then the King
Had virtuous uncles to protect his Grace.

FIRST CITIZEN
Why, so hath this, both by his father and mother.

Yes, young Edward has both *chachas* and *mamas* (though 'virtuous' might be a stretch). So when Richard-*chacha* is there to welcome the newly arrived young prince to London, he remarks upon the boy's demeanour:

RICHARD
   . . . The weary way hath made you melancholy.
PRINCE
No, uncle, but our crosses on the way
Have made it tedious, wearisome and heavy.
I want more uncles here to welcome me.

The uncles he wants are his maternal ones, who are actually just about to be murdered, unfortunately – the 'uncle' at the start of the speech and the 'uncles' at the end of it are categorically different.

---

* My search for every 'uncle' in the complete works seemed initially to suggest that one might stumble upon these particular relatives in almost every play, but many proved on examination to be things *unclean* in *All's Well*, a *carbuncle* in *Cymbeline*; the unusual verb *unclew* in *Timon of Athens*, and so on. Never noticed these before, either.

Later in this same conversation – a short scene in which the kinship is emphasised, with the prince and his brother using the word *uncle/uncles* ten times – the younger boy remarks that he's scared of going to the Tower, because his uncle Clarence was killed there, and his ghost might still be about.

I fear no uncles dead.

says his brave older brother.

Nor none that live, I hope.

replies uncle Richard. Murdered Clarence was his brother, so the living and dead uncles in this conversation are paternal both, meaning this exchange, at least, would potentially work in Bangla, though ruling out the possibility that either of them could be referring to the other side of the family.

We Anglophones *can* specify 'maternal uncle' or – even more exactly – 'mother's *younger/older* brother', but we aren't required to, and we don't have a single word for it should we choose to.

When it's not specified – what *exactly* is Sir Toby's relationship to Olivia in *Twelfth Night*? – the translator must make a choice, and the choice has consequences. Often Shakespeare can benefit from the imprecision; the translator can benefit from the specifying.

The Turkish word *amca* means specifically paternal uncle – but it can also be used to address other older men, not only uncles in blood. That was the word Emine used on p.79 when Lear's Fool calls him 'nuncle'.

In *Richard II*, Bolingbroke begins 'My gracious uncle—' but York cuts him off:

Grace me no grace, nor uncle me no uncle.
I am no traitor's uncle . . .

'Uncle me no uncle'? If you wanted another reason why this would cause trouble for a translator, look at that first *uncle* – Shakespeare's decided it's a verb now.

There is ample ingenuity to be found in translations of Shakespeare. I have shared examples in this book, and there are more to come. But along with our translators' ingenuity, I would like to salute their boldness, too. There has long been a sense, at least in the English-speaking world, that translators would do well to restrain themselves from making their language do anything it is not in the habit of doing. Not to try to get away with anything that is – lexically, syntactically, idiomatically – too new. To be only constrained by their language, in other words, rather than pushing at its limits. Part of this comes from nervous publishing, and part from a sort of pre-emptive self-defence – a writer doing something uncommon with a phrase might be excitingly doing Style, but if you're reading a translated work, well, it just sounds a bit funny, doesn't it? Just a bit off, kind of clunky? Probably just something wrong with the translation. (The number of times I've had people question weirdnesses in a translation and resisted the temptation to say, *Oh god, you should see the original . . .*)

I've heard the translator-writer Jeremy Tiang say that when he receives nervous editorial comments on a bold translation to the effect that 'But English doesn't do that . . .', he responds, 'Well, English hasn't done that *yet*.' Shakespeare is constantly making English do things that English doesn't do, after all. A brave translator will stretch their language just the same.

One of my proudest translating moments came when a friend shared a 'word-a-day' email they'd received, and the word in question was supported by a citation from one of my translations. My decision to import a Portuguese word into my translation of an Angolan novel meant that the thing we call the English language was now just a tiny bit richer.*

---

* My feeling of pride didn't last for long, I feel bound to say, because not long after this, a Google Alert notified me that I'd been cited in another online dictionary. This one was for the word 'miasma', which, as I've mentioned, is a word I do like and use when I can. I was less proud when I visited the site in question and saw that they were supporting the word with a *Washington Post* citation that said: 'But to get there, a reader has to wade through a miasma of awkward phrasing in this clunky English translation by Daniel Hahn . . .'

Meanwhile . . .

Hamlet describes some bad acting he's seen, concluding:

> I would have such a fellow whipped for o'erdoing Termagant – it out-Herods Herod. Pray you, avoid it.

In his Yiddish translation, Y. Goldberg renders 'it out-Herods Herod' as

איבערטיראנעווען א טיראן און איבערגאזלענען א גאזלען

[*ibertiraneven a tiran un ibergazlenen a gazlen*]

You might guess from a scan of the transliteration that Herod is no longer named; the line is 'out-tyrants a tyrant and out-thieves a thief'. Yiddish-speaking friends tell me that איבערטיראנעווען (*ibertiraneven*) is not a previously existing word that one would find in a dictionary, and nor does *tiran* conventionally operate as a verb at all. Clearly, then, this is unacceptable. Also, impeccably Shakespearean.

Chapter 14

jIH jIH 'e' yInISQo'. 'ej chochoH 'e' yInIDQo'

(on pronouns)

When you decide to translate something into a new language, you accept that the language will bring with it a very particular set of grammatical, syntactical and historical complexities. There's a lot that *te reo* Māori can't really do that the English language can, and there's a lot that English can't do that *te reo* finds easy. The question is how much a translator will lean into the opportunities that these challenges present. Sometimes a translator will do something that the source language would have found impossible. Why limit yourself to losses when you have the option of compensating gains?

When Edmund in *King Lear* plays on the words *bastard*, *base* and *baseness* (and, in a recent production, also *bass*, with Fra Fee playing a low note on an onstage piano), the Portuguese words – *bastardo*, *abjeto* – can't create the same effect. In the same scene, however, Lawrence translates:

An admirable evasion of whoremaster man, to lay his goatish disposition on the charge of a star!

as

Que escapada notável de um homem putanheiro imputar aos astros sua propria putaria!

Here even the verb he's chosen – *imputar*, related to our English *impute* – contains an extra echo of that 'whore' word, *puta*. As with those *Asterix* and *Harry Potter* examples we saw above, the translator will take advantage of those things a language will allow them, doing the sorts of thing our authors probably would have done, had they but been possible; just as Shakespeare only did those things English allowed because English happened to allow them. Translation is all loss and all gain; sometimes I need to lose a witty ambiguity on p.240, but I can instead slip an acrostic onto p.241, when it's in the same spirit, because English lets me. (I made just such an exchange only this week.)

But here's where – again! – it gets tough for the translators: those things that different languages *allow* are often also things that languages firmly *require*. In English it's not only the case that we're able to differentiate between fingers and toes, between story and history, between waiting and hoping, we are *compelled* to. Plenty of languages don't insist on such things.

In which spirit, I would now like to talk about *you*.

You ~~are~~ is the only standard pronoun that most forms of modern English have for addressing other people.

'How are you?'

I'd use that *you* for somebody I have just met, or for somebody I am on very intimate terms with. I'd use it for an individual, or a group. We should arrange something with you and your whole family – are you free on Thursday?

The languages from which I translate all differentiate between at least two pronouns of address, of differing formality / familiarity, a distinction I need to find ways of marking in English. If, for example, two characters are in conversation and one uses the *tu* form, while the other addresses his interlocutor with *vous* – what does the distinction indicate?

Should a reader assume a difference in age, in status, a deference in one man and a confident familiarity in the other? This splitting allows for greater precision – and it's there in Shakespeare's English, too. He can do more with 'you' and 'thou' than we can do with 'you' alone.

Of course, I have other ways of specifying a plural should I choose to – what are *you guys* doing tomorrow? (Other people with other Englishes might use *y'all, ye* or *youse*.) And I can use register to differentiate between degrees of formality, only not by varying the pronoun itself. (*I do hope you are keeping quite well?* vs *Y'alright?*)

The difficulty most often arises in transitions, as a switch in pronouns amplifies distance or erases it. At a moment of growing familiarity between characters, say, where one Spanish character politely addresses another as *usted*, and their interlocutor says: 'oh, please, feel free to address me as *tu*!'

In unmarked English, this would be:

'And how are you?'
'Oh no, please, no need for all the "you" stuff. Do call me "you"!'
'Ah, thank you – in that case, how are *you*?'

If you're ever reading a translation in which one character suddenly calls another 'sir', and are told 'Oh, please, there's no need to call me "sir"!', that's what the translator is attempting to get away with. (It is not a solution I like at all. It is, however, one to which I have occasionally resorted in some desperation, *faute de mieux*.)

One piece of good news for the translator of Shakespeare (it's almost all bad news otherwise) is that this particular marker is easy to correlate because Shakespeare does have two options, and they correspond pretty neatly to, say, the French *tu* and *vous*. Shakespeare uses 'you' (your, yours) for the plural (*Friends, Romans, countrymen, lend me your ears!*) and the reasonably formal/reserved (*Good pilgrim, you do wrong your hand too much*); and 'thou' (thee, thy, thine) for the singular and intimate or junior or subservient. *Wherefore art thou*

Romeo? Shall I compare thee to a summer's day? In the great intimacy of prayer, that's what was used for God, too. Hallowed be thy name . . . thine is the kingdom, the power and the glory, for ever and ever . . .*

For a French translator, then, every Shakespearean *thou* can be a *tu*, every *you* a *vous*. And unlike most English-speaking audiences today, a French audience would notice. In a language where people are attuned to these usages, being introduced to the President of the Republic and immediately presuming to be on *tu* terms would be *obviously* improper.

And it's not just that these second persons give you options, and therefore ways of marking intimacies, hierarchy, etc. It's also that – the flipside of this – there is no *unmarked* second person as we have in English today. It's not just that some languages (Shakespeare's included) will allow a user to specify, they will *require* it.

Here's a brief exchange from *Pericles*, between Pericles himself (the King) and Helicanus (a lord at his court):

— . . . What wouldst thou have me do?
—   To bear with patience
    Such griefs as you yourself do lay upon yourself.
—   Thou speak'st like a physician . . .

You could guess which line belongs to which character just by the pronouns – the first speaker is talking down to the second, the second is talking up to the first. Again, English-language audiences today

---

* Though not, actually, for ever and ever – some recent translations say 'The kingdom, the power and the glory are yours', which is presumably intended to avoid archaism, but also ends up flattening out the specificity of the relationship. 'Thy' is not *only* an old word now fallen into disuse, it's also telling us something that is distinct from 'your'. Ancient and koine (biblical) Greek differentiated: in the Orthodox liturgy, God is addressed in the second-person *singular*: τὰ σὰ ἐκ τῶν σῶν σοὶ προσφέρομεν (ta sa ek ton son si prospheromen). *Thine own from thine own we offer unto thee.*

are less likely to be sensitive to such clues. Not so a Turkish audience, for whom each thing marked here indicates the characters' relative status:

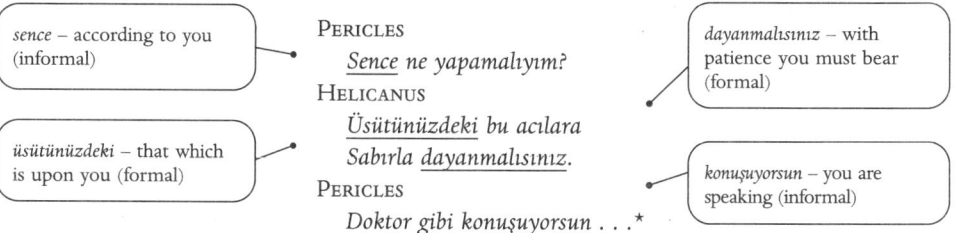

PERICLES
Sence ne yapamalıyım?
HELICANUS
Üsütünüzdeki bu acılara
Sabırla *dayanmalısınız*.
PERICLES
Doktor gibi *konuşuyorsun* . . .*

In Turkish, verbs ending with with -in, -un, etc. mark the informal second person; verbs ending -iz, ız, or -uz, -üz, etc. the formal second person. Those marker units can also appear in the middle of long composite words, too (which might each take the place of several words in English).

When translating *A Midsummer Night's Dream*, Ádám noticed that the mechanicals all use the less casual form – they're lower-middle class, he explained, and do want to be polite. In Hungarian, it's an amusing trait that audiences will notice – 'or maybe not exactly *notice*, but it's like a musical soundtrack to a film'. An English speaker today might know the difference between *thou* and *you* as employed on the Shakespearean stage; in Hungarian, the distinction is *felt*.

Social hierarchies notwithstanding, relational pronouns aren't always fixed, and they can vary from moment to moment. ('I knew old married couples in Hungarian who would do this,' said Ádám.) So the modulating of the warmth in any relationship, as built into the pronouns that characters use for each other, would be felt in many contemporary languages in a way that it seldom is in contemporary English. Perhaps this means that those languages where a comparable distinction is naturally drawn are a better fit for a play like *Macbeth*, where you might map the volatile relationship between the Thane and his Lady through their constantly fluctuating second-person pronouns – our contemporary English would struggle to do that.

* Translated here by Hamdi Koç.

Within moments of their first appearance on stage – with that speech we've seen about hours being cups of sack, minutes capons etc. – Falstaff has addressed the Prince of Wales as 'thou':

Marry, then, sweet wag, when thou art king . . .

which immediately tells an audience much about their relationship. It's a casual, teasing relationship. It is also socially inappropriate (calling a prince 'thou'?!), an impertinence frowned upon by king and court.

When the Hostess reports that the Prince said Falstaff's oh-so-valuable ring was actually copper, the old man blusters, ''Sblood, an [if] he were here, I would cudgel him like a dog if he would say so.' This is not a relationship of simple deference.

The French Falstaff (in the translation by François-Victor Hugo) says this upon our first acquaintance:

Effectivement, Hal, <u>vous arrivez</u> a me comprendre, Car nous autres, preneurs de bourses, noun nous réglons sur la lune es les sept planets, et non sur Phébus, le blond chevalier errant. Et je <u>t'</u>en prie, doux railleur, quand <u>tu seras</u> roi . . . que Dieu garde <u>Ta</u> Grâce! . . . <u>Ta</u> Majesté, devrais-je dire, car, pour la grâce, <u>tu</u> n'en <u>auras</u> pas . . .

The initial instance of the second person is an appropriate 'vous' – then we have five uses of *tu*. Including *Ta majesté* – the equivalent of 'Thy Majesty', a peculiar mash-up that seems to be formal but undermines it.

In *Twelfth Night*, Sir Andrew is about to write Cesario a challenge, and Sir Toby suggests he might 'thou' him as a way of insulting his honour:

Taunt him with the licence of ink. If thou thou'st him some thrice, it shall not be amiss and as many lies as will lie in thy sheet of paper, although the sheet were big enough for the bed of Ware in England, set 'em down.*

In those languages where pronouns don't split in this particular manner, an observant translator can create similar effects in other ways, of course. The second-person singular in Swahili (*wewe*), says JC Niala, doesn't itself distinguish between *thou* and *you*; but 'shifts in formality or intimacy can be marked contextually through tone, vocabulary, or the use of honorifics. For example, *wewe* can be modified by respectful terms like *bwana* (for *sir*) or *mama* (for *madam*) to indicate deference, or by omitting such terms for intimacy.' In her *Macbeth*, for example, Lady Macbeth greets her husband on his heroic return using a 'bwana' (Bwana Glamis), but later challenges his courage ('When you durst do it, then you were a man') dropping the 'bwana' thus: *Ulipothubutu kufanya hivyo, ndipo ulikuwa mwanaume kweli.*

'The stark directness,' JC says, 'gives the intimacy (and even aggression) of a wife pushing her husband, making it closer to "thou" than "you".'

You'd be surprised how tricky translating even a seemingly simple pronoun can be. Well, you wouldn't be surprised if you were a translator into, say, Japanese, a language with several distinct ways of saying 'I' – which means that every English 'I' in *Hamlet* could require a potentially hard and revealing choice.

So the second-person pronoun isn't the only trouble-maker. Yes, Shakespeare has two variants of the second person, a distinction that should ideally be rendered in a translated text, but plenty of languages have far more complex and nuanced systems of pronoun usage than that.

---

* Also note, incidentally, how he's making the 'thou' into a verb, not unlike what we've just seen another character do with 'uncle'. The problem here is that in French, say, the word 'tutoyer', meaning 'to address someone by 'tu' – *Si tu le tutoies deux ou trois fois* (Vivé/Llesta) or *quelques tutoiements ne seront pas mauvais* (Noël) – is an entirely normal, everyday-use verb already.

The English 'I', as we've seen, causes trouble because when spoken aloud it sounds like several other things. But at least it doesn't change – almost every English-speaking person, in almost every English-speaking context, would use what *Yes, Minister*'s Sir Humphrey calls 'the perpendicular pronoun' to refer to themselves as the subject of a verb. (The occasional 'we' for royalty and Margaret Thatcher; the occasional third person for Julius Caesar and other illeists.) But in Japanese, the first-person pronoun can be many different things, and each of these tells us something about its user.

First of all, how assertive do I want to be? Will *I* sound more or less arrogant, overbearing, submissive? Is the *I* of:

Shall I compare thee to a summer's day?

positioning himself identically to the *I* of Romeo's:

If I profane with my unworthiest hand . . .

or the new king Henry V's:

Presume not that I am the thing I was?

How assertive, on a scale of one to five? As far as the pronouns are concerned, they're all the same in English; the Japanese can – must – convey much more.

Assumptions about gender roles play a part in this self-expression, too. When Matsuoka-san came to translate *Romeo and Juliet*, she knew that she wanted to avoid female-coded first-person pronouns for Juliet, presenting her as a stronger character with more agency – not just weak, humble and put-upon – simply by giving her language that resembles Romeo's, through the assertiveness of her chosen I. Once again, a translator doesn't just have the option of choosing one pronoun or another, they are *required* to – to make choices for Hamlet, to make choices for Juliet. Many women in Shakespeare assert their right to be at the centre of their story – the modes of language they use can be a part of how they do this. Matsuoka-san was notably the first female translator to complete the Shakespeare canon in Japanese.

Japanese has multiple second-person pronouns, too, (of course) – some of these suggesting or assuming intimacy or casual friendship, or being respectful, or rude – though these are used less often nowadays in favour of addressing people by their given names, but here, too, it is possible to add different suffixes (among other features) to indicate, say, whether in that moment one is looking up or down at someone. (Just as I've done, out of respect, with Matsuoka-san.) King Lear might accuse Cordelia of disrespecting him, but in the crucial scene she *always* addresses him in the appropriate, respectful form.

There is so much that all these languages can do that's so supple, and so *useful*. I don't want to be disloyal, but doesn't modern English feel rather inflexible when it comes to dealing with *you* and *I*? Yet we typically only notice the inadequacies when we encounter other ways for language to be.

Chapter 15

እዚሁ ላይ ነው ችግሩ

(on 'To be . . .')

When Edith Grossman embarked upon her magnificent *Don Quixote*, she was careful not to look at any previous translations, to ensure that hers derived with maximum integrity from the source rather than from other people's interpretations of it. But some familiarity would have been inevitable with a text that has – in translation – buried itself so deep into English-language culture.

Pity the poor *Hamlet* translator, then, who wants to produce a text unencumbered by foreknowledge of other attempts. If you were to imagine completing this line – 'To be, or not to be, that is the . . . um, . . .' – in English, you might boldly consider multiple options, but you would struggle to un-know that there's a pre-existing default with a strong gravitational pull. Shakespeare's Hamlet has been speaking for 400 years (doing it in more than one language for about 300), and we can't help knowing what he said.

At least, 'To be, or not to be – that is the question' is straightforward enough. It's simple, unambiguous, unadorned. There are no obscure or complex words, no obvious forks in the road where a choice needs making. At least for a language like Spanish, close enough to English as it is, a like-for-like swap should work uncontroversially.

It's true, Spanish has two common verbs for *to be* – *ser* and *estar* –

but there's little question of which is appropriate here. The former is about essential or long-term being, the latter temporary / circumstantial. I am (*soy*) a writer; I am (*estoy*) in danger of missing this deadline. (How odd that we don't differentiate in English. It's really useful.) If Hamlet's question were 'To be in love, or not to be in love', it would be a different matter. But his question is about being – existing, essentially. So:

Ser or *no ser*. That is the question.

But as of the year 2000, there were already over forty Spanish translations of *Hamlet* published in Spain, and the other day, my friend Aurora posted this little sampling of fifteen lines on Facebook:

- *Existir o no existir, esa es la cuestión.* (Leandro Fernández de Moratín)
- *Ser o no ser, ¡ay! ése es el problema.* (Patricio Canto)
- *Ser o no ser, tal es aquí el enigma.* (Jaime Clark)
- *¡Ser o no ser, la alternativa es esa!* (Guillermo Macpherson)
- *Ser o no ser . . . La alternativa es esa.* (Idea Villariño)
- *¡Ser o no ser: he aquí el problema!* (Luis Astrana Marín)
- *Ser o no ser: he ahí el dilema.* (Juan Carriola Larrain)
- *Ser, o no ser: ésta es la cuestión.* (José María Valverde)
- *Ser o no ser: de eso se trata.* (Tomás Segovia)
- *Ser o no ser, esa es la cuestión.* (Carlos Gamerro)
- *Ser, o no ser: he ahí el problema.* (Rolando Costa Picazo)
- *Ser, o no ser, allí reside la cuestión.* (Pablo Ingberg)
- *¡Ser o no ser, la alternativa es ésa!* (Lluís Pasqual)
- *¡Ser o no ser, la alternativa es ésa!* (María Enriqueta González Padilla)
- *Ser o no ser, esa es la duda.* (Raúl Zurita)

We have here some general consensus about the verb *to be* (though shout-out to a more explicit 'to exist' outlying from Leandro Fernández de Moratín in the late eighteenth century). Then there's either *that is the question*, or *this is the question*, or *I have here the question*. Patricio Canto gives us a somewhat despairing ¡ay! – which gives an actor something to act, and handily plugs a syllabic gap in the verse line.

And to be or not to be is, apparently, the *cuestión*, the *problema*, the *alternativa*, the *dilema*, or the *duda*.* Tomás Segovia does away with a noun entirely – *that*, he says, *is what it's about*. Hamlet is not, after all, *asking a question* exactly – or at least, not the kind to which he expects an answer. Not one of the 'Ser o no ser' bits is presented with question marks.

In many other respects, though, the punctuation does vary. The punctuation is the only thing differentiating MacPherson and Villariño, but that difference is not inconsiderable. Some translators chose to put a comma after that first 'to be', which is potentially instructive for an actor deciding how to measure out his pacing. The two parts of the line are variously separated by a comma, a colon and an ellipsis, making the relationship between the halves quite different. Some have a rather bold exclamation mark, too, and this being Spanish, the terminal mark needs to be matched by an opening one, which, brilliantly, ¡makes it even punchier!

Now, if you're wondering how the source text is punctuated, naturally there isn't a single, simple answer. For one thing, the First Quarto (Q1) says:

To be, or not to be, I there's the point,[†]

Q2 is:

To be, or not to be, that is the question,

And the first Folio is:

To be, or not to be, that is the Question:

---

* Incidentally, a Spanish learner would be taught that the word for 'question' is '*pregunta*', which features nowhere on this list.

[†] The Patricio Canto translation above, produced in the late 1930s, was the first to be done from Q1. This might explain his 'ay!', though it's worth noting that 'ay' in English and '*ay*' in Spanish are quite different beasts.

(Oh, and there's another factor for us to revisit later: yes, these are all translations into Spanish, but the translators are variously Spanish, Argentinian, Anglo-Spanish, Mexican, Chilean, Basque, Catalan and Uruguayan. 'Spanish' is many different things.)

It's useful in this instance to be able to avoid pinning things down too much. It allows for the openness of interpretation that the source text intentionally has. Is Hamlet contemplating the wisdom of killing his uncle? Or of killing himself? Or is he just considering the point of life in general terms? To be, or not to be – that is a usefully vague question. In English.

For the latter part of the line, the Schlegel-Tieck German has '*das ist hier die Frage*'. Péter Vajda did the same thing in Hungarian, because, says Ádám, 'there's an architectural problem, a brick missing from the wall'. So in Vajda's line:

Lenni vagy nem lenni – ez itt a kérdés.

itt means 'here' – which one might dispute, since that isn't necessarily what Hamlet is saying. To Ádám's reading, the question is more general, not just about this moment – or about whether to let his uncle live or die – and so narrowing things to the particular situation is 'a mistake in dramaturgy'. Yet the Hungarian does need a syllable in there somewhere, for the metre, so Ádám added the word *nagy*, which means *big*. It is, after all, not just a question but *the* question.

Lenni vagy nem lenni: ez a nagy kérdés;

It's quite natural, colloquial. I mean, yeah, *that's the big question*, isn't it?

János Arany, another early Hungarian translator, did something different. His version:

A lét, vagy a nem-lét kérdése ez

is nominalised; that is to say, it's built around nouns rather than verbs, a question of *existence or non-existence*. Which is clever and interesting, said Ádám, but unpoetic, 'so much so that in his second edition, he actually put this down in a footnote and borrowed the Vajda translation in his main text' (i.e. Arany capitulated to the force of a pre-existing translation).

To be is such a fundamental verb – often among the first words we learn in a new language, but once you attempt to find a perfect match in another vocabulary, you find it's not always definitionally straightforward. Does it mean the same as *to exist*, and if not, what's the difference? Or maybe it does in this particular context? What else might it mean, otherwise?

But – as we've seen so often before – meaning is often the least of our worries.

One of the more memorable events in the Royal Shakespeare Company's commemorations of the 400th anniversary of Shakespeare's death was a sketch that featured nine rival Hamlets on stage together, each attempting to imbue Shakespeare's most famous line with a different emphasis. To be or not *to* be? *That* is the question. Or That *is* the question? (Hamlets included Judi Dench, David Tennant, Prince Charles, etc.) Silly as that conceit may sound, it inadvertently drew unusual attention to the exact components that make up the line; I mean, how many times have we heard that line, yet how often have we really ever given any thought to that second 'to'? The actors could only do what they did because of the units into which the English happens to divide. The fact, for example, that 'to be' is an infinitive presented in two discrete bits, which some languages happen to allow (e.g. Romanian) and many do not. Some languages indicate infinitives with single words marked, say, by a distinctive ending.* The comedy in the RSC sketch derived partly from the relative plausibility of some

---

* As we know, languages split ideas into multiple words differently (*madrugada*), or join them into composites. We will soon look at a scene from Shakespeare's brilliantly German-titled *Ein Sommernachtstraum*.

readings (To *be*, or *not* to be) over others (To be, or not *to* be), but the natural rhythm of other languages would land on different parts of the line, unless the translator could find an ingenious way of avoiding the change. All this assuming their verb for 'to be' even encompasses the same breadth of meanings as ours (living, general existence), or indeed that they have a verb for 'to be' at all, of course. Or, you know, not.

Chapter 16

(on words and their effects)

Beyond bare meaning, words have many other properties. The words *electricity* and *moon* don't just denote different things, they also sound different and resonate differently and taste different when you speak them. (A long sequence of short tight vowels and sharp consonants vs soft consonants and a long soft *ooooo* . . .) A translator might be lucky, finding that a translation of meaning doesn't entail losing all the rest, but most words for the moon are not much like *moon*. Greek has two different words for that big thing in the night sky – σελήνη (*selíni*) and φεγγάρι (*fengári*) – neither of which is *moon*-like at all.

Here's Hamlet, beginning his instructions to the visiting troupe of players on how to speak their lines:

> Speak the speech, I pray you, as I pronounced it to you –
> trippingly on the tongue . . .

To my ear, *trippingly* is the key word in this sentence. And it gets its effect through sound. It's a light-footed sort of word.

And here we have the line in Portuguese:

(a) *Não esqueças de dizer aquele trecho, tal qual o declamei na tua presença; mais que tudo fogo e energia . . .*

(a translation from Portugal, dated 1877, translator unnamed*)

And this:

(b) *Pronunciae a falla, por graça, como eu vol-a pronunciei, a dançar sobre a lingua . . .*

(early twentieth-century Brazil, tr. Tristão da Cunha)

And this:

(c) *Peço uma coisa, falem essas falas como eu as pronunciei, língua ágil, bem claro . . .*

(late twentieth-century Brazil, tr. Millôr Fernandes)

And this:

(d) *Repeti o trecho, por favor, como eu o pronunciei, com naturalidade . . .*

(late twentieth-century/early twenty-first century Brazil, tr. Barbara Heliodora and Anna Amélia Queiroz Carneiro de Mendonça)

---

* This used to happen often. We try to do better nowadays.

And finally this:

(e) *Por favor, repitam a fala como a pronunciei, com língua bem ágil . . .*

(2015 Brazil, tr. Lawrence Flores Pereira)

The translations above render the *trippingly on the tongue* – in semantic terms – as

- (a) *fire and energy most of all*
- (b) *dancing on your tongue*
- (c) *agile tongue, nice and clear*
- (d) *with naturalness*
- (e) *really agile-tongued*

The meanings are slightly different, but they're all within range, with the possible exception of the first – but even there, while the meaning conveys potency rather than delicacy, the language at least isn't a bad match for it. But in any case, I care rather less about meaning in this case than I do about the translator's ability to make a line *sound* right, to make it dance just as English *trippingly* dances.

We're in prose now, so the translators don't have the constraints that come with verse, but nor do they have the benefit – a verse line helps you (the actor) to find out how to speak it, where the beats are.

Lawrence, who produced that final version, is currently hard at work on a new *Midsummer Night's Dream*. In that play, Oberon leads his fairies into Theseus's royal palace, late at night, with these lines:

> Through the house give glimmering light
> By the dead and drowsy fire.
> Every elf and fairy sprite
> Hop as light as bird from brier,

And this ditty after me
Sing and dance it trippingly.

It's Shakespeare's only other *trippingly*.

Sometimes a translator will want to privilege consistency within translations – if a word is translated as *x* in one instance, then I'll try to make it the same word throughout. The repetition of a word, patterned through a text, might be significant. But in this case, there's no reason for our Brazilian Oberon to be echoing our Brazilian Hamlet. Lawrence's priorities for this second 'trippingly' are quite different. Yes, we need lightness – this is about fairies dancing, after all – but other things, too. Not least, in this instance it's got something to rhyme with. This is what Lawrence produced:

E me seguindo neste canto
Entoem, dancem saltitando.

Saltitando is a very trippingly sort of word, too.

A note: these lines might not be the final version, as Lawrence is still wrangling this play. In Brazil, this *Sonho de uma noite de verão* is still quite plastic, still a work in progress.

So, 'trippingly' has a lightness when Hamlet uses it, which allows the actor to speak it as lightly as he's asking the Players to speak. The actor playing Hamlet experiences the effect of these tripping words, and the audience experiences it through them. Shakespeare might write words that trip across the *page*, but that's not their principle function.

Word sounds give actors ammunition just as their meanings do. Remember that speech that Mark Antony gave when standing over the emperor's dead body, referring to Caesar's killers:

O, pardon me, thou bleeding piece of earth,
That I am meek and gentle with these butchers.

That word 'butchers' is harsh, spittable. In a way that, say, 'That I am gentle with thy <u>enemies</u>' would not be. Insults need to *sound* like insults. Think back to that highly effective *Tempest* swearing from Chico in Chapter 8:

> *Morre enforcado, vira-lata! Vai te enforcar, filho duma prostituta, insolente boca-suja.*

So many fantastically spittable consonant sounds there.

Or the moment in *The Winter's Tale* when Leontes's language intensifies, phrases get shorter, words contract – *inch-thick, knee-deep* . . . – as we watch his sanity unravelling before our eyes . . .

Or how about that 'common cry of curs' we've also seen before, so very harsh with those alliterating c- sounds? This is what Jean-Michel made of it:

> *Abjecte meute de roquets, dont j'exècre l'haleine*
> *Comme les effleuves des marais croupis dont j'estime l'amour*
> *Comme les carcasses des morts sans sépulture,*
> *Qui infectent mon air . . .*

That opening phrase is unpleasant-sounding, with strained vowels and guttural consonants, but lots of harsh sounds continuing throughout, too (*exècre, croupis, carcasses, infectent*). It's not pretty, nor should it be.

Y. Goldberg's Yiddish translation of *Hamlet* does not manage to do the *trippingly* in any way trippingly, alas. But I feel he makes up for it soon enough. In the very next sentence, where Hamlet says:

> Nor do not saw the air too much with your hand, thus, but use all gently; <u>for in the very torrent, tempest</u> and, as I may say, whirlwind of your passion, you must acquire and beget a temperance . . .

the phrase underlined is:

אפילע אין דעם סאמע שטראָם, שטורעם

(*afile in dem same <u>shtrom, shturem</u>*)

beautifully enhancing the effect with the same slight sonic repetition. In *Othello*, these lines:

> Yet I'll not shed her blood
> Nor scar that whiter skin of hers than snow
> And smooth as monumental alabaster.

give us that monumental word *alabaster*, paralleled with the pure white simplicity of *snow*. It forces a change to the speed of the line. Smoooooth as monumental alabaster! (The lucky actor playing Othello gets to use the delicious word *mandragora* at one point, too.) In French, that pair of words finds a comparably nice match – the simple *neige*, the grand *albâtre* with a big open A in the middle.*

An actor playing Iago, meanwhile, gets to speak this sequence of words:

> The food that to him now is as luscious as locusts shall be to him shortly as acerb as coloquintida.

Jean-Michel has him say:

> *L'aliment qui lui est aujourd'hui aussi savoureux que le fruit du caroubier lui paraîtra bientôt aussi amer que la coloquinte.*

---

* *Albâtre* is one of those easy-to-guess French words where the circumflex accent marks the place where French once had an 's', and where its English relative still does. Thus: *bête*/beast, *prêtre*/priest, *plâtre*/plaster, *maître*/master, *guêpe*/wasp, *abîme*/abyss, *côte*/coast, and so on.

Despite the fact that a French audience would have no better idea of what that last word means than an English audience would know *coloquintida*, keeping the exotic flavour of the word mattered more. You can tell from the context that it's a *bitter* thing of some kind; the greater detail of the meaning an audience can live without. What matters to Jean-Michel here is that it's the right *sort* of word.

We looked earlier at how the word *love* can cause semantic problems, with meanings that don't perfectly match across languages. But it, too, has its own set of sonic and associative characteristics (we've already referenced old *prove* rhymes and new *above/dove* ones), just as any word will in any language. And it turns out, love is also a tricky matter for the Danes; Niels had a choice between two *love* words that are the same in meaning but in no other respect:

- *Kærlighed* – rather unwieldy, three syllables, not very beautiful
- *Elskov* – a nicer sound, but now very old-fashioned

Elskov used to be the common word, and is the one mostly used by Niels's predecessor Edvard Lembcke, who finished his complete Shakespeare in the 1870s. But Niels avoided the archaism, and mostly uses *kærlighed*, today's more-common-but-less-lovely word. And no, it's not beautiful, but it does rhyme with *ærlighed*, which means honesty, offering a nice opportunity for a translator to enjoy whenever that presents itself.

In our conversation, Jean-Michel refers to 'Shakespeare's theatrical score', and he isn't the only translator to express his aims in these musical terms. Shakespeare chooses words that allow an actor to speak them with particular effect; they are extraordinarily *kinetic*. The linguistic effects of his writing are dense – *density* being another word that many of our translators use. But the writing is dense, not in terms of impenetrability of meaning, but how much effect is packed into every burst of speech. The old French translations by François-Victor Hugo (like the Baldini prose ones we've seen already) can be useful for a student, but they do tend to sprawl. They are not texts for an actor. A new text that preserves meaning but loses that kinetic energy, or which unnecessarily sacrifices the effective density of the writing, might be a reasonable explication of what Shakespeare *means*, but language is multifaceted, and Shakespeare is not only meaning, so translation must always be more, too. This is language that doesn't feel like it's being heightened artificially, but has organic richness and inherent dynamism. And – I repeat myself, I know – *so then must the translation.*

Chapter 17

нуждата превръща всичко . . .

(on gender and other opportunities)

Languages aren't just collections of discrete words, of course – they're hugely complex, often highly eccentric operational systems. For those of us who translate into English from Romance languages – as with many others languages – one of the places where our textual transfers generate the most friction is in the matter of gender: all nouns in my source languages are gendered, and adjectives indicate the gender of the nouns they agree with. Other languages employ other markers – none of which are found in English. English allows non-specificity even for people: you can talk about a servant, a teacher, a friend, without the noun revealing too much. But as with those varying formal/intimate 'you' forms we've already seen, those other languages don't just allow a user to gender nouns, they compel them to.

At a recent production of *All's Well That Ends Well*, I watched the Countess enter the stage alone reading (aloud) a letter she has just received. It begins thus:

> I am Saint Jacques' pilgrim, thither gone.
> Ambitious love hath so in me offended
> That barefoot plod I the cold ground upon,
> With sainted vow my faults to have amended.

The Countess has two plausible correspondents – her son, Bertram, and Helena, the woman who's in love with him. At this point in the letter you're hearing, you cannot be 100 per cent sure which of them it's from. In the unabridged version of the scene, Shakespeare doesn't allow for this doubt, prefacing the letter with some words to a Steward:

> Alas! And would you take the letter of <u>her</u>?
> Might you not know <u>she</u> would do as <u>she</u> has done
> By sending me a letter?

Removing this bit of context for this production means we experience the start of the letter with a few lines' uncertainty.

Not so in Romanian. In Ion Frunzetti's translation, the letter begins thus:

> <u>Primită</u> de Sînt-Iacov pelerin,
> <u>Desculță</u> mă tîrăsc pe țărna rece,
> Prin pocăință grea să-mi poată trece
> Iubirea ce m-a sîngerat din plin.

I've underlined a couple of words that tell you the gender of the letter writer. The very first word does it: 'received' (f.), as does the first of line two 'barefoot' (f.).

(Oh, I underlined all the words in the English letter on the last page that revealed the gender, too, not that it makes any difference.)

English is a less gendered language than many. We use gender for pronouns when referring to people, and sometimes to other animate beings, but most common nouns aren't inherently gendered, and we don't mark any other parts of speech. In German, every noun has one of three genders (as Old English did a thousand years ago, incidentally); in my three Romance languages, nouns are allocated to one of two and every adjective adjusts to match. In the Arabic examples we looked at in Chapter 12, we saw those verbs of love bearing prefixes and suffixes that identify the gender of that verb's subject and object. Russian verbs, meanwhile, reveal the gender of their subject, though only in the past tense. (He played – он играл; she played – она играла.)

Translate *I'm tired* into Spanish, and you have a choice – is this a person who would identify as male, saying *Estoy cansado*? Do they identify as female, in which case, *Estoy cansada*? In English, so long as you avoid third-person singular pronouns, it's easy enough not to specify.

> When I stepped outside, I found my neighbour clearing the thick snow from the driveway.
> 'Morning!' I said, and got a cheerful wave in reply. 'Out early today!'
> 'Yeah, got to run the kids to the new school – apparently their teacher's giving them a hard time about being late this week.'

At this point, you Anglophones don't know the gender of the speaker, or of the neighbour, or of the children or of the teacher. In Spanish, you'd know the gender of the neighbour, the teacher and at least one of the children; in Russian, the verbs tell you the speaker's gender, too.

Additionally, in Spanish, the snow will be feminine, the school either masculine or feminine depending on what type of school, the week feminine; and so the adjective *thick* would be feminine to agree with *snow*, *new* masculine or feminine to agree with *school*. There is no predictable or deducible logic to any of this. In Russian, the snow will be masculine, the school and week both feminine.

As a reader, I often find myself ten pages into a first-person story and wondering if the translator has noticed they haven't yet told me the gender of the narrator, which I know would have had to be unambiguous in the source from line one. Many languages include this information, very simply, in their adjectives. The word 'barren' appears three times in *Twelfth Night*, twice to refer to a male character, once to a female. Adjectives match the gender of their nouns in Greek, so the word shifts – άγονος (ágonos) in the masculine, άγονη (ágoni) in the feminine.

Because each language encodes information differently, a translator might also find themselves being *more* helpful than they perhaps intended – as in that Romanian letter. Since gender can require that words adjust to match each other – *thick* with *snow*, *new* with *school* – this can help to articulate bits of sentences that might otherwise be complex and hard to follow. At the very start of *All's Well*, we meet Lafew, a lord, who is in conversation with the newly widowed countess and her son. Lafew's first speech (within the play's first minute) goes as follows:

> You shall find of the King a husband, madam; you, sir, a father. He that so generally is at all times good must of necessity hold his virtue to you, whose worthiness would stir it up where it wanted rather than lack it where there is such abundance.

Did you understand that second sentence?

Now, I believe – but only because I read it twice – the 'whose' refers to his interlocutor/s, the 'it' refers to the king's virtue. The meaning, then, is as follows: The king is very good ('He that so generally is at all times good' is not an elegant phrase), so he will maintain his kindness towards you – you who are so worthy that you'd prompt it even where it was in short supply, and certainly not lack it from someone as abundantly good as him. (Or more simply still: He's very good and also you're very worthy; these things combined mean he will most *definitely* favour you.)

It's not an easy sentence to *say* – for one thing, unless you stress 'his virtue to *you*', the 'whose' becomes difficult – but it is possible, I think, for an actor to make sense of it when speaking (once they've figured out what it means themselves). Keeping in mind with total clarity that the king's virtue is the repeated 'it' helps a great deal. (Not that there are other obvious nouns it could be referring to, but so much of the unhelpful phrasing – 'hold his virtue to you' – makes it hard to keep one's bearings.)

Here it is now in François Guizot's French (based on an earlier translation by Pierre Le Tourneur):

Un roi, qui dans tous les temps est si universellement bon, doit nécessairement conserver sa <u>bienveillance</u> pour vous, dont le mérite <u>la</u> ferait naître là où <u>elle</u> manquerait bien loin de ne <u>la</u> pas trouver là où <u>elle</u> abonde.

The word *bienveillance* is a feminine noun meaning kindness/benevolence. The two uses of *la* and the two uses of *elle* that follow all stand in for English's slightly-hard-to-place 'it', except that here, these 'it' words are coded as feminine, and so can *only* correspond to the sole feminine noun in the sentence. A French ear will naturally hook these things together – the *bienveillance* is the *it* we're talking about, unquestionably.

Once again, there are potential benefits both ways – Shakespeare can choose to personify a non-person noun, and *choose* to assign a gender. The 'Shall I compare thee . . .' sonnet includes the line 'Nor shall death brag thou wander'st in his shade', and the sun has 'his gold complexion dimmed' – *his*, note. In Chapter 10, when we heard that 'sun' from Prince Hal, which was supposed to put us in mind of the word 'son', Shakespeare could attach the sun to a 'his' (*smother up <u>his</u> beauty*). Meanwhile in the opening to Chapter 2 we saw the moon presented as a 'she', *her* beauty being compared unfavourably to Juliet's. It's a sort of literary convention: suns and moons in English poetic language have come to be gendered as respectively male and female. (In this, we take after our Romance-language cousins, and unlike our Germanic side.)

Gender may be a complex issue in terms of personal identity, of how categories are divided and assigned, what is deemed to be the default and the political questions around all of these. But from a linguistic perspective, it's a simple example of the way some languages have in-built structural features determining what they will allow, and require, a user to express, and what can or cannot be kept concealed. With a highly grammatically gendered language, it might sometimes be hard to do deliberate ambiguity – not giving too much away with your 'poor fool', say), but we know that linguistic constraints offer opportunities too. (Remember what a Japanese translator could convey about Juliet by a simple pronoun swap . . .)

And we're not just talking about nouns referring to people (those characters in comedies in a cross-gender disguise) but everything. In a play like *The Taming of the Shrew*, which stages a power struggle between male and female, every noun, every object, is not an *it* but a *he* or a *she*.* And spare a final thought for compulsorily gendered-language translators trying not to give too much away when Orlando falls in love with a male actor dressed as Rosalind disguised as Ganymede pretending to be Rosalind, in the play that – as if it wasn't complicated enough – the French have little choice but to call: *As You Like Him*.

---

* The gender struggles in *The Taming of the Shrew* seem to have met with slightly too much approval by one misguided Hindi translator, whose translator's note – it's Rangeya Raghav again – refers thus to Katherine's capitulation speech at the end: 'When the Shrew speaks at the end of the play about relations between the man and woman, it's as if Shakespeare himself is speaking. And this outlook of Shakespeare's is similar to the Hindu perspective. He gives a lot of weight to being a faithful, devoted wife – things that modern women won't pay any heed to'.

Chapter 18

不用多说了

(on economy)

In Julian Clary's recent cosy-crime novel *Curtain Call to Murder*, a *Metro* journalist is interviewing a comedian, Simon Gaunt, about whether he plans to do any more theatre acting:

M: What about Shakespeare?
S: Nah, too many long words, innit?

This chapter is all about why a minor fictional character in a very amusing Julian Clary novel is wrong about Shakespeare.

So moving from that to the sublime, we start with *King Lear*.

When Lear appears at the end of his play, howling with grief, carrying the body of his dead daughter Cordelia, these are the words he enters with:

Howl, howl, howl, howl! O, you are men of stones!
Had I your tongues and eyes, I'd use them so
That heaven's vault should crack: she's gone for ever.
I know when one is dead and when one lives;
She's dead as earth.

Minutes later, he speaks for the last time, and he dies – mid-line – unable to comprehend his loss, or to believe that his beloved child is dead:

> And my poor fool is hanged. No, no, no life!
> Why should a dog, a horse, a rat, have life
> And thou no breath at all? O thou'lt come no more,
> Never, never, never, never, never!
> Pray you undo this button. Thank you, sir.
> Do you see this? Look on her: look, her lips,
> Look there, look there!

Such a painful thing to watch. But this chapter is not about Lear's experience or about human suffering; it's about syllables.

Have a look at those two pieces again – a dozen lines in total, 110 syllables, and the only words longer than one syllable are 'heaven', 'ever', 'never' (repeated), 'undo' and 'button'. It is absolutely stark. The absolute height of drama is conveyed almost entirely in monosyllables. The question could not be simpler: 'Why should a dog, a horse, a rat, have life, / And thou no breath at all?'*

This is not lush, heightened, show-offy, 'poetic' language.

Simply: where is Cordelia?

She's dead as earth.

Shakespeare can do wondrous things with a monosyllable, and English allows him to. The possibility is a factor of the language – often drawing on its hoard of old Anglo-Saxon vocabulary. It's one of the things that enables the compactness of his writing, when you can fit all this information into just ten syllables:

> Love looks not with the eyes, but with the mind . . .

Romeo dies addressing the apothecary who sold him poison:

---

* Also: *To be or not to be?* That is the other question. Massively consequential, but all in the simplest monosyllables.

> Thy drugs are quick. Thus with a kiss I die.

That's ten syllables. Juliet dies addressing the knife in her hand:

> This is thy sheath; there rust, and let me die.

Ten again. Lady Macbeth challenges her husband, and does it in four:

> Are you a man?

Here, then, are some useful English nouns for you:

man	life
child	light
love	word
world	death
home	god

Such small words for such big things!* That list is ten monosyllables. You could, should you so choose, pack all those vast things into a single line of iambic pentameter.

Some more uncommonly useful English nouns: girl, boy, day, night, dog, horse, book, house, earth, space, sea, sky. Monosyllables all! As are head and heart, life and death, you and me, eyes, ears, mouth and nose, fire, ice, time, peace, dark, etc.† Well over twenty of those I've listed are also monosyllables in German or Danish. Only two – light and earth – are monosyllables in Greek.

To get an idea of the problem some translators might face, I acquired *My First Hundred Words* books in eight languages. Each of them presents children – or other introductory language-learners – with largely the

---

* Such/small/words/for/such/big/things.
† Many of our most used verbs are, too, incidentally: walk, run, like, talk, have, be, go, see, say, stay, eat, pray, love . . .

same set of very common, basic, kid-friendly words. They're mostly nouns (apple, elbow, horse, train) plus a few colours and numbers.

The Greek and Italian vocabulary books had one paltry monosyllable apiece among their hundred basic words. The Italian being the word *tre* (for the number three), and the Greek being the delightfully silly loan-word κέικ (whose meaning you'll discover if you attempt a phonetic pronunciation in a silly accent). Then come Russian and Polish, each of which have thirteen monosyllables among their introductory hundred.

The hundred words in the Chinese set include twenty-five that comprise a single character, equivalent to a single syllable when spoken. French and German are higher still, with, respectively, forty-six and forty-seven monosyllables out of a hundred. Making them quite compact as languages go.

And English? Seventy-five of those hundred foundational words are monosyllabic. (All the rest are two syllables, except for *banana* and *bicycle*.) And just to repeat for emphasis, to these seventy-five English basic monosyllables, Greek has one.

I have not yet seen *Hamlet* in Greek but the idea worries me.*

(An English speaker might assume that some basic things obviously demand short words – I'm thinking about, say, our basic pronouns, which are unsurprisingly, monosyllabic – I, me, my, you, your, she, her, he, it, they, them, etc. But even these aren't inevitable – apart from the possessives, not one of those is a monosyllable in Greek.)

I might have been critical of Gabriele Baldini's work earlier, but it's true that there are linguistic realities that force an expansion, which aren't just a factor of an individual translator's prolixity. In the opening of *Twelfth Night*, Orsino – listening to his music aka the food of love – says:

---

* Even my first-*thousand*-Italian-words book only has seven monosyllables – or eight, depending how we identify them – and many are loan-words from other languages. (If my editor was wondering why I delivered this manuscript so late, one of the reasons was that I was doing stuff like counting these.)

That strain again . . .

In Baldini, this becomes:

Ancora una volta quella stessa melodia!

I do feel sorry for him, truly.

Now, studies have shown that different languages are typically spoken at different syllabic paces – Italian might have far more syllables to get through, but they manage to speak more of them per minute than English speakers. According to the 2019 Coupé study, in very general terms, languages that are less efficient in terms of amount of information conveyed per syllable make up for it by speaking more syllables per minute. But the difference in pacing still is not such that one could stage a Baldini translation without several intervals and a pretty big chunk of a day.

A rose by any other name might smell as sweet, though it might take rather longer to say. The Greek word is lovely – τριαντάφυλλο. It's pronounced *triandáphilo* (the stress is on that second accented á – it's definitely a word for speaking trippingly), and it's made up of *trianda* (thirty) and *phylo* (leaf). I think *rose* is a lovely word, too. But they do quite different things.

Τριαντάφυλλο – that's all well and good. The problem comes when you want to squeeze it into one syllable.

> Of all flowers
> Methinks a rose is best . . .

says Emilia in *The Two Noble Kinsmen*. Or Berowne in *Love's Labour's Lost*:

> At Christmas I no more desire a rose
> Than wish a snow in May's newfangled shows;
> But like of each thing that in season grows.

Quite apart from the rhyme problem (*rose*, *shows* and *grows* is neat), *rose* is such a short word! Our beautiful Τρι-αν-τά-φυ-λλο not so much.

Greek, as it happens, does have a more literary/poetic, high-register word for rose: ρόδο (rodo) – which is short and simple. Go figure.

English can be very compressed, then. As Alexander pointed out, even *Heav'n* is sometimes a monosyllable when Shakespeare uses it, and *ev'l*, too – which even the most mild-mannered of Bulgarian translators might think is frankly a bit much. Shakespeare has options for voicing the endings of past-tense verbs, or not bothering. Depending on the shape of your iambic lines and the available space,

> these endings can be voicèd or unvoiced.

And we've already seen some slippery elisions, like *reek o'th' rotten fen*, and *you kiss by th' book* and *put 'em i'th' paste* and *heat o'th' sun*. And what would Laertes be prepared to do to Hamlet to avenge his sister's death?

> To cut his throat i'th' church.

As a translator, you'll despair for a moment, then get to work. Do what you can.

Consider that *Richard III* opening with the strong, arresting, monosyllabic *Now!* – for which the French *maintenant* won't do at all. But Jean-Michel reached back to an older literary French, where he found 'Ores', an alternative word for *now* (today mostly obsolete, though still found in the occasional set phrase – *d'ores et déjà*). Jean-Michel's translations are not pointedly archaic, like the Tristão da Cunha we saw in Chapter 6, but the older language is a useful resource to plunder when the more contemporary word hoard doesn't give you what you need. (In this case, basically a word that means 'now' but does it quickly.)

> <u>Ores</u> voici l'hiver de notre déplaisir
> Changé en glorieux été par ce soleil de York . . .

Richard should not start slow, low-energy. And besides, *now* deserves to be noticed; it's such a good word for theatre, too – the artform of in-the-room, present-tense experience. Maybe a translator cannot always retain a monosyllable, as Jean-Michel does here, but you find a way to preserve a line that leads with a stress, that propels.

Often, target languages that are less favoured with monosyllables than English will force expansions, at least in syllable count if not in word count. But they will allow economies of other kinds. Certainly Richard's 'A horse, a horse, my kingdom for a horse!' will cause trouble. Shakespeare does the whole big thing in ten syllables; if your word for *horse* alone is three syllables or more – yes, I'm looking at you, Finnish – then you'll struggle to get much change out of a ten-syllable line if you want to name the animal three times. But other characteristics of a language might help. Finnish, like Russian, has no articles, so immediately every line slims down (*Horse! Horse! My kingdom for horse!*).

English has its superfluities, too. It does insist on using pronouns that aren't needed in many languages whose verbs adapt to tell you automatically who's doing the verbing. (Spanish, say. I go: *Voy*. You go: *Vas*. They go: *Van*.) And while I feel the nature of English generally means that our writers can cram a lot in, Ádám Nádasdy sees it differently. He made the decision, simply, that Shakespeare was the one with the unfortunate problem, that his need to fill every line – despite having such small chunks of language to do it with – means his redundancies are frequent. ('You call it compact – I call it prolix . . .') Where Shakespeare has 'attend and mark!', the Hungarian Puck uses just the one verb. Do we really need to describe someone as 'fair *and* beauteous'? What, both? The occasional 'In sooth' and 'My lord' can go, too.

When Lear says:

> . . . your disordered rabble
> Make servants of their betters . . .

Ádám dispatches this briskly: '*disordered* is omitted, but the meaning remains the same.' Unless there's a reason for superfluity, the superfluity can be pared away – because, unlike Shakespeare's English, Hungarian doesn't need the padding.

When Cordelia says 'Nothing, my lord', Sho also takes the opportunity to cut the 'my lord' from his Japanese translation, but the Japanese *nothing* that he uses:

ございません
[*gozai-masen*]

is already conveying Cordelia's respect through the manner of language she's employing, so there's nothing to be lost by removing those extraneous words to free up space for something else.

Economy and simplicity just look different in different languages.

Swahili, Georgian and Turkish are agglutinative languages, which means they combine roots with prefixes and suffixes into single words that can be cumulatively quite succinct. JC offers the example of Macbeth's 'I have done the deed'. What was a sentence in English, becomes a word in Swahili, with one pentasyllabic word standing in for five monosyllables: *Nimelifanya*, where 'fanya' is the basic verb for doing, and all the rest specifies:

- Ni- (subject prefix for 'I')
- -me- (present perfect tense marker, 'have')
- li (object marker for 'it'/'the deed')
- -fanya (root verb 'do')

In an agglutinative language, then, it's possible to have a word that's five or six syllables long, but where each syllable is adding something functional – a possessive (where Anglophones need possessive pronouns), noun cases (where we need prepositions), a verb aspect (pending, completed, etc.), and so on. In Chapter 8, we saw *Lear*'s Fool dramatically increasing his character count in Turkish in this way. Here's a couple of lines from Portia in *The Merchant of Venice*, about the ring she gave Bassanio as a pledge of their love, in the English and the Turkish:

I gave my love a ring and made him swear	*Ben de bir yüzük verdim aşkıma ve yemin ettirdim*
Never to part with it, and here he stands.	*Çıkarmayacağına, işte kendisi de burada.*

Çıkarmayacağına is not a short word. Even if you're not a Turkish speaker, I don't need to tell you that it is unlikely to be a monosyllable. But as words go, it's actually an extremely efficient one. It stands in for 'that he might never take it off',* or thereabouts.

A word might be six syllables long, but you might only need a couple such words to convey what English does in a whole line of fiddly monosyllables. Simplicity, as I say, looks different in Turkish.

Danish is one of those languages with the possibility of composites; true composite words are much rarer in English, but they're a good way of telescoping meanings into tighter space. When Lady Anne curses Gloucester (the soon-to-be Richard III) – 'Blush, blush, thou *lump of foul deformity*' (she's so great) – Niels found a way of condensing this long multisyllablic phrase. Here's his line:

Rødm, din krøbbelkrump . . .

where the word *krøbbelkrump* mashes together *krøbbel* (old word equivalent to the English *cripple*) and a back-formation from the adjective *krumpen* (crooked, stooped) – which is an obsolete form of *krympet* (shrunk). Says Niels, 'Turning an adjective into a noun (or vice versa, for that matter) is something that Shakespeare does frequently, so why shouldn't a Shakespeare translator follow in his footsteps?'

Krøbbelkrump is a fierce word to speak. 'The Danish *r* in this position

---

* = Verb for take off (*Çıkarmak*) + not + future (and all used as a verbal noun) + his + to. With the hard k before the suffix mutating into a soft g for flow.

is an uvular fricative, a throaty sound like in German, so you can't say this word without a kind of growl and a lot of disdainful consonants'. The actor playing Anne would later be asked on a radio programme to choose a word that meant a lot to her, and she chose *krøbbelkrump*. It's a potent word that did not exist till Niels assembled it; it does now.

Ádám leans into Hungarian's relatively longer words, too, exploiting that asset. When Petruchio in *The Taming of the Shrew* says:

> But for my bonny Kate, she must with me.
> Nay, look not big, nor stamp, nor stare, nor fret,
> I will be master of what is mine own.

that middle line – ten monosyllables – becomes this

> *ne bámuljanak, ne dühöngjenek*

Only four words, of which two 'are monstrous verbs of four syllables each ("stare" and "rage"), with a nice contrast in vowel harmony: á-u-a-a vs ü-ö-e-e.'

Well, said Ádám, 'Shakespeare uses his language like a machine gun, I use mine like a cannon. What can I do? I have a different gun!'

English has words that are there for structural reasons; you don't even separately register them, and those little words of English sentence architecture are mostly monosyllables (will, to, etc.). 'It's like one of those Renaissance marble statues,' says Ádám. You don't immediately notice that 'the guy is leaning on a trunk or something, because otherwise the statue would topple.'

We've seen other things that are good for compression already, like those old Māori exclamations that squeeze great feeling into a two-letter exclamation. Alexander, meanwhile, had ideas about how to exploit the workings of Bulgarian to replicate some sort of spatial economy. Occasional Bulgarian words, including some pronouns, can be rendered in a sort of naturally degraded form as they're actually heard in everyday speech – even if, as he explains, these shortened forms 'are usually shunned in metrical compositions'. (Just as we English speakers can get away with barely pronouncing some unstressed syllables in our language – an unstressed 'the' is sometimes allowed only fractions of a second.)

When Edgar, in *King Lear*, adopts his sort of West Country disguise, he speaks like this:

keep out, che vor ye, or I'se try whether <u>your</u> costard or <u>my</u> ballow [baton] be the harder.

Don't worry if you can't follow the meaning – we'll come back to it. But do just notice that *your* and *my* that I've highlighted. Now here is Alexander's translation:

Стой надалеч, думам ти, че да не опиташ кое е по-яко –
<u>твойта</u> кратуна или <u>мойта</u> тояга.

Those two highlighted words, *твойта* and *мойта* (tvoyta / moyta), are being used instead of the proper/correct *твоята* and *моята*, which have an extra vowel sound in the middle (tvo<u>ya</u>ta / mo<u>ya</u>ta).*

Or where Edgar, again, says:

Fathom and half, fathom and half: Poor Tom!

Alexander gives him:

Бой и <u>полвина</u>, бой и <u>полвина</u>!
О, бедни Том!

With a naturally compressed *полвина* (polvina) instead of *пол<u>о</u>вина*

---

* Though note of course that this speech is in prose, so in this case, *твойта* and *мойта* aren't being used to meet specific metrical constraints.

(polovina) – the latter is the one in my dictionary – he's using what is informally spoken rather than what is formally written, and saving himself a syllable in the process.

Additionally, Bulgarian – like other Slavic languages – makes clever use of prefixes to shift meanings of root words. What in English might require a phrase modifying a verb can be rendered with a prefix. Taking the variations on the basic verb чета – *read* – as an example, says Alexander:

> To translate '*Той <u>за</u>чете книгата*' into English, for instance, you'd have to say: 'He <u>started reading</u> the book'. '*Той <u>из</u>чете книгата*' should be translated as 'He <u>finished reading</u> the book'. '*Той <u>се за</u>чете <u>в</u> книгата*' – 'He <u>was absorbed in reading</u> the book', etc.

Prefixes can steer a verb meaning towards beginning, ending, undoing, overdoing, direction, combination, etc. They're supple in expression, but also rather good for saving space.

Here's another bit of Edgar – still on the run, but back in his own voice now:

> I heard myself proclaimed,
> And by the happy hollow of a tree
> Escaped the hunt. No port is free, no place
> That guard and most unusual vigilance
> Does not attend my taking. Whiles I may scape
> I will preserve myself, and am bethought
> To take the basest and most poorest shape
> That ever penury in contempt of man
> Brought near to beast . . .

Now in Alexander's Bulgarian:

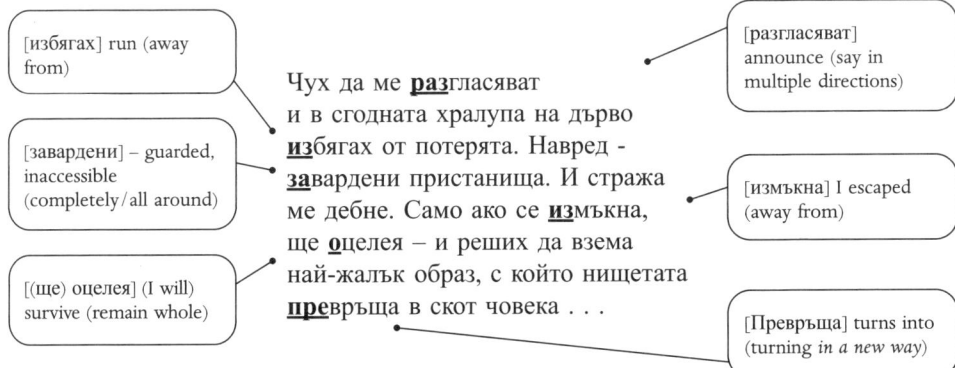

Remarkably, the Bulgarian has actually come out slightly more compact than the Shakespeare. (Even though Shakespeare is doing sneaky things like *'scape* . . .) And each of the elements in bold is a prefix that adjusts the verb to which it's attached. (On verbs, a prefix typically suggests a finished/completed action, too, rather than something still in a state of happening.)

Of course, our compact English words can have prefixes in their etymologies, too; the Latinate words in the same speech include *proclaimed, escape, attend, preserve, contempt* . . .

And prefixes can – again as in English – be used in combination. Here's Hamlet, persuading his mother (in Bulgarian) that he is not mad:

Но моят пулс не е по-учестен
от вашия и произвежда също
тъй свястна музика. Което казах
не е безумство. Всичко туй аз мога
да преизкажа пак, а лудостта
би заподскачала встрани. О, майко,
не се церете с благия мехлем
на утешителното обяснение,
че не простъпката ви тъй говори,
а лудостта ми. Язвата ви той
ще позамаже, докато отвътре
заразното гноило ще разяжда
плътта незримо.

Exactly the same number of words here as in the source, albeit on average the words are longer. But the efficiencies come in places like those words marked, each of which is constructed using two or even three *consecutive* prefixes from the list below:

- про – the result of the action + continuously performing an action until achieving a result;
- из – result of the action + action beyond a threshold + sudden action + from
- пре – repeating an action
- за – starting an action + short action + action beyond a threshold
- под – starting an action, a downward action or an action over an object
- с – starting an action, the result of the action
- по – low-intensity action

So, for instance, the last underlined word corresponds to the line where Shakespeare has the verb pair 'skin and film' (*It will but skin and film the ulcerous place.*)

Alexander's verb combination is made up of по + за + маже, where мажа is the infinitive of the root meaning 'to cover the surface of an object or part of it with a substance usually in liquid or semi-liquid state'. Hence if we want a verb meaning 'to lightly cover something with a substance usually in liquid or semi-liquid state without putting in too much effort, also figuratively to lightly conceal something', specifically in the third person singular.

позамаже

Pretty efficient. As so often, what we're talking about is not how a translator replicates what a writer does, but how they recreate the *effect* that they have sought to create.

Because Turkish tends towards longer words than English, Emine didn't have the option of making her King Lear die so monosyllabically.

So instead she made that last speech of his operate with a variety of word lengths (the longest being *gelmeyeceksin*, standing in for *you will not come*) – but then the Turkish breaks into a hard drumbeat of monosyllables for the *Never, never, never, never, never* line, just as Shakespeare is breaking away from them.

> *Benim garip soytarımı astılar. Yok, yok, hayat yok!**
> *Köpeğin, atın, farenin bile hayatı var da,*
> *Sende niye hiç nefes yok, ha?*
> *Ah, bir daha hiç gelmeyeceksin, yok!* <u>Hiç</u>, <u>hiç</u>, <u>hiç</u>, <u>hiç</u>, <u>hiç</u>.

Hiç is a strong, heavy word. Shakespeare's shift from monosyllables to the disyllabic *nevers* isn't the same as Emine's shift in the other direction, but the latter still makes for a strikingly different line.

Hiç does not simply mean 'never'. It means 'nothing'. But Emine set up the previous line in such a way that it could now open into a repeated 'nothing' in order to create this effect. And besides, 'nothing' is an important word in the play, as in several other Shakespeare plays. In the Turkish *Lear* – because this doesn't happen in the English – Emine's fivefold *hiç* will send audiences all the way back to the play's first scene, where a 'nothing' triggers the whole tragic plot. Because when Cordelia's father asks her to express her love for him, all she has to say for herself – to her father's disbelief – is simply 'Nothing, my lord.'

CORDELIA
   <u>Hiç</u>bir şey, efendimiz.
LEAR
   <u>Hiç</u>bir şey mi?
CORDELIA
   <u>Hiç</u>bir şey.

---

* *Yok* is *no* (or *not*, or *there isn't*, etc.).

As it happened, when Emine and I met, sitting outside a theatre in Istanbul one evening, increasingly struggling to make out the texts we were looking at as night drew in around us, she had another *nothing* on her mind. She had just finished writing her translation of *Macbeth* (she seemed surprisingly cheerful and well rested for somebody who had just finished writing a *Macbeth*) and I was due to watch her text – fresh and still warm – being performed that night. We talked, among other things, about the 'Tomorrow, and tomorrow, and tomorrow . . .' speech. Which requires that a translator figure out how to leave her audience with the full impact of another great Shakespearean *nothing*. In this case – and it's a bleak one – life being, after all, just a tale told by an idiot, full of sound and fury . . .

Signifying *nothing*.

If possible, an ending with that same powerful monosyllabic Turkish *hiç* would be the ideal concluding *nothing* here. *Nothing* is a tricky word in Shakespeare, incidentally, being homophonous with *noting* and also a sexual euphemism (so *Much Ado about Nothing* is a punnier title than you might have noticed) – but still, I'm constantly surprised which bits will cause translators trouble . . .

Chapter 19

Und sein so schlichter Schein herbergt Verrat

(on deceptive simplicity)

During the banquet scene in *Macbeth*, Lady M takes her skittish husband aside and challenges him with the words: 'Are you a man?'

For most of us (except that one director we met in a footnote in Chapter 10), it's not hard to see all the ways in which, say, complex wordplay would be hard to translate. Fine – but how about 'Are you a man?' Easy enough, surely? But no, great simplicity – annoyingly – can be curiously difficult, too. Don't forget, we've already seen what trouble-makers *you* and *I* can be.

When I set out translating a book, I always think I'll know where the snags will be. I am usually wrong. At least the Shakespeare translators I've spoken to have – mostly – known what they're letting themselves in for. As I've mentioned, Chico, the Brazilian translator whose *Tempest*, *Romeo and Juliet* and *Julius Caesar* we've seen glimpses of, is keen to do the *Henry IV* plays next (he's a Falstaff fan), as well as *Henry V*. The reason he has not done *Henry V* before now, he says, is this one famous line:

> We few, we happy few, we band of brothers . . .

He's been pondering those eleven syllables for two years.

We few,

i.e. those people who are defined as – and limited to – *us*, who are not many in number. (Except conveyed in two tiny syllables.)
Then:

we happy few,

which adds one word, meaning not just glad but *fortunate*.

The first word is doable in Portuguese – *nós*. But the most obvious solution for *we few* in Portuguese is *nós poucos*, which is bigger than *we few* and rather unlovely. (Maybe *Só nós* – Just us?) Portuguese has the word *venturosos*, which covers both glad and lucky, but you'll never have the space for it. At this point we're still supposed to be barely halfway through a single line, and still leaving room for *we band of brothers* – with its unifying alliteration, and so on. Chico doesn't want to lose the repetition, and he does want to keep his translation to one line. I don't think any of us like accepting impossibilities in our translation work, even if the fault is entirely with our limited language rather than our own limited skill. So I'm quite sure that Chico is going to keep staring at this line for a while longer. Anyway, he's still got to do the *Henry IV*s before he gets to that line, so he has some time yet. I have faith.

The phrase weighs in at nine words/syllables in So's Chinese, too.

我们几个，幸运的几个

However – and far be it for me to want to foster a spirit of envy, or competition, between translators I greatly like and admire, but . . . – hey, Chico, look what Niels has done!

vi få, vi muntre få, vi flok af brødre . . .

Neat, huh?

We must acknowledge, though, that this solution is not *only* a matter of this individual translator's customary brilliance; it is also a possibility contained within Danish, and simply not available to translators elsewhere. Danish allows things that other languages simply would not, because for this line, English-language Shakespeare is mostly using words that have Danish near-equivalents. You can see our *brothers* in his *brødre*; he has *få* for our *few*, and his *flok* (for Shakespeare's *band*) is a direct cognate of the English word *flock*. No other language will accommodate Shakespeare *easily*, of course, but our cousin Danish at least has its moments.

For another seemingly straightforward example, how about that 'The rest is silence' line that we know *did* cause plenty of trouble in Danish? Well, Ádám cited it as one of the enduring inadequacies in his Hungarian, too, about which he keeps changing his mind, never quite satisfied.

He admires the earlier Arany translation, which has *Néma csend* – very idiomatic, very normal. (*Néma* is *silent/mute* – an adjective.) Ádám didn't want a complete sentence, though. He too uses *csend* for silence, but needs an article (*the* silence) just to keep the iambic pattern. *Csak a csend* might be best. Nothing but silence.

When I met Te Haumihiata, her *Romeo and Juliet* was finished and she was deep into a new *te reo* Māori translation. This time, she was grappling with *Macbeth*. ('That must be difficult,' I said, insightfully.) Apparently one line in particular was causing trouble, and I racked my brains to come up with a good guess – what would be especially tricky? The bit about the multitudinous seas incarnadine? The witches' tightly formal rhyming spells?

None of these. Apparently the big problem is found in:

Are you a man?

Which was not what I was expecting. I mentioned this to Alexander, another of my *flok af oversættere*,* whose Bulgarian *Macbeth* I'd been studying. 'Oh yes,' he said, 'that line! It's one of the most difficult moments in the play.'

Man in English is so meaningful, and so short, and rhymes so obligingly . . .

In this case, Lady M is not actually asking her husband for a piece of information, she is challenging his manhood. But in Bulgarian, Alexander had a choice between two different, inadequate simplifications:

ти човек ли си?
[*ti <u>chovek</u> li si?*]

– are you a man, as opposed to some other species? (which is not what Lady Macbeth means) and:

ти мъж ли си?
[*ti <u>muzh</u> li si?*]

– are you a man, as in simply male? (Which is *also* not what Lady Macbeth means.)

On the day Te Haumihiata and I met, her working draft had Lady Macbeth say:

He raho rānei ōu?

This means 'Have you got balls?'

Though, since I gather that this *rānei* has some attitude in it, we might perhaps translate it as 'So have you got balls or what?'

Which is *exactly* what Lady M is asking.

Macbeth's response: *He raho tonu kē ōku.* Yeah, I've still got 'em.

---

* band of translators

She had the option of 'What kind of a man are you?', but felt that came out too long in *te reo* – *He aha hoki tēnā momo tangata i a koe nā?* Ideally, the line should be quick, muttered in a way that the other characters on stage don't notice.

Alexander went with something closer to his second option: Вие мъж ли сте?,* even if it meant that not using the same word as he used for 'I dare do all that may become a *man*' earlier in the play.

Swahili has a similar problem with a lack of specific constructions for gender roles; JC chose to have her Lady Macbeth use *mwanaume* rather than *mtu* (*man* rather than *person*), but brought it closer to Lady M's intentions by adding one word:

Je, wewe ni mwanaume kweli?

The *kweli* means *truly* – 'it's stronger', says JC, more clearly accusatory.

Are you a man *really*?

When Iago says to Rodrigo, *Come, be a man!*, this is just the sort of man he has in mind. But when he challenges Othello with the very same question that Lady M asked her husband – *Are you a man?* – the context suggests he's not asking the same thing she was. Iago's is a question principally about Othello's humanity, rather than his macho virility. The complete line is *Are you a man? have you a soul, or sense?*

In *King Lear*, meanwhile, when Kent says:

> Since I was man,
> Such sheets of fire, such bursts of horrid thunder,
> Such groans of roaring wind and rain I never
> Remember to have heard.

the word 'man' is being used to designate adult-ness. This is man as opposed to 'boy', rather than as opposed to woman, or as opposed to

---

* And yes, in the polite form – *вий* rather than *mu* – thus corresponding to Lady M's 'you'.

some other animal species, or as opposed to a human male who isn't sufficiently stereotypically *manly*. Kent has not heard these fearsome things since he attained manhood. But when Lear says: 'Is man no more but this?', it is man standing in for every member of the human species. And when the cross-dressed Viola, in *Twelfth Night*, says: 'I am the man', she means 'the man in question, the one Olivia's fallen in love with' – though there is an extra layer, and an audience laugh, because she is not, of course, any kind of man at all.

Man is another one of those monosyllables, another one of those first-words-you-learn, which surely couldn't be simpler. Surely! And yet, what a piece of work . . .

Chapter 20

Todas sus palabras son meritorias

(on Latinate vocabulary)

English is a fantastically hybrid tongue, whose vocabulary has gradually accommodated words from other languages with which it's come into contact, whether through trade or empire or immigration. It is not simply a smooth evolution of Anglo-Saxon (Old English), but a wild collection of supplementary bits and pieces that have accreted over the centuries. Every contact point (Romans, Normans, British colonial rule of India in the mid-nineteenth century, Polish immigrants arriving in the UK in the early 2000s, etc.) has complicated and enriched it.

The majority of our vocabulary today is Latinate, coming either direct from Latin or via French. With the arrival of the Normans in 1066, and all that, their language wove in with the tongue spoken by the Anglo-Saxons to form a sort of double language – for centuries, there was Anglo-Norman for the ruling class of society, English for the ruled-over. So today's English, still structurally a Germanic language, has a resilient old word stock deriving from our Anglo-Saxon ancestors, related to German, Dutch and the Scandinavian languages, but also a larger strand of Latinate words, whose close cousins are in French, Italian, Romanian, and so on. (And older Greek words usually via this Latin strand, too.) Often, for a single meaning, we have a choice between the two vocabularies – is this relationship *fraternal* (Latinate), or *brotherly* (Anglo-Saxon)?

Generalising slightly, you'll find that where we have synonym pairs of that kind, the longer and more formal-sounding words are often the Latin ones; things shorter and more plain-spoken, Anglo-Saxon/Germanic. I walk up stairs. I don't usually ascend them ambulating, unless I want to sound *very* grand. I wait and hope in one kind of English, but anticipate expectantly in the other. Is this T-shirt *verdant* – or just plain green?

The play of these two main registers is one of the English language's particular assets, so – as a writer who really takes advantage of everything his language will allow him – it is something Shakespeare uses. Sometimes he will use both together – that's what the 'attend and mark' streamlined by Ádám was about; sometimes his writing can be entirely simple, Anglo-Saxon.

Lines made up of shorter words will often map more neatly onto a German translation, so when tomorrow, and tomorrow, and tomorrow,

> Creeps in this petty pace from day to day,*

you can see the same shape in the Schlegel-Tieck translation where it:

> Kriecht so mit kleinem Schritt von Tag zu Tag

I know a bank where the wild thyme blows, says Oberon, using all monosyllables and again, very little Latin. In German/Danish/Dutch, you'll see some similarity:

- *Ik weet een plekje, waar de thym nu bloeit* (Dutch, tr. Burgersdijk)
- *Ich weiß 'nen Hügel, wo man Quendel pflückt* (German, tr. Schlegel)
- *Jeg ved en skrænt med timian i flor* (Danish, tr. Brunse)

---

* The only two-syllable word here is one of the only two Latinate words (*petty*, from old French).

Because we're all humans here, we do context, so we know this 'bank' is not an establishment for depositing money. It's also, as it happens, not a riverbank, but rather a grassy mound or slope. One of Lawrence's current options for this line in Latinate Portuguese is 'Sei de uma _encosta_ onde o tomilho-bravo brota.' With _encosta_ we're still in the realms of languages closely related to English, but you can see there's no kinship to our _bank_, which comes from another branch of the family.

Meanwhile, a language like Welsh is not fundamentally Latinate or Anglo-Saxon based, so a rocky Welsh hillside looks unconnected to anything we'd recognise: _llechwedd_.*

That _encosta_ is of course related to various side-ish things in English – _coasts_ and such like. A Portuguese coast might also be a _litoral_ – and while we do have the related word _littoral_ in English, it's a far fancier word than I'd normally use – I'd use _shore_, of course (a cognate with the Middle Low German word _schore_). Because of the imbalance of registers, our _shore_ is invariably a better translation of the Portuguese _litoral_ than our _littoral_ is.

Also, if I were to make a joke here about littoral translations – I'll admit, I shamelessly considered one – my Portuguese translator would be able to recycle it (_litoral_/_literal_), and my German or Welsh translator would not.

The Anglophone Othello says this:

> I would not my <u>unhoused free</u> condition
> Put into <u>circumscription and confine</u>
> For the sea's worth.

And this:

---

* While I know only a handful of Welsh words, _llechwedd_/_hillside_ happens to be one of them, only because I live in Lewes and there's a theory that that's where this hilly town gets its name – from the Old Welsh via the Old English word _lexowia_.

> But once put out thy light, . . .
> Thou cunning'st pattern of excelling nature,
> I know not where is that Promethean heat
> That can thy light <u>relume</u>.

He doubles up words with similar meanings, and he uses language that nobody else would ever use. I've underlined the relevant words, so please attend and mark . . . I mean, seriously, *relume*? Nobody else in the play would use this word, and no character in any other play ever uses it either. Do you? The effect of all this is that he seems to be over-talking, using more words than he really needs and trying to impress. (Weren't we just talking about how much English can do with a tight handful of monosyllables? And *circumscription* is what he does instead?)

Jean-Michel did try to make Othello's language different from Iago's, and found the key to the distinction in the 'It is the cause . . .' speech, when the Latinate vs non-Latinate features were pointed out to him by an academic at a conference. Jean-Michel can't replicate the same exact device, giving Othello disproportionately Latinate words where Shakespeare does, French being a fundamentally Latinate language; 'but I can decide to use shorter words, those with a more muscular impetus, more consonant force, for the Anglo-Saxon parts.' There are limits to the variety, of course, which are the limits of the language. As you can imagine, Othello in Italian is quite something.

(Jean-Michel also references an old theory that Shakespeare uses synonyms aimed at different parts of his audience. *Fairy king, attend and mark . . .*   that's *attend* for those of you educated folk seated in the galleries, just plain *mark* for you lot in the yard.)

It's not unusual to hear Latinate language from characters who are trying to impress – we've seen the mechanicals in the *Dream* do this, clumsily – whereas Othello is dignified and quite intellectual and his language shows this, when he's telling his stories. It's only when he gets hit by disaster that his language frays. Niels gives him language that's conspicuously grand, not only trying to impress, but also, yes, genuinely dignified. He can take advantage of the fact that Danish is a language of many layers – old Norse, low German, and a later French influence. The word 'fremmendord' means 'foreign/alien word', to identify words of Greek or Latin origin as outsiders, he explains. 'All the bookish words of Greek or Latin origin are clearly felt as strangers in the Danish world.'

He also cites the example of the courtiers at the start of *The Winter's Tale* in heightened discussion of the meeting of two kings – 'and they're really talking on stilts':

> Verily, I speak it in the freedom of my knowledge. We cannot with such magnificence – in so rare – I know not what to say. We will give you sleepy drinks, that your senses, unintelligent of our insufficience, may, though they cannot praise us, as little accuse us.

Unintelligent of our insufficience, you say? The whole conversation is of a ludicrously complicated formality, clearly designed to show off their position as courtiers. Most of the characters – including those speaking verse in the next scene – don't sound like this. Niels here didn't just raise the level of the vocabulary, but made the courtier *syntax* extra-complex to create this effect. Ádám said the same – you can't always do register with vocab, but greater complexity in sentence structure works instead.

As we've seen is so often the case in Shakespeare, effect is created by contrast. You notice the grounded punchiness of one register, because it's juxtaposed with the loftier florid diction of (put next to the higher flowery words of) another. Macbeth kills the king then wonders whether there's enough water in the sea to wash the blood from off his hands.

> No, this my hand will rather
> The multitudinous seas incarnadine,
> Making the green, one red.

The shock effect of 'making the green, one red' comes from the ways is it not like 'the multitudinous seas incarnadine'.

The multitudinous seas incarnadine is not something I would say, and nor would you. Like *relume* or *insufficience*, *incarnadine* has just this one appearance in Shakespeare.* But its polysyllabic poetic grandiosity sets you up to notice the *green one red*.†

Here's Othello again:

> This hand of yours <u>requires</u>
> <u>A sequester from liberty</u>, fasting and prayer,
> Much castigation, exercise devout,
> For here's a young and sweating devil, here
> That commonly rebels. 'Tis a good hand,
> A frank one.

"'Tis a good hand, a frank one' is one sort of language; the fact that this hand 'requires a sequester from liberty' feels like quite another.

In a speech with lots of short and simple non-Latinate words, Shakespeare/Othello still chooses *requires* over *needs*, and Latinate *liberty* over Germanic *freedom*. Whereas if you're an Italian speaker or a French speaker, the Latinate *libertà* or *liberté* would be the first word you'd reach for. (See also *fraternité*/*brotherhood*.)

Now, there's nothing *inherently* high-register about Latinate words and plain about Anglo-Saxon ones; but English has evolved historically to read in that way. Esperanto mixes both word groups, but there's seldom an equivalent duplication of synonyms. Here's that line we saw from Reto Rossetti's *Othello*:

> *Zorgu la domon, sakojn kaj filinon!*

---

* If you were wondering, there is one other *multitudinous*, spoken by the haughty hero of *Coriolanus*.

† 'The splendid word "incarnadine",' wrote Virginia Woolf – 'who can use it without remembering also "multitudinous seas"?'

There is a comparable mix of etymologies – the three nouns (*domon, sakojn, filinon*) are Latinate;* the imperative verb *zorgu* is German (from *sorgen*); conjunction *kai* is Greek (και, *and*); but it has no such register-hopping effect on the Esperanto ear.

But even if a translator happens not to be working in a language that is woven from two parallel strands that have evolved to suggest different registers, they needn't despair. Because different languages have different resources, it's usually possible to convey loftiness of speech vs plainness of speech *somehow*.

Emine has lately been working on a few bits of *Richard III*,† and for old Queen Margaret's speeches, she's experimented with using more words that have come down from Ottoman Turkish, and an Ottoman Turkish rhyme scheme. Queen Margaret, says Emine, is 'a character echoing the ancient Senecan tragic world', and from her role in the historical narrative – she's the widow of Henry VI, who looms from the backstory, seeming to be stepping into this play from another time. When working on the Porter scene from *Macbeth*, Emine used the vernacular language we've referenced already; but this is likewise dotted with old Ottoman words and expressions – she wanted some of this language for him too, especially when his speech has religious/Biblical references, as he imagines himself the gatekeeper of hell.

In his *Masala Shakespeare*, Jonathan Gil Harris points out that the Hindi of Bollywood (sprinkled with English, and laced through with words of many other origins – Persian, etc.) isn't a bad fit for the hybrid language of *Romeo and Juliet* – especially when you notice that the *collar/choler/collier* trio from Chapter 11 all come to English from different etymological strands.

---

* So in my Esperanto–Portuguese dictionary (of course I have an Esperanto–Portuguese dictionary), two out of these three nouns have evident kinships: *filino/filha, sako/saco*. (And *domon* relates to plenty of Latinate *house* words of our own, too.)

† Emine usually translates plays on commission for theatres intending to produce them. These bits of *Richard III* she just did *for fun*. I feel I will need to address the translator's psychopathology at some point.

The Scottish Gaelic *Julius Caesar*, made by U.M. MacGilleMhoire in 1911, uses language that my friend Mairi described as slightly 'religiously inflected'. In part by design, with MacGilleMhoire translating the whole play at some height, using deliberately antique words; but also for historical reasons relating to this language's use. Gaelic was by law replaced by English in certain contexts in 1609 (we'll see England do a similar violence to Welsh in Chapter 27); the long subsequent suppression of the vernacular language meant that comfort with the literary language was largely the domain of those with a link to religion.

Meanwhile, the Kurdish translator Kareem Abdulrahman talked to me about a phenomenon where his language's translations add an extra sheen of highbrow 'literariness' to classic work – all the more so in the theatre, where text was especially heightened. The language Kareem heard spoken on the stage when growing up was unusually formal, artificial, it was highbrow and declamatory, always, regardless of the speaker. Beautiful, perhaps, but Shakespeare's language is not only grand – it is also everyday, and simple, it's funny and coarse, his characters are occasionally kings but they're also servants. Dramatic characters should be differentiated. Using a consistent high-poetic style, all rhyming verse, removes many possibilities from what Shakespeare is doing. That's where the problem comes, then, not when you're creating one big distinctive voice for Othello, but when everybody around him talks like that, too. That's where things get tricky, where a translator has made *everyone* sound grand.

Most early translations into Arabic wrestled Shakespeare into formal language, with many critics believing that Shakespeare deserved only the loftiest, most elevated poetry – these being critics who *revered* Shakespeare. The translator Fatma Moussa Mahmoud broke with tradition in 1985 to produce an Arabic *Lear* that shifted between formal Arabic (*fushā*) and colloquial, making it at once more accessible to a twenty-first-century Arabic-speaking audience, and in the process, much closer to the shifting textures of Shakespeare's play. In the words of her daughter, the novelist Ahdaf Soueif, this replacing of an English verse/prose split with two distinct kinds of

Arabic 'liberated her from the need to strong-arm her text into metrics and allowed full scope for the richness, density and drama of the language.' One of our important principles, yet again: often translators change things in order to keep things the same.

Many people succumb to this temptation to make Shakespeare grander than he is – and this isn't always done with linguistic register. Sometimes you merely need to tweak some of the botany. In his essay 'The Art of Translation', Nabokov made his feelings quite clear:

> . . . here he comes strutting and shooting out his bejewelled cuffs, the slick translator who arranges Scheherazade's boudoir according to his own taste and with professional elegance tries to improve the looks of his victims. Thus it was the rule with Russian versions of Shakespeare to give Ophelia richer flowers than the poor weeds she found. The Russian rendering of:
>
> > There with fantastic garlands did she come
> > Of crowflowers, nettles, daisies and long purples
>
> if translated back into English would run like this:
>
> > There with most lovely garlands did she come
> > Of violets, carnations, roses, lilies.
>
> [. . .] how anyone could make such a botanical collection beside the Helje or the Avon is another question . . .

Nabokov is objecting to the wilful heightening of something that wasn't originally very grand. But because English is not the only language with multiple synonyms sitting at different registers, translators are constantly blessed with options. So, finally, leaving that Danish riverbank now, to return to the Athenian court . . . We've seen before that Greek has two distinct options for our *moon*, so a translator at each occurrence of that English word will have a choice.

Here's Theseus, at the start of *A Midsummer Night's Dream*, and Dionysis Kapsalis's translation:

> Four happy days bring in
> Another moon . . .

> Μένουν μόνο
> τέσσερεις μέρες πρόσχαρες που φέρνουν
> τη νέα σελήνη . . .

In Greek, four happy days bring on another *selíni*, not another *fengári* – Theseus is given the more poetic word. It comes from Selene, the moon personified as ancient Greek mythological goddess. It is lunar, rather than moon-like. An elevated Hellenic poetic trisyllable for our good old English *moon*.

Chapter 21

kad jūsų iždas kupinas žodžių

(on influences, kinships and etymologies)

Let's jump ahead by an act or so from Theseus's moons, till we're about a quarter of the way into *A Midsummer Night's Dream*. Where we rejoin the story, Oberon, the fairy king, has just dispatched Puck to fetch a magical flower, and he's now describing what will happen once he has dropped this flower's juice into sleeping Titania's eyes. In Hindi, first:

> नयन खोलते ही जिसको देखेगी, तब वह
> **सिंह, भेड़िया, बैल, नकलची बन्दर, या लंगूर भले ही**
> पीछे दौड़ेगी वह उसके भरे प्रेम आत्मा में अपनी।
> [*Nayan kholte hi jisko dekhegi, tab vah*
> ***Singh, bhediya, bail, nakalchi bandar, ya langoor bhaley hi***
> *peeche daudegi vah uske bharey prem aatma mein apni*]

That was from Rangeya Raghav's translation of the *Dream*, entitled *Ek Sapna*.

And now in Turkish, translated by Emine Ayhan and Aysun Şişik:

Uyanır uyanmaz karşısına ne çıkarsa,
(Bu bir aslan mı olur, ayı mı olur yoksa
Bir kurt ya da boğa mı olur bilemem, meraklı bir maymun
Yahut yerinde duramayan bir şebek de olabilir tabii)
Artık ne olursa, büyük bir aşkla düşecek peşine.

(Note: we've seen *yok* (no/not) before – here *yoksa* is *if not*, or *otherwise*.)

Next, those four lines (or five, according to the Turkish exchange rate, or three if you're working in Hindi) in our Greek translation by Dionisis Kapsalis:

Τον πρώτο που θα δει όταν ξυπνήσει,
Θες λύκο, αρκούδα, ταύρο, λιοντάρι,
πίθηκο ή αδιάκριτη μαϊμού,
θα τον ποθεί και δεν θα ξεκολλάει.

And finally, Gwyn Thomas's translation into Welsh:

Wrth ddeffro, y peth cynraf welith hi –
Boed hwnnw'n llew, neu arth, neu flaidd, neu darw,
Neu fwnci, neu epa sy'n busnesa –
Fe wnaiff hi ei ddilyn gydag enaid serch.

Oh, and in case you think you didn't recognise a word of any of those (though you'd be wrong), here's English, where they all started:

The next thing then she, waking, looks upon,
Be it on lion, bear, or wolf, or bull,
On meddling monkey or on busy ape,
She shall pursue it with the soul of love.

The English, you'll see, has those monosyllables we talked about, so this was always going to stretch the Turkish (hence the translators sneaking in an extra line). Though the 'ors' leave Shakespeare scope to add or subtract bits in the building of the ten-syllable unit. (Ádám would see these as typical English redundancy, I suspect.) Greek has a similar economy problem, but Dionysis Kapsalis saves space by losing an adjective in line three – our monkey has no epithet, though the ape is still αδιάκριτη (indiscreet/inquisitive).*

You should be able to spot the bull in this line of the Greek:

θες λύκο, αρκούδα, ταύρο, λιοντάρι, . . .

It's that word ταύρο, a cognate of the Latin *taurus*, and hence our Taurus star sign, taurine, toreador, etc.). The first word of the next line is πίθηκο – in Latin script, that'd be *píthiko*, and it's the Greek word for ape (whence our southern ape *Australopithecus*).

In the Welsh lines, meanwhile, you'll see the word 'llew'. In Chapter 28 we'll be meeting a Welsh captain by the name of Fluellen – an Anglicised version of Llewellyn, a name still common today – the *llew* in question being a *lion*. (See also, relatedly, *leo*, *lion*, and the archaic/poetic German *Leu* that we'll meet in the next chapter.)

The name *Lewis*, incidentally, has a few different independent origins, but one of them – when in Wales – is as an adaptation of Llewellyn. I assume, then, that this would be the origin of C.S. Lewis's surname, his paternal grandfather Richard Lewis having been a Welshman.

And talking about C.S. Lewis, if you look at the first of the extracts on p.201, you'll find the Turkish word for 'lion' quickly enough . . .

Meanwhile, you might deduce the Welsh words for 'monkey' and 'ape' in this line

Neu fwnci, neu epa sy'n busnesa –

---

* Another neat little example of how economical this English is – consider that word 'waking', positioned as it is, within commas, ensuring we know that it means 'at the moment of waking' rather than 'while awake'. So efficient.

IF THIS BE MAGIC

if I tell you that *fwnci* is just a 'soft mutation' (because of the preceding 'neu') of the Welsh *mwnci*.* Both *mwnci* and *epa* are related to the English equivalents. (The Welsh w, as in *mwnci*, being pronounced as a *u* – a shortish oo in *moonki*.) The Welsh 'sy'n busnesa' means 'who pries or noses around' and echoes the relevant English word because it's borrowed from it. And that recurring 'neu' is simply 'or' – the character list names 'Puck, neu Robin Goodfellow'.

This translation keeps the English spelling of 'Puck', incidentally, so I presume it is to be pronounced in the English way with a short vowel. As opposed to the Welsh Pwk, I suppose, which would be a slightly longer Pook (rhyming with *book*)? And talking about Kipling . . .

Look at the Hindi extract on p.200. You'll see that all the parenthetical animals have been squeezed into a single line (three stand-alone nouns and a pair of little phrases), so that lines two and three are now comparable in syllables. But it means that our former quartet of lion/bear/wolf/bull has been reduced to a trio. No matter whether you speak Hindi, if you know your *Jungle Book*, you might be able to deduce who's missing. (Also which animal's Sanskrit-origin noun is now a common family name.)

A bonus if you know a Romance language: if you look at the last word of the Greek extract, you can find one of your words for 'glue'. Kapsalis's line means 'She will desire him and won't let him go', the final word being to un-glue: xe-kollaei.

Needless to say, though, not everything that looks related *is* related. The number of possible combinations of vowel-consonant sounds is very large but not infinite. Shakespeare sometimes uses *an* (or *an'*) to mean if.

Like this line that we've seen before, from Falstaff:

> 'Sblood, <u>an</u> he were here I would cudgel him like a dog if he would say so . . .

---

* A 'soft mutation' is also how we ended up with *bechu* for *sin* on p.39 – if it had been the unmutated *pechu*, the Latinate root would have been more visible. (We've seen *pecado* and the like before.)

The Greek word for *if* is also *an* (αν). So where the Shakespeare Pyramus says:

> Now will I to the chink,
> To spy <u>an</u> I can hear my Thisbe's face.

the Kapsalis Pyramus says:

> Πάω αμέσως
> στη χαραμάδα για να δω <u>αν</u> μπορώ
> το πρόσωπο της Θίσβης μου ν'ακούσω.

But the Shakespearean *an* is a shortening of *and*, and the resemblance to the Greek is purely, unhelpfully coincidental.

That's not to say that a translator cannot take advantage of echoes that might have no etymological basis but be pleasing nonetheless. I've mentioned Edith Grossman's *Don Quixote* already – and this was how, upon much deliberation, she chose to begin it:

> Somewhere in La Mancha, in a place whose name I do not care to remember . . .

Not 'I do not choose to remember', or 'I do not want to remember', or 'I would rather not remember', but 'care to'. Why? Because the Spanish word that Cervantes uses is *quiero* (we've seen this word meaning 'love' already), and she found it pleasing that her English echoed his sounds.

Chapter 22

קוקנדיק אַפֿ מיר, װערן שאַרפֿזיניק אױך אַנדערע

(on humour)

One of the more tiresome conversations into which translators get drawn concerns 'fidelity', treated as though it were a single spectrum – 'here are two translations, this one is very faithful, that one much less faithful'. The less faithful translation being perhaps more 'creative', where a translator takes liberties to do something effective but at the risk of somehow changing the source text, and thus traducing it. Leaving aside the question of what the hell a translation that didn't radically 'change' the source could actually look like, this suggests a view of the process that has an interest in meaning alone, and not in language's other characteristics. Because when a piece of writing has register and diction and rhythm and cultural resonances (and meaning), a translator is weighing these up at every moment and making choices about which to prioritise. To put it another way, every translator I know would consider themselves fundamentally and aspirationally 'faithful', but we will not always be faithful to the same thing.

If you were to take a speech from a play – written by Shakespeare to be spoken by an actor – and translate the meaning impeccably and comprehensively, to produce something that might be semantically 'correct' but is now, alas, almost un-speakable, I'd argue that you were being faithful to the wrong thing. When translating a joke, sure, we could simply translate the meaning of the joke, and simply pretend we don't know what jokes are *for*. Personally, I tend to dismantle them entirely, look at the moving parts, then reassemble them into what might be a quite different joke. It's a question of priority. I want to be as faithful as I can. Sometimes, I'm being faithful to the laugh.

A Midsummer Night's Dream is the play that Lawrence is working on now, and since he and I have talked about his dislike of 'pomposity' in poetry, I'm eager to see what he makes of 'Pyramus and Thisbe', in which much of the humour comes from a parodying of this very thing. It's a scene in which a group of amateur actors (Athenian tradesmen by day) perform their version of a great tragic love story from classical literature.

Lawrence's problem is not with writing that's just grandiose, which can be interesting, but pomposity as something empty, unthinking. The 'Pyramus and Thisbe' scene is full of it: terrible writing crammed with classical nonsense that thinks it's poetic, but it's really just inflated, totally without substance. Pyramus's death gives the impression of being grand and important – but there's nothing in the writing that tells you about Pyramus as a character. No one in the history of theatre has cried at the death of Pyramus. Lear's death should destroy you, but then, Lear is a person; with Pyramus, there's nothing there. To paraphrase Oscar Wilde on Little Nell, you'd have to have a heart of stone to watch Pyramus's death without laughing. The actors are out of their depths, and the script they've been given doesn't help at all . . .

To prepare for this chapter, I went up to London last Thursday to watch a terrific production of *A Midsummer Night's Dream*, in which I found the 'Pyramus and Thisbe' part of Act V especially delightful, taking advantage of every comic moment the text offered it. During the eleven or twelve minutes in question, I counted thirty-one discrete audible laughs. Of these, twenty-four were laughs that were triggered by the text itself, or at least enabled by it – where the text gave the actors something specific to work with, which in turn produced the laugh. (I am excluding, then, a handful of laughs that were, so to speak, entirely *performance-specific*.)

This is not an exact science; I apologise for writing about it as though it were.

Since there's nothing more joyous than dismantling jokes to examine their workings, this chapter will do just that. Because where these funny moments are text-derived, I'd expect any good translator to keep them funny, or rather, to make them funny again. Every day, countless *Dream* actors in countless different languages are attempting to elicit the same laughs from this scene, and each should, in short, be given the same material to work with.

There are some circumstances in which the challenges of translating humour are obvious: it might play upon certain cultural references unknown to a target audience, say, and yes, as we've seen already, wordplay is always going to be hard, because that sort of humour is precisely about highly specific properties *inherent in specific words*. But in truth, almost all humour is difficult to translate, because even when it doesn't fall into one of those categories, the effect comes from a control of writing that is so often tonal and rhythmic. You might write a sentence and it's *almost* funny, but would be *really* funny if you could only get to the last word two seconds faster and if only that last word you landed on could be a monosyllable.

So to *A Midsummer Night's Dream*, a really funny play, its humour culminating in the fifth act when our group of 'rude mechanicals' (a weaver, a joiner, a tailor, etc.) present themselves before the nobles to perform '*The most lamentable comedy and most cruel death of Pyramus and Thisbe.*' Over the course of the *Dream*, we have come to feel great affection for the performers, so it pains me to tell you that their show is not good. The inadequacies of their script and their performances are where most of the humour is to be found. Here, then, are the moments in Shakespeare's text that produced laughs on Thursday night. And how the great Frank Günther ensured that they would stay funny in German.

We begin with Quince's prologue, with line breaks and punctuation carefully constructed to encourage nonsensical pauses. We saw Ádám's Hungarian solution to this in Chapter 11. Here's Frank's:

SQUENZ (PROLOG)
Wenn wir missfallen, ist es unser Wille,
Dass ihr nicht denkt. Wir kommen zu missfallen,
Nur das ist unser Streben. Kunst in Fülle
Niemals. Soll euer Widerwille wallen.

The chaotic pausing has been duly retained, producing self-contained units like 'If we displease, it is our will that you should not think', or 'Art in abundance – never', or (my favourite) 'Let your revulsion surge.'

Quince introduces his cast of characters, and summarises what is going to happen. So:

This grisly beast, which Lion hight by name,
The trusty Thisbe, coming first by night,
Did scare away, or rather did affright

'Did scare away, or rather did affright' only exists to stretch us to the end of a line and a rhyme; it's the sort of padding Ádám referred to in Chapter 18, but here the artlessness is of course intentional.

Dies greulich Untier ist als Leu bekannt
Die treue Thisbe kommt bei Nacht gerannt –
Allein – der Löw' sie schreckt und scheucht – sie fleucht.

What did the German lion do? It *schreckt* und it also *scheucht* – that is to say, it frightens her away *and* it scares her off. Or possibly vice-versa.

Pyramus (the prologue continues) will kill himself, after which Thisbe, 'tarrying in mulberry shade' (to rhyme with blade) will kill herself, too. Though note that in German, you will not find her tarrying in mulberry shade, because that would not rhyme with a German dagger – *Dolch*. Instead, she 'versteckt war *wie ein Molch*'. It's true. Our Thisbe, as portrayed by Francis Flute, awaits her fate while *hiding like a newt*.

That *greulich* adjective for the lion is an old-fashioned spelling for what would more usually be *gräulich* today; *Leu* is that archaic/poetic word for lion. Like much of what's to come in this 'Pyramus and Thisbe' script, we have old-fashioned, lofty language ('which Lion hight by name'), and an outmoded rhetorical style. So at various points, Frank's German gives us these archaisms (including very subtle things, like using the spelling 'Phantasie' rather than the slightly more common contemporary spelling 'Fantasie' to translate the word 'imagination'*); and there's terrible over-alliteration we're just going to have to get used to in this scene, too. All these things are encouragements to overact, of course. This language is big but empty, full of sound and fury, signifying *hiç*.

This is our first sighting of the heroic Pyramus, addressing the night

O grim-looked night, O night, with hue so black,	*O dunkle Nacht, o Nacht so schwarz wie Nacht!*
O night, which ever art when day is not,	*O Nacht, die ewig währt bis auf die Tage!*
O night, O night, alack, alack, alack,	*O Nacht, o Nacht, o wehe, weh, o acht!*
I fear my Thisbe's promise is forgot.	*Vergisst mich Thisbe, das ist hier die Frage.*

The actors in this play seem often to be unaware of what they're saying. In this case, Frank has dropped in some extra nonsense for Bottom/Pyramus here, because:

---

* The more modern spelling of this German word gave its name to a sparkling orange-flavoured drink.

> *o Nacht so schwarz wie Nacht!*

means

> o night as black as night!

Then Pyramus addresses the wall that separates his garden from Thisbe's

> Thou Wall, O wall, O sweet, O lovely Wall, . . .   *Und du, o Wand, o süße Wand, o Wand, . . .*

From which you will deduce that the German word for 'wall' is 'Wand'. A straightforward choice – though Frank's fellow translator Maik Hamburger did once sneak a political dimension into this decision, for a production in divided Germany, by choosing *Mauer*, the word used for a more famous Wall then cutting through Berlin.

A couple of scenes earlier, we've seen Bottom muddling up his senses:

> The eye of man hath not heard, the ear of man hath not seen, man's hand is not able to taste, his tongue to conceive, nor his heart to report what my dream was.

And he does the same as Pyramus here:

> I see a voice . . .

That's just silly. And Frank's

> *Ich seh die Stimme . . .*

is also identically silly. Ten out of ten.

As they declare their love through the hole in the wall that parts them, our Pyramus and our Thisbe compare themselves to classical lovers, getting most of the names wrong:

BOTTOM/PYRAMUS
    ... And, like Limander, am I trusty still.
FLUTE/THISBE
    And I like Helen, till the Fates me kill.
BOTTOM/PYRAMUS
    Not Shafalus to Procrus was so true.
FLUTE/THISBE
    As Shafalus to Procrus, I to you.

'Shafalus' and 'Procrus' are Bottom and Flute's attempt at Cephalus and Procris. The line often gets a laugh, even though I suspect most Anglophone audiences today don't have the Cephalus and Procris reference to call upon. Nowadays, the laugh is wrung from the line because 'Shafalus to Procrus' has a consonant string that makes it hard to say, and actors often make much play of the struggle.

ZETTEL/PYRAMUS
    ... Denn dein ist alle Zeit mein ganzes Herz.
FLAUT/THISBE
    Und meins ist deins und fühlt wie du den Schmerz.
ZETTEL/PYRAMUS
    Dir ewig treu sei meines Triebes Liebe.
FLAUT/THISBE
    O dass mich treuer noch die Liebe triebe.

Frank isn't reconstructing the old joke exactly, but playing with the line-ending sounds, and trying far too hard.
    Next, this:

BOTTOM/PYRAMUS
O kiss me through the hole of this vile Wall.
FLUTE/THISBE
I kiss the wall's hole, not your lips at all.

This is simply setting up a physical gag, and so the translation is uncomplicated.

ZETTEL/PYRAMUS
O küss mich durch das Loch der schnöden Wand!
FLAUT/THISBE
Ich küss der Wand das Loch ganz dicht am Rand.

– though (because meaning is not everything) we should note that its effect is amplified in English by Flute's being forced to break the regular metre and really draw attention to the words 'wall's hole'.

As this conversation progresses, Bottom and Flute don't realise they've both referred to Ninus's tomb as 'Ninny's tomb' – it's a joke that was set up about an hour previously (and in Chapter 10 in Hungarian), where we watched this same scene in rehearsal:

Wilt thou at Ninny's tomb meet me straightway?	*Kommst du zum Kirschhof nachts als meine Sonne?*

In Frank's German, Bottom/Zettel/Pyramus is supposed to ask Flute/Flaut/Thisbe to meet in the churchyard. The German word for that is *Kirchhof*. That's not quite what he said, though. There's an extra 's' – in this version, Bottom is arranging a rendezvous in – randomly – a *Kirschhof* – a cherry orchard. We do know, as it happens, that there are mulberry trees in the vicinity when the lovers meet their end, but in this version it is apparently a cherry orchard filled with mulberry trees. Or something.

(With a further dash of supplementary German nonsense added – will you come to the cherry orchard tonight *as my sun?*)

Throughout the scene, Shakespeare gives us parenthetical interruptions from the noble audience who comment sarcastically and are only moderately amusing. These interjections puncture – in prose – the super-artificiality of the bad verse they're being subjected to. This is their response to the introduction of the lion:

THESEUS
   A very gentle beast, and of a good conscience.
DEMETRIUS
   The very best at a beast,* my lord, that e'er I saw.
LYSANDER
   This lion is a very fox for his valour.
THESEUS
   True, and a goose for his discretion.
DEMETRIUS
   Not so, my lord. For his valour cannot carry his discretion, and the fox carries the goose.
   [etc.]

This exchange was cut at Thursday's performance, not unusually. There is a lot of this sort of thing from the oh-so-clever play-watchers which has aged much less well than our lovely amateur troupe. This is the wit of educated people, in which the characters are happily amusing one another and themselves, and a diligent translator needs to plough through in the interests of completeness, but those of us who've paid good money for tickets really don't need to hear it.

Though the 'Pyramus and Thisbe' script is all in verse, with those prose interruptions from its spectators, Bottom himself does break into prose once, earning a laugh because he doesn't have the willpower to stay in character:

---

* *Das Beste an Bestie.* OK, Frank, sometimes it's just too easy.

BOTTOM / PYRAMUS
> . . . O wicked Wall, through whom I see no bliss,
> Curst be thy stones for thus deceiving me!

THESEUS
> The wall, methinks, being sensible, should curse again.

BOTTOM
> No, in truth, sir, he should not. 'Deceiving me' is Thisbe's cue. She is to enter now, and I am to spy her through the wall. You shall see it will fall. Pat as I told you: yonder she comes.

and he breaks likewise from German verse into German prose:

ZETTEL / PYRAMUS
> . . . O böse Wand, befalle dich der Schimmel:
> Fluch diesem Stein, er lügt mir ins Gesicht.

THESEUS
> Ich finde, wenn die Wand vernünftig ist, sollte sie zurückfluchen.

ZETTEL
> Nein, mit Erlaubnis, mein Fürst, das soll sie nicht. „Ins Gesicht' ist Thisbes Stichwort. Sie muss jetzt auftreten, . . .

All the interruptions will be enough to make poor Starveling ('Moonshine') lose patience, likewise breaking from verse into this:

> All that I have to say is to tell you that the lanthorn is the moon, I the man i'th' moon, this thorn-bush my thorn-bush, and this dog my dog.

He's lapsed into prose, gone off script and rattled off his whole part in one frustrated sentence. So it is here:

> Alles, was ich zu sagen habe, ist, Ihnen zu sagen, dass die Laterne der Mond ist und ich der Mann im Mond und dieses Reisigbündel mein Reisigbündel und dieser Hund mein Hund.

The German has firm rules about where commas must be used, including, for instance, always before a *dass*, as here. But once Frank's past that, he does the speech without any punctuation at all. And ending, abruptly, on those nice short words like the English.

<u>Und dieser Hund mein Hund</u>. *OK? Satisfied?* Tsk.

Now, we learned back in Act III of the *Dream* that the prologue to 'Pyramus and Thisbe' would be written in 'eight and six', which is to say, the old ballad metre: fourteen-line units broken up into eight syllables (four iambs) and six syllables (three iambs). It is old-fashioned and sing-song, easy to over-emphasise. And we now transition from regular pentameter into that. In both languages, *natürlich*:

Sweet Moon, I thank thee for thy sunny beams.	*O süßer Mond, du strahlst so sonnig helle!*
I thank thee, Moon, for shining now so bright.	*Ich dank dir, Mond, für deinen Sonnenschein.*
For by thy gracious, golden, glittering gleams,	*In deiner goldig-gelben Glitzergrelle*
I trust to take of truest Thisbe sight.	*Riech ich die treulich traute Thisbe mein.*
But stay: O spite!	*Doch halt – o Schreck!*
But mark, poor knight,	*Sieh da – ein Fleck!*
What dreadful dole is here?	*Welch greulich Graus mich lupft!*
Eyes, do you see?	*Ihr Augen mein,*
How can it be?	*Was kann das sein?*
O dainty duck, O dear!	*O zartes Huhn, gerupft!**

Even when Bottom and Flute do manage to stay on-script, it is clear that – despite certain similarities of plot – the script itself is no *Romeo and Juliet*. There is plenty of nonsense:

---

* I don't actually speak German, but these last half-a-dozen short lines are *really* fun to read aloud.

> Sweet Moon, I thank thee for thy sunny beams.*

where the humour is at least in part that Bottom doesn't even realise how illogical it is. Evidently, he isn't really listening to himself.

German is a pretty straightforward meaning-for-meaning swap.

> *O süßer Mond, du strahlst so sonnig helle!*

At various points, the register of their script lurches about hilariously – moving from 'What dreadful dole is here?' to 'O dainty duck, O dear!' – which Frank replicates at each turn. (Unlike the Schlegel-Tieck translation, where 'O dainty duck! O dear!' is the rather more neutral, clichéd *Mein Herz, mein Liebchen süß . . .*)

In addition, the unlucky actors' script continues to be massively over-alliterative, that easily mockable old style:

For by thy gracious, golden, glittering gleams,	*In deiner goldig-gelben Glitzergrelle*
I trust to take of truest Thisbe sight.	*Riech ich die treulich traute Thisbe mein.*

(Alliteration being, after all, how you do poetry and serious writing, innit?)

The German words for *golden* and *glitter* both obligingly begin with a 'g' too, but Frank chose to replace *gracious* (which would have been *gnädig*) with *yellow*. These are golden-*yellow* glittering gleams. Or, to put it another way, **g**oldig-**g**elbe **G**litzer**g**relle.

We had a similarly bad bit in Quince's prologue:

> Whereat, with blade, with bloody blameful blade,
> He bravely broached his boiling bloody breast.

---

* This is Jean-Michel's favourite line.

Some really silly over-alliteration, which the German kept bad – bad being what was called for:

> Er nimmt den Dolch, den dampfend düstern Dolch,
> Und bricht sich brav den blutvoll bangen Busen.

But now, we come to the moment of maximum drama, where Pyramus finds Thisbe's bloodstained cloak!

> Thy mantle good,
> What, stained with blood?
> Approach, ye Furies fell.
> O Fates, come, come,
> Cut thread and thrum,
> Quail, crush, conclude, and quell!

I'm certain Frank felt it was a good day when he worked out that he could turn those verbs into

> Knack, hack und packe . . .

Oh, but first:

'Thy mantle good – what, stained with blood?' That 'What?' maximises the opportunity for Bottom to overact.

> . . . Whaaat [sharp intake of breath]?! Stained with blood?!

Not in the German, however, where both syllables that replace 'what, stained' are occupied by a single word – *befleckt*. Though I can't help feeling 'befleckt' is an inherently funny word already.*

---

* Maybe it's just me. And as any translator knows, context is everything. Listen to Schubert's 'Ave Maria', and you will hear the word *unbefleckt* there, and it is not even the tiniest bit amusing.

> *Dein Mantel gut –*
> *Befleckt mit Blut!**

The whole script of 'Pyramus and Thisbe' has been written by someone who – worse even than Orlando, whose efforts we've already sneered at a little unkindly – is prepared to contort language in the interests of a solid rhyme.

But we also have these:

> And this the cranny is, right and sinister,
> Through which the fearful lovers are to whisper.

and

> Come, tears, confound;
> Out, sword, and wound
> The pap of Pyramus . . .

Thursday's actor got laughs from the first of these, by apparently trying to wrestle an imperfectly formed rhyme into something neater – *right and sinister / are to . . . whis-isper?* It fits with the audience experience – we're watching bad actors trying hard to deliver what is also bad writing.

But – *sinister* had a stress on its second syllable when spoken by Shakespeare – and for some time afterwards; so the word we're hearing isn't SIN-is-ter, but sin-IS-ter; so the rhyme is OK! And the word *wound* (for an injury) was a perfect rhyme with *confound* – again, spoken as it was then. (Shakespeare makes rhymes with *-ound* words very commonly; even the *wound/confound* pair is a recurring one.)

---

* This line, in fact, is identical in the Schlegel-Tieck version, but for the middle dash, and was a high point of the production that my friend Abi and I once saw in Berlin.

There's humorous potential in an imperfect rhyme, especially if unexpected, even if it's only a factor of our contemporary pronunciation, not an effect inherent in what Shakespeare was writing. A translator has a choice – translate the new accidental joke, or translate the old lack-of-joke. Frank resists the temptation, and does as Shakespeare does:

> *Das ist der Spalt, waagrecht und eng und düster,*
> *Hier wispeln beide schüchtern ihr – Geflüster.*

OK, maybe he didn't *totally* resist the temptation. The script is trying not to repeat itself, but what it means is 'The two of them shyly whisper their . . . whisperings.'

So back to

Thy mantle good,	*Dein Mantel gut –*
What, stained with blood?	*Befleckt mit Blut!*

Gut and *blut* are a perfect rhyme in German. I have seen productions where mantle good/stained with blood are forced into a rhyme by an actor who would normally pronounce them differently – as would I, indeed, being a Londoner – as if to demonstrate the incompetence of Peter Quince's writing. But I should remind myself that the Shakespeare lines are still a perfect rhyme nowadays if you're from the Midlands, say, or from Liverpool. So having in Chapter 4 mentioned that couplet from a Beatles song that only rhymes in a Liverpool accent, so 'Pyramus and Thisbe' as performed by The Beatles would comfortably rhyme blood and good without forcing it into comedy. I'm thinking Paul as Pyramus, John as Thisbe, George as Moonshine and Ringo as the Lion?

If you're having trouble imagining that for yourself, hie thee at once to Google – such a performance does in fact exist. Yes, really.

Bottom/Pyramus continues, distraught:

> O wherefore, Nature, didst thou lions frame?
> Since Lion vile hath here deflowered my dear.
> Which is – no, no, which was – the fairest dame
> That lived, that loved, that liked, that looked with cheer.

That *no, no!* is – once again – a gift to a performer looking for bad overacting opportunities. There's slightly less to it in the German, because the syllables are needed for something else

> *Sie ist – nein, war – die schönste aller Frauen*

But he does keep that not altogether sensible alliteration at the end:

> *Sie lachte, lebte, liebte ungeniert.*

One rare example where at least the alliterative effect is an easy one to maintain, because some of the English words – *lived, loved, liked* – are cognates of the German. The German verbs, in this case, are actually *laughed* (also a cognate of the English word), *lived, loved*, and we're down from four to a trio so as to be able to fit that big word *ungeniert* ('unabashedly') into this incredibly tight line.

And so we come to the lovers' tragic end, where first Pyramus and then Thisbe stab themselves. But the emptiness of the language means that the pathos it seems to expect is unearned. (Plenty of *bathos*, though, if that's what you're after?) And so the death of Pyramus is not experienced by an audience as altogether tragic.

> Come, tears, confound!
> Out, sword, and wound
> The pap of Pyramus:
> Ay, that left pap,
> Where heart doth hop.
> Thus die I, thus, thus, thus!

And he duly stabs himself *in that left pap where heart doth hop* (sob . . .).

Frank's German doesn't have the benefit of those ludicrous hop/pap sounds, so he does this instead:

> *Aug, träne nich'!*
> *Stich, Dolch, und brich*
> *Den Busen Pyramus'.*
> *Ja, links den Bus',*
> *Dem Herz zum Gruß,*
> *Ich sterben muss, muss, muss.*

If we were interested in meaning alone, we might translate that as 'Eyes, no tears; / Stab, dagger, and break / the breast of Pyramus. / Yes, the breast to the left, / As a greeting to the heart. / Die I must, must, must.' But look down the right-hand side, and you'll see Frank has Pyramus drag the rhyme out over four lines. Previously his lines have rhymed in pairs (the previous speech has lines ending *Schreck, Fleck, lupft, mein, sein, gerupft, gut, Blut, fürchterlich, Hirn, Lebenszwirn, mich*) – but now he just keeps going.

Pyram-us', first. To rhyme with *Bus'*.

Oh, and *Gruß*.

Oh, and also *muss, muss, muss*.

The apostrophes at the end of the lines show contractions where he has to curtail words artificially to make those rhymes almost-work. It's terrible. (I love it.)

And we have that reliably foolish repetition – that gift to an actor – and there's more to come.

> Now am I dead,
> Now am I fled;
> My soul is in the sky.
> Tongue, lose the light.

Moon, take thy flight.
Now die, die, die, die, die.

Nun stirb, nun stirb, nun stirb.

Writing about precision, back in Chapter 1, I said that nobody dies generically. Pyramus is an exception – *now die die die – now am I dead* . . . – but this is not supposed to be good playwriting. Obviously nobody cries.

Pyramus's death – with, as his speech suggests, not one but multiple stab wounds – is exaggerated and potentially very gory.* Into this scene of appalling bloody carnage trips young Thisbe, with the delightfully simple entrance line:

Asleep, my love?

(One of the biggest laughs of the night, as it often is.)

Du schläfst, mein Schatz?

Flute/Thisbe now gets carried away with metaphors when describing her lost love, and waxes horticultural:

These lily lips,
This cherry nose,
These yellow cowslip cheeks
Are gone, are gone:
Lovers, make moan.
His eyes were green as leeks.

---

* Copious visible blood is an absolute requirement. The most famous prior telling of the Pyramus and Thisbe story, in Ovid's *Metamorphoses*, describes how it is his blood that gives the mulberries their colour. (These being the mulberry trees that – inexplicably – comprise the above-mentioned cherry orchard.) In *Titus Andronicus* (a play that knows a lot of blood when it sees it), Martius makes reference to Pyramus, 'When he by night lay bathed in maiden blood . . .'

Most evocative. The German metaphors are likewise not altogether controlled:

> *Dein Lilienmund,*
> *Die Nase bunt,*
> *Dein Ohr wie Rosenkohl,*
> *Dein Aug, so rot,*
> *Ist tot, ist tot,*
> *Wie wird dein Kopf so hohl.*

Yes, he has lily lips. But now he also has a Brussels-sprout ear? The German means:

> Your lily mouth
> Your colourful nose
> Your ear like a Brussels sprout,
> Your eye so red
> Is dead, is dead,
> How hollow is your head.

Sounds like a proper beauty, that Pyramus.

Dein Aug, so rot, / Ist tot, ist tot . . . is a lovely replication of *are gone, are gone* . . ., I think.

Thisbe's ending is unlike the rest of the scene, however. I feel it is mostly *not* funny. Apart from the brief interruption for the leek simile, which is irresistible, it is not full of laughs. I always admire an actor who can resist being borne along by the momentum of the audience's laughter, and draw it back – and hold just a moment of poignancy. There is a control, restraint here, the briefest moment of genuine human pathos, just a touch of proper Thisbe magic. And if Thisbe magic is . . .

 . . . well, it's the name of the book. Oh. Words are funny things when you stop to notice them.

And a postscript, while we're on the subject of *not* laughing . . .

One of the prose heckles from the Very Clever audience is as follows, responding to Snout as the talking Wall:

> It is the wittiest partition that ever I heard discourse, my lord.

There is a joke in there, and I'm grateful to the footnote in the new Arden edition for explaining it because I didn't know it even existed. The note begins:

> **partition** punning on the meanings (1) wall; (2) a section of an academic treatise. Demetrius may imply that even Snout's lines are more intelligent than such learned treaties . . .

And here is Frank's German:

> *Ich hab mein Lebtag keine Wand so witzig reden hören, mein Fürst.*

in which you can see he ignores the *partition* specifics and reverts to that word *Wand* – wall – so there is no double meaning in the German, and so no joke. I find it hard to care about this one. The line was played uncut on Thursday (despite not being funny any more, it still makes sense in its simple single meaning), but nobody laughed at Demetrius's erudite double meaning that night, nor at any performance I have ever seen. This particular joke was lost well before the translation.

As ever, of course, the confident translator takes opportunities when they are presented to him, even if they aren't in the source text because they simply couldn't be. Shakespeare was at least partly limited by the possibilities of English, just as Frank is by German. And Shakespeare was also in the unfortunate position of writing this play in the mid-1590s, and therefore unable to give his audience little metatheatrical winks about other texts that hadn't been written yet. Frank, on the other hand . . .

>Shakespeare: I fear my Thisbe's promise is forgot.
>Günther: *Vergisst mich Thisbe, das ist hier die Frage.*

Will Thisbe forget me? wonders Pyramus.
>Ah . . . – he muses – *that is the question . . .*

Chapter 23

Red' gelahrt on weise

(on research)

> *As Shafalus to Procrus, I to you!*

We've just seen how Frank Günther created an equivalent effect for his German actors to milk from this line. And, while I'll admit I'd never actually looked up Shafalus and Procrus before now, you can bet Frank did when figuring out what to do about them.

Almost every translator I spoke to mentioned the research that informed their work. They described translating from well-footnoted modern editions; expressed gratitude for digital access to the world's libraries; name-checked Google. When Chico was working out how to activate his *Cry havoc!* exclamation, it was access to footage of Marlon Brando delivering the line that unlocked it for him.

If you were a translator trying to decide how to replace the apparent code 'MOAI' on the love letter Malvolio finds in *Twelfth Night*, there are places you could go to read about all the multiple interpretations that have been suggested for its significance, in order to commit to a theory.*

---

* One of the theories is that it's a mistake caused by a mistranslation. We'll not dwell on that.

You could find out from a footnote or an online dictionary that when Othello intends to prove Desdemona 'haggard', he's drawing on hawking vocabulary. (It's a hawk caught when already an adult. Maybe you knew that – I didn't.) But we'll look later at a bit of *Romeo and Juliet* in Boris Pasternak's translation, and I can't help wondering how on earth *he* knew what a 'tithe-pig' was, working in the early 1940s and without access to a great and specialised library. In part, the answer comes from the old translators having had access to even *older* translations, into their language and others – likely to have been Pasternak's case.

I asked several interviewees how their Google-less predecessors had fared. Jean-Michel cited the moment in the old Laplace translation of *Macbeth*, in which a king appears who 'bears a glass', which was translated to suggest that he's holding a glass of wine or similar (it's a mirror). And Niels described one challenge faced by his nineteenth-century predecessor Edvard Lembcke, at the moment in *King Lear* when:

> the old king complains enigmatically about 'this mother', the '*hysterica passio*', which swells up towards his heart. Lear is male and cannot suffer from a female disease originating from the womb. Various editors have made various attempts at explaining this, but in my opinion, a satisfactory explanation was not achieved until Kaara L. Peterson published her article 'Historica Passio: Early Modern Medicine, *King Lear*, and Editorial Practice'.

Neither Lembcke, working on the play in the 1870s, nor Niels, who completed his translation in 1993, could access this piece of research.

Translators will draw on any annotated edition they can get their hands on, but nowadays most, as I've mentioned, work principally from the Arden. Some are quite devout in their adherence. We've referred already to the 'nunnery' question in *Hamlet* ('Get thee to a nunnery!') and the disputed possibility that it was a reference to a brothel, but Ádám follows the Arden (2nd series), edited by Harold Jenkins, 'and if Jenkins says no, I say no.'

Niels also refers to these lines in *The Merchant of Venice*:

> Bring them, I pray thee, with imagined speed
> Unto the tranect, to the common ferry
> Which trades to Venice.

The word *tranect* appears here – in the Quarto edition – for the first and last time in Shakespeare, or anywhere else. There's a possibility that this is a typesetter error, a rare variant on another word, or a bit of carelessness in writing.* Today's Arden and most other editions now go with 'traject', but the footnote Niels found back when he was mid-translation confirmed it was a sort of ferry across a river – and without that footnote, a translator might be quite lost. (Though, OK, the prefix is at least a part of a clue here, as is the following phrase.)

An Arden *Two Gentlemen of Verona* footnote helpfully points out a possible confusion in the line we quoted at the start of the book – *There is a lady in Verona here* . . . because the conversation in question is actually taking place in Milan – had Shakespeare forgotten where his play's set? Is it just a slip of the quill? In the Danish version you saw on p.21, Niels did the playwright a favour and discreetly tidied it up for him – *Der er en dame fra Verona her* – the woman in question, who's here, is now just a lady *from* Verona, perfectly normal, nothing to see, move on . . .

Emine mentioned doing background reading that included law, state theory, contract terms, etc. For pre-internet translation – including the earlier works by those translators still working today – there will always be a specific bird or a flower or a Bed of Ware that you don't know.†

---

* It does appear in the *OED*, but the entry says: '*Obs.* Known only in the passage quoted [from *MofV*], and prob. only a misreading or misprint of *traiect*, TRAJECT, in It. *traghetto* a ferry.'

† The Great Bed of Ware, from the *Twelfth Night* quotation on pp.144–145, is a famously large bed (you might have guessed that), currently on display at London's Victoria and Albert Museum.

So spare a thought for those translators I sometimes find myself too quick to criticise for their sloppiness, but who were working without access to any of the resources we take for granted.

I look back at a few lines in the first act of *Hamlet*.

> Perhaps he loves you now,
> And now no soil nor <u>cautel</u> doth besmirch
> The virtue of his will

> Whiles, a puffed and reckless libertine,
> Himself the primrose path of dalliance treads
> And <u>recks not his own rede</u>.

> Upon my secure hour thy uncle stole
> With juice of cursed <u>hebona</u> in a vial . . .

> . . . a most instant <u>tetter</u> barked about,
> Most <u>lazar</u>-like with vile and loathsome crust
> All my smooth body

I know what all those underlined things mean. But only because I've looked them up, in annotated editions to which I have ready access, or online.

- 'Cautel' means trickery – here is what we find in great-grandfather Tristão's Brazilian translation, published in pre-Google 1933: *e óra nenhuma jaca e <u>machinação</u> manche a virtude ao seu querer*. Yes, machination will do nicely.
- He 'recks not his own rede' means that he pays no notice to his own advice (reck being an Old English word – to take notice of); Tristão has him treading the primrose path of dalliance, *<u>descuidoso da propria doutrina</u>* – careless of his own teaching.
- 'Hebona' (also 'hebenon') is some kind of poison, though we can't know for sure which it is – possibly hemlock. Tristão uses damned

cicuta, which is indeed hemlock – though there's at least some context for this one and he might have made a sensible guess, since this is the substance used to kill the king.
- 'Tetter' covers various kinds of itchy skin disease – Tristão takes a clue from Lazar-like, hence leprous: *uma instantanea lepra, de aspecto lazarento, estendeu a sua vil e repugnante crosta sobre todo o meu liso corpo* . . .

All these words of Tristão's are accurate to the meaning of the source text, as best we can confirm it now. I have no earthly idea how he managed to know what he knew. He was working from William Aldis Wright's 1904 'Cambridge edition', which has no glossary or explanatory notes, and his own personal copy is not significantly annotated. I have inherited quite a bit of his library, and it's overwhelmingly primary literary texts, not reference material – this obscure information sure as hell isn't in there either. I probably ought to give him a break.

Scholarship continues to evolve, though, and the grounds on which even diligent translators make their decisions can prove shakier than they've anticipated. I've mentioned the pleasing theory that the 'chimney-sweepers' in the *Cymbeline* song were supposed to be dandelions. As I said, though, doubt has been cast on that thesis, and nowadays it's not given much credence. In the interim, however, there were enough translators who were keeping abreast of evolving Shakespearean interpretations but who were not fortune tellers, so there are translations that can be dated to that span of years when the belief was confidently circulating. Jean-Michel's 2000 translation keeps chimney-sweepers (*'Tous, beaux garçons, filles fières, / Tels de ramoneurs devientront poussière.'*), but there's a note by Margaret Jones-Davies referencing what was then believed to be the alternative meaning. Niels's translation of the stanza ends with this couplet:

Mælkebøtter blomstrer kort
går i fnug og blæses bort.

Mælkebøtte means 'dandelions'. The translation was done in 2017, one of the years in which this reading was widely believed correct. Like most translators I know, Niels keeps a note of potential amendments for future editions. Though his astonishing six-volume complete plays was concluded and the final volume published in 2018, the work goes on.

Incidentally, I once asked him what sort of things were on that list he was keeping of slip-ups to amend in future editions. He told me about the absolute worst mistake, an unforgiveable moment in one of the plays where one of the lines is 'defective' because it's unaccountably missing two syllables. It is so *embarrassing* (his word).

Two entire syllables. The shame! I honestly don't know how he sleeps at night.

Chapter 24

che l'ordine va spezzato . . .

(on word order)

We all know how *Romeo and Juliet* ends.

There is a lot of dying, with Juliet the last to go. After her death, however, we still have about 150 lines left in the play, as the other characters discover the tragic scene, and matters are sadly concluded. The play ends with a sombre rounding-up speech by Prince Escalus, three slow rhymed couplets, coming to rest on

> For never was a story of more woe
> Than this of Juliet and her Romeo.

More than one translator was adamant that their translation should conclude on Romeo's name, and not Juliet's – sure, he gets the flashy ending with the rhyme, but it's Juliet to whom the line should actually give pre-eminence. The boy's name might come first in the title (as boys typically do, in Shakespeare's *Antony and Cleopatra*, 'Pyramus and Thisbe', *Troilus and Cressida*), but Juliet is arguably the central character who evolves the most dramatically in the play, and whose death concludes it, and Shakespeare ends his script with this story of 'Juliet and *her* Romeo'. It's about Juliet, and someone who in this story exists in relation to Juliet.

Niels speaks highly of the old Lembcke translation:

En større Sorg i Verden ingen ved
end Romeos og Julies Kærlighed*
[A greater sorrow in the world nobody knows
than Romeo and Juliet's love]

But Niels himself prioritised putting Juliet's name first:

For ingen ofred mer for større tro
end <u>Julie</u> og hendes Romeo.

The Thai translation maintains it, too. As I've mentioned, the play is called:

โรเมโอและจูเลียต

So if you happen to know that the Thai word for *and* is **และ** (pronounced láe) then you can deduce its closing words:

จูเลียตและโรเมโอ

Some translations do end with Juliet because, simply, there are some languages in which she's easier to rhyme. (Never was a tale of such regret, / Than this of . . . etc.) But woe/Romeo was an easy win for Shakespeare, so he didn't need to construct anything overly forced.

The three languages I translate are closely related, and all have some kinship to English. Things like word order and sentence structure work very similarly (as they do not when compared to most of the world's languages). If I wanted to, I could start translating a sentence without knowing where it's going, and discover it along the way. I could follow the thread of the source language, unspooling it as I translate in real time, and still end up with an English that's constructed plausibly.

---

* Ah, we've met this troublesome Danish word for 'love' before.

That last sentence in Spanish, say, might be:

Podría seguir el hilo del idioma original, desenrollándolo mientras lo traduzco en tiempo real, y aún así terminar con un inglés construido de manera plausible.

It doesn't mirror the English exactly word for word, but you can look at the components and see it's close, at least in structural terms. But that is not always the case. Some languages have much greater flexibility of word order, particularly languages that are inflected and can therefore signal what syntactical part a word plays in the sentence by its ending (so where you actually *position* it doesn't matter). Latin is one such. So when we were talking about the Brazilian translator trying to draw the maximum impact from the battle-cry in the line *Cry havoc and let slip the dogs of war*, a Latin translator could simply bring the word to the front of the line. *Cladem* proclamabit!

Word order in some languages is governed by very specific rules that are unlike English. (Japanese and Korean verbs should sit at the end of their sentences, say.) Others are built of quite different units. The different rules are – as so often with languages – also what bring different possibilities. English strongly encourages subject-verb-object in most sentences, facilitating a big reveal of a surprising object noun. For instance: today, for breakfast, I had a croissant, a cup of coffee and a snowmobile. But in English, it's harder to deliver a big reveal of a surprising verb. We English speakers can't do 'I went into town today, where I a movie watched, and a pair of shoes bought, and a quick cup of coffee and a sandwich poisoned.'

It's odd to force one language arbitrarily to abide by the constraints of another.* But it's a circle that translators are for ever trying to square.

---

* Though we do it. Which is why I said 'arbitrarily to abide' rather than 'to arbitrarily abide', because one of the less convincing historic explanations for our funny ideas about splitting infinitives in English came from the idea that *Latin* doesn't allow for such a thing – despite the fact that I am not writing this in Latin now.

Shakespeare wrote a particular line because the materials and conventions of English meant that he could; my language does not encourage the same sort of behaviour, yet I do need to make it work somehow . . .

Take a look at these three high-intensity dramatic moments:

1)
Methinks I should know you and know this man,
Yet I am doubtful; for I am mainly ignorant
What place this is and all the skill I have
Remembers not these garments; nor I know not
Where I did lodge last night. Do not laugh at me,
For, as I am a man, I think this lady
To be my child Cordelia.

(Lear, *King Lear*)

2)
Were you a woman, as the rest goes even,
I should my tears let fall upon your cheek
And say, 'Thrice welcome, drowned Viola.'

(Sebastian, *Twelfth Night*)

3)
. . . And say besides, that in Aleppo once,
Where a malignant and a turbanned Turk
Beat a Venetian and traduced the state,
I took by th' throat the circumcised dog,
And smote him – thus!

(Othello, *Othello*)

All three are moments of high dramatic charge, from late in their respective plays. In the first, Lear is waking from his madness and at last he sees clearly again, and is confronted with his daughter whom he has so mistreated. The second is another reunion – twins Sebastian and Viola, separated by a shipwreck, re-find one another, though there's a moment of confusion as Viola is dressed as a boy, so they look (so goes the conceit) very alike. And Othello, at the end of a big narrative speech, suddenly draws a dagger that nobody knew he had, and stabs himself.

All three depend for their effect on where the line ends, on the actor being able to land on the right word.

Lear needs to speak haltingly – the speech is fragmented, the lines mostly irregular. – . . . [pause] – *And to speak plainly* . . . – [pause] . . . He's just recovering consciousness, waking from what Cordelia calls 'his ungoverned* rage', and we who are listening to him need to be unsure that he really is restored, that he really is going to recognise his daughter. Emotionally it's one of the highest-stakes moments of the play. And we don't know for sure that the recognition will happen until the very last word of the sentence (he stops speaking there, never finishing his line) – *I think this lady / To be my child* . . . [yes? . . . yes?] . . . Cordelia. [Yes!] Shakespeare is giving his actor great potential here.

The reunion in the second is different – inasmuch as, this being a comedy about separated twins, we all knew they'd be reunited eventually, didn't we? But it's a touching moment, for the characters' disbelief (and Sebastian's confusion) – though this is not quite the final moment, as it develops further, and it'll be a little while before they share a hug . . . But now, when Sebastian speaks his sister's name, this is actually the first time we've ever heard it. We're only a few minutes from the end of the play, and he recognises her, and she – who has been pretending to be 'Cesario' for most of the last couple of performance hours – has her name again. *Thrice welcome*, . . . *drowned* . . . *Viola*. (Aaaah.)

And finally Othello, who quickly draws a knife and stabs himself on the word *thus*. And so the *thus* in question sits at the end of the speech. Shakespeare is not always naturalistic (Othello will yet die on a rhyming couplet, and few people do that), but he is playable. It would be asking a lot of an actor to stab himself to death and *then* do a whole massive speech.

An actor would struggle if the lines were ordered, say, like this:

---

* την ακυβέρνητη *ζωή* του in the Kapsalis translation, now his ungoverned *zoí* – life.

> And say beside that in Aleppo <u>thus</u>
> I smote a turbanned and malignant Turk,
> Who had traduced the state, beat a Venetian,
> For which offence, that circumcisèd dog
> I took by th' throat.

In that scenario, either you stab yourself on *thus* but then keep talking without breaking rhythm for four more lines, or you *say* you stabbed yourself *thus* but don't actually do anything until after all those other words. You might get away with the former if you're in a Verdi opera and need to finish your aria, but not here.* So Shakespeare does his actor a favour, and ends with the stabbing. Blah blah blah . . . *Thus*.

Though we acknowledge that after his dramatic *Thus!* stabbing and a couple of reaction lines by other characters, Othello does rally impressively for that final rhyming couplet on which to die. In Verdi's version there are only a few short lines to sing after 'Ho un'arma ancor!' – I still have a weapon! – but it's pretty hard to sing anything full-voiced when one is dragging oneself across the floor, even were one unstabbed . . .

(Timing is everything. Argentine novelist/translator Carlos Gamerro points to the scene where Hamlet discovers Polonius behind a curtain, and with a 'Dead for a ducat, dead!', he stabs him:

> it is quite possible to kill a man while saying these words. But if Hamlet has to get through, as in Rolando Costa Picazo's translation, with '¿*Qué es esto? ¿Una rata que espía? ¡Apuesto un ducado a que es hombre muerto!*' even the venerable counselor will have enough time to get away.)

Shakespeare creates his effects – or enables his actors to do so – using tools that English allows him. What happens, then, in a language where

---

* In the scene we've just looked at, Pyramus does exactly this – he stabs himself repeatedly and then makes his neatly rhyming valedictory speech, but that's the point: it is not supposed to be good playwriting.

ending on a 'Cordelia' or a 'Viola' or a 'thus' is against the rules?

Salah Baban's Sorani Kurdish translation of *Othello* doesn't retain the effect at all, but then the function of the translation is different – in a culture where classic plays are more likely to be the object of literary study than experienced in performance, this matters less.

Chinese is a language of great flexibility, allowing So easily to land his line home on 'Viola': 欢迎啊，淹死了的薇奥丽!

Just as Turkish could do it with Cordelia – . . . *Bu da benim evladım Cordelia*.

In Japanese, the pressure is to put Cordelia earlier in the line, with the verb at the end, and previous translations have indeed typically ended on the 'think'. But Sho manoeuvred things around to bring the main verb forward and end with Cordelia – or rather, Cordelia da to (コーディリアだと), ending on a noun and particle. Sho explained that this use of anastrophe (inversion) is unusual, but he did it anyway – and (like his use of uncommon-in-Japanese rhyme) in fact the unusualness actually draws more attention to it, the inversion is all the more dramatic, theatrical.

And finally, returning to that word-order question that Emine and I discussed outside the theatre back in Istanbul (. . . *signifying* nothing), she did indeed find a way to bring the whole speech to rest on that heavy monosyllable: *Gürültü patırtı işte baştan sona, anlamı yok* **hiç**. (It's all the more impactful because Emine creates a rhyme pattern for the speech and this is the line that sharply breaks it.) The other Japanese translator whose work we've seen, Kazuko Matsuoka, likewise finds a simple and elegant solution to this one, securing something resembling a terminal *nothing* for Macbeth, keeping to the Japanese convention of ending on a verb by concluding not with the terminal noun but with a verb of negation – ない – *nai*, a very final monosyllabic '*does not exist*', of which she's made *meaningfulness* the subject. Like Sho – and indeed like almost all the good contemporary translators we've seen here – she's mindful of dramatic effect. She was for years a regular collaborator with the director Yukio Ninagawa, whose productions I never got to see in Japanese, though I do nonetheless feel very attached to one moment in particular . . .

Chapter 25

Таква музика е слатка сал

(on languages of other kinds)

If you ever come round to my place, you'll see a large and striking print hanging over the entrance stairs. If I told you it depicted a character in a Shakespearean scene, you would know at once that you're looking at Puck.

The picture captures a moment from the Ninagawa production of *A Midsummer Night's Dream* when the setting is transitioning from the court to the fairies' forest, and suddenly there's white-clad Puck leaping through the air, against a backdrop that is mostly black but for a few columns of light (created by fine sand). That moment in the production, with the strange effect used to create those beams of light, was described by Nicholas Garland, the artist who made this picture, as one of the most exciting things he had ever seen on stage.

The picture is exhilarating, and it is full of movement. (It surprises me whenever I come home that Puck is *still* in mid-leap where I left him.) It is black and white – far more black than white – and it is a woodcut. Large amounts of black ink have been applied on a huge solid block of wood to create an impression of quick airborne movement and light. I don't really understand how it works, but it might just be magic.

Something about the Puck whom I know from Shakespeare's play is captured in that picture, something that the artist saw in him, too.

An observation, then an interpretation, then an expression. Faithful to something essential in the object, but a *personal* creation, too.

A nineteenth-century English painting of the encounter between Romeo and Juliet is one person's imaginative attempt to evoke – to express – two people and a moment. A beautiful print made in art deco-period France might have the same subject (it, too, depicts an embrace between these same two characters), but its artist, George Barbier, is using entirely different techniques (materials, colour palette, line . . .) and the image is configured differently, the characters differently balanced – using different-but-related languages to create an entirely different mood. You could not mistake one for the other, but both are readings and re-expressions of a common source.

In the text of Shakespeare's *Romeo and Juliet*, the first thing that Juliet says to her mother, Lady Capulet, is 'Madam, I am here.' The girl is presenting herself – not filled with warmth, but respectful, dutiful. In the Northern Ballet production of Prokofiev's *Romeo and Juliet*, Lady Capulet enters Juliet's chamber for their first encounter, and Juliet – Saeka Shirai, in the performance I saw in Stratford last summer – hurries to kneel a moment before her mother, her brow to her mother's hand. She says nothing in words, of course; what her body conveys is respectfulness, dutifulness. 'Madam,' she is saying, 'I am here.'

The Prokofiev version is the musical text chosen for Matthew Bourne's *Romeo and Juliet*, too. Here, at the first proper meeting between the lovers,* Romeo sees Juliet and holds out his hand to her, and they dance – beginning almost rigidly *palm to palm*, not unlike *holy palmers' kiss*. And here begins their sonnet. For the rest of the scene they move between formally matching the other partygoers, and getting a little carried away to something more sensual – though in fact barely touching – as the music moves. (They don't make it to the crucial kiss in this scene, but when they do, at the close of Act I, it is definitely more epic than sonnet.) Prokofiev's musical score, said Bourne, 'becomes the script or the words'.

---

* When I saw it at Sadlers Wells in 2024, Rory Macleod and Monique Jonas.

Melissa McCarthy described the moment forty minutes into this production when she gasped, 'because I realised that no one was talking.' The dancers 'so embodied their characters' pain and love and humour and fear,' she said, 'that my mind heard every line, every thought.' As if that were the greatest compliment one might pay this brilliant piece of storytelling – actual words would have been superfluous. (Bourne is a first-rate storyteller, apart from anything else.)

After all, the lines given to an actor do often serve to introduce – instruct – their movement. 'Farewell, farewell,' says talking-Romeo, in Juliet's bedroom. 'One kiss, and I'll descend.' And so that is what the actor does. In the final scene, Juliet discovers that Romeo has left her no poison – 'drunk all,' she says, 'and left no friendly drop / To help me after?' – the actor tips the bottle upside down and nothing comes out. In the ballet, Shirai did the same, but the action alone is enough – we don't miss the words.

There is already plenty of comedy in *A Midsummer Night's Dream* that is not purely linguistic, but rather situational – it has many narrative pleasures that can be followed without much language at all. When Hermia and Lysander are finally alone in the forest, there is a playful little exchange when Lysander discovers that he won't be allowed to sleep on the bank (*encosta!*) beside her. He tries more than once; she sweetly rebuffs him more than once.

> Nay, good Lysander; for my sake, my dear,
> Lie further off, yet. Do not lie so near.

At the revival of Frederick Ashton's one-act ballet, *The Dream*, in Covent Garden in summer 2024, using bodies and choreographed movement and Mendelssohn, dancers Isabel Lubach and Benjamin Ella got exactly the same laugh, in exactly the same place. No loss at all.

The music we hear and the performances we see combine to make the meaning. When a ballet Romeo holds out his arm to Juliet to begin, say, a *pas de deux*, does that gesture of his 'mean' 'I take thee at thy word. / Call me but love, and I'll be new baptized'? It is the equivalent invitation to engage, certainly. It is perhaps just a question of what sort of information can be conveyed with music, and how precisely, but the movement and the music in combination are a mode of expression both more and less capable than the words they replace.

Liszt's *Hamlet* symphonic poem summons a shifting mood, rather than an exact narrative, and it's not unusual for music to tell us a story, even if the story is only impressionistic and only formed in our heads as we listen. (You hear a turn to a minor key and don't think, 'ah, now we enter a minor key', you think 'uh-oh, things are getting bad . . .'). But in this case, there is a short *Hamlet and Ophelia* ballet (originally *Hamlet Prelude*, also choreographed by Ashton) that uses the music to shape a scene, as we watch the collapsing relationship of the two characters – danced by Cesar Corrales and Sarah Lamb, when I saw it.

After a brief initial moment of Ophelia pining, we watch Hamlet alone, in a wordless soliloquy, as it were – tormented, frustrated, confused – before he is joined by Ophelia to dance together. For Ophelia's return, the high drama ends on some fortississimo low strings to be replaced – after a long pause – by slow woodwind playing *dolce ed espressivo* (sweet and expressive), a moment of calm before they dance together. But they share only the occasional tender moment ('I did love you once'), and mostly dance without much closeness – Liszt marks the score with the word '*ironisch*' – moving to something dark and more dramatic, aggressive (he points, to send her away – *to a nunnery!*), and then Ophelia, trying to stay on *pointe*, finds she can't sustain that poise and stumbles off, dislocated, leaving him to his angst – they don't dance together again, though a little later she drifts past in the background. The music certainly *seems* to be telling the story.

The Winter's Tale has a ballet, too, with music by Joby Talbot. Where those 'inch-thick' moments with Leontes conveys the fraying of his self-control, in the ballet, this happens not with harsh packed consonants and short vowels and monosyllables, but with ominous percussive music, mostly low-pitch instrumentation plus what the composer described as 'shrieking E-flat clarinets', frantic, jagged, scuttling movement and a change to the lighting state.

The type of precision I've been writing about in this book is particular to language – or rather, the language of *words*. Words have a relationship to the world they describe that is not the same as music's. One cannot compose a piece of music that *means* 'Angels and ministers of grace defend us'. Or 'His eyes were green as leeks.' Though Mendelssohn himself thought about it differently; for him, words:

> seem to me so ambiguous, so vague, so unintelligible when compared with genuine music, which fills the soul with a thousand things better than words. What the music I love expresses to me, is not thought too *indefinite* to be put into words, but, on the contrary, too *definite*.

We know already that while translation is always about losses, it is also about gains. Any language can do things that English cannot; music can convey effects that are beyond even the most artfully turned words.

Most of us connect viscerally – and sentimentally – to music. If you hear an old song you love but played without any words, it will touch you more readily than hearing the lyrics spoken, unclothed in their music.

In *The Taming of the Shrew*, Petruchio has the lines:

> I come to wive it wealthily in Padua;
> If wealthily, then happily in Padua.

They are used verbatim in a *Kiss Me, Kate* song; even reading them on the page now, I hear the words paced according to that tune, and no syllable-counting examination of Shakespeare's verse will ever dislodge that from my ear. The rhythm is rigidly predetermined because the lines are scored to music. In the musical version, there are fewer heavy stresses.

> If <u>weal</u>thily, then <u>hap</u>pily in <u>Pa</u>dua.

The syllables *weal* . . . , *hap* . . . and *Pad* . . . are slightly longer-held notes – dotted crotchets at the start of their respective four-beat bars; the singer has no sense of obligation to speak alternate syllables with anything like iambic evenness.

(Certainly the way it's scored by Cole Porter is more natural to our speech rhythm than any attempt to stress alternate syllables – If <u>weal</u>-thi-<u>ly</u> then <u>hap</u>-pi-<u>ly</u> in <u>Pa</u>-du-<u>ah</u>?)

That *Midsummer Night's Dream* line I quoted on p.76 that was performed as 'I am amazed at your passionate words' (with the Folio's additional word), rather than the Quarto version without the 'passionate') demonstrates just such another constraint. It had to be changed for this performance not because English (the language of the play's writing) is different from English (the language of the play's performance), but because the adjusted text was designed to be set to music, as part of the Benjamin Britten/Peter Pears opera. You might have spotted it as the title to Chapter 16.

Like any language, there are many things music does better than any other. Music, for one thing, is unusual in being a language where many voices can happen at once doing different things – two themes interplaying with harmonies from somewhere else, repeatedly overlayered, weaving together fruitfully rather than distracting.

Shakespeare has a scene in his *Romeo and Juliet* that puts Mercutio and the Montagues, and also Tybalt and the Capulets, plus Romeo himself, all on the stage together. There's a fair bit going on. Now, imagine he had added Juliet, and also the Nurse, and then he'd made the scene come to a head with all of them *talking at the same time* – not saying the same things, mind – well, of course it would be impossible to hear anything meaningfully. In *West Side Story*, Leonard Bernstein can do just that, and what he makes out of that scene – three high-voltage minutes called the 'Tonight Quintet' – is as thrilling as anything in the source play. The language of *West Side Story* – which is the language of a decent-sized orchestra, as well as lots of actors and singers and Stephen Sondheim's English – has some serious capacities. There are opportunities to be taken, and once again, the transition is full of gains.

The different parts appear on the score as parallel notated lines, and in the libretto they run vertically side by side; they are not superimposed when they are captured in print, because the language of text cannot be read like that. But the *expression* of music does not work like most languages – on a musical stage, we process them all together.

When Balthasar, in *Much Ado*, begins to play his music (introduced with a whole series of those *notes/noting/nothing* puns), the cynical Benedick is not so much moved as baffled:

> Is it not strange that sheep's guts should hale souls out of men's bodies?

And of course he's right – the workings upon us of stringed instruments, or any other moving art, are mysterious. Shakespeare's writing has spawned countless operas, ballets, musicals, paintings of scenes, and each one finds what it can in the source, and uses whatever particular resources it has to tell a story in the language of oil paint or semiquavers or choreography. Handled with technique and skill, it's amazing what you can do with sheep guts, or a hunk of soft wood, a scalpel and a lot of black ink.

Chapter 26

正当な順序の継続

(on bridges)

Among many fascinating things in the collection at the Shakespeare Birthplace Trust library is Haşim Bukozirov's prose translation of *Othello* into Azeri, published in Baku in the Arabic script in 1904.*

I turn straight to the end. Yes, there's something potentially resembling a 'thus' at the end of Othello's penultimate speech. Phew – that's a relief.

But some other things I noticed in those last couple of pages:†

- Shakespeare's original Cassio says: *I found it in my chamber, / And he himself confessed but even now, . . .* ; whereas the translation names the perpetrator – *I found it in my room <u>but Iago</u> has now confessed.*
- Shakespeare's Othello berates himself simply with *O fool, fool, fool!*; in Azeri, there's a pronoun subject: *Oh! <u>I</u> am a fool! <u>I</u> am a fool!*

---

* As we've seen for Turkish – to which it's closely related – Azeri at the start of the twentieth century used predominantly the Arabic script, as it still does today in Iran.

† I say 'I' notice. I do not know Azeri, and I can't read Arabic script. As so often in this book, I called upon the kindness of a friend (John, in this case), to help me find what I was looking for.

- Shakespeare's Cassio says (of Rodrigo): *and even but now he spake, / After long seeming dead*; but in Azeri, Rodrigo didn't speak *just now*, he spoke *finally*; and Cassio says not only that Rodrigo *previously seemed dead* but explicitly that *he came back to life*.
- Then Lovodico begins his speech: *You must forsake this room and go with us . . .* – which is the same in Azeri, except with an added vocative to start: <u>Now, Othello</u>, *you must follow us*, etc. A minor enough change, no big deal.
- And Othello asks that they speak of him as *one that loved not wisely, but too well*, and one whose hand *Like the base Judean, threw a pearl away / Richer than all his tribe . . .* Though in the Azeri, he was just *a man crazed by love*, etc. (the 'not wisely but too well' isn't exactly replicated), and he says that *like an idiot* <u>Hindu</u> (huh?) *he threw away the most valuable pearl of* <u>all the treasures of his homeland</u>.
- Then Othello concludes, pre-stabbing, with that *malignant and a turbanned Turk* story – which in this version has become . . . something else entirely . . .
- And finally, at the end of the scene and the play, Shakespeare's Lodovico describes Iago as: *More fell* [meaning *savage*] *than anguish, hunger, or the sea . . .* – but there are only two comparators here – he's *more merciless than famines and plagues* (plagues?), and he says he'll relay the sad news to the state – or, in Azeri, specifically to *the Senate*.

There's a lot about this that confuses me – not least the fact that, since this translation is not in fixed verse lines, there are no formal constraints of space, so why would you cut things out, or add padding? And why would you change the sequencing of a list if you're not trying to fit into a rigid metre? And how did Shakespeare's 'Judean' become Bukozirov's 'Hindu'? Those are not the same thing at all.

For an explanation of these apparent eccentricities, we turn to *Отелло*, a Russian verse translation by P.I. Veinberg, first published in 1864 . . .

. . . in which Cassio names the perpetrator, and Othello calls himself a fool with an explicit pronoun, and 'even but now' has become 'finally', and Rodrigo suddenly revives, and Lodovico adds a vocative (*Now, Othello* . . .), and Othello says he loved madly, and the Judean has become an Indian, and the pearl's more precious than the treasures of his country; and, yes, admittedly Iago is still compared to three things, rather than the Azeri two, but they are the ocean, and famine *and plague*; and Lodovico says he'll take the news back home to the Senate. (Which in Veinberg's Russian rhymes, as it did in Shakespeare's English.)

I don't know whether Haşim Bukozirov knew any English; but what he produced was a translation of the Veinberg Russian Shakespeare – a second-hand translation that we call a 'bridge' or 'relay' translation. We can see a clear two-step process of evolution, two translations in series, where Veinberg's decisions feed Bukozirov's.

Shakespeare:

> Like the base Judean, threw a pearl away / Richer than all his tribe.

Veinberg's Shakespeare:

> как глупец-индиец, я отбросил / Жемчужину, дороже всех сокровищ / Его страны;
>
> (like a foolish Indian, I threw away / The pearl, dearer than all the treasures / of his country)

Bukozirov's Veinberg's Shakespeare:

> احمق هندو کمی وطنیمگ جمیع خزینه لریندن قیمتلو مروارینی توللادیم..

[*Ahmaq Hindu kimi vətənimæg cæmi xəzinə(-)lərindən qiymətlu
mərvarini tulladım*]

(like an idiot Hindu I threw away the most valuable pearl of
all the treasures of our homeland)

The 'treasure of the homeland' is in the Russian, which is the source for the Azeri. And the Azeri 'Hindu' came from Veinberg's 'Indian', because of the Russian translator's own choice of source text – the Folio seems to say *Judean*, but many more recent (including the Arden today) assume that *Indian* is what's intended; either way, it's clear that the big leap happened before the Russian, and the Azeri was cleaving to that.

There are two interesting features in the Azeri for which the Russian predecessor can't be blamed, incidentally.

Shakespeare has Othello recount his stabbing of a 'malignant and a turbanned Turk'; in Russian, he's merely a 'турок злой', an evil Turk (no sign of the turban anywhere) – but the Azeri has removed the man entirely.

And as the speech ends – where Shakespeare has his dramatic *thus* – we get the Azeri stage direction

(اوز بوغازین کسیر)

– he slits his throat.

Though rather wonderfully, it actually appears on the page like this:

(اوز بوغا

زین کسیر)

with the word for throat literally slit in two.

Now, the Russian has Othello simply stab himself (*Закалывается.*), as the English does, but the Azeri translator gets specific. This is arguably a bad idea. If you thought that as an actor you'd struggle to keep talking (in fixed rhyme!) after stabbing yourself, just try doing it after you've specifically *slit your own throat* . . .

When I wrote that my great-grandfather's *Hamlet* was the first translation of a Shakespeare play published in Brazil, one might argue that the statement was not exactly true. Shakespeare translations had appeared before; they were, however, translations of French translations, not directly of the Shakespeare texts themselves. Tristão's was the first from English, the first without a bridge.

Bridge translations, or relay translations, used to be commonplace, and they do still happen. They can be problematic in terms of power relations and politics, and distortions are inevitable, but they are sometimes all we have. It's unsurprising that a translator in Baku should have had readier access to Russian than to English. The Shakespeare Birthplace Trust library also holds an 1892 Armenian translation of *Macbeth*, 'translated from German and Russian' – again, the historical dominance of Russian among lettered Armenians makes it a natural source. The first ever Arabic Shakespeare, that *Hamlet* with the happy ending, was done from French. (According to Margaret Litvin, from a version by Alexandre Dumas *père*, no less.)

One of the translations I've most enjoyed muddling my way through lately was Emanuel Ribeiro's version of *Romeo and Juliet* in Cape Verdean Creole (*kriolu kabuverdianu*). The language is a very old Portuguese Creole, and though it's the principle language for most Cape Verdeans, Portuguese is still everywhere on the islands, so unsurprisingly Creole tends to rely on Portuguese texts for bridge translations. In this pair of lines,

Romeu
   Y Santa ma Romeiro ka ten lábius?
Julieta
   Sim, ma so pa razá purke ês ê sábius.

those rhyming word are *lips* and *wise* (remember them?), which are a sort of fingerprint telling me that, for example, Ribeiro wasn't using Chico's translation as his source. This translation is shaped by whichever specific distortions happened upstream.

The translator Gregory Rabassa preserved his thoughts about his work in an excellently titled book, *If This Be Treason*. In it, he explains how a translator's reading experience, while similar in some ways to other people's, is unusual in that it is recorded; this reader's observations and choices are set down to be experienced by a whole new wave of readers, their reading experience spawned by – and mediated by – his. (Shaped, also, by the new language's requirements and possibilities, of course.) It is that translated text – the one that's had all these personal and linguistic influences brought to bear upon it – that then becomes a new source. And now the *only* source. Any feature of the text that has been 'changed' (other than the usual translation process whereby, you know, *everything* is changed) is unlikely ever to be changed back.

Anglophone directors or editors might be in a position to choose between marginally variant but equally plausible editions of *Hamlet* to work from. Translators and publishers in some cases are choosing between source *languages*, too. Even as I write, a translation of mine is currently being used as a source text for a translation into Telugu. There are few – if any – experienced literary translators who can translate Portuguese into Telegu; somewhat more if the source language is English. It is not, perhaps, optimal, but deemed to be much better than nothing.

Though English is now a lingua franca in many parts of the world, it hasn't been for very long. Looking back, those points when Shakespeare translations switched from regular bridges (through French, Russian, German) to direct from English, feel like watershed moments. In Brazil, in 1933, it happened with my great-granddad Tristão – a well-travelled man, highly proficient in English, and an Anglophile as well as a Francophile. He translated *Hamlet* from English, and now there's no going back.

Chapter 27

ти људи бесконачног језика

(on Shakespeare's languages)

If you thought Othello speaking Italian was about as Latinate as it gets, wait till you see what Henry Denison has done. In 1856, Denison, who I've always assumed was a schoolmaster – because, really, what else would he be?* – translated Shakespeare's *Julius Caesar* into Latin.

Denison faces some of the challenges one might expect of a language that matches up with only half of English, so when Cinna cries 'Liberty! Freedom!', the translator has little choice but to render it 'Libertas! Libertas!' ('Liberty' being the Latinate one that we've seen Othello use previously.)

At a glance, the translation mirrors the English quite reliably. Here's the opening speech, to compare with Shakespeare's:

Hence! home, you idle creatures, get you home!	*Hinc, domum, ignāvī; apagite, domum.*
Is this a holiday? What, know you not	*Num hodiē fēriās agitis? Quid? Nescītisne*

---

* Turns out he was a lawyer and a cricketer.

(Being mechanical) you ought not walk	*nefās esse cuivīs artificī diē profēstō deambulāre,*
Upon a labouring day, without the sign	*nisi īnsignibus artis suae indūtō?*
Of your profession? Speak, what trade art thou?	*Heus tū! Cujusnam artis tū artifex?**

You quickly get a sense of what he's up to. Though the translation is essentially prose, it's published nowadays in facing pages with the English and broken up as I've given it here, each line corresponding to one of Shakespeare's, so we always know where we are.

Denison does indeed take advantage of the flexibility of Latin word order, as suggested earlier, to make his Antony cry *Havoc!* with the greatest impact. He's built quite an expansive line in syllable terms – *cladem proclamabit, Bellonaeque canes in praedam immittet* – but I'm fairly confident his translation will never need to be spoken aloud in its entirety, so no matter . . .

Now, halfway through the play, Shakespeare surprises us by assassinating his title character (the play is about that event's consequences more than about the living man). When Caesar is stabbed at the Senate, he has a moment before dying to see that one of his killers is Brutus, whom he believed loyal, and he cries:

Et tu, Brute? – Then fall, Caesar.

It might be the most famous line in the play. But the *nagy kérdés* – the big question, I mean – is how do you translate 'Et tu, Brute' into Latin?†

---

* Please note: the *cujus* is not to be mistaken here for the Old French word for testicles.

† That 'Brute' being Brutus in the vocative case, which we don't have in our declension-deprived English. It's nice to have the opportunity to use it, and it will also come in handy for 'Friends, Romans, countrymen . . .' Here's a nice Scottish Gaelic vocative for you: *A chàirdean, a Ròmhanacha is fheara mo dhùthcha, aomaibh ur cluasan rium-sa* . . .

As a translator into English, I encounter this problem frequently. Writers in other languages often drop English words into their text, and I need to be able to make their English words stand out when surrounded by my also English words. Do I translate those words into the *other* language? But that doesn't work – Portuguese words in an English novel don't have the same status as English words in a Portuguese one. Can I replicate whatever I imagine is those words intended *effect*? (When *War and Peace* opens not in Russian but in French, that's telling us something about the aristocrats we're meeting and the type of education they've had.) Or do I just leave everything in English?

Henry V, Shakespeare's play celebrating the English victory over those terrible French people, was – inexplicably! – not performed in a French translation until a few decades ago. Which is possibly for the best not just politically but also translationally, since this play includes French-speaking characters, including France's Princess Katherine, whom the king intends to marry, and who is given French-medium English lessons, and features a conversation between her and the King that moves between the two (often error-strewn) languages. The easiest solution – which might prove the *only* solution – is to create a scene where Henry is speaking French, in contrast with Katherine who is, um . . . oh, so she's also speaking French? Except they mysteriously can't understand one another. And just crave your audience's forgiveness.

This scene didn't cause So Kwok Wan any particular trouble in Chinese – he replaced the default English with default Chinese and left the French as French. But when the *default* language is French? You can't retain a differentiation between the fluent speakers and the halting language learners – if your English king is now speaking perfect French, you surely can't have the French people being the only people speaking *broken* French. Nor can you really have the French people uniquely speaking English. And Jean-Michel explains that this problem is compounded for a French translator by the fact that the Francophones in the play (principally Katherine, her lady-in-waiting Alice and a soldier) speak a rather unusual French – 'a mixture of fifteenth-century French that Shakespeare would have heard from Huguenot people he knew in

London, but with mistakes'. Presumably Shakespeare here is doing his best rather than making *deliberate* mistakes? Anny Crunelle Vanrigh, Jean-Michel's colleague at Nanterre, believes these apparent mistakes in the French are because what we're seeing is actually Anglo-Norman – which I think is fascinating, though for a translator it hardly helps.

When translating for the subtitling and dubbing of the Kenneth Branagh film, Jean-Michel preserved two slightly different Frenches – the French characters using the old Shakespearean version and the English characters speaking 'correctly'. (He references another translation, by Geneviève and François Bournet, who make the Shakespearean French mediaeval.) But for publication and for performance, he had all his characters speak modern French – modernising and correcting Shakespeare:

Shakespeare French text: *Je te prie m'enseignez, il faut que je apprend à parler. Comment appelle vous le main en anglais?**
Déprats French text: *Je te prie de me l'enseigner; il faut que j'apprenne à parler. Comment dit-on la main en anglais?*

That's it. Everyone is just speaking French.

And with this, he accepted defeat, at least in some respects. When writing about this scene, he uses the phrase 'the failure of translation' for the first and last time. It is inevitable, he decided, that in French you will lose that sense of misunderstanding – especially regrettable in a play that's about the battle between the French and the English, so the fact that Katherine is learning the language of the victor is not irrelevant.

Though to compensate for the loss, Jean-Michel did at least take greater advantage of the obscene French puns on body parts (Katherine's English lesson here resembling William's Latin lesson that we saw Jean-Michel relishing in Chapter 10). In an English-medium production, when Alice teaches Katherine the English word neck ('de nique?'), it will be obvious to few people how obscene that sounds to contemporary French

---

* This is as per the First Folio, with just some slight spelling adjustments.

ears. (*Niquer*, to fuck, a relatively recent borrowing from the Arabic word, نيك.) The foot and the gown are both funnier to a French audience, too – the comedy reinforced in the original French production by a certain amount of unsubtle gesturing . . .

I should note that Jean-Michel does retain at least a touch of the play's original bilingualism, in the scene with Henry and Katherine, where the king gets to keep the odd carefully chosen *English* phrase amid his otherwise perfect French dialogue.

We can only be grateful that *Merry Wives* is not a play that has been translated into Latin, to the best of my knowledge. Nor have I yet found a Welsh-language translation of *Henry IV, Part 1*, which features a Welsh-language character who cannot be understood by most of the characters around her. Her husband Mortimer says:

> This is the deadly spite that angers me:
> My wife can speak no English, I no Welsh.

Unlike Princess Katherine, though, Shakespeare makes no effort to pin down Lady Mortimer's dialogue. The First Folio simply includes stage directions like

> (Lady Mortimer speaks to Mortimer in Welsh.)

It's not like the audience is supposed to understand anyway.

The stage direction does, however, mean that translation is built into any production of the play unless Lady Mortimer is excised from it. The actor playing her part will need some lines in Welsh, and Shakespeare hasn't bothered to supply them – but we do know what they need to mean, because Glendower helpfully tells us.

> (The Lady speaks again in Welsh.)

MORTIMER
> O, I am ignorance itself in this!

GLENDOWER
> She bids you on the wanton rushes lay you down
> And rest your gentle head upon her lap,
> And she will sing the song that pleaseth you,
> And on your eyelids crown the god of sleep . . .
> [etc.]

Which is lovely, but someone's going to have to get those lines translated into Welsh if we're going to do this scene.

The Welsh in *Henry IV, Part 1*, is weaponised as part of the play's ongoing power struggle, used to mark us-and-them divisions. Glendower says he will forbid Hotspur from altering a map; Hotspur says contemptuously:

> Let me not understand you, then: speak it in Welsh.

Oh, but:

> I can speak English, lord, as well as you,

Glendower replies.

Note that Shakespeare was writing this play sixty years after the then queen's father, Henry VIII, had passed the Act of Union, determining that the administration, governance and judiciary of Wales should all operate exclusively in English. It would take the Deddf yr Iaith Gymraeg, the Welsh Language Act, to put the two languages officially on an equal footing in Wales. (The Welsh Language Act was passed in 1993.)

In addition to French, Latin and Welsh, Shakespeare drops bits of other languages into his plays (Italian, Spanish, etc.), with the characters' uses of these being suggestive, sometimes comically, of their status, their education, their outsider-ness, of the barriers between couples and so on. As with the Welsh/English encounters, there can be fervently felt political considerations. And when all the original play's default English is being transformed into default something-else, the switching between languages needs a new equivalent, too.

Of course, what matters, both in Shakespeare's plays and in their translations, is that we can buy into whatever language the characters are speaking, and what the relationship between those languages is; whether the language is *actually* a logical one is irrelevant. If you know your Shakespeare, you might think it's a little jarring hearing 'To be, or not to be' rewritten in Portuguese or 'Romeo, Romeo, wherefore art thou Romeo?' in Tamil, or 'Our revels now are ended' in Thai or 'All the world's a stage' in French. But isn't Hamlet a Dane, and Juliet from Verona, and Prospero from Milan? And surely Jaques *should* be speaking French because he's from the court of a French duke? We've accepted them as English speakers for all this time, because that's the deal we've done with the playwright. Shakespeare has a lovely moment in *Pericles* (an apposite quote for every eventuality) where, in a play that jumps around *from bourn to bourn, region to region* (Tyre, Antioch, Tarsus, Pentapolis, Ephesus etc.), Gower apologises for a necessary artifice:

> By you being pardoned, we commit no crime
> To use one language in each several clime
> Where our scenes seems to live.

Just pretend, OK? Just go with it. Sometimes, a translator – of *Henry V* into French, say – has to resort to this. *You know the deal.*

One of my favourite bits of interlingual interpolation in Shakespeare is the episode in *All's Well That Ends Well* where Parolles is 'captured' by his own fellow soldiers just *pretending* to be the enemy. They blindfold him and swap their English (which we're already pretending is French) to talk among themselves in a foreign tongue. But because Parolles is a gifted linguist, who *hath a smack of all neighbouring languages*, they need to invent one. *Boskos thromuldo boskos!* one of them shouts. *Boskos vauvado. Kerelybonto.* And also *Manka revania dulche.* To which the only sensible response is *Oscorbidulchos volivorco.*

A terrified Parolles promises to share the secrets of his camp with his captors – his enemies, as he believes. *Acordo linta*, he's told. So there.

These bits, at least, should be easy to translate. *Oscorbidulchos volivorco* does not have any hidden meaning, so any language with the same very rough palette of sounds as English can keep it. Except that a quick online search tells me that in Polish, bosko is a word meaning 'sublimely'; and in New Testament Greek, it is a verb meaning 'put out to pasture'. Barbara Heliodora kept the same pretend language in Portuguese, though that 'acordo linta' is unitalicised in the dialogue, where an unlucky proofreader was presumably misled by the fact that – by unfortunate chance – *acordo* is in fact a perfectly real Portuguese word.

The illustrator Carson Ellis has created a wonderful children's picture book called *Du Iz Tak?*, in which all of the characters speak in an insect language. One of the many reasons I love to use it in translation workshops is that the book's various editions around the world have translated Ellis's language into an alternative insect language that is, respectively, German-adjacent, Polish-adjacent, Chinese-adjacent, and so on. Where U.S. insects say 'Du Iz Tak?', German ones say 'Wazn Teez?', Polish ones 'Zu dę daś', Chinese ones '哆悉哒' (Duō xī dā), and so on.

Where Shakespeare invents *Oscorbidulchos volivorco* and *Boblibindo chicurmurco*, in a language that isn't English, Nikolaos Poriotis has the soldiers say Οσκόρμπι, δοῦλτσος βολιβόρκο and Μπομπλιμπίντο τσικουρμοῦρκο, speaking a language that isn't Greek.

Which reminds me . . .

I should tell you Denison's neat solution to the translating-Latin-into-Latin problem.

Where the English Caesar (Guglielmi Shaksperii) said:

Et tu, Brute? Then fall, Caesar.

Denison gives him this line:

Καὶ σὺ τέκνον? – *Tum cadat Caesar!*

With καὶ σύ τέκνον, he is making the predominantly Latin-speaking Caesar break out briefly into Greek. The words mean roughly 'And you too, child'.

It's not an invention on Denison's part, though; in Suetonius's telling of Caesar's assassination (written in the year 121 CE), the historian reported that some people believed those words – those Greek ones – to have been Caesar's last. Denison is returning to one of the story's sources; for those three words, he reverts to the *original* original to replace Shakespeare's Latin-adapted version.

I wonder, though, whether the effect of Greek embedded in Latin is the same as the effect of Latin embedded in English? Do we assume the other characters are supposed to know what's going on? There's one possible answer found in the play itself, as it happens, and it's proverbial. If 'et tu, Brute' is perhaps the play's most famous line, and the next is the equally vocative 'Friends, Romans, countrymen . . .', they're run a close third by the moment when a character reports meeting Cicero, but he has no idea what the famous orator was saying. Apparently Cicero spoke Greek, and:

for mine own part, it was Greek to me.

The alien, hard-to-understand, possibly rather rarefied connotations of Caesar's Greek usage in his dying half-line are set up here.

Only a relatively small proportion of Shakespeare's audience would have been well educated in Latin, but Shakespeare's Latin at least contains a helpfully recognisable name – and the performance can do a lot to help. (The line is also orderly: 'Et tu, *Brute*' neatly mirrors 'Then fall, *Caesar*'.) But I do think the Denison solution pleasing. It's not a perfect match in terms of effect, but then, much of the play's effect lies in how it can be delivered live on a stage, and the Denison isn't a translation for performance to a mass audience of undereducated, monolingually Latin-speaking working folk. His solution is a satisfying one in print, at least. And if καὶ σύ τέκνον was Greek to you, you're in good company.

Chapter 28

ანუ რაოდენ ჩვენთვის ჯერერთ უცნობ ენაზედ

(on accents, dialects and representation)

Near the end of *The Merry Wives of Windsor*, when Falstaff is in the woods about to be humiliated by a gang of people disguised as fairies (long story, not going into it here), one of his masked tormentors says to his companions:

> Pray you, lock hand in hand, yourselves in order set;
> And twenty glow-worms shall our lanterns be
> To guide our measure round about the tree.
> But stay, I smell a man of middle earth.

And Falstaff, watching, says, in an aside to the audience:

> Heavens defend me from that Welsh fairy, lest he transform
> me to a piece of cheese!

The disguised man in question is Hugh Evans, the parson, and he is indeed Welsh. Falstaff doesn't recognise him with his mask on, but hears he's Welsh from his accent. So my question is: what does a Welsh accent sound like in, say, Korean? And what does recognisably Welsh-inflected Korean look like on the page?

Merry Wives has a French character, too, Dr Caius, and both he and Evans have markers of their accent represented in the actual text. Here's the Welshman:

Ferry goot. I will make a prief of it in my notebook . . .

And the Frenchman:

You, Jack'nape: give-a this letter to Sir Hugh. By gar, it is a shallenge. I will cut his troat in de park.

Translators are often faced with this sort of shallenge, where multiple varieties of language appear in a source text and they need differentiating in a meaningful way. I've translated a novel set in Spain, for instance, whose Mexican protagonist has an Argentine roommate – each of these three Spanishes needs to be distinct in both usage and accent (not least because the characters keep drawing attention to the distinction themselves). Some translators will swap in existing variants of their own language, in the hope of replicating the associations a reader is supposed to bring (we're supposed to assume a character is naïve/sophisticated/foreign/educated/plain-spoken/arrogant or whatever). An English-language translator might make one character sound Cornish, one a Dubliner and one Texan, say. So a Slovenian translator embarking on *Merry Wives* might ask themselves: what is the Wales of Slovenia?*

But I think most readers know instinctively that this apparently like-for-like substitution is never adequate. Here we find that the word 'equivalent' I've been using throughout this book is problematic. Though it would be a convenient shorthand to pretend otherwise, Texas is *not* the same as Patagonia, nor are their respective relationships to the publishing centres of New York and Buenos Aires the same. Besides, from a purely practical point of view, it's *distracting*. If we're supposed

---

* You might think of the last chapter as having attempted to answer the question 'What is the Wales of *Wales*?'

to be living in late-sixteenth-century Windsor, we want the Slovenian audience to believe the character is actually from real Wales, not some other real place. If we're reading a Brazilian novel set in Rio and somebody's cousin visits from out of town, why should they suddenly sound like they've walked out of Thomas Hardy or *Trainspotting* or *Jersey Shore*?

Niels found the French doctor Caius easy to replicate for an audience with comparable familiarities: simply put, Danish people can imagine Danish with a French accent. (Helped, said Niels, by the fact that their late prince consort, Prince Henrik – né Henri – never lost his French accent and people found it charming.) So the translator could without much trouble render a stereotypical French-accented Danish, with slightly unusual stresses, more nasal vowels, and so on.

So instead of the Danish French (English) Caius saying:

Mon Dieu, *han har frelst sin sjæl ved ikke at komme; han har bedt godt på sin Bibel at han ikke er kommet;* mon Dieu, *Rugby, han er allerede død, hvis han kommer*

which would be conventional spelling of which Danish-teacher friend Paul would approve, this is the line that Niels gives him, newly accented:

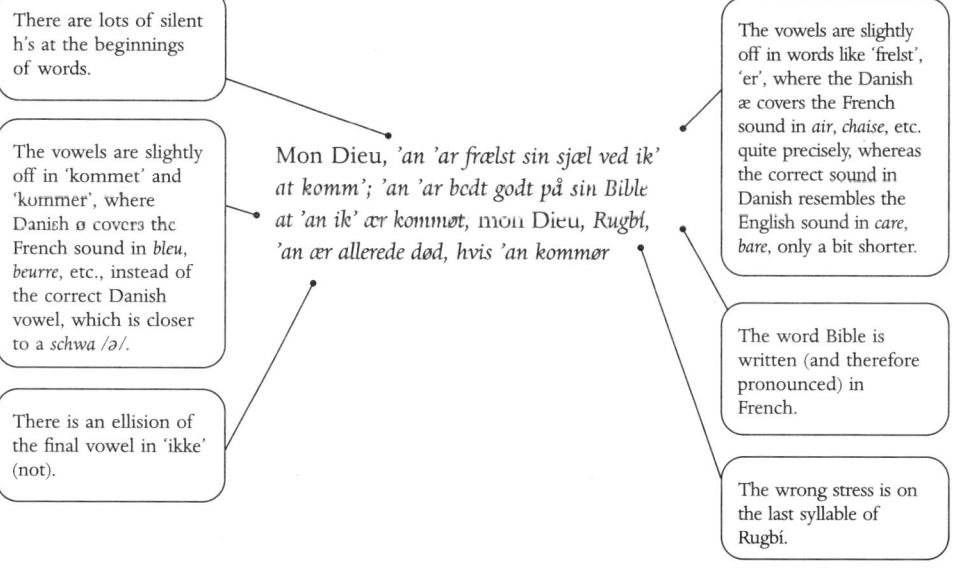

All of these, he says, are typical markers of Danish with a French accent.

Which is all well and good. But how many people in a Copenhagen audience could immediately and specifically recognise *Welsh*-accented Danish? How might a translator in Jakarta ensure that Welsh characters speak Indonesian with an accent that's universally recognisable as distinct from a *Devon* Indonesian accent?

In the Tintin album *The Black Island*, our Belgian hero finds himself in – of all places – Britain. While walking in Scotland, he gets directions from a local: 'It's no above fifteen miles tae Kiltoch. But mind ye keep tae the path thra' the glen.' This is a translation of Hergé's 'Kiltoch n'est qu'à 20 milles d'ici. Seulement, prenez garde de ne pas perdre le sentier.' This speaker's French is undifferentiated from every other speaker's French. Here, to borrow a line from that Shakespeare translation sceptic Borges, one can't help feeling the original is rather unfaithful to the translation. But Scottish English is worth the translators using here because it's obligingly recognisable; Scottish French less so.

Unable, then, to create a widely recognisable Welsh-Danish, Niels first tried for a sort of equivalence (hmm, that word again), making the Welsh parson *Norwegian*. But this begged the question, said Niels, 'What the hell is a Norwegian pastor doing in Elizabethan Windsor?'

It didn't work. The French doctor got all the laughs and the Norwegian-Welsh pastor got none. So they tried a German pastor, still without much luck. But much of the character's intended comedy resides in the accent, so the translator was reluctant to give up on it. Ultimately, the perfect solution was . . .

Actually, there isn't one, not yet. Maybe one day . . .

But – no. I am a natural translation optimist, but perhaps not *everything* is possible.

When Shakespeare transcribes one of Edgar's assumed accents with phonetic markers, an actor knows he's supposed to sound different from his default voice but in a way that's *specific*. Here's a bit we've seen previously in Bulgarian. Even if you can't understand the meaning exactly, you can hear the voice in it:

An 'ch'ud ha' bin zwaggered out of my life, 'twould not ha' been zo long as 'tis by a vortnight. Nay, come not near th'old man. Keep out, che vor ye, or I'se try whether your costard or my ballow be the harder. Ch'ill be plain with you. . . . Ch'ill pick your teeth, zir. Come, no matter vor your foins.

Sometimes the meaning is clear-ish if you speak it aloud (*it would not have been so long as it is by a fortnight* – it [i.e. my life] would have been a fortnight shorter), sometimes not so readily (*Keep out, che vor ye, or I'se try whether your costard or my ballow be the harder* – Keep out, I warn you, or I'll test whether your head or my cudgel is harder). Edgar is speaking these words to Oswald, who doesn't recognise him. Moments later, he's killed Oswald, and reverts instantly to unaccented verse:

I know thee well; a serviceable villain,
As duteous to the vices of thy mistress
As badness would desire.

(When I say that's unaccented, I of course mean *default-accented*. This is no less a distinct, marked voice than the other, it just happens to be less conspicuous being more Shakespeare-normative.)

What causes the trouble for a translator is an accent's *specificity*. So the job is creating an accent that might suggest what the original accent is suggesting (in terms of the prejudices we're supposed to have about it), but avoiding a new specificity that triggers the *why-are-we-suddenly-in-Jersey-Shore?* problem. The dilemma bedevils any translator handling two kinds of language – recreating the friction between, say, an omniscient narrative voice, on the one hand, and characters on the streets who banter casually, slangily. The translator Anthea Bell used to strive for what she called 'non-specific demotic' – that is, language that is clearly casual, informal, oral, but which doesn't immediately pin you down to a specific place. For our co-translation of *La Vorágine* (a 1924 Colombian novel), Victor Meadowcroft and I needed to mark out the way the plains-living characters spoke, without transplanting them to

Kent or Montana. We ended up with lots of dropped g's at the ends of words (*I'll be takin out the horses*), which felt spoken but helpfully non-specific; we avoided dropping h's at the start of words because it seemed to suck us specifically into stereotyped London. *I'll be takin out the 'orses.**

A scene in *Henry V* presents the encounter between Welsh, Irish and Scottish captains in the king's army – we know where they're from because they tell us, but also because their speech is marked to suggest their variously accented Englishes.

Again, some translators have chosen to transpose one regional accent to another 'equivalent' – as though these accents weren't specific, with a sense of community that's distinct and distinctive. And despite the fact that, as Jean-Michel points out, we're anyway dealing with 'stylized dialects, rather than historically accurate Welsh, Irish or Scottish', he says:

> . . . oddly, François-Victor Hugo gives [Scottish] Jamy a Creole accent, Marcel Sallé has Jamy lisp and gives [Welsh] Fluellen an Alsatian accent, [Irish] Macmorris translated by Jean-Claude Sallé has an Auvergnat accent. The excellent Sylvère Monod . . . also gives into temptation, giving Macmorris a *pied noir* accent . . .

Oddly is right.†

Unlike his difficulties with Evans, which is a pretty substantial part, Niels was less troubled by the trio of captains. It's only a short scene and not especially high-stakes (but again, yes, do please avoid specific Danish dialects, resist the temptation to make the Scotsman come from Jutland, etc.). Of the three of them, only Fluellen is a sustained character and the important thing, Niels said, is making his voice *personally*

---

* *guv'nor*

† There's an easier fit for Chinese, So explained, because while you'll inevitably lose specificities in e.g. the relationship between the Scots and the English, variant Chinese dialects/languages share the same writing system, so a translator can produce a single text that allows the *actors* flexibility in shaping how it's spoken.

distinctive; he is a sort of heroic character – brave and patriotic, not one who is there *only* for accent comedy.

In my experience, spoken accent is one of the very few things almost as hard to translate as ambiguity. So – yes – the captains in *Henry V* might need some attention, if we're to convey the differences between Scottish, Welsh and Irish Anglophones in Tamil meaningfully.

In the first part of *Henry VI*, the next play in the historical sequence, Joan La Pucelle (Joan of Arc) is about to enter Rouen with soldiers who are in disguise and whom she tells to: 'Talk like the vulgar sort of market men'. In other words, use the kind of language that will fool people into thinking you're market traders. Her own lines that follow need to reflect this, in whichever translation-language the new text is using. Whatever an equivalent might be, a market-men linguistic short-hand, helpfully specific but not *unhelpfully* specific.

Oh, as it happens, and to complicate matters, Joan's next line after this speech is actually in French . . .

Chapter 29

أرجوك ألا تفرضي القيود على لساني

(on reasons to translate)

In his book *The Anxiety of Influence*, American literary critic Harold Bloom considered the ways a writer of poetry might experience the influence of their precursors as inhibiting as well as generative. Not something translators would have to worry about, one might think – after all, producing work that is derivative is precisely what we're supposed to do. There's no such thing as being *too* influenced. But a deep anxiety about one's abilities to do justice to a genius fore-writer, not to let them down, well, that can be quite real.

The Czech translator Martin Hilský thinks in these terms:

> A translation must be related to the original in the way a child is to a parent. Children take after their parents but they also talk back. So I see all the Shakespearean translators of the world to be like Shakespeare's children, each in their own way different, each trying to do what they can.

I like this idea, and it gives a good sense of the challenge. Shakespeare's *Hamlet* is quite a hard parent for an aspiring nepo-play to live up to.

The greatest of literary giants I've translated myself is Machado de Assis, the one Brazilian writer who is the father to all others. As a translator, the job required being utterly subsumed into this great writer's work – but without being hamstrung by an awareness of that challenge and overwhelmed by his greatness. So as I talk to these Shakespeareans, I do have some sympathy.

More recent Brazilians on my own translating roster have included Antonio Prata (a fan, inevitably, of Machado de Assis). In his story 'Plan', the narrator proposes smuggling a new line into an edition of *Hamlet*. The line in question is apparently spoken as an aside by Hamlet to Claudius, his father's murderer, at the end of Act II. In the Portuguese source, Antonio used a line from a popular Brazilian song, which means something like 'Oh, if I catch you, oh, oh, if I catch you!' In my version, it became 'Oh, if I catch you – if I catch you, oh!', which is a little closer to one of those trochaic-beginning pentameters (though notice how redundant those 'ohs' are, only there to fill a line – oh!) – but it is not good. And *certainly* not good enough to pass for a bit of *Hamlet*, which is a high-ish bar.

The character in Antonio's story needs to give his newly 'discovered' line some scholarly credibility (even in my rather bloodless version), so he kidnaps the author of *Shakespeare: The Invention of the Human* – one Harold Bloom (b.1930) – and sticks him into an underground bunker where he is forced to devise some plausible justification for its earlier omission. Once Bloom's essay has been written, the bunker is blown up with the critic inside it.

Harold Bloom first saw Shakespeare performed in Yiddish.*

The late nineteenth and early twentieth centuries saw Yiddish-language literature flourish – coinciding with many Shakespeare translations into that language, just in time for the appearance of Harold Bloom. It is said – though I think apocryphally – that the title pages of these Yiddish translations bore the words *fartaytsht un farbesert* (פֿאַרטײַטשט און פֿאַרבעסערט): translated and improved.†

---

* The Shakespeare films of which he spoke most highly, incidentally, were Akira Kurosawa's *Ran* and *Throne of Blood*, Japanese-language re-fashionings of *King Lear* and *Macbeth*, respectively.

† Other Yiddish words you might want to learn include חוצפה, whence the English *chutzpah*.

The global Yiddish-speaking population was ravaged by the Holocaust, though much has been done in the decades since to preserve and revitalise the language. There are writers using it as their medium to this day. Of the post-war writers, the one to receive the most global attention (and the Nobel Prize) was Isaac Bashevis Singer, whose justification for continuing to write in the language, as explained in his Nobel banquet speech, was: 'I am sure that millions of Yiddish speaking corpses will rise from their graves one day and their first question will be: "Is there any new Yiddish book to read?"'

Bashevis Singer was himself a great reader. When asked if he would be interested in meeting Shakespeare, he replied, 'Not at all. Not for a moment. You see, I don't care if his work was written by Bacon or by some ghostwriter. Let the professors worry. I am still a reader. When you are really hungry, you don't try to find out the biography of the baker.'

The library of the Yiddish Book Center in Massachusetts holds several translations of Shakespeare (some of which we've quoted from already): *King Lear*, *Hamlet*, the sonnets, the two parts of *Henry IV*, *Richard III*, *Othello*, *Julius Caesar* and *The Merchant of Venice*, several of these in more than one variant translation.

In his introduction to his 1918 *Hamlet* in the YBC collection, Y.Y. Schwartz writes that 'it is a sign of poverty if a literature lacks Shakespeare in translation'* – it's a thing Yiddish could not even have dreamed of just decades before.

When I asked JC why she'd embarked on her Swahili *Macbeth*, she explained the reasoning in terms of her own relationship to the language (a complex one, as a multilingual person with 'kitchen Swahili' – not formally taught – as a child), but also as a project of language reclamation. She had been told in the past that a Bantu African language like Swahili would necessarily be too unsophisticated to convey complex ideas. (Based simply on racist assumptions about those people who speak them.) In 1963, Tanzanian president Julius Nyerere published

---

* עס איז א סמן דלות פאר א ליטעראטור וועלכע פערמאגט ניט שעקספיער'ן אין איבערזעצונג.
Unless otherwise specified, translations *from* Yiddish are by Claire Breger-Belsky.

Julius Kaizari, the first of his translations of Shakespeare, which some critics suggest – says JC:

> lean towards embellishment, occasionally prioritizing Swahili's idiomatic richness over strict adherence to the original text. Personally, I find this wonderful because it highlights Swahili's natural strengths – its lyricism and expressiveness.

(We've seen some of these strengths already, and there will be more.)

Emanuel Ribeiro, who produced that Cape Verdean Creole *Romeu ma Julieta* I've mentioned above, referred to the sense of extra responsibility inherent in the fact that:

> it begins with theoretically more advanced languages, such as English and Portuguese, to arrive at the Cape Verdean language, which is supposedly poorer in lexicon and idiomatic expression. But difficulties aside, having Creole as the target language also has the advantage of offering the translator a unique musicality and exuberance, which, when used well, result in a new sonority and harmony for Shakespeare's lyricism.

(There's a whole racist history in that *supposedly*, too.)

So we're talking here about languages with a desire/need to assert themselves. It's an assertion of – and enriching of – a strong literary tradition, too. Shakespeare translations have played a part in language reclamation movements across the globe, from Noongar to Frisian.

Several translators and publishers I spoke to cited a prestige effect – using Shakespeare and other texts perceived as high status to demonstrate a language's possibilities, and its seriousness. A publisher I once met who worked in a fascinating but undervalued and little-disseminated language (with only ten or fifteen million speakers) had lately engaged a translator to produce a *Ulysses* – not because he felt his readers were clamouring for it (sorry to disappoint you), but because, very explicitly, he wanted his language to be seen as the sort of language in which a book like *Ulysses* could be found. For many reasons – literary and also non-literary (e.g. Western European colonialism), Shakespeare is positioned high on global culture's prestige list.

In *The Universal Translator*, Yens Wahlgren identified this effect: 'The translation work done by the KLI – including *Hamlet*, *Much Ado about Nothing*, *The Epic of Gilgamesh* and *Tao Te Ching* – has also influenced the language's reputation among a wider audience. A language that can reproduce the classics of world literature is taken much more seriously than one that appears only on TV and in films.'*

I have occasionally heard the counter-argument, too, that this is an embarrassingly deferential pandering to white colonial notions of literary genius – why should we be amplifying *Shakespeare*, of all people, in our proudly postcolonial culture and language?

Even without needy monolinguals who require translators for basic literary access, another reason for 'why bother?' is about enabling a readership's appreciation of the skill of translation. I *could* sit at home and read a Shakespeare play to myself, but I do like to get out and see how other people have managed to reanimate them on stage; likewise, I read plenty of English-language books that have been translated from languages I could perfectly well read in the original, because the translator is someone whose (interpretative, creative, expressive) work excites me.

As I cast about for other plausible motivations, I also assume that the process of translating Shakespeare is just *fun*. Or at least, I did assume so, till I asked Frank about it:

'Fun' is a strange word to describe the task of translating Shakespeare. It's more on the line of subtle torture techniques for masochists. A German saying goes 'Viel Feind, viel Ehr', which could be translated

---

* The KLI mentioned here is the Klingon Language Institute, so I probably should have said 'galactic' rather than 'global'.

as something like 'Many foes, much honour'. Shakespeare's works are an overwhelming army of innumerable fierce and frightful foes to any translator. The achievement any Shakespeare translator has to be honoured for is that he doesn't run away from his desk for dear life, screaming.

And even if that sort of fun doesn't appeal, there are still other reasons to do it. Translating Shakespeare has often been deemed useful as a pedagogical exercise, for example. Gaelic-language writers in Ireland were encouraged to learn their craft by translating Shakespeare. I spent a happy afternoon in Oxford's Bodleian Library poring over the papers and notebooks of Gilbert Murray, which included not only his own handwritten drafts of Shakespearean scenes in ancient Greek, but also many college exams and competitions involving extracts from the ancient Greek *As You Like It*, *The Comedy of Errors* and so on. Murray won the 1886 Gaisford Prize for a bit of *Henry IV, Part 2* in Greek 'comic iambics'.

Henry Denison, our Latin translator, saw this value in the practice, too:

> The translator has long been persuaded that the very remarkable disproportion between the time and labour bestowed upon the teaching of the Greek and Latin languages, and the knowledge of either acquired by the average of English youth, is mainly owing to the neglect of translation, and to the preference shewn for what is styled, by courtesy, 'original composition'.
>
> Under this system, instead of acquiring new ideas, the young student learns to write without them; instead of enriching his language, he does everything to impoverish it; instead of learning nice grammatical distinctions, and attaining to choice expression and lucid arrangement, he runs off into vague generalities of phraseology, which evade all the difficulties of composition, and overcome none.

I do like Henry Denison.

One of my favourite discoveries while collecting translations for this book – albeit not the best translation in itself – was an edition published in Boston in 1870 of *La tragique histoire d'Hamlet, Prince de Danemark* 'translated by the graduating class of Miss Putnam's School'.*

In *The Merchant of Venice 1936*, Brigid Larmour's production of Shakespeare's play transported to the London of Oswald Mosley and rising anti-Semitism, Tracy-Ann Oberman's Shylock, in distress at her daughter's running away, speaks the line:

מײַן אייגן בלוט און פֿלייש
[*mayn eygn blut un fleysh*]

in Yiddish. Only then – for the benefit of those non-Jews around her – does she repeat it in English. 'I say my daughter is my flesh and blood.' For a semi-assimilated Jew in that time and that place, Yiddish is a natural language for Shylock's community.

It's harder to see how this might work when the whole play is in Yiddish translation, however. Yiddish being a curious language to hear in the mouths of most of *The Merchant of Venice*'s other characters, who are mostly non-Jews, and indeed many are expressly anti-Semites, including and especially Antonio, the titular Merchant himself.

Y. Bovshover's translation of *The Merchant of Venice* was the first Yiddish Shakespeare published in the US. When a cut-down version of this translation was used as the basis for a 1901 stage production starring Jacob Adler, a report in the *Jewish Exponent* seemed surprised to hear

---

* This is Miss M. Louise Putnam, who from the mid-1860s ran a school out of her home in Back Bay – a vibe that honestly would not be out-of-place in Back Bay today. When I wrote to my friend Paul K., who lives round the corner, to tell him about this local discovery, he just wrote back: 'Of course.'

a language which many of those who had heard it in the past had deemed harsh and raucous, but which seemed, as uttered by this actor, replete with gentle cadences and harmonies. It did not obtrude itself grotesquely, as many had feared it would, into the immortal English of Shakespeare, but proved a telling vindication . . .

In his introduction to the translation, Bovshover wrote of the play's universality, speaking as it does to the experience of 'any oppressed, derided or tormented person'. The Jewish presence at the play's heart, problematic though it might be, makes it a play translated into this language more often than almost any other.

Albeit with some tweaks. There is a moment in *Shakespeare in Love* where Ben Affleck's arrogant Ned Alleyn – who is in the company playing the role of Mercutio – is displeased at the size of the part he has been allocated. What's this play even called, anyway?, he asks. '*Mercutio*,' Shakespeare answers quickly. The Bovshover translation of *The Merchant of Venice* recentres the play with a change of title: *Shylock*.

Chapter 30

Jó hírnév nevű áru

(on names)

What's in a name?

When I meet Te Haumihiata for lunch, she is halfway through translating *Macbeth*. More specifically, on that day, she is trying to figure out how to recreate *Dunsinane* in *te reo* Māori.

Dunsinane is not a name for which *te reo* has a 'translation'. It has unwieldy sounds for a Māori ear, there is no *te reo* word that 'means' the same, and there is no standard analogue already existing as there is with some foreign names. *Romeo and Juliet* takes us to fair Whārona, where we lay our scene, as well as to Manatua – simply the translation of Mantua. But I assume nobody has ever had any cause to say *Birnam Wood* in *te reo* Māori before. And there are rules.

Dunsinane, Te Haumihiata told me later, ended up as *Tahinane*, which works in a language that doesn't allow for consonant clusters – a feature *te reo* shares with, say, Japanese. We've already seen 'strands afar remote' from *Henry IV, Part 1*; and 'bursts of horrid thunder' from Kent in *King Lear*. Stra<u>nds</u> and bu<u>rsts</u> are both sounds impossible to replicate in Japanese. Where we in English might very comfortably have consecutive consonant sounds (co<u>ns</u>ecutive co<u>ns</u>onant sou<u>nds</u>), Japanese splits such things into separate syllabic units with intercalated vowels. Macbeth becomes マクベス (Ma-ku-be-su) in Japanese, just as he's Matapēhi in *te* *reo* Māori. Hamlet expands even further to the five-part ハムレット (Ha-mu-re-t-to). Consonant-clustered A<u>nt</u>ony and <u>Cl</u>eopa<u>tr</u>a will cause similar trouble; likewise <u>Tr</u>oilus and <u>Cr</u>essida. Sha<u>kesp</u>eare's own surname won't stay two syllables for long either.*

(It's worth reminding you, of course, that English has its own limits. The Georgians can easily manage consonant clusters that would reduce an Anglophone like me to tears. And you might find your tolerance tested when travelling to pay tribute to Isaac Bashevis Singer's grandmother in her hometown of Szczebrzeszyn, a town that even in Polish is seen as meriting its own tongue-twister.†)

Even within a language's prevailing constraints, echoing the original sounds is still at the root of the reconstruction process – Te Haumihiata's opening scene of *Romeo and Juliet* is a wordplay-rich conversation about coals and choler and colliers between Kerekori and Hamahona – our old friends Gregory and Samson.

Our soft H doesn't exist in Russian, so something else must take its place. By old convention, the Prince of Denmark isn't transposed to a hard H (the bringing-up-phlegm sound, called the 'velar fricative' – the *ch* in *loch*, say – written in Russian as X) but to a G.

Это я, Гамлет Датчанин.

This is I, Gamlet the Dane.‡

Conventions do change, though. I have Greek Shakespeare editions where he goes by Γουλιέλμος Σαίξπηρ, others by Ούίλιαμ Σαίξπηρ (Goulielmos vs Ouiliam) – reflecting respectively an older habit of Greekifying names and a newer habit of simply transliterating them.

Italian, meanwhile, only very seldom ends a word with a consonant, so loan words/names get adapted. In Italy, I am Daniele. Hamlet becomes

---

* Conventionally 'Wiremu Hakipia' in Māori.
† *Chrząszcz brzmi w trzcinach w Szczebrzeszynie.* Good luck!
‡ This isn't common practice nowadays. If you're reading my book in its Russian translation, the author's name on the cover *will* likely be that harsher *-ch* sound – Хан rather than Ган.

Amleto – but even if you didn't change his name, an Italian would naturally pronounce an invisible third syllable in Am-lett-*a* anyway. You can keep the English spelling in French if you like, though there, too, it will still be pronounced as though it began with an 'a' ('amlet). Even if a language might allow something in theory, there's no reason to suppose that an actor raised on that language will find those sounds comfortable.

Some names will be unchangeable, or so you'd imagine. The name of a real, historical king, say. You can't decide, say, to rebaptise a King Henry as King Edward, just to suit your linguistic habits. (Those fighting-for-supremacy stories are complicated enough as it is, and we've got too many Edwards already.) But what if the existing name just won't work? The hell-raising Prince Hal[*] causes trouble for the Hungarians, not only because *Hal* is a difficult word to say – they need harder consonants to get their teeth into – but also because . . . Well, remember how I mentioned needing to avoid unintentional ambiguities? *Hal* is the Hungarian for *fish*.

When Falstaff insults Mistress Quickly by saying she is 'neither fish nor flesh', you can spot 'hal' in the Hungarian quip:

se hús, se hal, nem tudni, mire kapható . . .

So when Ádám was translating this play, he wanted to give the prince a name that wouldn't slip out of actors' mouths (in a slippery fishy sort of way), with nice consonants to get purchase on. In his translation, then, the prince is not nicknamed Hal, or Harry (or Heinz, as in the Schlegel-Tieck German translation) but Riki. Which – never fear – is not a nickname for Richard, but for *Henrik*. The first time we see them together on stage, Ádám gives the actor playing Falstaff an extra introductory exclamation, so that the nickname can be clearly introduced:

---

[*] Reading through this draft, I want to replace the word *hell-raising*, because I was irked by hell/Hal so close together in a way that's not controlled – if you needed yet another example of how the sometimes arbitrary particularities of a language's components will factor into what a writer can do . . .

Now, Hal, what time of day is it, lad?	Henrik! Riki! Te, mondd, hány óra van?

'I think in general I'm more impertinent than other translators,' Ádám told me, but 'when you play an instrument well, you can allow yourself a certain looseness'. (If this was not clear already, I entirely approve.)

While allowing an *inadvertent* fish to slip in would be regrettable, the meanings contained within some names are intentional, of course. Names – like everything else – need to be considered multidimensionally. They might suggest something about them (personality, background, class, nationality), and they'll have sonic properties like any word will. Desdemona already has four syllables and a particular stress pattern that will fit more easily into some verse lines than others. Juliet, Giulietta, Julia and Juliette don't all occupy the same space in a line.

A character in the first picture book I translated went from Miss Grumpy to Miss Mean when I realised I could only spare her one syllable; then from Miss Mean to Miss Stern when I spotted a handy rhyme with 'learn' two lines down. As is always the way with translation, we decide what is important, and prioritise keeping that. *Love's Labour's Lost* has a meaning (the labour of love is lost, assuming we're going with a much-discussed second apostrophe); but how about the alliteration? What if you felt that, for some reason, it was important to preserve that? What title would you give the play, in that case, in Greek?

No, I'm really asking.

Among the Greek words we've encountered in this book are:

- αγάπη (agápi) – love (on p.125)
- αγώνα (agóna) – fight/struggle (on p.44)
- άγονος (ágonos) – barren (on p.164)

The struggles of love are barren. Isn't that what we're after? Errikos Belies gave his translation the title:

Αγάπης Αγώνας Άγονος

Great-granddad Tristão translated some names sense-for-sense, Fortinbras becoming Fortebraço – the strong-armed meaning is more on the nose in Portuguese than in English, impossible to miss. Queen Mab in *te reo Māori* no longer goes by 'Mab', but Tahakura, which evokes both dreams and a reddish agate-like stone. And Te Haumihiata's 'Matapēhi' – the Macbeth avoiding impossible consonant clusters – perhaps also cleverly suggests that word *Mate*, which as we've seen already, has that whole versatile range of negative meanings.

One of most crowd-pleasing scenes in *Kiss Me, Kate* comes towards the end of the show, when a couple of gangsters who've been loitering backstage to intimidate an actor who owes their boss money find themselves suddenly *on* the stage. So they do what any self-respecting thugs would do: they sing a comic song about Shakespeare. 'Brush Up Your Shakespeare' is a bit of advice for men about why they ought to learn their Shakespeare – it's the only sure-fire way of seducing women, apparently. 'Just declaim a few lines from *Othella*, and they'll think you're a heck of a fella. When your blonde won't respond when you flatter 'er, tell her what Tony told Cleopater'er'. Every couplet rhymes on a Shakespearean title. Some are risqué (that would be *Coriolanus*). Some build their rhymes around multiple words (I wonder what we might do with a Washington Heights dream . . .); others are extra-forced for comic effect, like rhyming an ambassada with Shakespeare's *Troilus and*, um, *Crassada*.*

Begging the question, naturally: what happens to the song when you perform *Kiss Me, Kate* in another language?

Step forward the brave† Alain Marcel, who directed the show for the French stage in 1992, and remade Cole Porter's lyrics in French for his production. In his '*Décrasse ton Shakespeare*', we get something like this:

---

* When you read about forced rhymes in Chapter 4, I bet you didn't imagine they could get *this* bad.
† As in *courageous*, rather than as in 无与伦比.

> . . . *Tu enchaînes et confirmes qu'il y a pas de lézard,*
> *En scandant la tirade à Jules César.*
> *Si tu veux qu'elles se pointent en rangs par trois,*
> *Déclare leur en boîtant du Richard III* [. . .]
> *Si une dame distinguée demande quoi lire,*
> *Fais sortir d'un seul jet tout ton Roi Lear . . .*

As in English, the audience is assumed to know the references – indeed to see them coming. Only now, in the interest of maintaining not the lines' meaning but their *function*, Cole Porter's line

> Tell her what Tony told Cleopaterer,

has become:

> *En scandant la tirade à Jules César*

And Cole Porter's *Coriolanus* is now translated into Marcel's *Roi Lear*. This strikes me as just what a good translator ought to do.

Chapter 31

ते हे सुंदर नवं जग!

(on cultural adjustment)

Shall I compare thee to a summer's day? That is the question.
But it is not always a straightforward one.

> Shall I compare thee to a summer's day?
> Thou art more lovely and more temperate:
> Rough winds do shake the darling buds of May,
> (Except, well, not in the southern hemisphere they don't.)

Things don't typically bud in May if you're in Aotearoa. Rough winds do shake *the falling leaves of May*, perhaps? The darling buds of November?

What concessions must a translator make to their audience's understanding? What should they explain? How closely should the text be accommodated to its new home? What might be helpful to an audience, the people in this room right now?

To put it another way: does Verona always *have* to be in Italy? The decision to transpose a play from Shakespeare's world to some (precise) alternative is something directors do all the time, of course – *Richard III* in a proto-Nazi Germany; *Macbeth* as a Congolese warlord; Baz Luhrmann's *Romeo + Juliet* in California's 'Verona Beach'; and so on.

IF THIS BE MAGIC

In the world of translation studies, the terms you'll hear are 'domestication' and 'foreignisation' – the former makes adjustments to avoid alienating the new target audience, it goes to where they are; the latter is happy for them to keep being reminded that what they're reading is a translation, and if you don't understand everything, and it feels unfamiliar, well, that's fine, actually. Whether or not we think in those abstract terms, every translation is built out of things that are consequentially changed and things that seek to (pretend to) stay the same.

So: do we keep to Shakespeare's own northern-hemisphere seasons (summer in July, winter in January), and assume readers can figure it out? Or do we translate it to their seasonal cycle?

> Shall I compare thee to a summer's day?
> Thou art more lovely and more temperate:
> Rough winds do shake the darling buds of November,*
> And summer's lease hath all too short a date.

When Te Haumihiata was invited to translate this sonnet into *te reo* Māori – her first close engagement with Shakespeare – she was tempted to 'domesticate' that opening line of number XVIII, on the basis that having spring-like activity in May would only be unnecessarily confusing to an audience unfamiliar with Shakespeare, just as she had lately been herself.† Her translation chose to bring the text closer to her readers, rather than expecting them to cast their imaginations north. For her line three, then, she compromised, to this:

> *He hau tukipoho ka rui i te mata o te tau*

---

* Only using something that rhymes and scans.
† She remembered having seen the Burton/Taylor *Taming of the Shrew* movie when she was young, with no idea who Shakespeare was. 'But I did know Richard Burton and Elizabeth Taylor . . .'

Where *mata o te tau* is not explicitly May but the first new growth of spring.

The actor Malibongwe Mdwaba produced an isiXhosa translation of Sonnet 18,* but took the other decision – his reader might be living in autumn, but as long as you're in this sonnet, May is spring. His third line is:

> *Izivunguvungu ziye zivunguze zide zishukumisa amagqabi amahle kinyanga ka Canzibe*

Canzibe is May in the Xhosa calendar.

Likewise my southern-hemisphere Brazilian translation by Oscar Mendes keeps May as budding season (*Crestam ventos brutais de maio ou tenros brotos*†); as for that matter does every *English*-language southern-hemisphere edition I've ever seen . . .

We've previously seen this from *Love's Labour's Lost*:

> At Christmas I no more desire a rose
> Than wish a snow in May's new-fangled shows . . .

I don't expect Christmas in summer, or snow in May – that would be ludicrous! – says Berowne, who clearly never made it to Patagonia.

When Lysander refers to having met Hermia in the forest, where she'd gone to 'do observance to a morn of May', they're doing it because the play's setting is in and around Athens. Πρωτομαγιά (Protomagiá, 1 May) is an ancient holiday still celebrated today, with city dwellers making for the countryside to gather flowers to celebrate nature and spring. These characters live in Athens and do Athenian things. We don't need to pretend otherwise. Our audience in Melbourne will understand. Plenty of things exist in Shakespeare's Anglophone world that don't in other places (plants, animals, customs) – and indeed that don't exist in our own English today.

---

* This isn't published, but I stumbled upon him reading his own translations of two sonnets on Twitter/X. Worth checking out.

† Ooh, using *brutais* for the *rough* winds allows a very nice sonic link to *brotos* (buds).

One might argue, I suppose, that a sonnet is different? It's not 'set' somewhere, and fourteen lines isn't enough space to teach our readers a load of cultural/topographical context. And keep in mind that Shakespeare himself was constantly 'domesticating' for his audience, too. I said *A Midsummer Night's Dream* is set in and around Athens – but is it *really*? This is an Athens where the workers are called things like Bottom, Quince, Flute, Stout, Snug and Starveling, and they imagine that if their play had gone ahead, the Duke's favour might have earned Bottom 'sixpence a day' for the rest of his life. Accuracy of specific local culture is not the point.

And the Duke had not given him sixpence a day for playing Pyramus, I'll be hanged. He would have deserved it. Sixpence a day in Pyramus, or nothing.

Dionisis Kapsalis's Greek translation does this, incidentally:

Τέτοιο μεροκάματο που θα το ξανάβλεπε στη ζωή του. Δεν θα 'φευγε από δω με λιγότερο από μεροκάματο.

That repeated word μεροκάματο is the key here. Kapsalis apparently figured that while Londoners in 1600 might not be bothered by old Athenians inexplicably referring to *sixpence*, today's Athenians in today's Athens might well find it distracting. (We're now in a Greek-language version of an ostensibly Athens-set play.) At the same time, having a Shakespearean version of the heroic Theseus spending euros would be silly. A conversion into pre-euro drachmas would have been an option, and saved the anachronism (the sort of anachronism more noticeable to a new Greek audience than an old English one), since the drachma was an ancient currency before it returned in the nineteenth century, but instead, for minimum distraction, he goes casually with μεροκάματο – *merokamato* – simply 'a day's wage'. (Literally 'a day's toil'.)

The 'mero' at the start deriving from the Greek word for day (*kalimera*!). (When these same characters were trying to determine whether

the selini would shine on the night of their performance, they looked in an almanac – in Kostas Antoniou's translation, a ημερολόγιο.)
So:

Ένα μεροκάματο για τον Πύραμο η τίποτα.

[*Ena merokamato gia ton Pyramo i tipota.*
A day's wage for Pyramus or nothing.]

Sixpence a day, then, or *hiç*.

In Māori culture, *tikanga* is a traditional set of customs and values, and a behavioural code. So while Juliet asks Romeo 'what's in a name?', Hurieta asks Rōmeo, *He aha te tikanga o te ingoa?* What is the tikanga of your name? It means what the English means – and then some.

One of the arguments for adapting a play's internal culture rather than preserving it is about attitude. Not that seasons happen at different times of the year in different places, but that they *mean* different things. August is summer in Japan just as it is in Shakespeare-land, but as one translator explained, 'Sure, summer happens at the same time in Tokyo, that's not the problem – the problem is that in Tokyo, everyone *hates* summer.' It is categorically not a thing that everybody looks forward to. I mean, it's all very well if you're a a boy from balmy Stratford, of course. But there are Arabic translations and Bengali translations that make that first line about 'a spring day', because what those two translators' actual realities have in common is that summer is *hot*, so comparing somebody to a summer's day – unpleasant and, ugh, almost unbearably oppressive – might not be the compliment you think it is, Will.

Almost every translator I spoke to, even those whose translations were commissioned by a publisher rather than a theatre company, spoke of maintaining an awareness of what would be useful for *performance*. And translating a play for production – rather than, say, for publishing in a scholarly edition – does change the proposition. Not only because of the obvious ways the text has to be, for example, speakable (Shakespeare was a theatre man who wrote for actors, and even with his longest phrasing, he never forgot that they do need to breathe, so translators mustn't forget this either), but also because your audience is much more practically contained. The audience is not just anybody in the world who might buy the book now or ever; the audience is this group of people, in this room in Mumbai, every evening from tonight through to next Wednesday. Playwright and director Neil Bartlett, who has produced his own versions of Genet plays to serve his productions, argues that any theatre translation not only can be but *should be* bound by its specific moment. 'Every translation is a *pièce d'occasion* – a really good translation is one that is fantastic tonight but which will be out of date in two years.'

Shakespeare knew his audience well, of course, and he knew what they understood, and wrote for them. There wouldn't have been a person watching his *Henry VIII* who would have heard 'My King is tangled in affection to / A creature of the Queen's, Lady Anne Bullen' and wouldn't have known who this Anne character was or how well that was all going to work out. But what does a translator do to her text when the assumed knowledge is quite different? (Playing scenes set in Cheapside is different if you're at the Globe, which is five hundred yards from Cheapside, to staging them in Mozambique, where I wouldn't assume everybody has heard of it.) And conversely, how do things with foreign cultural glosses in the English adapt when they are translated 'back' to their settings? When the *Two Gentlemen* are back in Verona (with Romeo and Juliet), or Hamlet is speaking Danish again; when the lovers in the *Dream* are restored, with Timon, to their native Greek? When Lysander talks to Hermia about meeting in that place a league outside Athens, how do you phrase this for an audience who celebrate Πρωτομαγιά in that same spot today?

The sonnet of Romeo and Juliet's meeting is hard for a new audience to make sense of if they don't share the characters' understanding of pilgrims – and come to think of it, religious imagery (Christian and otherwise) poses problems all over the place. Do you take account of the religious context of your new audience, or are they all supposed to pretend somehow to be early seventeenth-century Londoners? When

Othello asks Desdemona if she is 'a strumpet' and she replies that, no, she is *a Christian*, the Arabic translator Khalil Mutran rendered that as '*a devout woman*'.* Beyond religion, so many other plays depend on sustained metaphor (the language of the theatre, of falconry, of the law), not to mention wide-ranging allusiveness that is of course similarly culturally specific. Some sort of attempted 'equivalence' (aargh, again!) is not uncommon: tribal chiefs for kings in some translations to African languages; or the slightly wilder title of Ibrāhīm Ramzī's 1930s Arabic translation: *The Taming of the Tigress*. Preti Taneja has written about a Bengali *Lear* in which an enraged Kent threatens Oswald not with 'I'll make a sop o'the moonshine of you' but with 'I'll make a *keema* of you', which was then returned to English as 'I'll make a *korma* of you'. '*Décrasse ton Shakespeare*' doesn't just swap a *Lear* joke for a *Coriolanus* joke, it also repositions the song culturally for a French audience. What associations would Washington Heights be supposed to evoke in them?

However, the aspects of culture embedded in Shakespeare's writing that might be unfamiliar to a reader geographically distant from his London probably mystify many readers who are far away not in space but in time. The chronological disconnect with which we Anglophones experience the Jacobethan Shakespeare is not insignificant. That Abraham Sybant translation of *The Taming of the Shrew* into Dutch in 1654 was probably made for a world far closer to Shakespeare's than ours is. The distance between sixteenth-century London and twenty-first-century London is already great enough – in some respects, I don't think moving it out of London to twenty-first-century Amsterdam or Lisbon significantly widens the chasm. Neither pilgrims nor falconry play a major role in the lives of most English speakers today, I suspect. And did you know what that 'sop o'the moonshine' of Kent's was referring to, I wonder?

One school of practice, then: you think of the audience from the very start, and you bring the work to them. You explain. You domesticate, like Shakespeare did. If necessary, you transpose wholesale.

---

* In Sameh F. Hanna's, *Decommercialising Shakespeare: Mutran's Translation of Othello.*

(Incidentally, one might think of this not only in terms of culture. When I spoke to theatre director Tim Supple about what foreign audiences recognise might in a play, he talked about making something 'true to the psychology of the people listening and speaking it'. Their 'psychology' is an interesting way to think about this, too.*)

At its best, cultural transposition vanishes the distance between audience and play, giving them access to more important things than having to wonder what a tithe-pig is. Verona is no longer in Italy – it's right here, wherever we are.

At worst, there's a reductiveness not only of the play but the target culture and the potential sophistication of an audience's experience. Incredibly, one *can* in fact enjoy a Shakespeare play in Brazil even if it doesn't feature football, favelas, carnival and beaches. I have never once seen an Ibsen play in London and lamented the absence of Morris dancing.

Naturally, every language has cultural/societal things it doesn't readily accommodate. We saw that earlier, with the annoying Spanish furniture. And a great cultural gap must be bridged somehow, whether we're talking about gaps across distance or across time. A translation into a language whose heyday predates Shakespeare will struggle, because there are plenty of things that exist in Elizabethan England that have no names in Latin or Ancient Greek. Even Shakespeare's *Julius Caesar*, which is supposed to be set, as one would expect, in The Time of Julius Caesar, has anachronisms. Most notoriously, a clock striking three, in a world where striking clocks had not yet been invented.

Most translators needn't worry about this; they can simply transpose it into an anachronistic clock of their own living language. Henry Denison can do no such thing in Latin, because the language cannot have the noun he needs, any more than there's a standard Latin term for a smartphone or an electric toaster or a Smurf. So Denison's Cassius needs to use a time-telling device that actually existed in his era and language; he says:

---

* Back to that questionable Raghav line about *Taming of the Shrew* for Indian audiences being specifically a good cultural match . . .

> BRUT —*Hora quota est?*
> CASS —*Clepsydra nonam indicat.*
> TREB —*Abeundum.*

The word here is *clepsydra*, a water clock – from the Greek κλεψύδρα, water stealer. Errikos Belies has one in his *Merchant of Venice* – and we've seen its components parts before: the <u>κλέ</u>β<u>ει</u> from 'stealing and giving odour', and <u>ύδωρ</u>, water, as in a fire <u>hydr</u>ant on the *Queen Mary 2*.

(Incidentally, you might have spotted an extra bit of helpful cultural adjustment by our diligent friend Denison: the clock that strikes three in English is indicating *nonam* in Latin; it's the ninth hour, by the Roman method.)

The Hindi translator Jason Grunebaum coined the useful term 'stealth gloss' to describe the phenomenon whereby a translator will smuggle in a bit of cultural information to scaffold your reading – but you won't notice the insertion has been made. Unlike a footnote, where you can tell that there's a helpful intervention, a stealth gloss is, as the name suggests, less conspicuous.

I might take this Brazilian sentence:

> *E na parede, atrás dele, um antigo retrato de Getúlio Vargas.*

and render it thus:

> And on the wall, behind him, an old portrait of President Getúlio Vargas.

Compare phrase by phrase, and I imagine you'll see where I have discreetly – *stealthily* – given you a bit of cultural information (which the original readership would be assumed to have). But if you were only reading my translation, you would have no idea that I'd done this; you'd simply read right through it.

(For this example, my Brazilian translator might want to translate Getúlio Vargas into François Mitterand.)

It's harder for a director or dramaturg to smuggle a bit of new information into the English-Shakespeare text (without upsetting the verse or the sensibilities of the very precious), but it's easy enough for a translator to change a 'Henry' to a 'King Henry', or a 'York' to a 'Duke of York' (or even 'his uncle York') – just a bit of help in keeping track of characters.

When William Shakespeare's competent translation* of *Much Ado about Nothing* was painstakingly restored to its original Klingon, the cultural markers it adopted were those of Klingon culture, not Shakespearean England/pseudo-Sicily. For:

and then there's a partridge wing saved

the translators have opted for:

vaj, reghuluS 'Iwghargh polchoHlu'

which literally means, of course, 'So a Regulan bloodworm has been conserved'.

Where Benedick is compared, for his valour, to Hector, a hero of terrestrial mythology, be'neDIq is compared to Aktuh, from the famous Klingon opera *Aktuh and Maylota*.

Whereas Margaret's request that Benedick write her a sonnet,

---

* When translated work gets reviewed, it is customary – if frustrating – for the translation to be entirely unconsidered, except for one vague, passing adverb or adjective. '*Book Title*, fluently translated by Daniel Hahn, is . . .' Or 'in a seamless translation by Daniel Hahn, . . .' (Why do you assume seamlessness is what I'm after?) *Limpid* is another favourite. I'm not even sure what 'limpid' means, but I once had two of them in the same week.

ghIq jI'IH 'e' DanaDmeH jIHvaD <u>Sonet</u> Daqon'a'? [emphasis mine]

does preserve the cultural specifics, because the sonnet form does apparently exist within Klingon poetry (I imagine the term itself is a loan word from Terran English).*

Bringing us back, then, to that sonnet from Juliet and Romeo's first meeting, which plays with ideas of pilgrims and palmers and saints. The translations we saw in Chapter 3 were made into languages whose audiences might be expected to have a basic familiarity with Catholicism. But when Juliet's Nurse exclaims, 'Jesu, what haste!', and 'Oh, God's lady, dear!' her Māori counterpart says to Hurieta, *E hine, he aha te whāwhai?* and *Ki a koe hoki, e hine!* – neither Jesus nor God are part of the exclamation. (The word *hine* is simply a way of addressing a girl.)

And their dawn conversation in *te reo* Māori is not about larks and nightingales, but about *tūī* and *ruru* (the latter being an onomatopoeic name for the morepork owl) – a translation not just of the words but of the species, to make sense within the new context's local fauna.

Some cultural adaptation is deliberate, but it's also easy to do a bit of cultural re-centering by accident. When Puck refers to a 'roasted crab', he is not referring to a crustacean but a crab *apple* – Abhijit had this mistake pointed out to him in the nick of time. In Bengal's seafood-eating culture, it's a mistake easily explained.

A translator must be aware of the context she's working in, the associations an audience might bring. And, as with the inadvertently added ambiguities we've discussed above, keep alert to uninvited details of new culture slipping in, too. (Ugh, *summer!*) It's surprisingly easy accidentally to add anachronistic or culturally inappropriate references that might distract.

When working on *La Vorágine*, Victor and I found one phrase that

---

* While we're in that cultural universe: Leonard Nimoy found himself in his later years missing his boyhood Yiddish, so memorised a Yiddish translation of 'To be or not to be'. I found this information pleasing.

would have been a nice translation in the context but ruled it out because it had an echo that would have been distracting. The phrase was 'pale fire' – the first translator of *La Vorágine* could have used it if he'd wanted to, because Nabokov's *Pale Fire* didn't exist at the time, but today it's a bit of interference we don't want. Likewise, the fact that the book's previous translators were able safely to preserve the narrator's 'tinder' metaphor when talking about his seductions. (On the other hand, we did sneak in a little Samuel Beckett joke which is equally anachronistic but it makes me laugh.*)

When the Potters had a kid and named him Harry, back in 1970, that's one thing; likewise any pre-1980s Kylie – or for that matter a pre-1930s Adolf. Choosing those names today is another matter, no longer associatively innocuous. As they travel between languages, Shakespeare's plays are also moving great distances in place and time; so we need to avoid inadvertent pollution, unhelpful echoes, if we can.

Unless you can control them, of course . . . What cultural enrichment might you *choose* to bring in from your culture – deliberately, positively – that is useful rather than distracting?

Let's go back to that Lembcke ending to *Romeo and Juliet* (we saw it when considering his sequencing of the lovers' names):

> *En større Sorg i Verden ingen ved*
> *end Romeos og Julies Kærlighed*

There's something extra happening here. An early-nineteenth-century short story called 'Hosckræmmeren' (The Stocking Pedlar) by Steen Steensen Blicher features a girl prevented from marrying the boy she loves; the unfortunate girl goes mad and sings a song that begins 'The greatest sorrow in this world':

> *Den største sorg i verden her . . .*

---

* No, not telling.

A line from a Danish story, written long after Shakespeare, but it's here, in a delicate little tribute stitched in by a Danish translator.

Similarly, Chico's lines for Juliet that we saw on p.124 (the nightingale/lark conversation) are actually referencing the work of an important twentieth-century Brazilian poet, João Cabral de Melo Neto, and his poem 'Tecendo a Manhã' – 'weaving the morning'. Most people won't even notice; to those who do, the quiet, respectful nod in the older poet's direction is lovely.

Culture lives in idioms, too – and again, a translator has the choice of translating an idiom's meaning (oh, it's raining female trolls!), or using a pre-existing one of their own (ugh, it's raining cats and dogs today . . .) – these cats and dogs in a translation are 'domesticating', the female trolls would be 'foreignising'. The latter has advantages: giving a reader a new way of looking at things is more interesting than just recycling a cliché. Back in the Prologue, I referenced the phrase 'just the tip of the iceberg', which is rather inert and you barely noticed it, but if I'd said – as they do in Afrikaans – 'our discussions were only *the ears of the hippopotamus*', well, *that* you would have noticed. The disadvantage, though, is that you're taking a textual moment that's inconspicuous and making it strange, which might not be the effect you want at that exact juncture.

In Spain you will typically find *Much Ado about Nothing* swapping out its English idiomatic title for a Spanish idiomatic title. In Spanish, the play is *Mucho ruido y pocas nueces*. A lot of noise, not many nuts. Most translators will keep the novelty when Shakespeare has produced novelty – a surprising image or juxtaposition, say, but they'll swap in a set phrase of theirs for a set phrase of his. As a bonus, it's a nice way to show off the richness of the language they're writing in.

So when Shakespeare has Juliet's Nurse say:

> dost thou fall upon thy face?

the Nurse in Te Haumihiata's translation says:

I te hopu kiore koe?

– an existing idiom that literally means 'were you trying to catch a rat?' (I love this.)

Or we might go to Bulgarian, another language that's idiomatically rich. When Anglophone Hamlet, discussing whether he will ever accede to the throne, begins quoting a proverb (but then stops himself) –

Ay, sir, but while the grass grows . . .

Alexander gives him this line

Да, сър, ама трай коньо . . .

which is the beginning of an existing Bulgarian proverb – Трай, коньо, за зелена трева – meaning 'Wait for ever for something promised to you'. The first couple of words should be enough for a Bulgarian audience to know where he's going . . .

When translating for publication rather than performance, of course, retaining any kind of obscurity, whether linguistic or contextual – cultural, horticultural, culinary, etc. – is easier to justify, since it's possible to footnote the translation as a way of filling out the reader's knowledge. Some of the translations we've looked at are footnoted quite comprehensively. King Rama's *Romeo and Juliet* has ocassional notes on characters (remarking that the Nurse uses a lot of rude language), and explaining literal translations, and on cultural things, often Christian ones, including a long note on various holidays prompted by the Nurse's mentioning Lammas. Page 103 of Kazuko Matsuoka's *Twelfth Night* has two helpful notes, on the line 'If thou thou'st him . . .' and on 'the bed of Ware'. But that's no use to an actor, who isn't supposed to interrupt himself every few lines to explain what you're missing.

It's a matter of taste, I suppose. When I'm translating, I do smuggle things in when I feel it's important, but I'm also quite comfortable with my readers not knowing everything. An editor wrote a note on a manuscript recently saying 'our readers won't know what this ref. is', and I tried to find a polite way of saying 'I honestly don't care'. True, not everyone in Poland will know what the Bed of Ware is, but not everyone in the Anglosphere knows it today either. Never mind. On we go . . .

Chapter 32

αν δεν την καταλαβαίνετε ούτε σεις, δεν πειράζει

(on understanding, and multilingualism)

For the last decade, I have raved about a Georgian-language production of *As You Like It* that I saw at Shakespeare's Globe (twice!) and loved. But today, before I go on, I must acknowledge that in my enthusiasm, I never tried to find the name of the translator whose work the Marjanishvili company was performing, and I really ought to know better. So first things first, making amends: it was a version by Lasha Bugadze, probably based on a translation by Mose Qarchava.

Always #namethetranslator.

I don't speak any Georgian, but that in no way impeded my enjoyment. At the time of writing this, I have seen Shakespeare in fifteen or twenty languages – most of them languages I don't understand, and many of these were presented without surtitles – and have often been thrilled by them. Now, *As You Like It* is a play I know pretty well, so although the Georgian company had made changes, I could follow it – and I mean follow it sometimes at every beat, not just broad narrative strokes. But what happens when you have less background knowledge to go on? How do you respond?

One of the exercises I regularly give students is to translate a text from a language with which they have little or no familiarity. I've said before that in literary translation, bald 'meaning' is often not the most important thing, and it's certainly not the *only* important thing. But the tyranny of meaning can be hard to prise oneself from. And it's amazing what you can notice if you don't have meaning to distract you.

When Maureen Freely and I were co-teaching a course in 2016, we gave our students a George Seferis poem to translate. Maureen and I both know some Greek, but no one else in the room did. They got the text in the original Greek and the same thing transliterated into Latin characters, we read it aloud to them a couple of times, and played the Theodorakis song setting. Then they produced their translations.

The poem contains the line:

διψάσαμε το μεσημέρι
[*dipsásame to mesiméri*]

which means:

we were thirsty at midday

The French translator Ruth Diver does *not* know Greek, but she did spot the comedic possibilities in a poem about a character called Messy Mary. Maureen and I had always been peskily distracted by knowing what *μεσημέρι* 'means' – those syllables conjured a time of day in our minds, not a nickname. Ruth privileged something different. Her translation was much funnier than mine.

I know *A Midsummer Night's Dream* well, but there was a bit of patterning I only noticed for the first time when looking at a speech in Welsh, a language I don't know at all. If you don't understand Spanish, you might have been better placed to notice every variant detail in those *To be* . . . speeches on p.149, just focusing on a game of spot-the-difference without being distracted by meaning/understanding. Apparently Frank Kermode would encourage his students to look at Shakespeare in French – I wonder if this useful alienation was one of the reasons?

Some Shakespeare plays lend themselves to language-less experiencing (or rather, experiencing without access to the *meaning* of the language) better than others. Plays where there are many turns in the plot, scenes with narrative momentum, clear moments of revelation and surprise – and not too many long speeches that are narratively static. If you want entertaining plot unhampered by people talking too much, I would not recommend watching *Love's Labour's Lost*, which has some scenes that are only there for language, and which is filled with our young playwright showing off how clever he is by writing lots of young characters showing off how clever they are . . .

Skilled performance can fill in many gaps, of course. Of the many things I've seen staged in a language that's not conventionally accessible to me, one of the most pleasing was the Māori *Troilus and Cressida* that visited Shakespeare's Globe in 2012. I was struck by how comfortable the actors were on that unusual stage, with that huge visible audience (Pandarus especially) – how engaging they were, telling a story. Because it's not a play I know well, or a language I know at all, I only meant to watch a few minutes – but ended up sitting there in the Globe archive watching all two hours on a small screen, as rapt as the live audience, right through till their whooping applause at the end.

A Midsummer Night's Dream, though, is particularly full of delightful things and they are not all dependent on detailed deciphering of complex language. As I've mentioned earlier, the dispute between Hermia and Lysander was just as funny in the ballet I saw as in any more word-based production.

Back in Chapter 21, we heard Oberon talk of his plans to squeeze the juice of a magical flower into the sleeping Titania's eyes, so we know that she is about to fall passionately in love with the first creature she sees on waking, but then we watch the weaver Nick Bottom being given an ass's head, and here he is now, pacing up and down beside her bower, singing loudly. We know, then, what will happen, that she will wake to this grotesque sight . . . and fall in love. Titania's first waking line is:

> What angel wakes me from my flowery bed?

It's a beautiful line, and it's in verse (remember that in this ill-matched relationship, Titania speaks verse and Bottom prose) and the phrase's lovely lightness – juxtaposed with Bottom's clumsy singing and the ludicrousness of the situation – only enhances the humour. Ass-headed Bottom is not an obvious subject for delicate love poetry. The line is not *inherently* funny – in most other contexts that exact sequence of words wouldn't be. But it contributes to an irresistibly good dramatic *moment*. And – as I can confirm, having seen this play in several languages I don't understand – even without the words, the moment is very funny indeed.

Similar things happen in *The Comedy of Errors* (once you can get past a very long speech at the top that is somebody just telling a very long backstory with words), where the plot is increasingly entangled and then we can delight in the characters' revelations. *Twelfth Night* is a much more complex play, but one of the many pleasures of its ending is not unlike *The Comedy of Errors* as each character in turn works out how wrong they've been and what the implications are. *Othello* has fewer jokes than *A Midsummer Night's Dream*, but it's pure drama, with many tightly wound scenes of dramatic revelation and changes of fortune, and many scenes of *I-know-something-you-don't-know*.

(Emine mentions in passing, in our conversation, that she is 'in love with Iago', because, she says, 'he is the essence of theatre'.)

Twelfth Night is the play I know best, to the point where in a translated production I can usually tell not just where we are in the overall story but which line we're on, give or take. When I saw *Vízkereszt* in Budapest – Ádám's Hungarian translation – I spent the first twenty minutes or so essentially running the parallel text in my head, monitoring our progress. (Though the director did swap two scenes at the opening, trying to throw me.) It's how I knew each time there was a good laugh coming, even if I didn't know how the translator was going to get it.

Then I let go of the mental handrail, and started actually watching the story that was being told, and that's when I started to enjoy myself.

When I described this experience to director Tim Supple, he said those were the moments he's looking for in his own work, where we access the thing that's beneath (or inside?) the language, and are not aware of the fact that we're processing language at all. Like boring for oil, he said, the translation is about:

> gaining access to something that lies within Shakespeare – which of itself is embodied in Shakespeare in a language that is not entirely familiar to us, so our experience is through this keyhole of limited comprehension. That's its magic and its mystery. What you're looking for is those moments that get to *the thing*, the thing that's inside it, which is not always reliant on detailed linguistic decoding.

Titania wakes, and the audience should laugh – not thinking about the words (even if it's the words that deliver it), but because they have a feeling for the relational and narrative moment. When Tim's *Dream* was played in a village in Tamil Nadu to an audience who would mostly not have understood the text being spoken, that exact moment, he said, 'crystallised a certain aspect of Shakespeare's genius . . . It was so clear from the audience's delight in that moment that it was deeply recognisable.'

Where *Love's Labour's Lost* has several scenes that can be hard to animate on stage (even on the contemporary English-language stage), because there is little to them but conversation, pretty much every scene in *A Midsummer Night's Dream* has a great narrative engine driving it. Jean-Michel cited this distinction to explain why we see so few plays by Racine staged in English – he's a writer for whom language is everything. A play like *Bérénice* has very little plot – 'it's all music, it's all language'. It's a beautiful literary play, but Racine never wrote anything as generously, theatrically user-friendly as *A Midsummer Night's Dream*.

Being one of Shakespeare's most effectively theatrical, most purely dramatic plays, full of those moments of narrative delight, in which an audience can follow the drama rather than the speeches, it's not for nothing that the *Dream* is a pretty classic first-introduction-to-Shakespeare play. It was my Shakespeare gateway as a kid, and quite possibly yours, for those who can't yet manage *Antony and Cleopatra* or *Cymbeline*, but that also makes it one of the better plays to watch in a language over which one doesn't have great mastery. Which was one of the things that made it ideal for Tim Supple's production, which used a script that *no* audience member could ever fully understand . . .

Tim's experience of directing Shakespeare in other languages has included a Turkish *Comedy of Errors*, a German *Much Ado about Nothing* and a Chinese *Tempest*. The first pair were relatively straightforward, though *Much Ado* was the more controversial of these in translation terms because the cast didn't get along with the pre-existing version chosen, wanting something more modern – so they staged an insurrection. ('A very friendly and stimulating, interesting insurrection,' Tim says.)

The Tempest is a denser play, demanding some understanding of a psychological, cultural, historical, philosophical world that inevitably proved more distant for a Chinese audience – quite apart from the huge gap between the languages themselves. Rehearsals involved much greater scrutiny of the translated text, which was newly commissioned for the production. Once they'd been encouraged to do so, Tim found his actors very ready to request small-scale changes to their lines – sometimes because a speech was convoluted (often Shakespeare's fault), or because the translator had replicated some of the archaism by using a word that might exist in Chinese vocabulary but is outside common usage. Here we're talking about a director who began with no sense of 'how Mandarin moves from the page to the voice', as he put it, nor any instinct for the stresses of the language (though that instinct is improved now, he says, having done the production twice). He did also use a revealing – if laborious and admittedly inadequate – process of back-translation to attempt to get a handle on it. Another part of the solution for the director is trust, of course, earned gradually by the translator.

The translator in question was So Kwok Wan, whose work we've seen already. So was the very last translator I talked to for this book – a happy conversation to end on. We met on Zoom – I was back home in Western Europe, he was in East Asia, smoking a cigarette and putting the finishing touches to his arts festival in Hong Kong. It was a busy moment in the programming cycle, but he took the time to meet, to share his positive translation memories.

Each of So's Shakespeare translations to date was done in close concert with an English-language director (through the RSC) who would be directing a Chinese-language production. Each director explained their vision and helped to unpack the text, and So's translation was based on those conversations. He referred to the 'Second Shakespeare' with whom he collaborated in each case – and he's sort of joking, but also sort of not, because his translation depended on their reading of the play – like a bridge – as well as Shakespeare's published words.

When a director was particularly committed to the detailed workings of the text, like Tim, or Owen Horsley, the conversations could be incredibly in-depth. If So had to choose between, maybe, five different Chinese options for 'virtue' or 'mercy', his understanding of the director's precise reading would inform that choice. 'Tim is a very thorough thinker,' So said, 'he wants to understand what *exactly* this [Chinese] word means.' The line-by-line consideration is slow and multidimensional, ensuring he's able to 'match the English intention, the rhythms, so the actor can understand how it can be delivered'. So is not using iambic pentameter, or rhyming in the same way as Shakespeare, but he is guided by sentence structure, thought, sound, by a wish to produce something that works for the actors, and by a trust in the guiding director – just as the director must trust him.

At the end of our conversation, I invited So to show off a bit – go on, tell me some specific part you're just *really proud of* – but he wouldn't. His answer, instead, was about gratitude, about how much he'd learned from this work with Tim and co. How it had taught him how text 'propels an actor, how it states an intention, how you get the actor all the clues.' It taught him 'how we read and understand a script.' What else? 'About theatre-making. Shakespeare is really about that. It's just wonderful.'

* * *

While Tim has worked a lot in translation, and is interested in the process and what it allows, translation per se is not the dramatic experiment he's engaged with. His projects begin with people – not 'I wonder how *A Comedy of Errors* functions in Turkish', but 'I have people in Turkey I want to work with, and in order to do that . . .' For a director, he says, this is the ideal way round.

The most translationally extreme case generated one of his most celebrated productions, a South Asian *Midsummer Night's Dream*, first performed in India in 2006. Tim began by casting whomever he thought best for the roles – regardless of the culture or state they came from – and worried about their language competencies afterwards. The production was ultimately spoken in seven different working languages.

Some actors were Anglophone, so could speak the source text; some spoke another South Asian language; many could move between English and one or more other languages, with varying degrees of comfort. Every actor got their lines translated into their respective language; then it became clear that they would also need their interlocutors' lines translated (so they didn't drift off when ostensibly in 'conversation' with someone they actually didn't understand), and then, of course each character's lines needed to be translated into the language(s) spoken by their understudy, too. Our Bangla translator Abhijit Gupta was a part of this project, which is why all the examples you've seen of his work come from Puck, a character who just happened to be understudied by a Bangla-speaking actor.

That production, then, was not translating into *a language*; it was a translation into a country's very particular linguistic context. For India, this means not only a multiplicity of languages, it also means there's English threaded throughout. As an English speaker in South Asia, you will regularly hear English words woven through other languages, infiltrating everything. So even a Bangla-speaking Puck is not purely Bangla-monolingual. Here's the end of the play, which we saw on p.40 – *so, good night unto you all*, etc., in Abhijit's translation:

নইলে মিথ্যেবাদী যেন হয় পাক,
এবার তাহলে **গুড নাইট** বলা যাক।*
সব শোধবোধ হবে, দৃঢ় হবে বন্ধন,
হাততালি দিয়ে যদি কর অভিনন্দন ॥

This is roughly what that sounds like

No'ilē mithyē bādī jē no hoẏ pāk,
ēbār tāholē guḍ nā'iṭ bolā jāk.
Sob śōdhbōdh hobē, dṛṛha hobē bandhan,
hātatāli diẏē jodi karo abhinandan.

Abhijit here is employing two words that Bangla speakers often use colloquially but aren't themselves Indo-Aryan words. I've picked them out of the second line: গুড নাইট – *guḍ nā'iṭ*.

A multilingual production means that different audience members will have quite different experiences (more than each person would have of any show anyway, I mean), depending on the access allowed by their particular language competencies. As will happen for readers of this book, which jumps around between languages and is untroubled by whether you – or I – know them, so different things will come into focus for each of us. If I write the word *norsu*, every reader will see the same ink marks, but some of you just pictured an elephant. As an audience member, you might understand only the words spoken by, say, Quince, Helena and Philostrate; while the person sitting next to you understands only Egeus and Titania. When the production toured, it became clear that most non-South Asian audiences treated this as a bilingual production, rather than a multilingual one; unable to differentiate instantly between Tamil and Hindi or between Bangla and Sinhala, they felt the production simply shifting between English and not-English. 'I really liked the bits *in Indian*,' some audience members said.

---

* Note the Bangla full stop we've seen before.

The multi-language nature of the Supple production was driven by collaborative ambitions, and it nicely expressed the multilingual realities of its setting. It was not designed to shore up an interpretation of the play – though multilingual, hybrid texts are used for that purpose often. The Globe's recent *Antony and Cleopatra*, say, where the play's two worlds are represented by English (Antony/Rome) and BSL (Cleopatra/Egypt). There's also been a *Winter's Tale* in Delhi, where the Sicilian court used the original English text, and rural Bohemia used Hindustani; an English-language *Dream* in Aotearoa/New Zealand featuring Māori-speaking fairies; the *Twelfth Night* now playing in New York where, in a default English-speaking world, Swahili is the common language shared by newly washed-ashore twins Viola and Sebastian; or Theatr Clwyd's *Romeo and Juliet* currently in rehearsal in bilingual Wales, where the Montagues mostly speak Welsh and the Capulets English (though being Wales, it's more fluid than this suggests, with Juliet's Welsh improving as the play progresses).

India has twenty-two so-called 'scheduled' languages (recognised by government through an article in the constitution) and countless others also spoken there. An Indian *Dream* was always going to be complicated. So let us move from the inherent unmanageability of such a place to a little patch of northern Europe. Southern Jutland is the territory where southern Denmark borders northern Germany, and a large proportion of its inhabitants are reasonably comfortable understanding both those countries' principal languages. What better place, then, for a production of *Romeo and Juliet* where Capulets and Montagues live in different but adjacent linguistic worlds?

You have seen a lot of Niels Brunse's and Frank Günther's work in this book already. For this *Romeo and Juliet*, staged in 2021, a translation was commissioned that brought their work together – a specific bilingual text produced for a specific bilingual audience. Juliet and the Capulets were German-speaking (using Frank's translation), Romeo and the Montagues Danish-speaking (using Niels's). Niels made the two translations slot together – which meant, among other things, creating lines in Danish that rhymed perfectly with lines in German. The languages have some phonetic similarities, but it required much invention. This is the sonnet of Romeo and Juliet's meeting:

ROMEO
Hvis min profane hånd kun vækker vrede
og byder denne helligdom imod,
er mine pilgrimslæber ydmygt rede
til rødmende med kys at gøre bod.

JULIE
Die Buße, Büßer, bleibt der Hand erlassen,
Die Anstand mit der Andacht schön verband.
Denn Büßerhand darf Heilgenhände fassen,
Beim Büßerkuß küßt nur die Hand die Hand.

ROMEO
Har da en helgen ikke læber røde?

JULIE
Doch, Büßer, fromme Lippen zum Gebet.

ROMEO
Min helgen, und da læberne det møde,
som mellem vores hænder her er sket.

JULIE
Das Bild erhört, doch unbeweglich, still.

ROMEO
Så giv mig stille det, som bønnen vil.
                              (Han kysser hende.)

I understand small German and less Danish, yet somehow I love this.

Chapter 33

bir kaç diyarda / Aynı dili kullanmakla

(on multipolar languages)

Depending on which edition of this book you're holding, you might have been presented on p.12 with the word 'Lego' or the word 'Legos', and on p.93 with 'colour' or 'color' – and indeed this sentence might be using single quotation marks or double. I'm fortunate to have two separate English-language publishers for this book, and you're unlikely to have noticed the thousand tiny accommodations that have been made to bring this text close to you. English is vast and variable (and ever-changing) – the occasional little 'u' is the least of it.

If I were writing a novel set in London, I would make my characters sound like they're in London. There are markers of idiom and vocabulary and pronunciation I could use to draw you into that setting. If my protagonist's friend wandered into the scene, and they were visiting from Glasgow, or Belfast or Texas, their way of expressing themselves could similarly be marked – that's easy enough. The distinctive features of Texas English are not the same as those for Glasgow English.

It's rarely that simple in translations.

Well-written characters will all sound distinct, of course. Hamlet doesn't sound like Falstaff, though both are speaking their default English. In French they should sound different, but their voices made up of . . . Paris French? North African French? Québec French?

I'm currently translating a novel set in Lima. So what's the default English that *my* characters speak? What are the distinctive features of urban Peruvian English? And how do I make my Lima characters sound different from their cousins who live in more rural parts of that country? What sort of markers would make you, my dear Anglophone reader, know instinctively that this is a character from Peru's north-east?

(Bringing us back to the Welsh accents marked in Shakespeare and his translations, where the effect presupposes that all surrounding text is what's normative, the baseline English from which this exceptional voice is deviating.)

The same word used by different writers does different things – what might be an archaic word in one Portuguese is a standard common use one in another. We see this in English, too – my friends in India use the word 'thrice' as a regular everyday word, while it hasn't been current in *my* part of the Anglosphere for ages. (You've seen it a few times in this book, but used by Shakespeare and Coleridge, not by me.)

Some of the examples I've used hitherto might fairly represent a translation language, but only within regional specificities. Claims that I made about the division of second-person pronouns in Spanish, say, are technically true in Spain; they are less true in Argentina, where the distinction is made differently – and actually, Argentine young people are only using that formal 'you' very seldom in everyday speech anyway, so it might not survive another generation. An Argentine Shakespeare in 2050 might erase the distinction altogether.

I've referenced Chico's 'translations into Portuguese' many times, but what does that 'Portuguese' even mean? Yes, Chico turns Shakespeare into Portuguese, but it's Brazilian Portuguese specifically, and it's not from Rio, which is where my Portuguese comes from. His language is not like mine, not quite. When he said there wasn't a way of moving between *you* and *thou* meaningfully ('I would need to change the language I'm translating into too much'), he was talking about an impossibility in his *specific* Portuguese – in his specific place, today.

And his choices about rhythm – that we saw on p.25 – are determined by what works when *he* speaks a line. Chico is from the southern state of Rio Grande do Sul, a part of the country, he says, where they tend to overstress some heavy syllables and de-emphasise the rest – so in his mouth, a line might have only three or four heavy beats, even if it's a dozen syllables long. This from Mercutio's Queen Mab speech (which we'll be looking at in Russian in the next chapter):

Seu carro é uma casca de avelã

usually sounds like a ten-syllable line (just like the source line: *Her chariot is an empty hazelnut*), but when Chico reads it back to me in a conversational tone, it's only got three noticeable stresses in it. Give the text to an actor who is not him, and it might test them.

Because features like, say, second-person pronouns are used differently across the lusophone world, creating something that works for every reader/audience is, well, maybe not impossible but pretty close.

Usually, when I say that English does/doesn't/is something or other, I'm talking about *my* English. I mentioned that *I* don't consider 'blood' and 'good' a perfect rhyming pair, but maybe, as the song goes, it's because I'm a Londoner; they are still a perfect match to 1960s Liverpudlians, say. As I discovered when writing song lyrics with some American friends, my 'better' and 'feta' are not a perfect rhyme for everybody. And beneath the accent, each of us has a language use that is particular to us, an idiolect, the combination of vocabulary, grammar and pronunciation whose usage is distinctively ours. When I asked my friend Susana to read a few of Chico's lines aloud, they didn't all rhyme quite as they do when I say them, because Susana is from Portugal, and therefore far too busy to pronounce vowels. (My family's from Rio – we even pronounce vowels that aren't there.)

In theory, one might aim for a sort of multi-continentally neutral translation – but neutrality never comes easily to these big (colonial) languages. However much people might want it – translators, publishers or even readers – *neutral* language does not exist. It's easy to assume the contrary, and I often encounter early-career Anglophone translators who are unaware of the ways in which their own translations are inflected – we all centre ourselves as a default. Not that I think translators should be trying to avoid this; on the contrary, a translator's own particular resources supply them with the tools to produce interesting work. But an awareness of this is useful, especially when translating for the stage. The Peruvian novel I'm currently translating will be read by anybody who happens to secure a copy, anywhere and at any time, now or in future. ('But why do all these Peruvians sound like they live in Sussex?') After this, I will be translating a play, which will be performed on a day, in a room.

Just as every audience member is different, so too is every book reader, but we cluster them based on assumptions that flatten those differences out. This version is for The American Market, that one for The Australian Market. Group A will know these things and have that sort of accent; Group B need pandering to in some other way.

Translators take account of their particular audiences or not (I work with publishers all over the Anglo world, each with their own sense of their distinct readership), but translators also have languages of their own. Should I translate to British, because that's the tool I wield most effectively, or American, because my publisher is based in Brooklyn, and my readers are assumed to be on their land mass?

In book publishing, there's usually a mix of the two – I might use my language, and make editorial concessions in conversation with a publisher elsewhere. Sometimes that opportunity doesn't arise because publishers increasingly publish single global editions for sale everywhere, so all bets are off. This can be a factor with small-press children's picture-book publishing especially (I had to forego 'colour/color' and 'marvellous/marvelous' entirely in a recent job). In the theatre, of course, one might have a better sense of who one's audience is, to inform one's choices. They are here and now, this audience, in this theatre in Rio tonight, they're the ones who need to be persuaded that these characters are real people, acting and interacting as real people do.

Chapter 34

Why, now you speak as I would have you speak

(on actors)

Boris Pasternak was a great poet, the author of *Doctor Zhivago* and – conveniently for me – a rather good translator of Shakespeare into Russian, producing translations of eight plays that have been much studied and admired. Perhaps my favourite Shakespeare film is Grigori Kozintsev's magnificently bleak *Korol Lir* – it's a *King Lear*, ostensibly by the English Jacobethan dramatist Уильям Шекспир, but in all Russian words, and it was Pasternak who made those words.

While Pasternak is a great admirer of Shakespeare's prose, he has doubts about the verse, which seems to him too often rushed. His own translations avoided the archaisms that others used before him, opting instead for what Kozintsev praised as 'natural contemporary language'. ('Natural' is an interesting notion in this context.) The translator, wrote Pasternak, must avoid anything that seems to be 'literary artifice', and 'create an impression of life'.

But the fixed metre of the verse in *Romeo and Juliet*, he wrote, 'is never obvious. There is no declamation. The form never asserts itself at the expense of the infinitely discreet content. This is poetry at its best, and, like all such poetry it has the freshness and simplicity of prose.' These are the properties of the original verse, so any new-wrought translated verse should be the same.

Translators work within odd constraints, as we know, making thousands upon thousands of choices, determining what to prioritise at each moment – lose *this* to gain *that*. So no two translators, good or bad, would ever independently produce the same translation of any substantial work. Each translation bears its translator's fingerprints, and that individuality is unavoidable – indeed, desirable. There's much to be said for allowing an individual translator's creativity free(-ish) rein. Kozintsev wrote that Pasternak's Shakespeare 'is all the voice of a great poet, and the rhythm of his breathing is always audible' – a line that pleases me because while I *think* Kozintsev is referring to the great poet Pasternak rather than the great poet Shakespeare, you can't be quite sure.

Anna Radlova was the same generation as Pasternak, and she, too, translated several Shakespeare plays into Russian. *Romeo and Juliet* was one of the plays on which the two translators overlapped, so I sat down with my friend Sasha to do a little comparison. We used the Queen Mab speech, in which Romeo's animated friend Mercutio riffs on the fairies' tiny midwife who rides around helping people to give birth to their dreams.

Here's how it begins in Shakespeare, with the first half-dozen lines of the speech:

ROMEO
   I dreamt a dream tonight.
MERCUTIO
                     And so did I.
ROMEO
   Well, what was yours?
MERCUTIO
                     That dreamers often lie.
ROMEO
   In bed asleep while they do dream things true.

Mercutio
> O, then I see Queen Mab hath been with you.
> She is the fairies' midwife, and she comes
> In shape no bigger than an agate stone
> On the forefinger of an alderman,
> Drawn with a team of little atomi
> Over men's noses as they lie asleep . . .

And now for the Russian:

Pasternak	**Radlova**
Всё королева Маб. Её проказы.	О, вижу, верно, королева Меб*
Она родоприемница у фей,	У вас была. Она у эльфов бабка
А по размерам — с камушек агата	И росту всего-навсего с агат
В кольце у мэра. По ночам она	У олдермена в перстне. Цугом ездит
На шестерне пылинок цугом ездит	Она на атомах по человечьим
Вдоль по носам у нас, пока мы спим.	Носам, когда они заснут покрепче.

Scan across it line by line – almost no words the same (though you can see 2 × королева – queen). In the first line, even Mab is different – Russian doesn't have a flat 'a' sound like English (hat, cap, Mab), so the options are a longer 'a' as Pasternak has it – *Maahb* – or a short 'e' for Radlova – *Meb*. Radlova gives the speech a nice exclamatory start (*O!*), as Shakespeare does. And that 'верно' is a natural-sounding parenthetical (like 'then' or 'truly').

---

* As far as I can tell Radlova's translation is sometimes published with *Меб*, sometimes with *Маб*. – I've encountered both versions.

Pasternak starts slower – the first line has a break in it (and it's a pause after that open-voweled *Мааb*) and it's end-stopped like the English. There will be more of this, especially in the latter part of the speech; over the whole speech, Pasternak ends fifteen sentences at the ends of lines, Radlova only ten. (Oh, and Pasternak starts only six lines with И [*And*], to Radlova's nine.)

Pasternak begins by saying: *the whole thing is Queen Mab*; Radlova says Queen Mab was *У вас* – with you (or *chez vous*, or similar). Her version of the speech has an explicit addressee, then; Pasternak's doesn't.

Three word-choice distinctions:

- For Shakespeare's *midwife*, we can choose between Pasternak's *родоприемница* vs Radlova's *бабка*. Russian commonly uses a borrowing of the French word *accoucheur*, but that's hard to fit metrically in here. Radlova's *бабка* is an old lady, a sort of folklorish word, but also part of *повивальная бабка* (midwife); whereas Pasternak's chosen word is incredibly long – something like *birth-receiver** (though remember this is a language that does without articles or the verb 'to be' in the present – the *zero copula* we've encountered before – so he saves space elsewhere).
- Pasternak uses *фей* (*fyey* – fairies); Radlova *эльфов* (*elfov* – elves) – though she'll use *фей* later.
- the signet ring is either on the finger of a *мэр* (mayor, Pasternak) or an *олдермена* (alderman, Radlova) – *alderman* is a loan word, and a foreignising feature of the faraway English-speaking world, which Radlova has preserved. (Pasternak's *мэр* could easily be Russian.)

That *всего-навсего* in Radlova's third line conveys the 'only' aspect of 'no bigger than' – it's very casual, and there's nothing like it in Pasternak. In general terms, his is quite compressed – not unusually for him. (What he is not, is loose, chatty.)

Oh, and look at that last line now:

---

* I haven't found this Russian word anywhere else – I wonder if it might be a neologism?

Pasternak: Вдоль по носам у нас, пока мы <u>спим</u>.
Radlova: Носам, когда они <u>заснут</u> покрепче.

The word I've marked is the *sleep* part of *'Over men's noses as they lie asleep'*. The Pasternak means *while we are asleep*, the Radlova *when they fall asleep*. The difference? спать is to sleep; заснуть is to fall asleep. One of those nifty Slavic prefixes we looked at in Chapter 18.

Incidentally, you might have noticed we changed pronouns between those variant lines. That's because, while Shakespeare's Mercutio has Mab's chariot riding *over men's noses as they lie asleep*, Radlova changes it to *humans' noses* (по человечьим / Носам), and Pasternak makes it into <u>our</u> *noses* (по носам у нас). Read into those choices what you will.

A bit more of Shakespeare's irrepressible Mercutio, now describing Queen Меб's chariot:

> Her wagon-spokes made of long spinners' legs,
> The cover of the wings of grasshoppers,
> Her traces of the smallest spider web,
> Her collars of the moonshine's watery beams,
> Her whip of cricket's bone, the lash of film,
> Her wagoner a small grey-coated gnat,
> Not half so big as a round little worm
> Pricked from the lazy finger of a maid. *

Pasternak
В колёсах – спицы из паучьих лапок,
Каретный верх – из крыльев саранчи,

Radlova
В колесах спицы – ноги пауков,
И крылышки кузнечика – верхушка.

---

* I'm stopping here, more or less arbitrarily, limiting us to the first fourteen lines of the speech. Needless to say, there are things to see in lines 15, 16, 17 . . . but this book is getting quite long already.

Ремни гужей – из ниток паутины,	Постромки из нежнейшей паутинки,
И хомуты – из капелек росы.	И хомуты из лунного луча,
На кость сверчка накручен хлыст из пены,	И бич из плёнки с косточкой сверчка;
Комар на козлах – ростом с червячка,	В ливрее серой маленький комарик
Из тех, которые от сонной лени	За кучера: он меньше червячка,
Заводятся в ногтях у мастериц.	Что по руке ленивой девки бродит.

This time, if you compare the first line in each, they do seem to start the same, albeit the dash sits somewhere different:

Pasternak: В колёсах – спицы из паучьих лапок,
Radlova: В колесах спицы – ноги пауков,

The subtle distinction is something like:

in the wheels – spokes of spiders legs
vs
in the wheels' spokes – spiders legs

But you'll also see that Pasternak has dashes running right through this section. Shakespeare has a lot of lines with the words 'is/are made' implied but not spoken; Pasternak's Russian fills the verbless gaps with dashes – the part of the carriage on the left, what it's made of on the right.

Ремни гужей – из ниток паутины
И хомуты – из лунного луча

[The harness straps – of cobweb threads
And collars – of a moonbeam]

(Dashes standing in for invisible to-be verbs are not uncommon in Russian. If you run this through Google Translate, it drops in verbs, because that's what *usually* happens when travelling from Russian to English: 'The harness straps <u>are made</u> of cobweb threads'.)
One last thing – look at the second line

Pasternak: Каретный <u>верх</u> – из <u>крыльев</u> саранчи,
Radlova: И <u>крылышки</u> кузнечика – <u>верхушка</u>.

When I'm translating a Brazilian writer, my messy first drafts always include the word 'little' too often, reflecting the Portuguese facility for producing diminutives of its nouns – done with a suffix that feels a much lighter touch than having to keep adding my extra qualifying adjective. (See the *caipira/caipirinha* on p.80.) A diminutive is an easy thing to do in Russian, too – here Radlova is using two of the same nouns as Pasternak, but she's made them both diminutives. (So eg. крыльев and крылышки – the former being wings, the latter something like . . . winglets?) His line is metrically impeccable, I think; but her diminutive brings a warmth, a softness.

In similar vein, look at the differences between the way they did those gossamer threads –

WS: Her traces of the smallest spider web,

Pasternak: Ремни гужей – из ниток паутины,
Radlova: Постромки из нежнейшей паутинки,

Pasternak's is another quite clipped statement of fact (he was after 'simplicity', remember?), Radlova's I think lovelier. We have паутины vs паутинки – hers is the diminutive again. And she's added the word нежнейшей, a superlative adjective meaning softest or tenderest – and could there be a softer-sounding word than *nyezhnyeyshyey*?

(Oh, and for a coachman, he gives Mab/Maab/Meb а комар, she's а маленький комарик – the added adjective *malenky* being *small*, as any Nadsat speakers know.)

Crucially, I think, a diminutive, expressing something that is so very small – not just a gnat but a minuscule, malenky little teeny-*tiny* gnat – is also an easy thing to *act*. And that's something that several of these textual variations have in common: in many instances, the theatrically minded Radlova is giving the *actor* something to work with; Pasternak might be making a poem. (Shakespeare may be writing verse here, but he's not writing a poem.) There are the diminutives (there's a lot of suggested gesturing – 'yeah, it was <u>this</u> small'), there's her beautifully inflected rhythm and the momentum that you get from running sentences across line endings, and the exclamatory opening, and the direct address, and the folklorish storytelling tone, etc. – all of these things are useful when you're on a stage telling a story . . .

I should say, in Pasternak's defence (because I do love Pasternak), that I'm not claiming these passages to be entirely representative of these two translators' work, but as a little snapshot, these moments are revealing, I think.

I've said before that translators need to concern themselves not merely with what a text says, but what it *does*. In the case of a play – a score for an actor to follow – it's partly about what it does *to an actor*, and what effect that has on their audience. A line break pushes an actor to emphasise a particular word; a listener laughs, surprised by what they hear.

Many of the features of language usage that we've seen in this book so far – whether word choice, rhythm, the lightness or heaviness of stress, hardness or softness of diction, are information for actors to use, whether consciously or not. Actors can learn how to present themselves from what their characters say, and what others say about them, of course; but the language they're given will also determine how it is spoken. Angels and ministers of grace!

Think back to those words in Chapter 16 – to Antony spitting out his reference to Caesar's *butchers*; to Hamlet telling the players, trippingly, to speak *trippingly*; to the Leontes *inch thick, knee-deep* breakdown. These sounds have an effect on an audience, because they have an effect on the mouths and breathing and voices of the actors.

Translations can be more or less obliging to the people who might one day have to speak them aloud, and every translator I spoke to about Shakespeare, without exception, cited this as a significant consideration. The translations are intended to be user-friendly, full of instructive *detail*.

Where Shakespeare has Macbeth shout 'Liar and slave', Jashwant Thaker's Gujarati translation gives the line as જૂઠ! ગુલામ! – which you can see is just a pair of exclaimed stand-alone words, rather than combined into a single exclamation as in English. These Gujarati words are 'Juutthaa! Guulaam!', so the line means (as you might guess) 'Liar! Slave!' The translator has dropped the *and* and given the actor two angrily shoutable words (explosive, big vowels, etc.). Thaker was himself a director and actor, and surely knew what was fittest for his purpose.

We've already seen Jean-Michel's translation of those *Coriolanus* lines, the harshness of:

> *Abjecte meute de roquets,*
> [etc.]

When the Belgian actor Jean-Claude Drouot was rehearsing this role, he asked the translator about some of the diction in the play, suggesting that it was unpleasant-sounding, not mellifluous to speak. Jean-Michel replied, yes, *that's sort of the point* – it's clashing, conflictual, violent. It is not supposed to be pretty. (Our 'You common cry of curs' is not a *pretty* line either.) The actor was encouraged to trust the detail of the translator's text, just as they would trust Shakespeare's.

I should note that while translations can (should) give an actor what they need, an actor can affect translations, too. Jean-Michel did rework some of his Shylock lines when the actor Jean-Luc Boutté said he was struggling with them, for example. And just as a playwright might – as

Shakespeare did – write with foreknowledge of his cast and their abilities, a translator working to a specific production can do the same.

Chaiti Mitra's Bangla translation of *Hamlet*, made for a specific production and specific cast, took inspiration for her courtier Polonius from a south Indian politician, J. Jayalalithaa (known as 'Amma') – making the character power-hungry and sort of absurd, but also motherly, concerned and rather down to earth. It was only the director's decision to cast a woman in the role of Polonia that suggested this connection to the translator at all.

We've previously seen Niels's disagreement with a director regarding his choice between two variant *silences*, and the way the director determined some of the translator's decisions. I did shudder in solidarity when reading an interview where director Terry Hands discussed a production of *Twelfth Night* he did once in France:

> . . . the alexandrine is their norm and we felt, because it was a lyrical play, we would use the alexandrine. And we did six or seven weeks of rehearsal, and the play was utterly dead. I then had to come back to England for ten days, and I said to the translator, 'While I'm away, please change the entire text into iambics . . .'

When I talked to Malibongwe Mdwaba, the South African actor who made those isiXhosa sonnet translations, he vividly described his process (he drew me a diagram over Zoom as we talked), in which he starts with Shakespeare's text and world and positions himself in such a way that it passes through him to become the thing that he then expresses to us (it's still eighty per cent Shakespeare, yes, but has picked up maybe twenty per cent of Malibongwe along the way). And as we talk, I realise, to my delight, that – as with the ambiguous Kozintsev line we've just seen – I'm not sure whether Malibongwe is talking about his acting process or his translation process. Acting is among the more popular items in our catalogue of translation metaphors.

I know many translators who think a lot about breath. The quicker the pace, the more you can say in a breath, but you also need to support the meaning by having the keyword somewhere you can comfortably add stress. Fine to breathe in the middle of a line, but not in the middle of a thought. And it has a lot to do with the body, too – are you moving around a lot, or standing still, eyeballing your arch-enemy? 'For me, it comes more or less instinctively,' said Niels, 'because I always *hear* the words when I translate. Some of the best productions of Shakespeare I've seen have taken place here in my head.'

A Danish actor cast as Buckingham in *Richard III* (a big part) was struggling to learn his lines. *Am I just getting old?*, he wondered. Then he swapped the previous translation for Niels's and it all came much more naturally – 'it was as if he was just thinking all these things himself'.

Those carefully chosen words are doing all the work.

One of the characteristics of Swahili that JC described to me is the way gesture is embedded into the language. This gives it a particular kind of expressiveness that is especially well suited to performance. It is, JC says, 'both a poetic language and an actor's language'. When Macbeth asks this question:

> Is this a dagger which I see before me,
> The handle toward my hand?

JC suggested this as a possible translation:

> *Je, hii ni kisu ninachoona mbele yangu,*
> *mpini <u>ukielekea</u> mkononi mwangu?*

Your Swahili–English dictionary might tell you that the word *ukielekea* means *towards*. It suggests the physical movement of the dagger *towards* the hand, but, JC says, it:

> [it] also subtly conveys the sense of embarking on a journey or choosing a direction. In Swahili, *elekea* is closely tied to travel or movement toward a destination . . . [This] translation suggests that

by reaching for the dagger, Macbeth is metaphorically choosing a particular path – one that leads inexorably to violence, guilt, and destruction. The act of grasping the dagger thus becomes not just a moment of hesitation but a fateful decision to set out on an irreversible journey.

All that is given to an actor, gesture included, all of it contained, already, in one word. Eat your heart out, Shakespeare . . .

Chapter 35

O, daardie verruklike speeltuig van haar gedagtes

(on thoughts, and more actors)

In every production of *Romeo and Juliet* I've seen, Mercutio is where the most intense charisma is, and that charisma is fuelled by the way Shakespeare has him use language. His death, sudden, out of the blue, robs the play of one of its gravitational centres, and marks the moment the play tips irrevocably into tragedy. Any scene that could otherwise have been dragged down by the lovesick Romeo moping tediously around Verona is enlivened by his teasing, joking, high-spirited friend.

Mercutio is brilliant, and highly educated – the Queen Mab speech whose opening we've just seen feels pre-formed, as if he knows exactly where he's going with it. (And paradoxically, like he could go on for ever if he wasn't interrupted.) It's entirely different, then, from this speech that Shakespeare gave the actor who plays Juliet's Nurse, just minutes earlier:

> Even or odd of all days in the year,
> Come Lammas Eve at night shall she be fourteen.
> Susan and she, God rest all Christian souls,
> Were of an age. Well, Susan is with God;
> She was too good for me. But as I said,
> On Lammas Eve at night shall she be fourteen,

That shall she, marry! I remember it well.
'Tis since the earthquake now eleven years,
And she was weaned, I never shall forget it,
Of all the days of the year upon that day.

(And on it goes.)

The Nurse's speech is based in iambic pentameter, just as Mercutio's was. But where Mercutio's is beautifully structured – but also varying elegantly as he goes – the Nurse is speaking just as she thinks. Unlike Mercutio, there's no delayed gratification, with a clause set carefully aside and picked up again three lines later – and no structure to speak of at all. We just follow the unspooling. And in its own way, it too is irresistible.

The Nurse just lets herself go where her thoughts lead her – if the mood takes her mid-sentence, she's going to digress and she's going to do it right now. It's funny, and it's chaotic. Of the ten lines I've quoted, seven have some bit of punctuation interrupting the flow, almost always changing direction mid-line. (Compare that with the chunks of Queen Mab I quoted on pp.314 and 316, which comprise fourteen lines, and all but a couple of these are spoken through without interruption.)

Creating a new-language playscript that's in keeping with the characters (hence giving the same to the actors) means representing their thoughts just as Shakespeare does – so if their words are ungoverned, chaotic, hurtling, or whatever they might be, so they should remain. A translator must inhabit each character distinctly just as a playwright must.

Niels talked particularly about the difference between those Mercutio and Nurse speeches, and his translations show the patterning (created and varied) in Mercutio, and follow the shape of the Nurse's ramblings, too. And he compared the pleasure of translating the words of Claudius – whom we see mostly as a smooth-talking politician-king,[*] making controlled speeches, with those of his nephew/stepson, Hamlet, who

---

[*] Even in Saxo Grammaticus, the story's source, this character is a man of 'smooth words'.

is always audibly *thinking*, in real time. A Claudius speech might hold back half a verb across a four-line parenthesis (Ádám isn't averse to helping actors out with just a bit of added structure when they're being asked to sustain a long thought like this); or consider this, where he suggests that Hamlet ought to stop mourning his father:

> But you must know your father lost a father,
> That father lost lost his, and the survivor bound
> In filial obligation for some term
> To do obsequious sorrow; but to persever
> In obstinate condolement is a course
> Of impious stubbornness,'tis unmanly grief,
> It shows a will most incorrect to heaven,
> A heart unfortified, or mind impatient,
> An understanding simple and unschooled . . .

Which might not be full of human empathy, but certainly has a logic to it. Claudius, said Niels, was easy to translate – 'because he's an impeccable speaker'. But this oratorically sturdy speech is followed soon by another, from a young man who is actually grieving. It's from Hamlet's first soliloquy – his first time left alone with *us* – and we get to witness whatever his synapses are doing, in a speech that is disordered, impassioned, distressed, with lines broken, self-interrupting, and so on.

>   O God, God,
> How weary, stale, flat and unprofitable
> Seem to me all the uses of this world!
> Fie on't, ah, fie, 'tis an unweeded garden
> That grows to seed, things rank and gross in nature
> Possess it merely. That it should come to this:
> But two months dead – nay, not so much, not two –
>   . . .
>   And yet, within a month
> (Let me not think on't – Frailty, thy name is Woman),

> A little month, or e'er those shoes were old
> With which she followed my poor father's body,
> Like Niobe, all tears. Why she –
> O God, a beast that wants discourse of reason
> Would have mourned longer – married with my uncle . . .

At one point, Claudius remarks coolly that Hamlet's talk doesn't sound like madness, 'though it *lacked form* a little . . .'

So very often, speech in Shakespeare seems to be travelling at the speed of thought;* and thoughts – as anyone who's experienced them can tell you – are not that tidy. They do not sit neatly, each in a self-contained line. A character – like any person – can have multiple, sometimes conflicting, thoughts in their head simultaneously. Motives aren't always direct. Iago wants to cause Othello pain, and he has many rational reasons for this, and also none. Lines can seem to argue with themselves, and people can change their minds. Orsino concludes his rapturous description of the beautiful tune he's hearing, then orders it to stop because he's fed up of it now, all before he's reached the end of his line.

> O, it came o'er my ear like the sweet south
> That breathes upon a bank of violets,
> <u>Stealing and giving odour. Enough, no more,</u>
> 'Tis not so sweet now as it was before.

(In that third line – which we've seen before, with the enforced pause in the middle, the extra syllable at the caesura – we witness his mood turning.)

The translator has to keep up, capture everything as it rushes past, and re-contain it, ideally within a plausibly compact form. When the British Centre for Literary Translation ran workshops translating the 'To be, or not to be' speech into Mandarin, Romanian, Spanish, etc., part of the translators' basic struggle was keeping up with the lightning-fast

---

* Or 'In motion of no less celerity / Than that of thought', as Shakespeare put it. Yeah, there's always a quote.

development of the character's thinking, while always observing the constraints of the line. The Polish translators spent a disproportionate amount of time fretting over the word 'shocks' ('the thousand natural shocks/That flesh is heir to'). What *exactly* was Szekspir on about at that precise monosyllabic moment?

In *The Tempest*, when Prospero tells his daughter Miranda how they came to be exiled, his speech is a bit more Hamlet than Claudius – there are self-interruptions, digressions, and it's not always easy to follow a through line in a long sentence . . . It's complex syntax – he's a clever, educated speaker – but it's also broken up by his emotional state in this moment. Here's how it starts:

> My brother and thy uncle, called Antonio –
> I pray thee, mark me, that a brother should
> Be so perfidious! – he, whom next thyself
> Of all the world I loved, and to him put
> The manage of my state . . .

Now here's Emine, with the whole passage in Turkish:

> Kardeşim, senin amcan, adı Antonio –
> N'olur can kulağıyla dinle beni, bir kardeş ki
> Böyle kalleş olsun – dünyada en sevdiğimdi senden sonra,
> Ben de devletimin idaresini emanet ettim ona,
> Ki o sıra tüm senyörlükler arasında
> En güçlüsüydü devletim,
> Prospero, düklerin Dükü; şerefimle ve
> Serbest sanatlardaki eşsiz irfanımla öyle nam salmıştım ki . . .
> Bütün işim gücüm bu çalışmalar olunca,
> Ben de kardeşime devrettim yönetimi
> Ve hepten batınî araştırmalara kaptırıp kendimi,
> Giderek boşladım devlet işlerini.
> İşte amcan olacak o hain de –
> Dinliyorsun, değil mi?

You can see the effect (and something of the state of mind) from the punctuation alone – dashes fragmenting it, a self-interrupting question, an ellipsis where he drifts momentarily . . .

When Jean-Michel embarked upon his translation of 'There is a willow grows askant the brook', the speech in *Hamlet* where Queen Gertrude reports the grim news of Ophelia's death,* he decided to begin it thus:

> *Un saule pousse en travers du ruisseau*
> *Qui montre ses feuilles blanches dans le miroir de l'eau.*
> *C'est là qu'elle <u>tressa</u> d'ingénieuses guirlandes*
> *[. . .]*
> *Là, aux rameaux inclinés se haussant pour suspendre*
> *Sa couronne de fleurs, une branche envieuse <u>cassa,</u>*
> *Et ses trophées herbeux comme elle*
> *Sont tombés dans le ruisseau en pleurs. Ses vêtements <u>s'ouvrirent</u> . . .*

I've underlined three verbs: *tressa* (she made garlands), *cassa* (a branch broke), *s'ouvrirent* (her clothes spread). They're all in the particular past tense called the *passé simple*, which is the *literary* past tense, not a tense that anyone lives in regularly; it's a writing-a-story tense rather than having-a-regular-chat tense, and by using this, Jean-Michel is heightening our sense of these lines being pre-formed, a pre-prepared narrative. This is not Gertrude casually free associating, this is Gertrude delivering a prepared report. It's scripted out, formal, careful, reconstructed. In particular, it's attempting to avoid saying in terms that Ophelia took her own life (this speculation will come later, and it has implications). There was this *branche*, you see, and unfortunately, this *branche* just inexplicably *cassa*.†

---

* This is the speech about which Nabokov complained in Chapter 20 that the Russian translators had poshed up the botany.

† Compare to Yiddish, in which the Goldberg translation says: האָט דערטרונקען זיך דײַן שוועסטער (*dayn shvester hot dertrunken zikh*) and Schwartz says: זיך דערטרונקען ס'האָט דײַן שוועסטער (*s'hot dayn shvester zikh dertrunken*). Both are reflexive constructions using *zikh*, so while the former is ordered in such a way as to be more forcefully explicit, they suggest the same thing: Ophelia dertrunken *zikh*. She definitely drowned *herself*.

One actor unilaterally transposed this entire speech into the present tense to make it more 'vivid'. Jean-Michel was not pleased.

And finally, this: a speech from the end of Act I of *Pericles*, in which the eponymous king reflects on the circumstances that led to his decision to leave Antioch rather than marry the princess – having discovered that the king and that same princess are incestuously involved.

Absent a consistently superb translation of *Pericles* into Brazilian Portuguese that I was able to find – though there's one by José Roberto O'Shea with many parts I like – Chico kindly produced a version of this speech for us specially.

(Apologies, this speech is a long one, but there are lots of different bits I'd like to look at . . .)

1	How courtesy would seem to cover sin,	1	Ah, como a cortesia enganadora
2	When what is done is like an hypocrite,	2	Acoberta o pecado, qual o hipócrita,
3	The which is good in nothing but in sight.	3	Que nada tem de bom, fora o semblante.
4	If it be true that I interpret false,	4	Quem dera, interpretando, me enganasse,
5	Then were it certain you were not so bad	5	Pois nesse caso não serias vil
6	As with foul incest to abuse your soul:	6a	[A ponto de injuriar tua própria alma
		6b	Com a nefasta mácula do incesto;]
7	Where now you're both a father and a son	7	Porém agora és genro de ti mesmo,
8	By your untimely claspings with your child,	8a	[Pelos feios abraços e apertões
		8b	Com que enroscas a tua própria filha,]

IF THIS BE MAGIC 331

9	Which pleasures fits a husband, not a father;	9	Em afagos de esposo, e não de pai,
10	And she an eater of her mother's flesh,	10	E ela devora a carne de sua mãe,
11	By the defiling of her parents' bed;	11	Ao conspurcar o leito parental;
12	And both like serpents are who, though they feed	12	E os dois, qual serpes, nutrem-se de flores
13	On sweetest flowers, yet they poison breed.	13	Para engendrar venenos e pavores.
14	Antioch, farewell! For wisdom sees, those men	14	Antioquia, adeus, pois a prudência ensina:
15	Blush not in actions blacker than the night	15	Quem entre as negras sombras se conduz,
16	Will 'schew no course to keep them from the light.	16	Tudo fará por se ocultar à luz.
17	One sin, I know, another doth provoke;	17	Pecado engendra sempre outro pecado;
18	Murder's as near to lust as flame to smoke.	18	Fogo e fumo: a luxúria e o assassinato.
19	Poison and treason are the hands of sin,	19	Traição e veneno são punhal
20	Ay, and the targets to put off the shame.	20	E escudo para resguardar o mal.
21	Then, lest my life be cropped to keep you clear	21a	[Assim, para não ter cerceada a vida
		21b	Por quem defende o engano e a mentira,]
22	By flight I'll shun the danger which I fear.	22a	[Devo agora partir: a fuga é o meio
		22b	De esquivar os perigos que receio.]

(Note that Chico's is twenty-six lines, as opposed to the English text's twenty-two. Where a single English line has opened out into a pair in Portuguese, I've marked these with square brackets.)

A quick look at the English first. There are a few rhetorical devices (*if it be true that I interpret false*); there is rhyme, though this tends towards the latter part of the speech; there's some rigid artifice, but also some passion to it fuelled by his unrestrained disgust (*foul incest, untimely claspings, defiling*), and so on. The regular iambic patterning is disrupted with choriambic openings at a few strategic moments: Ántioch, farewell (line 14, when the speech turns a corner), then Múrder (l.18) and Póison (l.19) – and that conversational Áy in the antepenultimate line (l.20). Lots of nice building of momentum, too.

Oh – before we go on, I should mention that *Pericles* was not a solo composition by Shakespeare, and at least the first section of the play is believed to have been written by another hand. So what we're looking at in this instance is probably a speech by George Wilkins, a pamphleteer, innkeeper, likely pimp, violent criminal and quite good playwright. Anyway . . .

The last *Pericles* I saw on stage was Tamara Harvey's gorgeous production at the Swan Theatre in Stratford, with Alfred Enoch in the title role; I'd seen Enoch on big and small screens before, but also doing several Shakespearean roles on stage, so wasn't surprised to find him giving a thoughtful, compelling performance here. To my good fortune, the actor is conveniently half-Brazilian and a fluent Portuguese speaker, so he sat down with me to look at Chico's translation, drawing on his particular insights. This is a speech he had lately been doing for the RSC eight times a week, so he knew it, in its English form, very well.

It took Alfie very little time in our conversation to find his way into the workings of the Portuguese – he's a clever and careful reader, and also someone who reads very differently to me. He talks a lot in terms of what is 'useful', about what, as an actor, the text 'gives you'. He was also, I was pleased to see, full of admiration for Chico's work – as I listen back to the recording of our conversation, it's punctuated quite regularly by one or other of us muttering 'yeah, it's *really* good'.

As we've seen elsewhere, Portuguese tends to have bigger words, so in the interest of avoiding sprawl, Chico's longer words here replace a larger number of shorter ones. (Even with the four extra lines, the Portuguese still has a dozen fewer words.) We start with the opening:

How courtesy would seem to cover sin,	*Ah, como a cortesia enganadora*
When what is done is like an hypocrite,	*Acoberta o pecado, qual o hipócrita,*

English *courtesy* and *hypocrite* have become Brazilian *cortesia* and *hipócrita* – clearly related, but now with an extra syllable apiece. Our Germanic word *sin* has swollen into the Latinate *pecado*. But we've managed to avoid the entire 'would seem to' phrase by making the courtesy *enganadora* – deceptive; and indeed the whole verb structure is streamlined – *deceptive courtesy covers sin like a hypocrite*, in Portuguese, with a single verb (rather than *courtesy seems to cover sin, and does this like a hypocrite*).

Those longer words notwithstanding, the lines end up sounding more compact than they look. We saw in Chapter 33 how Chico's own Portuguese tends towards the heavy stressing of fewer main syllables and the swallowing or elision of others. And as I could hear when Alfie read it through, plenty of syllables on the page are lost to vowels naturally eliding when these lines are spoken aloud:

Ah, como_a cortesia_enganadora
Acoberta o pecado, qual o hipócrita,

(Note that Wilkins drops an e- for his metre, too, hence *'schew* for the more common *eschew*.)

Chico isn't using archaic language here, though he does occasionally tend towards older usages, such as the word for 'like', in 'like an hypocrite' after that caesura: 'qual o hipocrita' wouldn't be the most common way of expressing that today, so it took us a moment ('Oh, it's 'qual' in *that* sense!'). A useful monosyllable, though.

Alfie talked about being able to follow Pericles's running-on thoughts in the English, conveying the sense in the first few lines that, oh, another thing – oh, and another thing . . . You can lean into the 'hypocrite', then use line 3 as a sort of afterthought. But this thing he wanted to do in the playing is now helped by the fact that line two in Portuguese has a new caesura. So now the first thought ends mid-line on *pecado* – sin . . . but actually it doesn't, because Pericles appends the 'like an hypocrite' – so that's *already* an afterthought – and things unfold from there with growing momentum. (There's more resolution in the latter part of the speech, when it gets aphoristic, not so much here when he's sorting his thoughts out.)

We talked a lot about line 9:

Which pleasures fits a husband, not a father,

which apart from being tricky to say (*which pleasures fits?*), disrupts the structure. The way Alfie wanted to deliver the speech in production involved doing lines 5–6

Then were it certain you were not so bad
As with foul incest to abuse your soul . . .

in one breath, then you move into a sort of sestet, three pairs of lines (ll.7–13, from *Where now* . . . to . . . *poison breed*.) . . . Except you don't, because that pesky '*Which pleasures* . . .' line gets in the way. So he and director Tamara Harvey agreed to cut that one, so you get three pairs of lines, and you ratchet up the pace two lines at a time (rather than pausing on that slightly longer line, making the audience hold a thought over).

Chico's version of that unloved line is:

Em afagos de esposo, e não de pai,

One benefit of keeping all the bits of the speech intact (rather than cutting line 9) is that the 'and another thing . . .' effect 'gives you a kind of unsteadiness . . .', but Alfie admitted he *still* wanted to cut it when he spoke the lines in Portuguese. Though obviously Chico wouldn't have been allowed to do that himself. (We translators are very well behaved, sometimes.)

The 'untimely claspings' line (l.8), in what we're now calling the sestet, is one of those singles that expanded into two in Portuguese:

Pelos feios abraços e apertões
Com que enroscas a tua própria filha

According to Chico this is an attempt to recreate its unsettling feeling 'by means of cumulative effect' – and it is indeed uncomfortable, starting with a hard stress, a series of hard consonants, etc. – though the expansion necessarily loses some of the *drive* through the speech that Alfie spoke about.

That 'claspings' is an ugly word, couldn't be less lovely, romantic, sensual, delicate – and indeed there are several points where it's entirely appropriate to have some ugly sounds in a speech like this, a speech that is expressing such revulsion. In Chico's translation, we were particularly taken by the word *conspurcar*, which neither of us had encountered before and means *to defile*. (The girl is *conspurcar*-ing the parental bed.) It's a good sound for the expressing of disgust – moreso than Wilkins' *defiling*, I think; and I imagine Chico chose it with care. (The O'Shea translation has the reasonably harmless sounding *desonrar*.)

While Alfie sight-read the translation beautifully, there was just one little slip, in line 11, in the middle pair of the sestet, where Shakespeare has *parents' bed* and Chico makes it an adjective – *leito parental*; Alfie read the Portuguese word *parental* as *paternal*. Which could work quite plausibly, too, in this case. Though what the Portuguese definitely can't have is the openness of the source meaning, where you can say *parents' bed* or *parent's bed*, and they'll sound indistinguishable to the audience.

And what about those irregularities I mentioned in the source? Chico saw the irregularity of the *Antioch, farewell* line (l.14), and stretched his own out (from decasyllable to alexandrine) to throw the pattern similarly:

Antioquia, adeus, pois a prudência ensina . . .

Not every irregularity can be like-for-like, of course – unfortunately Brazilian poison has a second-syllable stress, so it doesn't work like choryambic line 19, *Póison and tréason shall* . . . . But Chico does find a way of giving the murder line some rhythmic impact, and this one is apparently a special pleasure to play – by swapping around the two halves of the sentence, and dropping the verb entirely:

Murder's as near to lust as flame to smoke
Fogo e fumo: a luxúria e o assassinato

Two pairs of nouns, balanced up on either side of a colon. There's a stressed opening to the line, and a lengthened ending so we definitely notice the murdering. And since we're in the territory of almost proverbial language, stripping out a bit of grammatical scaffolding feels OK, too.
Fire and smoke: lust and murder.
('Yeah – that's *very* good – *muito* bom . . .')
In addition to that irregular *Pelos feios abraços* line, we paused on,

Traição e veneno são punhal

which feels abbreviated at the start. But apparently, Alfie said, *Pericles* has a lot of nine-syllable lines (dropping the first off-beat of an iambic pentameter), which are very useful, propulsive, giving its speaker a lot of options – he cited these from later in the play:

Here I charge your charity withal,
Leaving her the infant of your care . . .

I don't know whether Chico knew about this feature of *Pericles*, but it meant the anomaly in his Portuguese felt totally in keeping with the play as a whole.
Chico also maintains the source text's transition from more disordered

to more ordered, ending with things almost proverbial and mostly rhyming – but also never *quite* settled, as it insists on dropping in individual unrhymed lines. You keep feeling, said Alfie, like there are potential endings – often on a rhyming couplet – but he's not done yet, and starts up again:

> And both like serpents are who, though they feed
> On sweetest flowers, yet they poison breed.
> [OK. Pause. And . . .]
> Antioch, farewell! For wisdom sees . . .
> [etc.]

Most of the Portuguese rhymes match the English ones – the word *pavores* (fears) doesn't correspond to anything in the English, but it delivers a rhyme with *flores* (flowers), and it works well enough that you wouldn't guess it's a drop-in. I did wonder whether the *pecado*/*assasinato* rhyme was close enough, but Alfie said 'I'd take that, in performance'.

So to the ending . . .

If he were looking at the Portuguese text in rehearsal, Alfie said, he'd be tempted to cut line 21b, the antepenultimate line, too – leaving a bit of space for the previous thought to hang there before Pericles says: 'Right, I've got to go . . .'. (This part is expanded in the Portuguese anyway, so we could bear a trim.) But he was especially taken by Chico's final couplet, which goes as follows:

> *Devo agora partir: a fuga é o meio*
> *De esquivar os perigos que receio.*

It's another of the expansions – what used to be a single line now gets a couplet in Portuguese. That means Chico has space to use up, so when I saw the *Devo agora partir* ('I must now leave') added at the start, I assumed it was just filler – it doesn't correspond to anything in the English. But this ending was perhaps Alfie's favourite part of the whole translation – the quite particular effect of a rhyming couplet that has a break in the first line, so the rhyming unit is set up only over *a line and a half*. The way the thought 'transcends the line', as he put it, is really useful (and particularly enjoyable to speak, apparently). 'It's that energy you get when the thoughts don't align' – and it's an effect familiar in Shakespeare. (Chico was also thinking about Pope, apparently.)

Any actor playing Hamlet will be given a couple of great ones to conclude their first two acts with:

> The time is out of joint; O cursed spite
> That ever I was born to set it right!

and:

> . . . More relative than this. The play's the thing
> Wherein I'll catch the conscience of the King.

Yeah, that's *really* good.

Chapter 36

. . . galdramann, ramman að kynngi

(on all of it at once)

I'm a reasonably good literary translator. Not a great one, but good enough, I think, to recognise other people's greatness. I can discern the challenges in a piece of work, and the brilliance of somebody's solutions. I can't always tell *how* they did it – though this book has seen me try – but I know when the skill is there. Alongside Shakespeare, this book has been a celebration of some great translators.

What I've shared here has of course been selective, partial. I have mostly been looking at exceptional work – work that is literally *the exception*. I don't claim that every translator can do the things we've seen at every moment. This is a book about what is possible in translation, not what is inevitable. Not even, I think, what is typical.

And I hope it now goes without saying: languages being what they are, even the great translators – like any writers – are subject to the ways in which a language will impose its own non-negotiable constraints. My friend Paul K. is a structural engineer, and I'm sure he's a brilliant, inspired one – but the laws of physics are the laws of physics.

When discussing some of the strands that form a translator's work, I've often had to pick them apart to present the task as though we translators only need wrangle one problem at a time. Pronouns in the

*Henry IV*s, rhyme in *A Midsummer Night's Dream*, register in *Othello*, and so on. But good writing is never that simple, and so translation, which requires a parallel good-writing, is never that simple either. It is everything, everywhere, and yes, all at once.

All the general issues in this book are things that, to variously demanding degrees, I've had to deal with myself as a translator – wordplay, verse, cultural assumptions, ambiguity, economy, non-equivalence of meanings, archaism – I've even had to reconcile an annoying son/sun. And it happens constantly, in one place, crowded and overlapping. A text's problematic dimensions are many, and they are simultaneous.

So I'd like to spend some time on a single scene, one of my favourites. It's from *Twelfth Night*, it's about nine or ten minutes played, and it has everything.

The scene in question – Act II, Scene 4 – takes place in Count Orsino's palace, and it's mostly a conversation between Orsino and his servant 'Cesario' (our heroine Viola dressed as a boy). Orsino is talking about his love for Olivia, and Viola/Cesario is talking about love in the abstract and hoping her master won't realise she's really talking about her feelings for *him*. It is beautiful and poignant, crammed full of suppressed desire, and it's funny, too. There's blank verse, a little bit of rhyme and some prose. And there's even a song!

It begins with Orsino telling another of his servants, Curio, that he wishes to hear some nice atmospheric singing:

Enter ORSINO, VIOLA, CURIO, *and others*
ORSINO
    Give me some music. Now . . .

Sorry to interrupt so soon. But I just wanted to point out: we're starting with a trochee. For most of the scene, Orsino will be doing ten-syllable lines, pretty regular, but he begins with a stressed syllable, commandingly: <u>Give</u> me.

IF THIS BE MAGIC

Niels noticed this ('course he did . . .), and Danish is obligingly similar, so here's the start:

<u>Giv</u> mig musik – Godmorgen, mine venner . . .

Anyway – sorry – let's start again. The first part of the scene:

> მომასმენინეთ კვლავ მუსიკა, in Siko Pashalishvili's Georgian. We've seen before that Georgian's an agglutinative language. Well, that first word is *momasmeninet*. The verb root is სმენ, and this whole word means 'cause me to hear', formed thus: **mo** (prefix); **m** (first-person object-marker); **a** (preradical vowel); **smen** (verb root); **in** (causative formant); **e** (second-person subject-marker for imperative); **t** (plural subject-marker). I really, *really* want to learn Georgian.

> I'd like some <u>music</u>: *Kérnék zenét*, according to Ádám.

> Orsino begins in verse – not remarkable, except that Curio will answer in prose. Orsino is being quite self-absorbed here. (As often.) Most translations of the play I've seen allocate verse and prose as Shakespeare has done.

Enter ORSINO, VIOLA, CURIO, *and others*
ORSINO
Give me some music. Now, good morrow, friends.
Now good Cesario, but that piece of song,
That old and antic song we heard last night:

> As happens frequently in this play, Cesario has to be squeezed into three syllables to fit its line – cé-sá-r(i)ó – not every language will allow the eliding of that 'i'.

> For translator Jaime Clark, the piece of song is a 'trova' – much more specific than 'song', but since the nature of the song will be specified imminently, it's an appropriate guess. A *trova* is an old love song such as would have been sung by a *trovador* – a troubadour.

> In some editions, *old and antique*, using two adjectives that might not be *exactly* synonyms, but are pretty close. Close enough, at least, that certain translators can bear to lose one in order to keep things contained – true to form, our friend Ádám Nádasdy doesn't waste this space-saving opportunity, condensing to one adjective. It's *a régi dalt* – 'the old song'.

> 'antic' must be stressed on the first syllable, not how we'd stress *antique* today. Alison Carey's *Play On* modern rewriting, done as part of a series for the Oregon Shakespeare Festival, calls the 'old and antic song' an 'old unearthly hymn', which fits a contemporary stress, collapsing the distance between text and audience. Of course, *unearthly* doesn't mean the same as *antic*, but it's a nice word – sometimes that's enough for me.

Methought it did relieve my passion much,
More than light airs and recollected terms
Of these most brisk and giddy-paced times.
Come, but one verse.

CURIO
He is not here, so please your lordship, that should sing it.
ORSINO
Who was it?
CURIO
Feste the jester, my lord, a fool that the lady
Olivia's father took much delight in. He is about
the house.
ORSINO
Seek him out, and play the tune the while.
Music plays. Exit Curio.

> Is Orsino asking Cesario himself to sing it? Ambiguous, perhaps. You'd think not, from the fact that Curio replies 'the person who sings it isn't here' – though translator Jaime Clark clearly reads it the other way. For him, the 'Now, good Cesario' line that opened the speech was '*Canta, Cesario*'.

> Gabriele Baldini has Orsino asking Cesario to sing, too, though inevitably it takes him *aaaages* to get the request out: *E adesso, buon Cesario, canta appena un accenno di quella canzone, di quella vecchia canzone un po' fuori moda che abbiamo udita la notte scorsa*. Well, the meaning is certainly all there.

> When Feste appears in the dialogue markers, depending on the edition, he's sometimes called 'Feste', sometimes just 'Clown', but this is the sole time his name is *spoken*. Federico Patán's translation calls the character 'Fiestas'. Meaning *parties*. Which, yes, is what *feste* means in Italian, but it feels a bit on the nose for the name to show its meaning so blatantly *in the language of the play*. That said, most of the Italian translations keep him as Feste, which I suppose is no more subtle in Italian than making him Fiestas in Spanish. The old Italian translator Carlo Rusconi tweaked him to Fest<u>o</u>, which you might think an improvement. Of course, with the name only spoken once all evening, maybe (*whisper it*) it doesn't matter hugely what the translator does?

> But if you're going to change the name, do try something that keeps the almost-rhyme of Feste-the-jester, perhaps?

> The last line looks like part of the prose exchange, but to all intents and purposes it's a line of verse with one syllable missing. If you added a 'Go' at the start, it would be a full line; still, it feels like one of those imperatives that starts with a stressed syllable, like those choriambic openings do (Look to your house! Give me some music!). So Niels Brunse, again: *Find ham; spil melodien indtil da*.

IF THIS BE MAGIC

Now Curio goes to fetch Feste, and Orsino and Viola/Cesario are left alone . . .

ORSINO
Come hither, boy. If ever thou shalt love,
In the sweet pangs of it remember me;
For such as I am all true lovers are,
Unstaid and skittish in all motions else
Save in the constant image of the creature
That is beloved. How dost thou like this tune?

VIOLA
It gives a very echo to the seat
Where Love is throned.

ORSINO
Thou dost speak masterly.
My life upon't, young though thou art, thine eye
Hath stay'd upon some favour that it loves.
Hath it not, boy?

> In the Mikhail Lozinsky translation, it's 'Приди, мой мальчик; если сам полюбишь . . .' with some nice Slavic verb-prefix action. иди is go (imperative) – but here with a при- (towards) prefix; and любишь is to love (second-person singular) – but with по- prefix it suggests *falling in* love.

> Pashalishvili's Georgian translation doesn't have *pangs of love*, it has *burning with love*. Remember that thing about Georgian allowing consonant clusters? The word for burning here is ცეცხლმოდებული – *tsetskhlmodebuli*.

> *Skittish* is such a great word. Unstaid and skittish! It does appear one other time in Shakespeare, in *Troilus and Cressida*, whose prologue refers to expectation 'tickling skittish spirits'. Kazuko Matsuoka sees no benefit in having the word translated the same way in these two plays so the Japanese texts don't have any overlap as the English do. Meanwhile, *flyvske* is the Danish word here. Flyvske!

> Orsino may be speaking in structured verse, but the lines still follow his thought. He ends one long sentence mid-line before the question, starting another sentence mid-line as if the thought's just come to him, interrupting his flow. In Danish:
>
> > . . . ustadige og flyvske I alt andet
> > end deres tankers dvælen ved det væsen,
> > de elsker. Kan du li den melodi?
>
> *Elsker* being the verb form related to the old-fashioned word for love we saw on p.160. The translation deploys both *elskov* and *kærlighed* multiple times in this scene.

> *Beloved* – one of those words that sometimes has three syllables (belovèd), sometimes – as here – just two. (It appears as a noun early in the next scene – a letter addressed 'To the unknown beloved' – where it usually has its third syllable voiced.)

> The translator can do what they like with Viola's reply as far as I'm concerned, but whatever they do needs to be really good, because Orsino comments on how good it is. Just saying.

Viola

                A little, by your favour.

Orsino

  What kind of woman is't?

Viola

                    Of your complexion.

Orsino

  She is not worth thee then. What years, i' faith?

Viola

  About your years, my lord.

Orsino

  Too old, by heaven. Let still the woman take
  An elder than herself; so wears she to him,
  So sways she level in her husband's heart.
  For, boy, however we do praise ourselves,
  Our fancies are more giddy and unfirm,
  More longing wavering, sooner lost and worn,
  Than women's are.

Viola

                I think it well, my lord.

Orsino

  Then let thy love be younger than thyself,
  Or thy affection cannot hold the bent;
  For women are as roses, whose fair flower
  Being once display'd, doth fall that very hour.

Means 'by your leave'; but it's also picking up Orsino's 'some favour that it loves' in the previous line, where 'favour' is 'face' – and his is indeed the face she has fallen in love with. Not that he notices even now, of course. The *favour* double-meaning is a connection so particular to the English. Still – this is where Niels takes it:

> O . . . *dit blik har hvilet på et elsket ansigt;*
>   *nå, har jeg ret.*
> V   *Ja, lidt; det er jo Jeres –*
>   *helt klare ret at mene noget sådant*

Danish can use one word (*ret*) covering both *right* (correct) and *right* (entitlement). So Orsino asks if he's *right* in his assumption; Viola replies, 'Yes, it's your, um . . . absolute *right* to say such a thing. (She stops herself before saying 'Yes it's *your face!*')

Although Orsino and Viola mostly complete each other's verse lines, this line of V's is incomplete. Why? It might sound like it's completed by O's 'Too old, by heaven', but it isn't. The French translation by Pierre Leyris adds in an extra non-Shakespearean phrase just to plug the playwright's wayward gap, whereas Schlegel (the man himself this time) preserves the curtailed line – either he can see the reason for it, or he gives Shakespeare the benefit of the doubt and just assumes there must surely be one . . .

'unfirm' is not a word much used elsewhere either – not in Shakespeare (four uses in total) or indeed anywhere else. (In this usage, meaning *flighty*, the *Oxford English Dictionary* cites only this *Twelfth Night* line.) But it's formed in English in such a way that a hearer can guess what it means.

My Arden edition says this means 'stay strong', that it's an archery metaphor (stay taut like a drawn bow), so it's a phrase far away from any contemporary usage. Most translations will not perpetuate that sense of distance – the conveying of meaning to a contemporary audience will be more direct. Barbara Heliodora's *não resiste* (it won't *hold out*) is less interesting, less precise – but at least in terms of accessible meaning, it's usefully closer to an audience in Brazil today than 'hold the bent' is to us Anglophones.

VIOLA
And so they are. Alas, that they are so;
To die even when they to perfection grow.

> Not only do these two complete each other's lines, which is always significant and which always has some relational reason (and so they do in most of my verse translations), but after a lot of blank verse, Orsino moves into rhyme for a pair of lines – and then Viola echoes him. And again, so do they in the nineteenth-century German:
>
> *So sind sie auch: ach! Muss ihr Los so sein,*
> *Zu sterbenm grad im herrlichsten Gedeihn?*

Now Curio returns, bringing Feste:

ORSINO
O fellow, come, the song we had last night.
Mark it, Cesario, it is old and plain.
The spinsters and the knitters in the sun
And the free maids that weave their thread with bones
Do use to chant it. It is silly sooth

Incidentally, for Shakespeare here, the word 'silly' meant simple or innocent, rather than foolish. Translator Khachik Dashtents knows this, so Այնպան էլ խոր չէ is what Armenian audiences get. It's clear and contemporary and has shed any risk of anachronistic misunderstanding. Nice to be an Armenian audience. Anyway, sorry – moving on . . .

                    it is silly sooth
And dallies with the innocence of love,
Like the old age.
FESTE
    Are you ready, sir?
ORSINO
    I prithee sing.
FESTE (*Sings.*)
    Come away, come away, death,
    And in sad cypress let me be laid.
    Fie away, fie away breath,
    I am slain by a fair cruel maid.
    My shroud of white, stuck all with yew,
    O prepare it.
    My part of death, no one so true
    Did share it.

    Not a flower, not a flower sweet
    On my black coffin let there be strewn.
    Not a friend, not a friend greet
    My poor corpse, where my bones shall be thrown.
    A thousand thousand sighs to save,
    Lay me, O, where
    Sad true lover never find my grave,
    To weep there.

Not silly.

Come away, Fie away, Not a flower, Not a friend – each of these three-syllable line openings is repeated. No prizes for spotting the repetitions in the first line of Frank Günther's German, So Kwok Wan's Chinese or Brunse's Hungarian:

> *Nicht ein Blümlein, nicht ein Blümlein süß*
> 来吧，来吧，来吧死亡
> *Nem kell, ó, nem kell virág*

So kept the original form in Chinese, so it could be set to music; though you'll see his repetitions are threefold, not twofold. The Hungarian word for *flower* is *virág*. So Ádám's translation doesn't repeat the same thing (*Nem kell* means something like *There's no need . . .* , but more pithily than English) but the pattern is the same. This is a song, so a tune might have echoing phrases to carry these lines.

Matsuoka-san's published translation footnotes both *cypress* and *yew* for her Japanese readers; the notes in this instance are cultural rather than botanical – not assuming an unfamiliarity with the existence of these trees, but with their mostly death-related associations.

Özdemir Nutku ends his first verse '*Hiç kimse almadı üstüne ölüm rolünü*' and starts his second '*Hiçbir çiçek, hiçbir güzel çiçek.*' So many nice familiar *hiç*s for you.

Sometimes given as 'strown' (alternative old spelling). But that uncommon 'strown' is how it needs to be pronounced anyway, in order to rhyme obediently with 'thrown'. Frank can manage a perfect rhyme without dragging an audience out of their linguistic comfort zone: The modern sounds of . . . *Sarg mir gesteckt* rhyme simply enough with . . . *Erde es deckt*. (Also with my favourite *befleckt*.)

An emphatic, and poetic, and usefully syllable-filling way of saying 'a million sighs'. Would a translator bother to replicate this? Carlo Rusconi did something similar, with '*mille e mille sospiri*' – but his translation is entirely prose *including the song lyrics*, so doesn't get as many effect points for that.
    The thousand-thousand doesn't fit into Frank's German tight song metre, so he just goes with a single *tausend Seufzer*, as does Jean-Michel with *mille sanglots* – though arguably the precise number isn't the point anyway. A thousand sighs is still quite a lot of sighs.
    In Schlegel, it's:

> *Um Ach und Weh zu wenden ab*
> *Berge alleine*
> *Mich, wo keine Treuer wall ans Grab*
> *Und weine.*

so no sighs in particular, just general *pain and woe*. But in its favour, the metre isn't only very robust, it maps perfectly onto the English metre throughout.

IF THIS BE MAGIC   347

We're talking about a song here – in that last example, one way we can see that the German and English rhythms map onto each other perfectly is that the exact same musical setting by Brahms has been used for both.

After the song, Orsino and Feste banter a little:

ORSINO
  There's for thy pains.
FESTE
  No pains, sir. I take pleasure in singing, sir.
ORSINO
  I'll pay thy pleasure then.
FESTE
  Truly, sir, and pleasure will be paid, one time or another.
ORSINO
  Give me now leave to leave thee.
FESTE
  Now, the melancholy god protect thee, and the tailor make thy doublet of changeable taffeta, for thy mind is a very opal. I would have men of such constancy put to sea, that their business might be everything and their intent everywhere, for that's it that always makes a good voyage of nothing. Farewell.

> We're all in prose now; every *Twelfth Night* translation I have, in every language, does these bits in prose. The effect is only lost in those examples like François-Victor Hugo where the *entire* play is in prose, and we don't sense that key-change between Orsino and Viola, and Orsino and everyone else. So of course, in Gabriele Baldini's translation this section is prose, but so is everything. Viola's:
>
>   And so they are. Alas, that they are so,
>   To die, even when they to perfection grow.
>
> is now:
>
>   *Tali sono, ahimè! altro se le sono! Morire proprio nel punto in cui crescono a perfezione!*

> These prose bits were always going to be tricksy. Feste, like every Shakespearean Fool, is no fool. In this one instance, So Kwok Wan dodged a bullet – on those rare occasions when you're translating expressly for a director who's already decided which awkward chunks of scene he's going to cut, you can be spared the translating altogether . . .

And now, once again, Orsino dismisses everyone else – 'Let all the rest give place' – and is left alone with Viola. Potentially a great dramatic turning point in *Twelfth Night* (or *Was ihr wollt* – 'What you will' – in the Wieland translation). Will Viola lose patience, drop her disguise, and confess her true feelings?

ORSINO
    Once more, Cesario,
Get thee to yond same sovereign cruelty.
Tell her my love, more noble than the world,
Prizes not quantity of dirty lands.
The parts that fortune hath bestowed upon her
Tell her I hold as giddily as fortune;
But 'tis that miracle and queen of gems
That nature pranks her in attracts my soul.

VIOLA
But if she cannot love you, sir?

ORSINO
I cannot be so answered.

VIOLA
    Sooth, but you must.
Say that some lady, as perhaps there is,
Hath for your love a great pang of heart
As you have for Olivia. You cannot love her;
You tell her so. Must she not then be answered?

ORSINO
There is no woman's sides
Can bide the beating of so strong a passion
As love doth give my heart; no woman's heart
So big to hold so much – they lack retention.
Alas, their love may be call'd appetite,
No motion of the liver but the palate,
That suffer surfeit, cloyment and revolt.
But mine is all as hungry as the sea,
And can digest as much. Make no compare
Between that love a woman can bear me
And that I owe Olivia.

VIOLA
    Ay, but I know—

ORSINO
What dost thou know?

Orsino says: 'Get thee . . .' (trochaically), to which Viola will reply '. . . love you?' (one of the scene's curtailed lines) – but note, *thee* vs *you*. Viola is playing the part of a servant, not presuming to be Orsino's equal. In the Hindi prose translation, the former line is 'मैं **तुमसे** फिर प्रार्थना करता हूँ कि एक बार फिर उस निष्ठुरता की रानी के पास जाओ!', and the latter 'और यदि **आपसे** प्रेम न करे श्रीमान्?' I've bolded the two you's – तुम/*tum* and आप/*aap* – informal and formal, respectively, so those hierarchical positions are encoded in the translation just the same. (In comparison, when we first meet Viola, she is with the sea captain who saved her from the storm. With him she uses 'thee', and the captain speaks up to her with 'you'.)

In this speech, Orsino ends a lot of his phrases mid-line, running over at the ends – moments 'when the thoughts don't align,' as Alfie Enoch put it – and there's nice momentum when he gets going. Again, most translators into verse manage some version of this.

I have nothing to say about this phrase specifically in translation but it's very funny.

At this point in *Play On!* – not the Oregon modernising text series but the stage retelling of the story of *Twelfth Night* lately brought to life with Duke Ellington songs – our Orsino avatar tells his 'Vi' that only a man can really write great music because only a man really has the depth of feeling. He sings 'I Got It Bad (and That Ain't Good)' – a melancholy number that includes the line 'She don't love me like I love her – nobody could . . .'

We take for granted that Orsino can pick up Viola's exact word – but as we've seen before, with *love* in *The Two* (Spanish) *Gentlemen of Verona*, inflected verbs can prevent this. Federico Patán gives us: 'Y pese a todo sé'/'¿Saber? ¿Qué sabes?'

IF THIS BE MAGIC

VIOLA
    Too well what love women to men may owe.
    In faith, they are as true of heart as we.
    My father had a daughter loved a man,
    As it might be, perhaps, were I a woman,
    I should your lordship.
ORSINO
                And what's her history?
VIOLA
    A blank, my lord. She never told her love,
    But let concealment, like a worm i'th' bud,

> In the 1955 Russian film of *Twelfth Night*, this is what Viola (Klara Luchko) says:
>
> У моего отца была
> Дочь, и она любила человека,
> Как, будь я женщиной, и я, быть может,
> Любил бы вас.*
>
> That человек – My father had a daughter who loved . . . a person.
>   Also: we know Russian verbs reveal their subjects' gender in the past tense – so Viola says her imaginary sister once loved (любила) – whereas she, as a man, would love (Любил), back in male disguise. And she would love *you* – but specifically вас, in the formal (pretending to be a servant, addressing a count).

> Presented as two parts of one complete line but there's an extra syllable dropped in, to force a pause (we've seen before how Shakespeare sometime sneaks in an extra syllable where there's a significant caesura – *and by opposing end them. // To die . . .*).

> Finally a nice easy line! In French it's just 'Rien, Monseigneur.' That's how both Victor Bourgy *and* Bernard Noël translated it. We have agreement!
>
> Or it could be *Le néant, mon seigneur* (tr. Jean-Michel Déprats). Or just *Est néant* (tr. Pierre Leyris). Or *Un désert, Monseigneur!* (tr. Nathalie Vivé & Gabriel Llesta). Or *Un long effacement, monseigneur* (FVH). Or *Aucune histoire, monseigneur* (Pierre Messiaen). Or . . . etc.

> Annoyingly compressed, and not a lot most translators can do about it. Though Barbara Heliodora's Brazilian translation, *qual verme na flor*, manages similar compactness – partly because *in-the* combines in Portuguese to a single monosyllable (em + a = na), and partly because she replaces the *bud* with a *flower* (monosyllabic *flor* rather than disyllabic *broto/botão* (we've seen both 'broto' and a verb form 'brota' already); but also because rather than the usual comparator (*como um verme* – like a worm), she's gone with *qual verme* – where *qual* is that less common usage that Alfie spotted in the *Pericles* translation.

---

* No translator is #named; the only person with a script credit is director Yan Frid, but it looks like he's using the Mikhail Lozinsky translation – the speech is Lozinsky verbatim, just with one line excised. В них сердце верно, / Как в нас. – 'In faith, they are as true of heart as we.' (We've noted a related adverbial верно before in Radlova's Queen Mab.)

Feed on her damask cheek. She pined in thought,
And with a green and yellow melancholy
She sat like Patience on a monument,
Smiling at grief. Was not this love indeed?
We men may say more, swear more, but indeed
Our shows are more than will, for still we prove
Much in our vows, but little in our love.
ORSINO
But died thy sister of her love, my boy?

> ροδομάγουλα in Rotas's Greek – because as we already know, if you want a convenient Greek literary/poetic word for a rose, Greek gives us ρόδο.

> Vassilis Rotas makes a surprising choice here – rendering the line as *μες στη μαύρυ της μελαγχολία*, meaning 'in her black melancholy'. (It's not essential for rhyme or rigid metre or any other obvious formal constraint.) I thought I'd ask the translator why he'd gone for this; unfortunately, I got no answer, as this particular translator has been dead for forty-eight years. Probably we'll never know. There might be a good reason – perhaps to do with black bile (though black as the association is then much less interesting). As a translator myself, I know I'm inclined to give others the benefit of the doubt, so maybe there's something clever like that going on . . . or it could have been a momentary lapse. It happens.
> Hmm, interestingly, the Jaime Clark does something similar – *en negra, amarillenta pesadumbre* – her sorrow is *black, yellowish* – and I wondered briefly whether they might have been working from the same non-English source, but one of the novelties of the Clark translation in Spanish (apart from doing the verse in verse) was that it was *not* from a French bridge.

> In the *Manga Shakespeare* version (adapted by Richard Appignanesi, illustrated by Nana Li), the line is translated as 'with a green and yellow melancholy, sat smiling at grief' in the text; the 'monument' component isn't lost, however, but conveyed in the visual language (a drawing of a statue: a woman, sad and patient), which has its own possibilities.

> Oh, some of our translators are going to face the man problem again.

> This is not one of the play's rhymier scenes, but there are a handful of nice rhyming moments. Schlegel matches Shakespeare blank verse for blank verse and rhyme for rhyme. And for this couplet, we get *Doch der Verheißung steht der Wille nach. / Wir sind in Schwüren stark, doch in der Liebe schwach*. It's a perfect rhyme, just as it was in English in 1602. Shame that's been lost to English; for the closer experience, best to read a translation.

> Viola has the question 'Was not this love indeed?' Orsino asks 'But died thy sister of her love, my boy?' Rotas' Greek versions are: 'Αυτό δεν είναι αγάπη αληθινή;' and 'Κι η αδελφή σου πέθανε απ' τον έρωτα, παιδί μου;' – *agapi* and *erota* again.

IF THIS BE MAGIC

> I've heard Viola's heartbreaking response to Orsino's question about her 'sister' stressed on stage two different ways. Either:
>
> > **I** am **all** the **daugh**ters . . . (so beginning with a trochee)
>
> or:
>
> > I am **all** the **daugh**ters . . . (so beginning with an anapest: da-da-**dum**)
>
> The former makes more sense of the contextual meaning, the latter nudges it closer to a regular iambic pentameter, if your unstressed 'I am' is almost an 'I'm'. What it definitely isn't is a regular iambic pentameter as it stands.

VIOLA
I am all the daughters of my father's house,
And all the brothers too; and yet I know not.
Sir, shall I to this lady?

ORSINO
                    Ay, that's the theme:
To her in haste. Give her this jewel; say,
My love can give no place, bide no denay.

> After a couple of lines of irregular length, this one breaks out of the pattern entirely. There's a pause encouraged before it, for Viola to snap out of the sadness, back into the present. The manga version cleverly slots in a small wordless panel to force a beat before she resumes speaking. Agostino Lombardo's Italian breaks the line completely, even though in Italian the 'I know not' finishes midway through, so the pause couldn't be more obvious:
>
> > *Io sono tutte le figlie della casa*
> > *Di mio padre, e anche tutti i figli.*
> > *Eppure non so –*
> > *Signore, debbo andare da questa dama?*

> 'sag, / Dass ich nicht anders kann . . .' – Frank replacing the optional English comma with a compulsory German one.

Sorry, I probably should have paused earlier, but I didn't want to interrupt them. Much of this conversation is so lovely. It had better still be so lovely once the translators have done with it. Is that too much to ask? Please just don't break it!

Finally, when you're listening to that concluding couplet in performance, in the moment the scene closes, do you know for sure what 'bide no denay' means? Maybe it's approximately *guessable* in modern English, but in French the meaning is more easily – as Malvolio would say in the next scene – 'evident to any formal capacity'. Jean-Michel's translation is 'va l'assurer / Que mon amour constant ne souffre aucun rejet' – *rejet* meaning the same as *denay*, but with the added bonus of actually being understandable.

Carey's *Play On* script changes the meaning, turning 'denay' into 'delay'. James Anthony's *Shakespeare Retold* version clarifies the meaning, while also preserving the verse and the rhyme, ending the scene 'And get there quick. Give her this jewel. Say / She can't resist; my love won't go away.'

Concluding on a rhyme, that perfectly finished couplet is important, of course. Every verse translation I've found recreates it, or a half-rhyme at least. Some are better than others at preserving other features (more or less contained, with the particular momentum of where the line breaks, etc.) – but all of them are filled with impressive things when you take a look and try to work out what they're up to . . .

Ie, dyna'r pwnc!
Dos eto, ar frys; cyflwyna'r anrheg hon
I'r lân Olivia: a chais well ateb im'.
Nid yw nacâd, dwêd wrthi, yn tycio dim.
(Tr. J.T. Jones, Welsh)

Sì, questo é il tema. Corri da lei.
Dalle questo gioiello. Dille che il mio amore
Il suo posto non può lasciare né il rifiuto accettare.
(Tr. A. Lombardo, Italian)

Շտապիր իր մոտ, տուր այս գոհարը և ասա նրան,
Որ սիրուց բացի, սիրտրս չի ուզում մի այլ պատասխան:
(Tr. Kh. Dashtents, Armenian)

> Ay, that's the theme:
> To her in haste. Give her this jewel; say,
> My love can give no place, bide no denay.
> (W. Shakespeare, English)

The more time I spend on this book, the more I can't help feeling that Shakespeare knows what he is doing. And he's not the only one.

Chapter 37

No coneixem ses obres?

(on the literary canon)

When the curtain rises on young Will Shakespeare in the stage version of *Shakespeare in Love*, we find our playwright infatuated with the wrong girl (just as his Romeo is, at the start of *his* play), and he is attempting to write a sonnet to the girl in question. He starts: *Shall I compare* . . . *<thee>* . . . But he's struggling:

> Shall I compare thee! . . . to a . . . to a . . . ?
> Shall I compare thee to a . . . sum . . . a sum . . . a something, something . . .

Those of us watching are supposed to know where he's finally going to land. Every iteration is just a stop on his path to 'a summer's day'. (An autumn morning? An afternoon in springtime? A . . .)

He gets there eventually (with a little help from wing man Christopher Marlowe). A . . . summer's day?

> Thou are more . . . something, something, something . . .

The effect depends on the audience knowing where we're going, depends on the final version seeming inevitable to us from the start, even if it isn't to our frustrated Will. For *Shakespeare in Love* to work in Bogotá, we need a well-established sense of Spanish Sonnet 18 for Colombian Will to grope his way towards. The Vásquez translation begins thus:

> *He de comparar . . . Comparar . . .*
> *He de comparar . . . ¿te? ¡He de compararte! ¿A qué? ¿A . . .*
>   *? A un . . .*

Then he tries a few things:

> *¿He de compararte a un albor lejano?*
> *¿He de compararte a una mañana de otoño? ¿A una tarde de*
>   *primavera? Diablos.*

In the source, Will's first attempt is to compare his mistress to 'a mummer's play' (a mummer being a performer in a traditional seasonal folk play). In Vásquez's version, it's *un albor lejano*, meaning 'a distant dawn'. The translator has spotted that 'a mummer's play' rhymes with 'a summer's day', so the audience is being teased – Shall I compare thee to a mummer's play? – aargh, so close! So Vásquez does the same – his *albor lejano* rhyming with *un dia de verano*, which we all know is where we're going to end up.

Or at least, we know it if there's a Spanish Shakespeare well enough established in the canon. (This version, I believe, is Jorge Capriata.*)

Note that there's no dictionary in the world – nor, for that matter, is there any algorithm/software – that would translate 'a mummer's play' as 'un albor lejano'. It's great.

Translations can crystallise as canonical, just like source texts can.

---

* Oh, and note that we have something not unlike a trochaic opening here, too. Hé de comparárte . . .

We readers can become attached to them in just the same way, and it's hard to imagine the validity of alternative interchangeable versions. Just recall the stories that mattered most to you as a kid, when some of the strongest bonds were formed. For me, those books included classics that were definitely not called 'Gretel and Hansel' or 'Cindergirl', Lindgren's *Pippi Longsocks*, Hans Christian Andersen's 'Small Mermaid' . . .

In Tom Stoppard's *Arcadia*, young Thomasina is doing her Latin translation homework, which includes a passage describing a sighting of Cleopatra. Septimus takes the text from her and 'improvises' a translation, but we're supposed to recognise it as being Enobarbus's speech from Shakespeare's *Antony and Cleopatra* (which we saw on p.32).

Here's the Stoppard, playing with what we already know:

SEPTIMUS

Let me see if I can attempt a free translation for you. At Harrow I was better at this than Lord Byron. (*He takes the piece of paper from her and scrutinises it, testing one or two Latin phrases speculatively before committing himself*) Yes – 'The barge she sat in, like a burnished throne . . . burned on the water . . . the – something – the poop was beaten gold, purple the sails, and – what's this? – oh yes, so perfumed that' –

THOMASINA (*catching on and furious*)

Cheat!

SEPTIMUS (imperturbably)

– 'the winds were lovesick with them' –

THOMASINA

Cheat!

SEPTIMUS

– 'the oars were silver which to the tune of flutes kept stroke' –

THOMASINA (*jumping to her feet*)

Cheat! Cheat! Cheat!

In Jean-Marie Besset's translation, French Septimus begins his rendition with

> La barque où elle était assise, tel un trône éclatant, incendiait les eaux . . .

I haven't found this version anywhere else, so it might be that the lines that Septimus is 'improvising' are translations Besset produced with the rest of his *Arcadia*; they are not quoting anyone else's pre-familiar Shakespeare.

In German, though, the translator of Arcadia gave Septimus this:

> In Harrow was ich bei so was better als Lord Byron. [. . .] Ja – „ Die Bark', in der sie saß, ein Feuerthron, / . . . Brannt' auf dem Strom: " . . . äh – na – „ getriebnes Gold der Spiegel . . .'

The German translator of *Arcadia*, as it happened, was one Frank Günther. Ever mindful of anachronism, though, Frank modestly did not recycle his own *Antonius und Kleopatra* – he had one, of course (we've seen snippets on pp. 53 and 55), but it didn't exist to be quoted in Tomasina's early-nineteenth century. So the version he used is drawn from the pre-existing translation by Wolf Heinrich graf von Baudissin.*

(Cheat! Cheat!)

In the *Industry* season three finale, Harper and Petra are having a showdown meeting with Otto Mostyn, aiming to cut off professional relations. Petra keeps saying it's all 'amicable'. Otto replies:

> Hide not thy poison with such sugared words.

---

* Frank does help an audience who might not have spotted his source, though. When German Thomasina jumps to her feet, she cries out 'Schwindel, Schwindel, Schwindel, das ist Shakespeare!'

It's not a line many would recognise, coming as it does from *Henry VI, Part 2* (definitely a Shakespeare deep cut), but you can tell he's quoting something, and from the ten syllables and telltale 'thy', thou mightst guess it's Shakespeare.

Should you choose to watch the episode dubbed into German – and really, why wouldn't you? – you'll hear Otto say:

> Birg nicht dein Gift in solchen Zuckerworten.

Christian Kähler, who made the German script, had reached for Schlegel-Tieck.

The 1905 edition of the *New International Encyclopaedia* stated confidently that 'The Schlegel-Tieck translation is universally considered better than any other rendering of Shakespeare in a foreign language. Thanks to Schlegel and Tieck, Shakespeare has become a national poet of Germany.' In Germany, largely because of these translations, the playwright came to be called 'Unser Shakespeare' – our Shakespeare. The Schlegel-Tieck, it has been suggested by some, is actually rather an improvement on its source. Theirs is the version I called on – unthinkingly, by default – on p.191, for the bank where someone pflückt the wild thyme.

When I mentioned my intention to write this book to my friend Catherine, she launched straight into 'Morgen, und morgen, und dann wieder morgen' – it was specifically the Schlegel-Tieck that she was quoting, just as any of us might retrieve a scrap of remembered Shakespeare in English.

Just as everyday English carries idioms drawn from our own greatest canonical translation, the 1611 King James Bible (and its more quietly influential predecessors), so translated Shakespeare looms large in other languages, phrases from his work inflecting people's speech. According to the translation blog series at the Shakespeare Birthplace Trust, Carl August Hagberg's translation of the *Much Ado* title, *Mycket väsen för ingenting*, is used proverbially in Sweden; his version of Hamlet's 'pale cast of thought', too. I referenced *Something is rotten in the state of* in passing in the Prologue, and it's also proverbial in Hungarian – but specifically in Péter Vajda's rendering:

Valami bűzlik Dániában

Something *stinks* in Denmark. (*Bűzlik* – a great word with that long thin 'u' sound – means stench.) The *specific, individual translation* has its own afterlife.

The song 'Shakespeareana' by Brazilian composer Francis Hime is a setting of the words of Sonnet 18, but specifically Geraldo Carneiro's translation of the sonnet (*Te comparar com um dia de verão?*), adapted to fit Hime's song; meanwhile, if the words 'By the rivers of Babylon . . .' put a tune in your mind's ear, Boney M won't be singing in Hebrew, they'll be using phrasing from Psalm 137 that comes substantially from our deeply culturally established King James (too many translators to #name).

The wide cultural familiarity with Shakespeare can be useful to a translator. Cole Porter could rely on the fact that his listeners would be familiar with the titles that form the gag at the end of each line of 'Brush Up Your Shakespeare'; and Cole Porter's translator assumed the same of his. And as we saw with the Günther *Arcadia*, you use whatever existing cultural resources there are. A character in Elaine Feeney's *How to Build a Boat* learns some Shakespearean insults; the first thing Feeney's Dutch translator Astrid Huisman did was to reach for pre-existing Dutch Shakespeare. Conversely, if a character in a non-English novel quotes Shakespeare in their language (as they often do), I won't back-translate it for my English text, I'll return to the source and drop in the original Shakespeare line, as a German might do with their pre-existing Schlegel-Tieck.

Begging the even *more* awkward question: what happens when characters are quoting Shakespeare in two variant translations in, say, a contemporary Japanese play – and then you're tasked with translating that Japanese play into English? This nightmarish hypothetical was not so hypothetical for Rosie Fielding, who faced this issue when translating Kimura Ryūnosuke's HAMLET X SHIBUYA. Her solution? To retrofit the English by quoting variant Q1 and Q2 texts.

In Isabella Hammad's novel *Enter Ghost*, in which the characters are staging *Hamlet* in Palestine, the author needed to find a way of conveying a specific Arabic translation of *Hamlet*, in this entirely Anglophone novel. The narrator, Sonia, introduces it by telling us that she struggles with reading this text, because the translation (by Jabra Ibrahim Jabra) is in 'classical Arabic', while she's comfortable only with conversational family chat; and then she presents a suggestive English back-translation for all the transliterated Arabic quoted lines, defamiliarising them for us. *Akun am la akun?* Shall I be or not be?

So when you're embarking on your own new translation of a very familiar classic, how do you present a piece of writing that people know so well already, that rings in their memories whether you like it or not? That is the question.

Many global theatre audiences know their Shakespeare just as well as we English speakers do, so if you're a translator, how can you dare to alter a text that seems canonically fixed? Think of an iconic translation in English, and ask yourself: how readily would you adjust to a new English version of *Asterix* – or, for that matter, of the Bible – where all the names of the characters were suddenly different from the ones you grew up with? Yet one might argue that retranslation of something as rich as Shakespeare isn't just acceptable but necessary. Translation is always interpretation, which is why translators frequently compare their work to that of an actor, or a director. No production of *Hamlet* can bring out every possibility in the text, so we need it done again and again, exploring new choices. And so it is with translations and retranslations.

Even if you avoid examining previous translations while you're working – the Grossman approach, which seems to be common among the Shakespeareans I've talked to – you'll already know the famous bits, just as we Anglophones might know Shakespeare's famous bits in English. So do you recycle? Do you try to dislodge them?

One solution is to play with expectations, to translate *against* what people are expecting to hear. Directors and actors, after all, are constantly trying to find ways to make a text new – to take something like *Hamlet*, famously just 'a play full of quotes', and make an audience hear it afresh. This, for a translator, is also an opportunity.

There can't be a more globally familiar Shakespeare line than 'To be or not to be'. As we've seen, there are languages in which one particular translation is *relatively* straightforward (though never inevitable), others where the options seem endless. One of the places where the possibilities fan out is in the verb form itself – not the meaning of 'be', but the fact that infinitives (to run, to write, to go) don't work the same in every language.

In Bulgarian – as in demotic Greek – what takes the place of an English infinitive is tied to a specific person (there is no neutral 'to go', there's only for-me-to-go, for-you-to-go, for-them-to-go, etc.). So in Greek:

I want <u>to go</u>: Θέλω <u>να πάω</u>.
You want <u>to go</u>: Θέλεις <u>να πας</u>.

The infinitive or its equivalent is underlined – and it's formed in Greek using a να (marker of the subjunctive) and a verb that shifts according to the relevant going-person. (So also, *I want you* <u>to go</u>: Θέλω <u>να πας</u>. With the first-person verb and a second-person subjunctive.)

We return, then, to Hamlet's ultra-famous speech, and a new problem: *for whom* to be?

Is he asking 'for-me-to-be, or for-me-not-to-be'? Or 'for-you-to-be, or for-you-not-to-be' – a specific singular you, or the plural, addressing the audience? Or collectively 'for-*us*-to-be, or for-us-not-to-be?'

Alexander opted for:

Да бъдем или не – това се пита.

That бъдем is a plural, and tells us that Hamlet is asking a question about us all. What does it mean *for us* to be – or not?

He wanted to avoid a singular form of the verb, not least 'to distance the speech from the idea of suicide as the solution to Hamlet's personal problem and restore its more philosophical, generally existential slant, which is obvious from the further development of the soliloquy.' (Part of his justification when challenged at the time also related to the particular Renaissance sense of the individual's place within humanity.)

But there's another reason for his choice. The most famous prior translations of the lines began

Да бъдеш . . .

[For you to be . . .]

and Alexander was deliberate in not reusing it. He wanted the line to be noticed. Not for his ego, but because it is, in fact, an important line. It's such a big (*nagy*) question! And in its super-familiar form, it's too easy *not* to think about it; you hear it – that famous quotation – but it never gets any real purchase. Making a small alteration is enough to bring a listener up short – wait, what? *To be*, you're asking, *or not*?

That really *is* quite a profound question, now you mention it.

Alexander's new, canon-defying line went on the poster.

In short, translations can put down deep roots in their new homes, just as a canonised text can in its own. When the Hungarian director Arthur Bardos came to England in 1949, he said of *Hamlet*: 'It's strange to hear the text in English because I'm used to the original version, translated by János Arany'.

In the interview series *Of Beauty and Consolation*, hosted by the Dutch journalist Wim Kayzer, critic George Steiner tells a story that I like very much. I do not believe it is literally true, but that is irrelevant. Steiner takes us to the 1930s, to the Soviet Writers' Congress, at a time when being a writer was not good for one's life expectancy. Pasternak's friends asked him to speak – he was likely to be arrested anyway, so why not?

Now, he was over six feet as you know, incredibly beautiful, and when Pasternak got up, everyone knew. He gets up . . . I'm told you can hear the silence till Vladivostok . . . And he gives a number. And two thousand people got up. It was the number of a certain Shakespeare sonnet, of which he had done a translation, which the Russians say with Pushkin is one of their greatest texts . . . And they recited it by heart, the two thousand people, the Pasternak translation. It said everything. It said: you can't touch us, you can't destroy Shakespeare, you can't destroy the Russian language, you can't destroy the fact we know by heart what Pasternak has given us . . . And they didn't arrest him. It's one of the very great stories . . . In that case, the sons of bitches don't arrest you – or if they do, it's too late. The other people have your treasure with them.

Like I said, I don't think it's literally true. But it's a story about translation as a thing worth doing, an act of potentially profound human connection, and a great and enduring gift. So it certainly *should* be true.

Chapter 38

Сколь естеству твои дела противны

(on translations without translators)

I drafted this book in the closing months of 2024 and early 2025. Since AI was the prevailing topic of conversation among most of my acquaintances, and since translators are always deemed to be especially imperilled by this sort of thing (because what we do is basically mechanical and requires no individual human creativity or sensitivity or unexpected left-field inspiration, apparently), it seemed important that a book about translation consider it. So – reluctantly, I'll admit – I allocated Chapter 38 to 'AI and translation', and duly wrote a few thousand words on the subject. This is not that chapter.

That Chapter 38 – the one that this isn't – presented a pair of experiments, just to see how a couple of different AI tools could handle a bit of Shakespeare translation. According to a line often misattributed to Einstein, creativity is 'intelligence having fun'. Or rather, that Kreativität ist „*Intelligenz, die Spaß hat*". That seems aptly to describe much of what I've found *our* translators doing. So I asked AI to deploy its much vaunted 'intelligence' (sure, keep calling it that if you like) – while having what I can only assume is some kind of . . . *artificial* fun?*

I used a piece from *Hamlet* (*There is a willow grows askant the brook*

---

* There was no fun.

. . .), and a piece from *King John* (the words of Prince Arthur, who leaps from his prison wall, hoping to escape, but dies in the act); the former very widely translated and easily found, the latter less familiar, though not an especially tricky piece of writing. I chose to be kind, and requested translations into French, one of the better resourced languages. (We've seen a French version of the former text already.)

The results were not surprising. It seemed to me – though I'm not an expert – that what both tools produced for the famous speech was substantially derived in chunks from existing translations (translators obviously unnamed, uncredited, unremunerated, yadda yadda . . .). The *King John* passage was closer to being an 'original' translation, as far as I could tell, but also more inadequate to anyone who examined the details of the source. It was possible to get from a bad translation to a better one, of course, or a reasonable one even to a good one, by sharpening the focus of the prompts. With each new refinement (respect line lengths, simpler vocabulary, make last two couplets rhyme) it inched closer to what I would not be ashamed of – if I were a machine pretending to take the remotest interest in Shakespeare, language and the truthful expression of human grief.

The analysis in my original Chapter 38 was long and involved, and almost instantly out of date. But even a year ago, AI translations – at least between well-resourced languages – already broadly *made sense*. They were good at processing and clearly re-expressing units of meaning (though not ambiguity), and at some formal features (especially if explicitly instructed). They were missing a lot, but – AI tools being excellent at bullshitting to present their work with such seeming certainty – you wouldn't always know it without careful comparison. Even where flawed, they were irresponsibly plausible.

As the prompts were refined, so too was the output. The tools depended for their incremental improvement on human instruction – not that they can't identify rhyme without my help, but *I* had to decide when rhyme was the thing that mattered in that moment and when to disregard it in favour of some other feature I thought better worth privileging. Any translator appraises options and determines compromises, and sometimes would do well to *not* reconstruct the rhyme. I knew what I liked or didn't about the translations, and – because I could tell the difference, and could read the source myself – AI could serve as a tool of sorts for me. If you can tell this tool *exactly* what to do, it can do it.*

The question, then, isn't whether a machine can perhaps do a great job. Sure it can, sometimes. But only if we humans know the exact qualities of the product we're after. The potential volume to choose from is infinite. In theory, those infinite typewriters staffed by infinite mwncis (this idiosyncratic human does like using that word) could eventually, and hopefully before the heat death of the universe, produce not just *Hamlet* but a great new play – a masterpiece of *Hamlet*'s stature – through enough arbitrary keystrokes, but that is not enough. The masterpiece needs to be recognised amid all the crap – narrowing down to select *this* sequence of keystrokes. Someone needs to wade through all the possible keystroke sequences across infinity, and identify this cluster (not the adjacent, similar one) as the precise keystrokes to make up the speech; if you can select this exact line out of all the possible arbitrarily arranged lines, then – especially because good writing is often *not* the normative stuff – to all intents and purposes you're being a Shakespeare. (Or one of his human translators.) Anyone literate in Shakespeare's day *could* have written 'O, what a rogue and peasant slave am I!' (rather than 'Gosh, what am I like!'), if only they'd known that was what was required.

Most people use translation tools because they can't otherwise read the source, but it is only if you *can* read the source, closely, and compare, that you can see the difference. The true effectiveness of the tool is limited by the expertise, judgment and actual skill of its user. I wish all the enthusiastic bandwagon jumpers understood that part.

We're rapidly accelerating over the brow of this tipping point now. Today, a general assumption might still prevail that the most complex literary writing remains a last bastion – surely, we want to believe,

---

* It has no pretensions whatever to *originate* anything. It can do whatever *we know how to order it* to perform. (Is what Ada Lovelace wrote about the Analytical Engine in 1843.)

cyber-translators* cannot yet do Literature? (I have been taken to task by a translator friend for that *yet*, but stand by it.) The machines are fine for many things, but even in the best resourced languages like mine, it's not as if they can do, like, *Shakespeare*, right? Well, it depends what you think that task entails. Translate it to my admittedly super-demanding standards? No. But they will give you *something*.

Even under the current regulatory systems that don't require even the most basic transparency, we know that the tech companies have been able to teach their tools by scraping pirated copies of my work, and that of my friends, and of most writers whose books have given you pleasure, and the work of probably every translator we've met in these pages. The work of human translators – like human fiction writers and human illustrators and all the rest of us – is the actual intelligence from which a handful of other people are making their runaway billions. And we're also complicit, of course; I've used generative AI as rarely as I can, but I know that even the brief experiments I've described above will have taught it something. Like it or not, we are all getting better at teaching it. And however much its author might object, this book you're reading now will find its way into the machine soon enough, too.

(One of the benefits – certainly to you, reader – of my having left this subject to the end of this book is that it avoids the risk of all 400 pages being filled by a rant about this. Really, don't get me started.)

Of course, human translators – even some of the great masters we've met in these pages – also make mistakes. As a human translator myself, I can admit to plenty. But even human mistakes are more interesting and more revealing than algorithmically determined ones. The humanity is surely the point.

We know how different the translations of complex writing tend to be – look at those Portuguese 'Speak the speech' variants on p.155, or the Spanish 'To be's' on p.149. Convergence is not inevitable. In human

---

* cyber- coming from 'cybernetic' from the Greek κυβερνήτης meaning pilot, steersman; we saw it in Lear's ακυβέρνητη (ungoverned) life on p.236.

translation, variation is the norm. Nobody – or nothing – just accidentally, randomly, by pure coincidence produces a translation that's the same as mine.*

I celebrate the fact that I can only produce *a* translation of a book, rather than *the* translation. The fact that multiple translations exist, each processed through a different human brain (and body, set of experiences, idiolect, etc.), is a thrilling feature of translation, not a bug. Want to learn more about the workings of the Queen Mab speech? Read it in a great translation as well as in its English form. Want to learn *much* more about it? Read it in three variant translations, or ten.

That old acting metaphor applies, once again. Each new *Hamlet* I see gives me new points of access to Shakespeare's *Hamlet*. Human interpretations are multiple and increasingly *expansive*. Again – *the humanity is the point*.

Where it comes to literature, AI can be a handy tool for humans, not a bargain substitute for them. I don't think even the most sophisticated machine can yet do what I do, still less what we can *all* do. (The threat is not that it will replace me, but that it will replace the diversity of a huge multitude of us.) But what worries me today is that people believe it can, or soon will; once people buy in, the battle might be lost. If enough people do, the rest is moot. Maybe we should just save some money and time and human brain-racking, and settle for a supremely confident-sounding, reliable eighty per cent? Maybe, as the baseline shifts, we'll feel that eighty per cent – never more – is good enough? Maybe allowing everything to tend towards everything else is fine! Settle for the gist. I mean, who cares?

I'm really asking, though. For some of us, this is no longer a rhetorical question.

---

* My friend Antonia once went to the birthday party of a Shakespeare scholar in Kraków, where people read out sonnets in various translations, and the expert had to guess whose was by which translator. See? We human translators know how to party.

Chapter 39

doni al li sian vočon per sia propra lango

(on the translators)

I have been saying all along that this is a book about translation, and so it is. But it is also about translators, the people who do the magic.*
One of the pleasures of working on it has been meeting some of them, and discovering the work of many others.

As a translator from three European Romance languages, I've been asked countless times in interviews which other language I'd translate if I could choose one. And my answers used to vary, but one way or another I was always wishing for a new proficiency in something quite different from my usual repertoire – Arabic, perhaps. Or Bengali. But recently I realised that the truth is simpler: deep down, I wish I could translate English. With English as my target language, I could in theory work to develop new reading proficiencies and translate other things *towards* it; but since it's my only really competent writing language (my only plausible *in-bound* language, then), I'll never be able to translate *Middlemarch*, or P.G. Wodehouse, or *Where the Wild Things Are* (this one feels particularly cruel), and I'll never be able to translate Shakespeare. So I've been writing this book about these translators because I am their Number One Fan, but I ought to acknowledge another truth: I am also very jealous of them.

---

* Not actually magic.

It seems sometimes like these fortunate souls are everywhere. I was recently watching a YouTube interview with the pianist Evgeny Kissin, and was surprised to see him suddenly reciting, in its entirety, his own Yiddish translation of 'To be, or not to be'. (Now published!) On 15 August 2025, at the ceremony to mark the eightieth anniversary of VJ Day, a 104-year-old British Indian Army veteran by the name of Yavar Abbas went off-script and moved King Charles to tears with his words of tribute. I mention him because – you might have guessed – Abbas once translated *Othello* and *Macbeth* into Urdu.

In the week I signed my deal to write this book, I attended an event in London with the Czech novelist Jáchym Topol and his translator Alex Zucker to discuss their latest novel, *A Sensitive Person*. The book includes many Shakespeare quotations, and Topol mentioned in passing that he didn't go with a famous canonical Czech version because, oh, his dad had also translated Shakespeare (obviously) so he'd just used those. Not long after, I mentioned this project to a Colombian scholar who was helping me with a translation I was working on, and she said, 'Oh, yeah, my ex-husband and I did one of those.' (That was a *Romeo and Juliet*, using the Spanish version of the alexandrine form, each line made of two seven-syllable halves.) Yes, writers everywhere are at it.

Part of the appeal, I think, is the difficulty. Evidently, Shakespeare is very good (Stanisław Barańczak wrote: 'Translating Shakespeare, one should remember that he wasn't a stupid fellow'), and therefore he is very demanding; and I think, quite simply, that many translators are attracted to difficulty. This translation even more than most is a huge *writerly* challenge. And it's no surprise that this impossible task has often been approached not by people you'd think of as professional linguists or scholars, but by professional writers. It's a challenge taken up by hundreds of poets and novelists ranging from the barely known to twentieth-century superstars. While it's relatively rare for Anglophone writers to translate, writers in other languages (for whom a bit of functional bilingualism or multilingualism is common) will often also do the odd bit of translation to fund their novel/poetry-writing habit. And in Shakespeare, at the top of the tree, they find a very juicy challenge.

(In the UK, to be fair, a handful of often monolingual playwrights do produce a seemingly endless supply of new translations of Chekhov, García Lorca, Ibsen and co., but their process is quite different – and I suspect many of us would feel some discomfort on learning that a foreign production of a Shakespeare play had been based on a sort of high-status prettying up of a so-called 'literal' translation. Seriously, don't get me started on that, either . . .)

Writers translate, among other reasons, to exercise a linguistic muscle in order to improve their own writing. Once Carlos Gamerro had finished translating *Henry VIII*, he discovered his own writing transformed:

> I found, to my amazement, that when writing in Spanish prose, my ear had become acutely sensitive to the rhythmical patterns of the language, that it was automatically measuring lines, paying attention to weak and strong endings, to alliteration and internal rhyme, in a way it had never done before. All my novels written after my translating of Shakespeare were affected in this way.

There's also that question of prestige, of course. Just as people want Shakespeare to exist in their language (I've mentioned those people who saw it as a sort of affirmation of their language's significance – 'if our Armenian or Gaelic is to be taken seriously as a literary language, we should have Shakespeare in it . . .'), so the sense of referred prestige can be appealing to the translators themselves, too. Why wouldn't you want to engage in a four-century-spanning collaboration to become one of the authors of *Hamlet*, of all things?

Though you might think that extra, borrowed prestige would hardly be necessary for some of those who've taken it on. The uncredited Portuguese translation I referred to on p.155 was done by a man who, in his day job, was Dom Luís I, the King of Portugal. (He followed up his *Hamlet* with a *Merchant of Venice*, a *Richard III* and an *Othello*.) I've mentioned President Julius Nyerere's Swahili translations already. And we've met King Rama VI of Siam, of course, too. Meanwhile, French translations – and there are so many hundreds – have been done by Victor Hugo's son, and by Voltaire, and by André Gide, and by the father of Olivier Messiaen . . .

Some of them have what it takes. Others have two languages and a bit of education and therefore assume that they have adequate wit and skill even though most people don't.* To put it very mildly – and I hope I don't really need to say this again, at this point in the book, translating Shakespeare is *not easy*.

While I can see the appeal, there's the pressure, too, of course. As a translator, I might start a piece of work on an almost blank page, but there's some other guy's name at the top – I have some responsibility for a reputation that isn't my own. Albeit with Shakespeare there is, at least, less risk of permanent damage. Many of us translators have the unenviable responsibility for a whole branch of a contemporary writer's international career, but even *Titus Andronicus* will survive for posterity if one sloppy translator butchers it.

Great writers can be great translators (Pasternak certainly has his moments and then some), but it's certainly not guaranteed. Sometimes the very best struggle to write as someone other than themselves, to disengage some aspects of their regular craft and produce writing that is entirely unlike their own. Some don't even try. One Spanish translator, when I asked them about the (heavily abridged) Neruda *Romeo and Juliet*, commented, 'Well, he basically just translates everything into *Veinte Poemas de Amor*, doesn't he?'

However much a translator might wish to limit the influences on their work – I want this to be Shakespeare *only*, not corrupted by the earworm I was humming over breakfast this morning – we all use what we have,

---

* As the saying goes, claiming that you can be a literary translator because you know two languages is true, just as you can be a concert pianist because you have two hands.

and we are all suggestible. I ended a chapter of my own first translation with what turned out to be a direct quotation from *My Fair Lady*. If only I'd realised this before the translation was published.

You might deduce from Chapter 37 that I'm a fan of Tom Stoppard, and I do like *Kiss Me, Kate*, and Astrid Lindgren was a childhood favourite, and I happened to be watching the last season of *Industry* while I was writing it. Another writer at another time would have drawn on different resources, as would another version of me.

When the actor Corin Redgrave was reading his father's autobiography, he was struck by Michael's use of the word 'discomfortable' – a highly uncommon word. (It gets a squiggly red line in this manuscript.) Then Corin realised that when the passage in question was written, Michael had just lately played *Richard II*, and that word – which we saw way back on p.20 – had just seeped through.

Incidentally, Michael Redgrave, a great actor who was a veteran of many Shakespearean roles, always maintained that *King Lear*, at least, sounded better in German.

Lilian Gish, the Hollywood silent movie actress, used to say in interviews that she 'tried never to get caught acting'. There's an assumption that translators should think the same – sure, I want you to admire and enjoy my translations, but I also don't want you to notice I'm in there with you.

But even if I believed that sort of translator neutrality were desirable (I do not), it wouldn't be possible. Individual translators have fingerprints, just like any writers. We have words we like, that we're grateful for an opportunity to use. That's what 'ruefully' is doing on p.43, by the way. We might want to subsume our style to the work we're translating (Anthea Bell translated *Asterix* and she translated W.G. Sebald and it was imperative that they not sound the same), but that doesn't mean translators are interchangeable. We humans notice different things, prioritise different things, draw on different resources and different sensibilities of our own.

What comes out of any translator, any writer, will be influenced more or less subtly by whatever's buzzing in our minds at the time the work is being created. Ask twenty people to tell the story of Little Red Riding Hood in 150 words and the twenty versions will be different, even if their plots and their basic intentions are the same. If a translation is alive, it'll be the translator's blood running through its veins.

In his 2012 Sebald Lecture on translation, the poet Sean O'Brien used one of my favourite analogies, from an old TV ad:

> In the advertisement a hapless customer sits down in the chair of a sinister, very ugly barber who had a crazed ferocious stare and a haircut so appalling and lumpy and damaged that it looks as if he's contracted mange. The barber tells the customer that he can have the same haircut, a 'Lionel Blair' (for anyone who doesn't know, Lionel Blair, now in his eighties, was a famous dancer and variety artist, dapper and always beautifully groomed). The customer protests that Lionel Blair doesn't have a haircut like the barber's. At this the barber brandishes the clippers and says: 'He does when he comes in here.' So poet X may not say what I attribute to him – but he does when he comes in here.

A translator is a reader, and her reading will be an individual one. The critical difference between us and the majority of readers, of course, is in that Rabassa line we've seen – about how our own reading is recorded, preserved, then forms the basis for readings by other people. My translations will be the sum of my micro-choices, my priorities will be informed by my tastes, my politics and much more. Whether we acknowledge this or not, we translate in a moment, and from a human position.

Jean-Michel referenced the translations of his predecessor François-Victor Hugo, where we can see FVH's personal prudishness in his transformation of the opening scene of *All's Well That Ends Well*, in which Shakespeare fills several pages with banter (puns, etc.) about chastity and virginity, into an entirely literal conversation the deeper meaning of which is now almost totally obscure.

János Arany, originally a country boy and an admirer of rural life, made a *Dream* where the mechanicals talked like rural peasants, rather than the

Athenian lower-middle class. And his *Hamlet* contains a reading that's disputable but revealing: in the 'To be, or not to be' speech, when Hamlet bemoans 'the insolence of office', Ádám's predecessor interpreted this as being a complaint about petty local bureaucracy. But is that quite what the line means? Our Hamlet might not have had the easiest time of it, but he did not have to wrestle with the paperwork of the mid-nineteenth-century Hungarian state. This is something of which Arany had considerable experience himself, however, and, said Ádám, 'he was temporarily blinded by his own experience of bureaucratic abuse'. (Even without Google, the relevant meaning of the word office should have been known to Arany in his day, not least through Latin legal phrases including 'officium'; and besides, said Ádám, 'he would always have had slagel tea'.*)

We all make our own personally driven adjustments, whether intended or otherwise. Ádám himself made the old-fashioned and somewhat ridiculous Polonius just a little less ridiculous. 'I felt sorry for him,' he explained, simply.

Pasternak, meanwhile, took the Queen Mab line about the fingers of lawyers 'who straight dream on fees' and wrote: Усы судей, которым снятся взятки – the moustaches (?!) of judges who dream of bribes. He looked at Shakespeare's *fees* and what he saw were *bribes*. Surprisingly, his contemporary Radlova saw a bribe (взятка), too. Also revealing, I feel?

That one overlapping Russian noun notwithstanding, two translators are unlikely to produce identical translations of a single couplet, let alone of a whole play. Oscar Wilde once wrote that is no such thing as Shakespeare's Hamlet, 'there are as many Hamlets as there are melancholies'. Hence something new for each interpreting actor to present. Likewise there are as many *Hamlet*s as there are translators from English, and then some.

When I talked to our Brazilian translator Lawrence Flores Pereira, the incidental biographical facts that he is also a poet, and a musician,

---

* Shortly before completing this book, just wanting to check I hadn't missed anything, I ran a few of my early interview recordings through a bit of automated transcription software to see if it was worth employing. If you're wondering, Ádám here is talking about Schlegel-Tieck.

and part French, all came up in our conversation to help me understand why he was as he was. Translators will reveal things about themselves in their work. The fact, frankly, that someone even countenances the wild notion of trying to translate Shakespeare in the first place tells you something about them, doesn't it?*

Back in Chapter 2, we looked at Gabriele Baldini's version of *Cymbeline*, in that laboriously expansive prose translation – but a translation that came suddenly into focus in that nicely written song, remember? It's the song that added a fear of a hot *August* where Shakespeare had *sun*, and which spelled the Italian word for *tears* in the old style – *lagrime*, where the rest of the translation has *lacrime*. There has to be a reason, surely?

Oh, changing the subject completely, I'd encourage you to read the work of Natalia Ginzburg, the amazing Italian novelist, a writer of great clarity, of an un-self-indulgent, unembellished style, who wrote passionately about how much she hated August more than any other time of year (the first half of the month especially), and who throughout her career favoured, just idiosyncratically, the *lagrime* spelling when writing about tears. Oh, and did I mention she was married to Gabriele Baldini?

But anyway.

The King of Portugal was not the only translator to have his work appear uncredited.

Those revered Schlegel-Tieck translations appeared with August Wilhelm Schlegel and Ludwig Tieck on the title page, but among the worthy names that were *not* on the title page, spare a thought for von Baudissin, whose *Antony and Cleopatra* we saw recently, and Dorothea Tieck (Ludwig's daughter), whose many substantial contributions to the collection included *Macbeth*, from which my friend Catherine quoted on p.358.†

---

* I was teaching last year with Tejaswini Niranjana and she mentioned having done a *Julius Caesar* translation into Kannada when she was just nineteen or twenty. We all do foolish things in our youth, I suppose, but . . .

† In similar vein, if you want to know who *actually* did the work on the Thomas Bowdler edition referenced on p.16, that would be his sister, Henrietta.

Given how much a translation is shaped by its creator – the source author who inspired the translation is one of its begetters, but not the onlie one – it continues to baffle me that even translators of Shakespeare can still go unnoticed. When Emine and I met in Istanbul, her *Macbeth* had received its first few reviews – up to that point, not one of them had yet mentioned her. (Bad news for the Germans – turns out Shakespeare's actually *Turkish*.)

Either that, or the translations are acknowledged, but assumed to be interchangeable. Niels recalled a production of one of his translations getting reviewed, but with the reviewer quoting lines from Lembcke's translation, which he presumably happened to have on the shelf, and anyway, how different could they be? Either the critic didn't know there was a difference, or they didn't care. As Niels said, 'As a translator, I can't understand how they would *not* care about which words are used.'*

One of the things this book has sought to do is throw a little light on the under-noticed authors of these amazing new (old) works.

After all, as Sir Toby Belch asks in *Twelfth Night*:

Wel, pam mae'r pethau hyn yn guddiedig? Pam y rhoir llen i guddio'r fath ddoniau? . . . Ai man yw'r byd hwn i guddio rhinweddau?†

– or to put it another way:

Wherefore are these things hid? Wherefore have these gifts a curtain before 'em? . . . Is it a world to hide virtues in?

While the challenges of translating Shakespeare abound, it's not hard to see the appeal. In addition to the potential improvements to one's

---

* This happens less in reviews of plays translated into English, partly because, well, we stage them so seldom, and partly because, as I've mentioned, what we still see so often are old plays 'translated' by a famous Anglo dramatist with an agenda quite different to that of the translators I know, and the translators in this book, and the translator I aspire to be.

† As translated by J.T. Jones.

own writing from this vigorous workout, and the satisfaction of problem solving, and the benefits of consolidating and expanding one's own language and culture, it's about the opportunity to live, for many months, more *deeply* than anyone else, inside writing of a generosity that is unparalleled. The translators in these pages have had the chance to contend – more closely than anybody, ever – with the work of the most brilliant and bountiful writer I know.

Incidentally . . . it should go without saying that there are countless, countless great global writers I *don't* know. And the world is full of other languages with great writers who might deserve to be in that same pantheon, but we have no access to them. The Anglosphere is exceptionally good at exporting culture, and historically bad at welcoming anybody else's in. Fortunately, this English-speaking world – the world in which I do most of my reading – does at least have its own share of great literary translators working to change that, making it possible for me to read some of my favourite writers. As a part of that translator community myself, I'm lucky to count many of these fellow human translators as my friends. Those translators haven't translated Shakespeare, and so most of them are not named in these pages, but this book has been about them, too.

Epilogue
If this be magic . . .

I do not, for the avoidance of doubt, believe in magic. But like most people, I do experience wonder, and the sense that no logical explanation for a certain encountered phenomenon can exist, surely? A response to what feels like the *effects* of magic, even if the cause is actually ingenuity or sleight of hand. Translating Shakespeare is . . . *something*, but actual magic it is not.

Many of the translators you've read about in these chapters make work that baffles me. Genius is the closest thing to magic I can recognise in the real world. These people cast their spells – or play their tricks, if you prefer – through expert manipulation of their all-powerful languages. Prospero, in *The Tempest*, derives much of his magic from books, which are quasi-living companions to him in his island exile; in the final act, he surrenders his magical powers, with this great gesture:

> But this rough magic
> I here abjure; and when I have required
> Some heavenly music (which even now I do)
> To work mine end upon their senses that
> This airy charm is for, I'll break my staff,

> Bury it certain fathoms in the earth,
> And deeper than did ever plummet sound
> I'll drown my book . . .

The Tempest, first performed in 1611, was likely Shakespeare's last solo play. (Those that followed, *Henry VIII* and *The Two Noble Kinsmen*, were collaborations with fellow playwright John Fletcher.) But earlier that year, the King's Men had staged his dark, troubling, beautiful story of loss and redemption, *The Winter's Tale*.

At around the midpoint of *The Winter's Tale*, Leontes, the King of Sicilia, is told – as are we – that his wife Hermione has died. By the time we reach Act V, much dramatic time has passed, so she's been dead for sixteen years – but somebody brings Leontes word that there is a new statue of his late queen, and it's a wonder. He absolutely must take a look.

Leontes knows it's only a statue, of course. It will have Hermione's general form, her outward appearance, but it is made of stone, not flesh, so it will be cold, bloodless. It might be an impressive approximation, but it will not have a pulse. It will not *be* Hermione.

And then he sees it.

As a theatre spectator, you know the whole scene is pretend, you do know this, deep down; yet still it's implausibly affecting. Leontes is overwhelmed, but there's also some humour – tonally there's so much to the scene, and it seems to change almost with every line. There's a richness such as you find with actual human conversations – not sixteen lines of uninterrupted miscellaneous melancholy, or twenty-four lines of just someone being-jealous-in-a-vague-way. The light is always shifting.

Sitting quietly in the theatre, we realise before Leontes does that what we're looking at is no statue, but rather Hermione – or rather, the actor who was playing her before the interval – standing motionless (maybe on a little pedestal, maybe in an alcove?), statue-like.

But Leontes does not know this and is astonished by what he sees. His teenaged daughter wants to reach out and touch the figure, and

Paulina (Hermione's friend, who brought them here) has to stop her – no, the paint's not yet dry!

Leontes remarks that – hmm, that's odd . . . – the statue of his queen has rather more wrinkles than he remembers. (Ah, explains Paulina quickly, that just shows you how brilliant the re-creating sculptor is – he's rendered her *as she would have looked today*.)

Then Paulina performs her great enchantment. *It is required* (she says, as all great artists say) *you do awake your faith*. She calls for music, and bids the statue move.

> Music, awake her; strike!
> 'Tis time; descend; be stone no more; approach.
> Strike all that look upon with marvel. Come,
> I'll fill your grave up. Stir – nay, come away;
> Bequeath to death your numbness, for from him
> Dear life redeems you.

And Hermione moves, steps down from her pedestal.

So realistic is this statue that Leontes can almost believe his original, authentic queen has been restored to him. *If this be magic*, he says, *let it be an art / Lawful as eating*.

The statue, it turns out, is no block of lifeless stone. *Oh*, cries Leontes when he reaches out and touches her, *she's warm!* Through great care, through clever trickery, through Leontes's own willingness to believe in what he's experiencing, Paulina has conjured up for us – in this room, today   a copy as living as its source.

Maybe just the occasional new wrinkle, to enhance the beauty.

Appendix

(on chapter titles)

I've quoted Shakespeare for my chapter titles, in a great range of languages (among them, a few languages I wasn't able otherwise to include in the book). This is where all those title quotations came from:

Prologue: Hvis du ku glæde mig ved at tale til mig . . .
'If thou couldst please me with speaking to me . . .' (*Timon of Athens*), translated into Danish by Niels Brunse

1. this storie/The World may reade in me (*on translation*)
'this story/The world may read in me' (*Cymbeline*) – English, First Folio

2. Comment mettre cela en vers? (*on verse*)
'What verse for it?' (*Troilus and Cressida*), translated into French by Jean-Pierre Maquerlot

3. O teu beijo é um soneto (*on Juliet and Romeo's sonnet*)
'You kiss by th' book' (*Romeo and Juliet*), translated into Portuguese by José Francisco Botelho

4. ये दोनों एण्टीफोलस शक्ल से एक-से ही हैं (*on rhyming*)
'these two so like . . .' (*The Comedy of Errors*), translated into Hindi by Rangeya Raghav

5. . . . Om nieuwe raadzelen mijn zelven in te scherpen (*on irregularity*)
'To change true rules for odd inventions' (*The Taming of the Shrew*), translated into Dutch by Abraham Sybant

IF THIS BE MAGIC 383

6. **그가 얘기를 다시 하게 만들겠습니다** (*on archaism*)
'I will make him tell the tale anew' (*Othello*), translated into Korean by Jong-Chul Choi

7. **Milý pane, mluvte i vy téż jenom jako dřiv** (*on translating into English*)
'Let me entreat you speak the former language' (*Measure for Measure*), translated into Czech by Bohumil Štěpánek

8. **Podrę wiersz. Proza lepiej usposobi** (*on prose*)
'These numbers I will tear and write in prose' (*Love's Labour's Lost*), translated into Polish by Maciej Słomczyński

9. **Սպասիր, շունչ առ** (*on commas, and other things*)
'Pause, and take thy breath' (*Henry VI, Part 1*), translated into Armenian by Khachik Dashtents and Henry Sevan

10. **Thou ferlies at my words, but haud thee still** (*on ambiguity and wordplay*)
'Thou marvell'st at my words: but hold thee still' (*Macbeth*), translated into Scots by R.L.C. Lorimer

11. **Ni chaiff peryglon fy nychrynu ddim** (*on extreme wordplay*)
'Danger shall seem sport' (*Twelfth Night*), translated into Welsh by J.T. Jones

12. **Uthando ayilothando** (*on meaning/s*)
'love is not love' (*Sonnet 116*), translated into isiXhosa by Malibongwe Mdwaba

13. **จะเลยยกเอาเปนญาติวงศาของเจ้าเองเสียกระมัง** (*on uncles, and boldness*)
'Thou wilt say anon he is some kin to thee' (*The Merchant of Venice*), translated into Thai by King Rama VI of Siam

14. jIH jIH 'e' yInISQo'. 'ej chochoH 'e' yInIDQo' (*on pronouns*)
'let me be that I am, and seek not to alter me' (*Much Ado about Nothing*), restored to the original Klingon by Nick Nicholas

15. እዚሁ ላይ ነው ችግሩ (*on 'To be . . .'*)
'that is the question' (*Hamlet*), translated into Amharic by Tseggaye Gebre-Medhin

16.
(*on words and their effects*)
'I am amazed at your words' (*A Midsummer Night's Dream*), translated into music and libretto by Benjamin Britten and Peter Pears

17. нуждата превръща всичко . . . (*on gender and other opportunities*)
'The art of our necessities is strange' (*King Lear*), translated into Bulgarian by Alexander Shurbanov

18. 不用多说了 (*on economy*)
'What needs more words?' (*Antony and Cleopatra*), translated into Chinese by Yuanchong Xu

19. Und sein so schlichter Schein herbergt Verrat (*on deceptive simplicity*)
'in his simple show he harbours treason' (*Henry VI, Part 2*), translated into German by A.W. von Schlegel

20. Todas sus palabras son meritorias (*on Latinate vocabulary*)
'All his words are worthy' (*The Two Noble Kinsmen*), translated into Spanish by Amir Hamed

21. kad jūsų iždas kupinas žodžių (*on influences, kinships and etymologies*)
'You have an exchequer of words' (*The Two Gentlemen of Verona*), translated into Lithuanian by Antanas Danielius

22. קוקנדיק אפ מיר, ווערנ שארפזיניק אויכ אנדערע (on humour)
'the cause that wit is in other men' (Henry IV, Part 2), translated into Yiddish by Y. Goldberg

23. **Red' gelahrt on weise** (on research)
'Speak scholarly and wisely' (The Merry Wives of Windsor), translated into Low German by Robert Dorr

24. **che l'ordine va spezzato . . .** (on word order)
'How order should be quelled . . .' (Sir Thomas More), translated into Italian by Edoardo Rialti

25. **Таква музика е слатка сал** (on languages of other kinds)
'In sweet music is such art' (Henry VIII), translated into Macedonian by Bogomil Gjuzel

26. **正当な順序の継続** (on bridges)
'by fair sequence and succession' (Richard II), translated into Japanese by Kazuko Matsuoka

27. **ти људи бесконачног језика** (on Shakespeare's languages)
'these fellows of infinite tongue' (Henry V), translated into Serbian by Živojin Simić and Trifun Đukić

28. **ანუ რაოდენ ჩვენთვის ჯერერთ უცნობ ენაზედ** (on accents, dialects and representation)
'accents yet unknown' (Julius Caesar), translated into Georgian by Ivane Machabeli

29. أرجوك ألا تفرضي القيود على لسان (on reasons to translate)
'I prithee, give no limits to my tongue' (Henry VI, Part 3), translated into Arabic by Mohammed Badran

30. Jó hírnév nevű áru (*on names*)
'a commodity of good names' (*Henry IV, Part 1*), translated into Hungarian by Ádám Nádasdy

31. ते हे सुंदर नवं जग! (*on cultural adjustment*)
'O brave new world' (*The Tempest*), translated into Marathi by Mangesh Padgaonkar

32. αν δεν την καταλαβαίνετε ούτε σεις, δεν πειράζει (*on understanding, and multilingualism*)
'Though you understand it not yourselves, no matter . . .' (*All's Well That Ends Well*), translated into modern Greek by Nikolaos Poriotis

33. bir kaç diyarda / Aynı dili kullanmakla (*on multipolar languages*)
'To use one language in each several clime' (*Pericles*), translated into Turkish by Hamdi Koç

34. Why, now you speak as I would have you speak (*on actors*)
'Why, now thou speak'st as I would have thee speak' (*Edward III*), translated into contemporary English by Octavio Solis

35. O, daardie verruklike speeltuig van haar gedagtes (*on thoughts*)
'O, that delightful engine of her thoughts' (*Titus Andronicus*), translated into Afrikaans by Breyten Breytenbach

36. . . . galdramann, ramman að kynngi (*on all of it at once*)
'. . . a magician, most profound in his art' (*As You Like It*), translated into Icelandic by Helgi Hálfdanarson

37. No coneixem ses obres? (*on the literary canon*)
'We know his handiwork' (*King John*), translated into Catalan by Josep Martí Sábat

38. Сколь естеству твои дела противны (*on translations without translators*)
'Thy deeds, inhuman and unnatural' (*Richard III*), translated into Russian by Mikhail Donskoy

39. doni al li sian voĉon per sia propra lango (*on the translators*)
'our own voices with our own tongues' (*Coriolanus*), translated into Esperanto by Marjorie Boulton and Humphrey Tonkin

Epilogue: If this be magic . . .
'If this be magic . . .' (*The Winter's Tale*)

P.S. I should add a confession. But first, let me say: if you were contemplating writing a book using translated lines of Shakespeare as chapter titles, don't. It causes such problems. Quite apart from the choosing and finding, which is more trouble than you can imagine – don't even ask . . . – the translatedness is almost insurmountably inconvenient. Just because my carefully identified source text would have worked as a title, its selected translation sometimes does not. In several cases, a perfectly good dramatic translation just isn't translating *the relevant aspect/s of the word*. My title for Chapter 30, for example, doesn't really work if you actually know Hungarian; because, while the English source would have worked fine for me (it refers to 'good names', which are indeed the subject of the chapter), the translation – quite reasonably – uses *hírnév*: the Hungarian word for 'reputation' (the line indeed being about one's 'good name' in *that* sense), so while the translated line does what's needed in its speech, in its scene, serving a Hungarian actor and audience very well in that moment, it no longer really suits *my* purposes. The translator kept what mattered for their needs and discarded what was incidental and irrelevant. Or Chapter 36! Icelandic is an inflected language, so while the *magician* I wanted to reference is still there, he appears now in the accusative case, which makes it odd when isolated in my title. Again, the translation does what is required of it, but doesn't work perfectly for *my* unusual purposes. And there are others. I'm keeping them all anyway, as I can't resist a #teachablemoment about the challenges of translation – so here you have it. But it is annoying . . .

Further Reading and References

This book has been built around my readings of Shakespeare in various languages and on conversations with his translators, much more than on other secondary materials, but if you want to read more widely or deeply, you will find there is both very little on the subject and a huge amount. There aren't dozens of other books that seek to cover Shakespeare translation very broadly as this one does (so I've been telling my publishers), but there's a lot to be found on specific aspects of it, each dealt with much more comprehensively than I could here.

The existing work on Shakespeare translation has usually been produced with a much more detailed focus than in this overview – most of it is essay/chapter-length pieces published in academic contexts. (But then you also have occasional books like, say, Dirk Delabastita's *There's a Double Tongue*, a 500-page analysis of translating Shakespeare's wordplay, with particular attention to *Hamlet* – that one's fascinating.) There have been more or less enduring journal series on related subjects: *Shakespeare Translation,* published annually in Tokyo from 1974; *Multilingual Shakespeare: Translation, Appropriation and Performance,* published at Łódź from 2004 (this was previously *Shakespeare Worldwide*), etc. There are also a handful of essay collections that bring together a few different perspectives to create a composite picture: Arden's *Shakespeare and the Language of Translation* (2004) is a very good place to start – it's edited by Ton Hoenselaars, a name to follow if you want to read more on this subject. That volume includes pieces by Jean-Michel Déprats and Alexander Shurbanov: two translators whose work you've come to know in these pages; as well as a twenty-five-page 'Further Reading' section supplied by Delabastita, which far exceeds both my space in this volume and my expertise – it's recommended.

There's also the recent *Shakespeare in Succession: Translation and Time*, a volume of essays edited by Michael Saenger and Sergio Costola, where you'll find pieces by José Francisco Botelho and Niels Brunse.

There are, of course, countless books that touch on Shakespeare translation as a small component within focused examinations of his performance, dissemination and reception in all sorts of contexts (at first glance, on my shelf, I can see *Shakespeare's Hamlet in Romania, 1778–2008; Shakespeare on the Noongar Stage; Shakespeare on the German Stage (vol. 1, 1586–1914): Shakespeare in East Asian Education* . . .), which all have interesting things to say in passing about translation/s, as well as countless general studies of his global influence, his unusual universality, his ubiquity, his international afterlife.

When this book quotes from Shakespeare in his English-language incarnation, unless otherwise specified, quotations are given as they appear in the Arden edition (third series). Obviously, do read him in English at every opportunity. He's as good as they all say. If you're lucky enough to be able to read him in another language additionally, reading Shakespeare while *simultaneously* reading Nádasdy/Mason/Ayhan/Kawai, or other equally brilliant double-acts, so much the better. As Ton Hoenselaars puts it in his preface to his above-mentioned volume, 'to study Shakespeare in translation is just another way to find him'.

If This Be Magic is written by a translator, rather than a scholar, so as I said, it's fed primarily on actual translations of Shakespeare rather than existing appraisals by others. And so most of the quotations that appear in this book are from translations of Shakespeare, into one of about fifty languages. The Shakespeare translators whose words appear in this book are listed below, naming the translated play(s) that I've cited and, where possible, giving details of where that the translation in question might be found in published form.

Translations of Shakespeare Quoted*

Yuri Andrukhovych (Ukrainian), ill. Vladyslav Yerko: *King Lear* (A-BA-BA-HA-LA-MA-HA, 2023)

James Anthony (contemporary English): *Twelfth Night* (*Shakespeare Retold* series, Redbrick books, 2021)

Kostas Antoniou (Greek): *A Midsummer Night's Dream* (Αιγόκερως, 2007)

Richard Appignanesi (graphic novel, English), ill. Nana Li: *Twelfth Night* (Manga Shakespeare, SelfMadeHero, 2009)

János Arany (Hungarian): *Hamlet* (Osiris Kiadó, 2023)

Emine Ayhan (Turkish): *King Lear* (Alfa, 2019); *Macbeth* (Akademim Yayınları, 2025, and version supplied by translator); *The Tempest* (Alfa, 2019); *The Merchant of Venice* (Alfa, 2019); *A Midsummer Night's Dream* (with **Aysun Şişik**, Alfa, 2018)

Salah Baban (Sorani Kurdish): *Othello* (Aras, 2012)

Mohammed Badran (Arabic): *Henry VI, Part 3* (Dār al-Maʿārif, 1959)

Gabriele Baldini (Italian): *Cymbeline* (Bur/Rizzoli, 1989); *Twelfth Night* (Bur/Rizzoli, 1979)

Stanisław Barańcak (Polish): *Romeo and Juliet*, *Hamlet* (both Znac, 2021)

Wolf Graf von Baudissin (German): see Schlegel-Tieck edition, below

Mohammed Ayad Ibrahim Bek (Arabic): *As You Like It* (al-Maaref, 1944)

Errikos Belies (Greek): *The Merchant of Venice* (Το Βήμα, 2016)

José Francisco Botelho (Portuguese): *Romeo and Juliet, Julius Caesar, The Tempest* (all Penguin/Companhia das Letras, 2016, 2018 and 2022, respectively); *Pericles* (unpublished, supplied by translator)

Marjorie Boulton and Humphrey Tonkin (Esperanto): *Coriolanus* (Esperanto-Asocio de Britio, 2023)

Y. Bovshover (Yiddish): *The Merchant of Venice* (Hebrew Publishing Co., 1899)

Bülent Bozkurt (Turkish): *Richard III* (Remzi Kitabevi, 2010)

Breyten Breytenbach (Afrikaans): *Titus Andronicus* (Buren, 1970)

Benjamin Britten and Peter Pears (opera, English): *A Midsummer Night's Dream* (Boosey & Hawkes, 1960)

Niels Brunse (Danish): *Cymbeline, The Two Gentlemen of Verona, The Taming of the Shrew, Hamlet, Richard II, Richard III, Henry V, Macbeth, Romeo and Juliet, The Merry Wives of Windsor, Twelfth Night, King Lear* (all in complete plays, six vols., Gyldendal, 2010–18)

Niels Brunse & Frank Günther (Danish/German): *Romeo and Juliet* (unpublished, supplied by Niels Brunse, 2021)

---

* Listed alphabetically by translator family name. For consistency, all are presented in this book using the Western convention where given names precede family names.

Haşim Bukozirov (Azeri): *Othello* (Типографія Перваго Типографскаго Товарищества, 1904)

L.A.J. Burgersdijk (Dutch): *Macbeth* (in complete works, Brill, 1884–8)

Alison Carey (contemporary English): *Twelfth Night* (ACMRS, 2023)

Geraldo Carneiro (Portuguese): *Sonnets*

Jong-Chul Choi (Korean): *Othello* (Minunmsa, 2001)

Jaime Clark (Spanish): *Twelfth Night* (in *'Twelfth Night' llega a España*, tirant humanidades, 2023)

Tristão da Cunha (Portuguese): *Hamlet* (in *Obras* vol. 2, Agir, 1979)

Antanas Danielius (Lithuanian): *The Two Gentlemen of Verona* (Vaga, 1983)

Khachik Dashtents (Armenian): *Twelfth Night* (Haypethrat/Armenian State Publishing House, 1953); *Henry VI, Part 1* (with **Henry Sevan**) (Armenian Academy of Sciences, 1972)

Henry Denison (Latin): *Julius Caesar* (incl. preface) (Contubernales, 2023)

Onestaldo de Pennafort (Portuguese): *Romeo and Juliet* (Edição da Livraria do Globo, 1947)

Jean-Michel Déprats (French): *A Midsummer Night's Dream* (Actes Sud, 1990); *The Winter's Tale* (in *Comédies III*, Pléiade/Gallimard, 2016); *Richard III* (Gallimard, 1995); *Henry V* (Folio/Gallimard, 2000); *King Lear, Twelfth Night* (Éditions Théâtrales, 1996); *Love's Labour's Lost* (Folio/Gallimard, 2013); *Macbeth, Coriolanus, Hamlet, King Lear, Othello* (all in *Tragédies I and II*, Pléiade/Gallimard, 2002); *The Merry Wives of Windsor*, (with **Jean-Pierre Richard**, Gallimard, 2010); *Cymbeline* (Éditions Théâtrales, 2000)

Mikhail Donskoy (Russian): *Richard III* (Izdatelstvo AST, 2017)

Robert Dorr (Low German): *The Merry Wives of Windsor* (Verlag der Th. Kaulfuss'schen Buchhandlung, 1877)

Raphael Eliaz (Hebrew): *Romeo and Juliet* (Hakibbutz Hameuchad – Sifriat Poalim, 1971)

Millôr Fernandes (Portuguese): *Hamlet* (L&PM, 1997)

Lawrence Flores Pereira (Portuguese): *Hamlet, King Lear* (both Penguin/Companhia das Letras, 2015 and 2020, respectively)

Ion Frunzetti (Romanian): *All's Well That Ends Well* (Editura de Stat Pentru Literatură şi Artě, 1960)

Tsuneari Fukuda (Japanese): *Hamlet* (Schinchosha, 1960)

Tsegaye Gebre-Medhin (Amharic): *Hamlet* (Oxford University Press, 1964/1972)

Mihnea Gheorghiu (Romanian): *King Lear* (Univers Enciclopedic, 1997)

Bogomil Gjuzel (Macedonian): *Henry VIII* (Makedonska akademija na naukite i umetnost, 2015)

Y. Goldberg (Yiddish): *Hamlet* (Melukhe-farlag, 1934); *Henry IV, Part 2* (Melukhe-farlag, 1936)

François Guizot (French): *All's Well That Ends Well* (in the complete works, publ. Didier, vol. III, 1861)

Frank Günther (German): *Romeo and Juliet* (dtv, 1995); *Antony and Cleopatra* (dtv, 2003); *A Midsummer Night's Dream* (ars vivendi, 2000); *Twelfth Night* (ars vivendi, 2001)

Abhijit Gupta (Bengali): *A Midsummer Night's Dream* (unpublished, supplied by translator)

Carl August Hagberg (Swedish): *Much Ado about Nothing* (C.W.K. Gleerup Förlag, 1861)

Helgi Hálfdanarson (Icelandic): *As You Like It* (manuscript at Shakespeare Birthplace Trust, 1951)

Amir Hamed (Spanish): *The Two Noble Kinsmen* (in *Romances*, Penguin Clásicos, 2016)

Barbara Heliodora (Portuguese): *The Two Gentlemen of Verona, Hamlet* (with **Amélia Queiroz Carneiro de Mendonça**), *Twelfth Night, All's Well That Ends Well* (all in *Teatro Completo*, Editora Nova Aguilar, 2016)

José Mendez Herrera (Spanish): *The Two Gentlemen of Verona* (Aguilar, 1962)

François-Victor Hugo (French): *Henry IV, Part 1* (in *Oeuvres complètes I*, Pléiade/Gallimard, 1959); *Twelfth Night* (Flammarion, 1966)

Jabra Ibrahim Jabra (Arabic): *Hamlet* (Al-Muʾassasah al-ʿArabīyah lil-Dirāsāt wa-al-Nashr, 2000)

Josep María Jaumà (Spanish): *Romeo and Juliet* (in *Tragedias*, Penguin Clásicos, 2016)

J.T. Jones (Welsh): *Twelfth Night* (Cymdeithas Lyfrau Ceredigion Gyf, 1970)

Yrjö Jylhä (Finnish): *King Lear* (Suomalaisen Kirjallisuuden Seura, 1936)

Dionysis Kapsalis (Greek): *King Lear* (Agra, 2020); *A Midsummer Night's Dream* (Agra, 2012)

Shoichiro Kawai (Japanese): *A Midsummer Night's Dream* (Kadokawa, 2013); *The Merchant of Venice* (Kadokawa, 2005)

Hamdi Koç (Turkish): *Pericles* (Yapı Kredi Yayınları, 1993)

Mikhail Kuzmin (Russian): *King Lear* (Izdatelstvo AST, 2020)

So Kwok Wan (Chinese): *Henry V, Twelfth Night* (unpublished, supplied by the translator)

Hyon-u Lee (Korean): *Hamlet* (found at <https://globalshakespeares.mit.edu/hamlet-q1-lee-hyonu-2009/#video=hamlet-q1-lee-hyonu-2009>

Edvard Lembcke (Danish): *Romeo and Juliet* (in complete plays, Det Schubotheske Forlag, 1897–1900)

Pierre Leyris (French): *Twelfth Night* (Flammarion, 1994)

Agostino Lombardo (Italian): *Twelfth Night* (Feltrinelli, 1993)

R.L.C. Lorimer (Scots): *Macbeth* (Canongate, 1992)

Mikhail Lozinsky (Russian): *Twelfth Night* (in complete works, Academia, 1937)

Dom Luís I, King of Portugal (Portuguese): *Hamlet* (Imprensa Nacional, 1877)

U.M. MacGilleMhoire (Scottish Gaelic): *Julius Caesar* (Akerbeltz, 2016)

Ivane Machabeli (Georgian): *Julius Caesar* (in complete works, Kelovneba, 1983–7)

Jean-Pierre Maquerlot (French): *Troilus and Cressida* (in *Tragédies I and II*, Pléiade/Gallimard, 2002)

Samuil Marshak (Russian): *Sonnets* (Izdatelstvo Khudozhestvennaya Literatura, 1963)
Josep Martí Sàbat (Catalan): *King John* (Estampa d'E. Domènech, 1909)
Te Haumihiata Mason (te reo Māori): *Romeo and Juliet* (Auckland University Press, 2023); *Macbeth* (Auckland University Press, 2025, and drafts supplied by translator); Sonnet 18 (supplied by the translator)
Kazuko Matsuoka (Japanese): *Richard II, Twelfth Night, Macbeth, Troilus and Cressida, Romeo and Juliet* (Chikumashobo, in 2015, 1998, 1996, 2012, 1996, respectively)
Malibongwe Mdwaba (IsiXhosa): Sonnet 18, Sonnet 116 (unpublished, found at <https://www.youtube.com/watch?v=aoqUTNYTL4A> and <https://www.youtube.com/watch?v=RV4XZPy-J_k>, text supplied by translator)
Oscar Mendes (Portuguese): *Sonnets* (in complete works, José Aguilar, 1969)
Pierre Messiaen (French): *Twelfth Night* (in complete works, Desclée, de Brouwer, 1945)
Giorgio Melchiori (Italian): *King Lear* (Mondadori, 2019)
Chaiti Mitra (Bengali): *Hamlet* (unpublished, supplied by translator)
Vicente Molina Foix (Spanish): *King Lear* (in *Tragedias*, Penguin Clásicos, 2016); *The Merchant of Venice* (in *Comedias*, Penguin Clásicos, 2016)
Conrad Murray (contemporary English): *Romeo and Juliet* (Methuen/Bloomsbury, 2024)
Khalil Mutran (Arabic): *Othello* (Matba'at al Ma'arif, 1912; quoted in Sameh Hanna)
Ádám Nádasdy (Hungarian): *Romeo and Juliet. Hamlet. A Midsummer Night's Dream, Twelfth Night, The Taming of the Shrew, Henry IV, part 2, King Lear* (all in Shakespeare Drámák series, Magvető: vol. I, 2001 [incl. *Shrew, Dream, Hamlet*], vol. II, 2008 [*Twelfth Night, Romeo and Juliet*], vol. III, 2018 [*Lear, Henry IV*])
JC Niala (Swahili): *Macbeth* (unpublished, supplied by translator)
Nick Nicholas (Klingon): *Much Ado about Nothing* (Klingon Language Institute, 2001)
Carlos Alberto Nunes (Portuguese): *Romeo and Juliet* (Peixoto Neto, 2017)
Özdemir Nutku (Turkish): *Twelfth Night* (Remzi Kitabevi, 1988); *King Lear* (İş Bankası Kültür Yayınları, 2009)
Mangesh Padgaonkar (Marathi): *The Tempest* (Mouj Prakashan Griha, 2006)
Siko Pashalishvili (Georgian): *Twelfth Night* (in complete works, Kelovneba, 1983-7)
Boris Pasternak (Russian): *Romeo and Juliet, King Lear* (both Vremya, 2017)
Józef Paszkowski (Polish): *Hamlet* and *King Lear* (publ. in one vol., Państwowy Instytut Wydawniczy, 1974)
Federico Patán (Spanish): *Twelfth Night* (in *Comedias*, Penguin Clásicos, 2016)
Edmundo Paz Soldán (Spanish): *Much Ado about Nothing* (in *Comedias*, Penguin Clásicos, 2016)
Nikolaos Poriotis (Greek): *All's Well That Ends Well* (Οι φίλοι του βιβλίου, 1945)
Anna Radlova (Russian): *Romeo and Juliet* (Tsedram, 1935)
Rangeya Raghav (Hindi): *The Comedy of Errors* (Rajpal, 2016); *A Midsummer Night's Dream* (Rajpal, 1957); *The Taming of the Shrew* (Rajpal, 2015); *Twelfth Night* (Rajpal,

2017) (Translator's note to *The Taming of the Shrew* quoted in a translation by Aditya Vikram.)

Rama VI, King of Siam (Thai): *Romeo and Juliet* (1922), *The Merchant of Venice* (1916), publishers unknown

Edoardo Rialti (Italian): *Thomas More* (Lindau, 2014)

Emanuel Ribeiro (Cape Verdean Creole): *Romeo and Juliet* (including preface) (unpublished, 2017)

Reto Rossetti (Esperanto): *Othello* (Stafeto/J. Régulo, 1960)

Vassilis Rotas (Greek): *Twelfth Night* (Επικαιρότητα, 1989)

Carlo Rusconi (Italian): *Twelfth Night* (in *Teatro completo*, vol. 7, Unione Tipografico-Editrice Torinese, 1923)

Schlegel-Tieck edition (German): *Antony and Cleopatra* (tr. Wolf Graf von Baudissin); *Macbeth* (tr. Dorothea Tieck); *Twelfth Night* (tr. A.W. von Schlegel); *A Midsummer Night's Dream* (tr. A.W. von Schlegel); *King Lear* (tr. Wolf Graf von Baudissin); *Henry VI, Part 2* (tr. A.W. von Schlegel); *Hamlet* (tr. A.W. von Schlegel) (all in complete works, Reimer, 1825–33)

Y.Y. Schwartz (Yiddish): *Hamlet* (incl. preface) (Forverts, 1918)

'will.i.was shookspear' (contemporary English): *Sonnets* (publ. as *sonnets that slap: a collection of the littest shakespearean sonnets translated for a new generation*, 2023)

Alexander Shurbanov (Bulgarian): *Hamlet*, *King Lear*, *Macbeth* (all Iztok-Zapad [East-West] Publishers, 2016)

Živojin Simić and Trifun Đukić (Serbian): *Henry V* ((Latin-script version, Kultura, 1963)

Maciej Słomczyński (Polish): *Love's Labour's Lost* (Wydawnictwo Literackie, 1984)

Octavio Solis (contemporary English): *Edward III* (ACMRS, 2022)

Bohumil Štěpánek (Czech): *Measure for Measure* (Fr. Borový, 1928)

Abraham Sybant (Dutch): *The Taming of the Shrew* (Dirk Cornelisz, 1654)

Jashwant Thaker (Gujarati): *Macbeth* (Saraswati Prakashan, 1964)

Dorothea Tieck (German): see Schlegel-Tieck edition, above

Gwyn Thomas (Welsh): *The Tempest* (Gwasg Gee, 1996); *A Midsummer Night's Dream* (CBAC, 1999)

Péter Vajda (Hungarian): *Hamlet* (1839, unpublished, quoted in Nádasdy *Hamlet*, q.v.)

P.I. Veinberg (Russian): *Othello* (Library of Great Writers/Brockhaus/Efron, 1903)

Nathalie Vivé and Gabriel Llesta (French): *Twelfth Night* (Éditions Espaces 34, 1998)

Yuanchong Xu (Chinese): *Antony and Cleopatra* (Dolphin Press, 2016)

Shenghao Zhu (Chinese): *Titus Andronicus*, *Timon of Athens* (in complete works, People's Literature Publishing House, 1978)

Also, too many Spanish 'To be . . .' versions to list.

Other Quoted Sources

Unless otherwise specified, quotations from translators about their work have been taken from interviews I carried out for this book. In addition, quotations from the following sources appear in the text and are listed by page of first appearance.

(**p.7**) *Kiss Me, Kate* – original book by Bella and Samuel Spewack, music and lyrics by Cole Porter, dir. Bartlett Sher (Barbican Theatre, London, 2024)

(**p.8**) *The Compact Oxford English Dictionary* (Clarendon Press, 1991)

(**p.8**) Robert Frost – 'that which is lost out of both prose and verse in translation', from *Conversations on the Craft of Poetry*, Cleanth Brooks (Holt, Rinehart & Winston, 1961)

(**p.10**) Arundhati Roy – from *The Algebra of Infinite Justice* (Flamingo, 2002)

(**p.16**) *The Family Shakespeare*, ed. Thomas & Harriet Bowdler (Hatchard, 1807)

(**p.18**) John Ruskin quoted from his Lectures on Art (Lecture 3, *The Relation of Art to Morals* (delivered in Oxford, 1870; publ. in *The Works of John Ruskin*, Longman, 1905)

(**pp.26–7**) Aira preface to *Cymbeline*, tr. the 'Textured Translation' Challenge Lab (*Latin American Literature Today*, issue 30, 2024)

(**p.34**) *Shakespeare in Love* – adapted for the stage by Lee Hall, based on the 1998 screenplay by Marc Norman and Tom Stoppard (Faber & Faber, 2014); also, Spanish translation by Juan Gabriel Vásquez, unpublished, supplied by the translator

(**p.43**) Samuel Taylor Coleridge, 'Kubla Khan' from *Christabel; Kubla Khan, a Vision; The Pains of Sleep* (John Murray, 1816)

(**p.43**) Victor Hugo – from 'Booz endormi', in *La Légende des siècles* (first series, Hetzel, 1859)

(**pp.64–5**) Frank Günther – from 'Ten Questions for Frank Günther', *In Other Words* issue 41 (British Centre for Literary Translation, 2013)

(**p.71**) *Player Kings* – adapted by Robert Icke from Shakespeare's *Henry IVs* (Nick Hern Books, 2024)

(**p.72**) 'The sin of smoothing Out Shakespeare', *Guardian* letters (8 Jan 2016)

(**p.75**) Jorge Luis Borges quotation – from his lecture 'The Riddle of Shakespeare', delivered in Washington D.C. on 23 April 1976; available at <https://folgerpedia.folger.edu/Shakespeare%27s_Birthday_Lecture:_%22The_Riddle_of_Shakespeare%22>

(**p.81**) João Guimarães Rosa, tr. Alison Entrekin – from *Vastlands: The Crossing*, (Bloomsbury, 2027)

(**p.91**) *Richard II* folio note – Nick de Somogyi ed. 'Shakespeare Folios' edition of *Richard II* (Nick Hern Books, 2003)

(**p.100**) Hyon-u Lee, Folger *Shakespeare Unlimited* podcast, ep.6, July 2014

(**p.104**) J. Dover Wilson, *What Happens in* Hamlet (Cambridge University Press, 1935)

(**p.105**) J.K. Rowling, tr. Jean-François Ménard, *Harry Potter à l'École des Sorciers*, (Gallimard Jeunesse, 1998) (**p.105**) René Goscinny & Albert Uderzo, tr. Anthea Bell & Derek Hockridge, *Asterix the Gaul*, (Orion, rev. edn. 2004)

(**p.106**) Thurber's line about his work losing something in the original is widely quoted, but I am still in search of a good source. The exchange might be apocryphal, but I shall give it the benefit of the doubt in the meantime. He did, however, use a version of this joke in a cartoon caption – 'He's having all his books translated into French. They lose something in the original.' (in *Thurber & Company*, Harper & Row, 1966.) Thanks to the Thurber House for this source.

(**p.132**) William Empson, *The Structure of Complex Words* (The Hogarth Press, 1985)

(**p.146**) Antony Jay & Jonathan Lynn, 'The Skeleton in the Cupboard', *Yes, Minister* (season 3, episode 3)

(**p.148**) Miguel de Cervantes, tr. Edith Grossman, *Don Quixote*, (Vintage, 2005)

(**p.168**) Julian Clary, *Curtain Call to Murder* (Orion, 2024)

(**pp.170–171**) Heather Amery & Richard Cartwright, *First Hundred Words in English* (Usborne, 1988); other language editions: French & German, 1988; Polish, Chinese & Italian, 2008; Russian, 2017 (all Usborne)

(**p.172**) Christophe Coupé et al. – 'Different languages, similar encoding efficiency: Comparable information rates across the human communicative niche' (*Scientific Advances*, V/9, 2019)

(**p.196**) Jonathan Gil Harris, *Masala Shakespeare* (Aleph, 2018)

(**pp.197–8**) Ahdaf Soueif – from 'Radical Choices', *In Other Words* issue 41 (British Centre for Literary Translation, 2013)

(**pp.197–8**) Vladimir Nabokov – from 'The Art of Translation', *New Republic*, 1941

(**p.219**) Beatles 'Pyramus and Thisbe', *Around the Beatles* TV special, 1964; at <https://www.youtube.com/watch?v=H_8Mr2OT6Ac>

(**p.224**) Note from Arden *Dream* – from *A Midsummer Night's Dream*, Arden edition (3rd series), ed. Sukanta Chaudhuri (Bloomsbury, 2017)

(**p.227**) Kaara L. Peterson, 'Historica Passio: Early Modern Medicine, *King Lear*, and Editorial Practice', in *Shakespeare Quarterly*, Vol.57, no.1, 2006

(**p.237**) Carlos Gamerro – from 'Will, Thou Art Translated', *In Other Words* issue 41 (British Centre for Literary Translation, 2013)

(**p.241**) Melissa McCarthy – at the Center Theatre Group Gala 2024, at https://www.youtube.com/watch?v=E7p_2mb9stU

(**p.242**) Joby Talbot – quoted in Stephanie Jordan's 'The Timing of Jealousy', in the programme for the Royal Ballet production, Covent Garden 2024

(**p.243**) Mendelssohn letter – from 'Letter to Marc-André Souchay' (1842), in *Letters of Felix Mendelssohn Bartholdy, from 1833 to 1847*, tr. Lady Wallace (Longman, Green, Longman, Roberts & Green, 1863)

(**p.251**) Gregory Rabassa, *If This Be Treason: Translation and its Dyscontents* (New Directions, 2005) (**p.264**) *L'Île Noire (Les Aventures de Tintin)*, Hergé (Casterman, 1956); English translation, *The Black Island*, by Leslie Lonsdale-Cooper & Michael Turner (Methuen, 1966)

(**p.264**) Borges's 'el original es infiel a la traducción' appears in his 1943 essay 'Sobre el Vathek de William Beckford' [On William Beckford's Vathek]

(**p.265**) José Eustasio Rivera, tr. Daniel Hahn & Victor Meadowcroft, *The Vortex (La Vorágine)* (Charco Press, 2024)

(**p.266**) Jean-Michel Déprats – from 'Do You Speak Franglais? The hotchpotch of languages in *Henry V*', in *Critical Quarterly*, July 2022

(**p.268**) Harold Bloom, *The Anxiety of Influence* (Oxford University Press, 1997)

(**p.268**) Martin Hilský – quoted from 2012 expats.cz interview with Ryan Scott, at <https://www.expats.cz/czech-news/article/interview-with-martin-hilsky>

(**p.269**) Antonio Prata, tr. Daniel Hahn, 'Plan' (in *Four Short Tales*, Words Without Borders, 2013)

(**p.270**) Isaac Bashevis Singer: first quotation is taken from his Nobel lecture, 1978, at <https://www.nobelprize.org/prizes/literature/1978/singer/lecture/>; second quotation is from 'Isaac Bashevis Singer Talks . . . About Everything' (*New York Times*, 26 November 1978)

(**p.272**) Yens Wahlgren, tr. A.A. Prime, *The Universal Translator* (The History Press, 2021)

(**p.274**) Joel Berkowitz, *'Jewish Exponent', Shakespeare on the American Yiddish Stage* (U. Iowa, 2002)

(**p.280**) Cole Porter, 'Brush Up Your Shakespeare' – from *Kiss Me, Kate*, 1948

(**pp.280–81**) 'Décrasse ton Shakespeare' – translated from Cole Porter's 'Brush Up Your Shakespeare' by Alain Marcel, 1992

(**p.287**) Neil Bartlett – from the 'Jean Genet: Translation and Censorship' conference, International Translators' Federation, Paris 2010

(**p.288**) Khalil Mutran, 'devout woman' quoted in Sameh Hanna's 'Decommercialising Shakespeare: Mutran's Translation of *Othello*', in *Shakespeare & the Arab World*, ed. Katherine Hennessey & Margaret Litvin (Berghahn, 2019)

(**p.288**) Preti Taneja – from 'Does Shakespeare's Text Even Matter?', in *Performing Shakespeare in India*, ed. Shormishtha Panja & Babli Moitra Saraf (Sage, 2016)

(**p.290**) Jason Grunebaum, 'stealth gloss' from 'Choosing an English for Hindi', in *In Translation: Translators on Their Work and What It Means*, ed. Esther Allen & Susan Bernofsky (Columbia U.P., 2013)

(**p.293**) Steen Steensen Blicher *Hosekræmmeren* (Stocking Peddler) in *Hosekræmmeren og andre noveller* (Gyldendal, 2016)

(**p.294**) João Cabral de Melo Neto, 'Tecendo a manhã' in *A educação pela pedra* (Alfaguara, 2008)

(**p.298**) George Seferis – from 'Ἄρνηση' (Arnisi), in Στροφή, 1931

(**p.312**) Boris Pasternak – from 'Translating Shakespeare', tr. Manya Harari, in *I Remember* (Pantheon, 1959) (**pp.312–13**) Grigori Kozintsev tr. Mary Mackintosh – from *King Lear: The Space of Tragedy* (Heinemann, 1977)

(**p.321**) Terry Hands – quoted in *Directors' Shakespeare: Twelfth Night*, ed. Michael Billington (Nick Hern Books, 1990)

(**p.325**) Saxo Grammaticus, tr. Oliver Elton, *Amleth Prince of Denmark* (Kessinger, no date)

(**p.348**) Line quoted from 'I Got It Bad (And That Ain't Good)', lyric by Paul Francis Webster to music by Duke Ellington (1941)

(**p.356**) Tom Stoppard, *Arcadia* (Samuel French, 1993)

(**p.357**) Tom Stoppard, tr. Jean-Marie Besset, *Arcadie* (Actes Sud, 1998)

(**p.357**) Tom Stoppard, tr. Frank Günther, *Arkadien* (Jussenhoven/PROJEKT, 1993)

(**p.357**) Mickey Down and Konrad Kay, *Industry – Industry*, Season 3, Episode 8 'Infinite Largesse', 2024

(**p.358**) *The New International Encyclopaedia* (Dodd, Mead and Co., 1905)

(**p.358**) Carl August Hagberg's translation of *Much Ado about Nothing*, referenced in 'Shakespeare in Swedish' by Karin de Figueiredo, Shakespeare Birthplace Trust blog (2017); at <https://www.shakespeare.org.uk/explore-shakespeare/blogs/shakespeare-swedish/>

(**p.359**) HAMLET X SHIBUYA, tr. Rosalind Fielding, in *Re-imagining Shakespeare in Contemporary Japan* (Arden/Bloomsbury, 2021)

(**p.359**) Elaine Feeney, *How to Build a Boat* (Harvill Secker, 2023)

(**p.360**) Isabella Hammad, *Enter Ghost* (Jonathan Cape, 2023)

(**p.362**) Arthur Bardos, BBC interview, 1949, on the occasion of his visit to England to direct *Hamlet* there

(**pp.362–3**) George Steiner – from *Of Beauty and Consolation*, episode 4 (2000), at https://www.youtube.com/watch?v=LJhsuwg5Jns

(**p.366**) Ada Lovelace, notes on Babbage's Analytical Engine, publ. to supplement her translation of an article by Luigi Federico Menabrea, in *Scientific Memoirs* (Taylor, Sept. 1843)

(**p.370**) Jáchym Topol, tr. Alex Zucker, *A Sensitive Person* (Yale/Margellos, 2023)

(**p.370**) Stanisław Barańczak, tr. Antonia Lloyd-Jones – the quotation is one of his 'three translation truisms' from Part IV of his *Ocalone w tłumaczeniu* (Saved in Translation) (Wydawnictwo a5, 2004)

(**p.373**) Corin Redgrave, *Michael Redgrave: My Father* (Richard Cohen Books, 1995)

(**p.374**) Sean O'Brien – from the 2012 Sebald Lecture, 'Making the Crossing: the Poet as Translator', in *In Other Words* issue 39 (British Centre for Literary Translation, 2012)

(**p.375**) Oscar Wilde – 'as many Hamlets . . .' line is taken from his essay 'The Critic as Artist (part II)', in his *Intentions* (Methuen, 1891)

(**p.390**) *Shakespeare and the Language of Translation*, ed. Ton Hoenselaars (Methuen/Arden, 2004)

Acknowledgements

My greatest debt, naturally, is to the Shakespeare translators who agreed to talk to me about their work. I met some in person, some on Zoom; I met many of them more than once, and lots of these conversations lasted *hours*. (And then there were all the follow-up questions and the follow-ups to those, for which I can only apologise.) So my principal thanks go to Abhijit Gupta, Ádám Nádasdy, Chaiti Mitra, José Francisco ('Chico') Botelho, Emine Ayhan, JC Niala, Jean-Michel Déprats, Lawrence Flores Pereira, Niels Brunse, Shoichiro ('Sho') Kawai, So Kwok Wan and Te Haumihiata Mason. Also, the late Frank Günther, who sadly died in 2020, but whom I was lucky to meet a decade earlier and interview about his work. This book is a tribute to all these brilliant humans and the extraordinary things they can do. Alongside those translators of Shakespeare's plays, I also got to chat to Rosie Fielding, Alfred Enoch, Tim Supple, Malibongwe Mdwaba, Jonathan Gil Harris and others about their respective relationships to Shakespeare in/and translation. My thanks to them all.

Many of those conversations happened because I'm lucky to know people who are ready to say 'Ooh, y'know who you should meet?' then make introductions. Mark Baczoni introduced me to Ádám; Yana Genova introduced me to Alexander; Max Porter to Tim, and Tim to So; Jean-Michel to Sho. It's thanks to Patrick Spottiswoode at the Globe that I first met Niels and Frank. Debanjan Chakrabarti and Debnita Chakravarti put me in touch with Abhijit and Chaiti. Gitanjali Patel introduced me to Alfie. Maureen Freely introduced me to Philip Arditti, who introduced me to Emine. Lyndsey Fineran sent me to Mike Dreaver, the mastermind behind an inspiring Māori-language publishing project, who not only introduced me in turn to Te Haumihiata, but drove me down from Auckland to Rotorua for a lovely lunch with her and her granddaughter/co-translator Meretūahiahi Ward, pointing out fascinating things to look at along the way.

I'm also lucky to have the sort of friends – many of them translators themselves – to whom one might drop a note that says: 'Hey, do you have time to grab a coffee and explain how Hungarian commas work?' or: 'If you've got a sec, a quick question about the effect of etymological streams in Esperanto . . .' And they not only agree, but send replies like: 'OK, *now* you've got my attention.' Or: 'Ooh, this sounds like the time I spent a couple of hours explaining things to the Czech translator of *Cats*.' Translators are hilarious and weird people. (If you've read this book, you'll have figured that out for yourself, obviously.)

I had language-specific questions small and large answered by: Bethlehem Attfield (Amharic); Sawad Hussain, Ruth Ahmedzai Kemp and Ibrahim Fawzy (Arabic); Nairi Hakhverdi (Armenian); Nicky Harman and Daniel Li (Chinese); Mattho Mandersloot (Dutch); Sebastian Schulman (Esperanto); Maria Turtschaninoff (Finnish); Elizabeth Heighway (Georgian); Karen Emmerich (Greek); Jenny Bhatt (Gujarati); Mark Baczoni (Hungarian); Victoria Cribb (Icelandic); Lucy North (Japanese); Anton Hur (Korean); Phillip Dupesovski (Latin); Ishaan Anavkar (Marathi); Marina Sofia (Romanian); Anna Novokhatko (Russian); Ellen Elias-Bursać (Serbian); Emyr Wallace Humphreys (Welsh); Yankl Krakovsky (Yiddish, including Leonard Nimoy).

Noga Applebaum, Jessica Cohen and Evan Fallenberg all pitched in generously on Hebrew; Aditya Vikram Shrivastava, Jason Grunebaum and Daisy Rockwell helped with Hindi. Antonia Lloyd-Jones shared her substantial expertise in handling Polish stress.* Andrea Reece and Camille Rivière helped me *décrasser* a bit of French singing. For most things Greek, it was Iannis Carras, my friend of many moons, σελήνη and φεγγάρι particularly.

Sasha Dugdale read Pasternak and Radlova with me; Thea Lenarduzzi read Baldini and Ginzburg (and throughout the process made me feel

---

* I mean Polish *syllabic* stress, obviously.

better about my first draft's out-of-control word count); Mui Poopoksakul talked me through King Rama VI's translations into Thai; and Charlotte Collins helped me to see the funny side of 'Pyramus and Thisbe' in German. Maureen Freely sat with me for hours on what otherwise would have been a grim day and explained some of the mysteries of Turkish. I read bits of the Tristão da Cunha *Hamlet* alongside Tristão's granddaughter, Ignês Sodré – a woman whose manifold qualities include being my mother, and so I have plenty else to thank her for besides, so we will be coming back to her.

Mairi Kidd introduced me to Gaelic, and Kareem Abdulrahman to Sorani Kurdish. Paul Russell Garrett was knowledgeable and helpful on Danish commas and Danish pronunciation and other Danish things (even if neither he nor Nielsine knows how to post a Danish letter). I can't say I know *very* much about Bulgarian prefixes, but everything I do know, I learned from Petya Pavlova. John Angliss took great pains to help me understand what was going on in a piece of Azeri. (Telling me, first, that it *was* a bit of Azeri, because I didn't even know that.) Hend Saeed helped me to decode variations on the word 'love' in an Arabic *As You Like It*. Claire Breger-Belsky kindly agreed to check a couple of little Yiddish things for me, and ended up doing what I suspect was weeks of work. They are the main reason there are so many fascinating Yiddish bits and pieces included. (Though as my regular host at the Yiddish Book Center, I feel Mindl Cohen has a lot to answer for, too.)

Lydia Aers contributed a small act of production espionage. Brigid Larmour answered a question about her excellent *The Merchant of Venice 1936*, as did Ceri Williams about the bilingual Theatr Clwyd *Romeo and Juliet*, and the Barbican's Toni Racklin about *Kiss Me, Kate*. My friend Nick de Somogyi explained First Folio italics. My uncle Ricardo sent me Francis Hime's lovely 'Shakespeareana'. I learned of the Steiner story from Tiago Rodrigues's *By Heart*. Silvina Katz updated me on modes of address in Argentina.

Other suggestions and answers and observations and bits of surprisingly relevant trivia came from Aneesa Abbas Higgins, Anna Halas, Anne Rooney, Astrid Huisman, Aurora Humarán, Bryan Karetnyk,

Daniel Medin, David Sanderson, Davit Gabunia, Deepa Bhasthi, Elif Shafak, Erna von der Walde, Gioia Guerzoni, Helder Lopes, Jean Louis Steuerman, Juan Gabriel Vásquez, Julian Sedgwick, Kate Mosse, Khairani Barokka, Lasha Bugadze, Leslie Howard, Lucie Campos, Mahesh Rao, Mara Faye Lethem, Neil Jordan, Nick Garland, Petr Horáček, Polly Toynbee, Ruth Diver, Ruth Jones, Steve Crawshaw, Susan Bassnett, Susan Bernofsky and Susana Moreira Marques. Embarrassingly, a few of these offered suggestions I never had a chance to follow up (for last-minute time and space and circumstances) – for which my apologies. There is an alternative universe in which this is a better book thanks to you.

My school-days' appreciation of Shakespeare came mostly from Peter Holmes. I've talked about Shakespeare in performance with my friend Abigail Anderson, who is one of my favourite directors and also one of my favourite directors (and who features in the book). Yzanne Mackay studied Shakespeare with me, once upon a time, and I've been thinking about her while writing this because she loves translation more than anything. The *Arcadia* example in chapter 37 is there for Tanweena. (She is also referenced herself in the book, though anonymously.) My friends Joe, David, Anton, Sophy, Ed, Tim and many others named above listened patiently while I bored them about irregular meter and Anglo-Saxon monosyllables over the last two years of drinks and dinners. The Pyrenean branch of BTS cooked while I edited.

I spent far too much of these past years digging around in library collections, usually for quite recherché things. The number of books I requested with still uncut pages attests to this. (I would like to write an article someday on different libraries' attitudes to dealing with these.) I'm grateful to the helpful staff at the British Library – especially in the difficult times that coincided with my research; to those at the Shakespeare Institute, the London Library, the Shakespeare Collection at the Library of Birmingham, the Cambridge University Library, the Bodleian Library, the Folger Shakespeare Library, the Shakespeare's Globe archives, and especially the ever-patient library team at the Shakespeare Birthplace Trust.

IF THIS BE MAGIC

My title echoes Gregory Rabassa's excellent translation book, *If This Be Treason* – Greg's daughters Kate and Clara were kind enough to allow me to make the connection. This book is a tribute to the work of great translators, and their dad was one of the best.

Shakespeare in translation is a subject I've been thinking about intermittently for a long time, and have had several opportunities to share initial thoughts over the years – a panel at the RSC (and conversations there with Réjane Collard-Walker), a series of events in partnership with Shakespeare's Globe and the British Centre for Literary Translation, a more-or-less impromptu talk at the Hay Festival thanks to Peter Florence instantly seeing the appeal of the subject, a commission from Nick Robins to write about it for *Around the Globe*. Nell Leyshon and Max Porter were among the first people in the book world to whom I mentioned this concrete book idea, and their interest and enthusiasm meant a great deal. My initial proposal was read by Araminta Whitley and James Reynolds who both gave me the sort of encouragement I needed to believe this book might one day appeal to a publisher.

And the publisher who immediately knew exactly what I wanted it to be was Francis Bickmore. Francis acquired this unlikely book and welcomed it into the Canongate family, for which I will be always grateful. It could not have landed in a better home. There is not a more hospitable publisher around, largely thanks to Jamie Byng, whose boundless enthusiasm for this book – as for all things – has been joyous and invigorating. To my great good fortune, Maddy Price joined Canongate at just the right moment to take over editorial duties. I've been so lucky to have her as this book's new guide and champion. The thoughtful feedback I received from her, as well as from John Freeman and Sierra Fang-Horvath at Knopf, made this a better book in literally hundreds of little ways.

Most writers will know how much a good copy-editor can improve a book, too, and Seán Costello is just about the best. Both he and Edward Crossan, our proofreader, had to handle an unusually complicated text (45 languages, I think?) and I am grateful to both for their care. Louise Tyler steered this whole awkward process with all the patience, clarity, flexibility, reassurance that this book and its author needed. I've never created more trouble for a typesetter than with this book, so thank you – and *sorry* – to Les and everyone at Palimpsest Book Production, who have been heroic. The gorgeous jackets are by Gill Heeley (for Canongate) and Ariel Harari (for Knopf) – thank you both. Seeing those first designs in my inbox was a thrill, a highlight of the whole adventure. As I write, five months out from publication, Lucy Zhou is preparing a campaign to get the book noticed when it appears; and Jessica Neale and the rights team are working hard to find it homes in other languages. Truly, every part of Canongate works so hard and so well for their books. My gratitude to them all.

This book was written during a complicated year for our family. I have come to learn that my sister, Emily, and her husband, Ed, are absolutely the best people to share the difficult times with, as well as the good ones. Unsurprisingly, their Alice and Jesse are just amazing, too – they were one of their granny's greatest joys in recent years. (As they are their uncle's, of course.) Elena has looked after our dad throughout it all, along with Adi, whom he adores more than anyone in the world. We've had huge love and support through these years from our clan of Brazilians, and from Cristobal and our Chileans.

And so, finally, to my parents, to whom this book is dedicated. My mum is the reason I became a reader and a translator. My dad took me to the theatre to see Shakespeare, early and often. Gabriel honestly has no particular interest in Shakespeare or literary translation, but spent the last two years caring for my mum with great devotion, which is far more important than any of those things.

My mum is the main reason I wrote this book, and she died this summer before being able to read it. But when I finished writing my very first book, back in 2002, I handed her the fresh manuscript to read and she said, 'Sweetheart, I'll read it this weekend, but I want to tell you now, I *love* it.' So I shall be cheered by the certainty that she loved this one, too.

Thank you for everything. x